Secrets of Grandmaster Play

Secrets of Grandmaster Play

JOHN NUNN and
PETER GRIFFITHS

B. T. Batsford Ltd, *London*

First published 1987

ISBN 0 7134 5789 9

Typeset by W. Turner & Son Ltd, Halifax
and printed in Great Britain by Billings Ltd, Worcester
for the publishers, B. T. Batsford Ltd,
4 Fitzhardinge Street, London W1H 0AH

A BATSFORD CHESS BOOK
Adviser: R. D. Keene, OBE, GM
Technical Editor: P. A. Lamford

Contents

Preface

The purpose of this preface is twofold; to describe how this book came to be written and to answer some of the questions which might occur to the reader.

When Peter Griffiths approached me with the basic idea of the book, my interest was immediately captured. Books containing deep and careful analysis of games are admittedly few and far between, but Alekhine, Fischer and Timman had all produced far better analysis than I could ever hope to. Peter proposed something a little bit different, namely to use the analysis in a more overtly educational manner, to instruct players of many different levels. As a chess teacher of thirteen years experience, he was ideally qualified to emphasise this aspect of the book. Many teaching books tend to oversimplify the process of chess thought, but by taking genuine tournament games in their entirety we hope to show what really happens, pointing out the errors as well as the good moves.

As with all jointly authored books, readers will inevitably wonder who did what. In general, the moves are mine and the words Peter's, but the actual production was far more complex than this might suggest. First of all I would analyse the games, Peter would check it and when we had chased all the analytical problems to ground, Peter would write the game up. Then we would meet to discuss the draft and a lively debate would often ensue as to which aspects of the game should be emphasised. The final product would gradually emerge in a form which both authors were happy with.

Readers will notice that many of the games have been published and analysed before, but each one was thoroughly re-examined for this book. I spent between three days and two weeks on each game before posting the analysis off for Peter to check. Needless to say, such a detailed inspection turned up a number of new and sometimes embarrassing points. Chess is not an exact science and alert readers will no doubt find analytical flaws in this book; with such a large quantity of analysis some mistakes are inevitable. However, every effort has been made to reduce the number of errors as much as possible.

The choice of games was itself a time-consuming process. From a shortlist of 100, the number was gradually whittled down to the twenty-four you will find in the book. A number of criteria were applied, but the main one was that there should be many different types of game in the book, covering the full range of chess experience. A certain bias in favour of tactics remains, but this is a realistic reflection of my personal style. Nevertheless, there are endings and positional games too. For the most part we have chosen 'best' games, although such a judgement is inevitably subjective. You will find well-known grandmaster opponents from big internationals, but also weekend Swiss games against less august opposition – so long as the chess is interesting and instructive it doesn't matter.

John Nunn
April 1986

Introduction

In presenting two dozen of John Nunn's best games, and in trying to explain his thought processes as clearly as possible, I should make the point at once that it is not our intention to give the reader an easy time! This book is designed for a wide range of players who wish to improve their chess and are willing to put in some hard work to achieve that end. One of the main aims has been to highlight the differences in approach between a Grandmaster and a weaker player, and to try to narrow the gap. To some extent this comes down to technical matters – more accurate analysis, superior opening knowledge, better endgame technique and so forth; but in other respects the difference goes deeper and many readers will find that they need to rethink much of their basic attitude to the game. One example of this would be the tremendous emphasis which is placed on the dynamic use of the pieces, if necessary at the expense of the pawn structure, or even of material. This is no mere question of style; it is a characteristic of the games of all the strongest players.

A great deal of analysis has been done on each game. There are two schools of thought on this. Some hold that light analysis is preferable and that a student benefits more from having to work out the tactics for himself, others maintain that this approach simply leaves the inexperienced reader mystified. There is something to be said for both points of view, but (in this book at least) we have come down firmly on the side of the second theory. In so doing we have not only presented the analysis itself, but have tried to show **how** a position should be analysed; what a thorough and systematic analysis looks like. As a result of that the book has turned out to be almost as much a manual of tactics as an orthodox collection of games.

On this subject I might perhaps offer a word of warning. It should not be imagined for a moment that even a Grandmaster could analyse during a game to the kind of depths which we have plumbed here. I shudder to think what would happen if readers laboured under that illusion and tried to play accordingly! John's style tends to be analytical and he can see a great deal over the board – in several places I have indicated approximately how much he worked out during play – but on many occasions the tactics are not clear-cut and there is still a vast gulf between what he saw and a complete analysis.

The games appear in chronological order and cover the period 1974-85, from around the time of John's first entry into international play and his promotion to International Master (1975) until the present, culminating in the superb game against Belyavsky, probably his best effort to date. During this time the evolution of his style is interesting to trace, from the very direct tactician of the early games to the more complete player of today. One of the most striking features of the later period is his deeper approach to positional problems, especially in the field of opening theory. He became a Grandmaster in 1978.

Probably the most useful way to tackle each game would be to play through the main moves first, to get an idea of the outline, and then go back to study the notes. And above all do this critically; in that way you may get the best of both worlds – you will to some degree be working things out for yourself and at the same time you will not (we hope) be mystified!

Peter Griffiths

Symbols

+	check
!	strong or imaginative move
?	bad move
(?)	inaccurate move

Game 1

Vienna Game
Teesside 1974
(World Student Team Championship)

J. Øst-Hansen v. J. Nunn

1	**e4**	**e5**
2	**♘c3**	

The best-laid schemes of mice and men . . . ! First of all Nunn was expecting 1 g3, which his opponent had employed consistently in previous rounds. Øst-Hansen in turn was anticipating Nunn's usual Pirc Defence (1 . . . d6) and intended to meet it by a g3 system, transposing back into positions with which he would be familiar. Unfortunately, 1 . . . e5 wrecks this little plan; so White, having almost no detailed knowledge of the open game, chooses the only variation with which he happens to be acquainted, a very sharp line of the Vienna. Nunn also knows this variation; so for the time being both players are convinced that the other is in uncharted territory!

2	**. . .**	**♘f6**
3	**♗c4**	**♘×e4**
4	**♕h5**	**♘d6**
5	**♗b3**	

White can simplify if he wishes by 5 ♕×e5+ ♕e7 6 ♕×e7+ ♗×e7 7 ♗b3; while Black, after 5 ♗b3, can also avoid the critical line by 5 . . . ♗e7 6 ♘f3 0–0. But of course neither player intends to let his opponent get away that easily!

5	**. . .**	**♘c6**
6	**♘b5**	**g6**
7	**♕f3**	**f5**
8	**♕d5**	**♕e7**
9	**♘×c7+**	**♔d8**
10	**♘×a8**	**b6** *(1)*

If you have not come across this peculiar variation before, it amounts to an exchange sacrifice by Black, in return for which he gets a substantial lead in development and attacking chances against the uncastled king. Neither side has had much choice during the previous few moves: White obviously has to keep making threats after his original pawn sacrifice, while Black cannot play . . . ♕e7 any earlier because the aggressive centre pawns which he now possesses are an essential element in the initiative which he hopes to maintain.

1
W

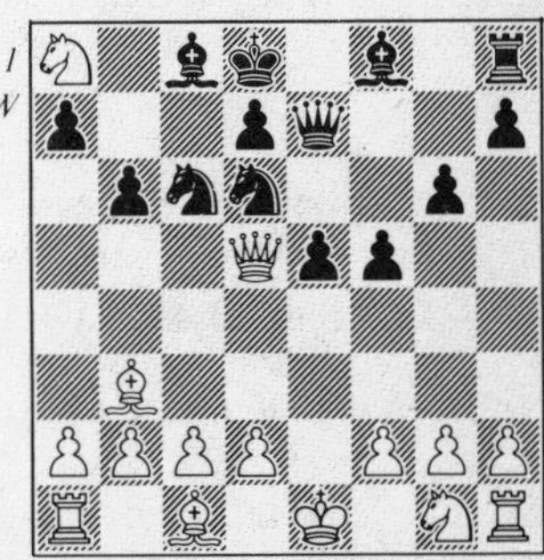

The knight, of course, is trapped and Black will round it up by . . . ♗b7, which will also force White to waste more time avoiding the threat to his queen (. . . ♘d4). Black will probably delay the capture of the knight for quite a long time, though: not only will it cost what could be a vital tempo, but after . . . ♗×a8 Black's own knight at c6 is likely to be pinned by the queen.

It would take us too far afield to discuss all White's 11th move alternatives (11 a4, ♘f3, ♕f3, ♘×b6, ♕d3, ♘e2, in addition to the move chosen, 11 d3). Much midnight oil has been devoted to the variation, as you might imagine, and theoretical advances occur very slowly. It is above all the domain of the correspondence players, who will not be rushed into anything. Suffice to say that in 1974 11 d3 was most highly regarded, while more recently opinion has swung towards 11 ♘×b6.

11 d3 ♗b7

We might say a few words here to compare Black's exchange sacrifice with others which you will find in this book. Black is reckoned in theory to have approximate compensation for the material, but there is nothing clear-cut about it. He is not thinking in terms of a winning combination, or even of analysing precise variations. He is saying: 'My minor pieces are going to be superior to the white rooks for a long time and I have much better control of the centre than White. I can start making threats quite soon, and as a guideline my attack will be based on the pawn thrust . . . e4. In the time he takes to organise his position I should be able to achieve something more concrete.' And, without overestimating Black's chances, if you have ever played White in this type of position, you will know how awkward it is to develop satisfactorily. Getting the pieces off the back rank may not be too difficult; making them work effectively and thus countering Black's initiative is another matter.

So much for theory. In a moment we shall demonstrate the opportunities open to Black's pieces by means of some variations.

12 h4

He must counter the threat of . . . ♘d4, but can delay the queen's retreat by preparing his own pin, ♗g5. In that way he provokes . . . f4, so that the safe square g4 will be available for his queen. If Black replies 12 . . . h6, then 13 ♕f3 ♘d4 14 ♕g3 is a slight nuisance.

12 . . . f4

13 ♕f3 ♗h6

Nunn is becoming uneasy about his mysterious '1 g3' opponent who displays such an intimate knowledge of an obscure Vienna line; so he deliberately bypasses the theoretical continuation. In 1974 this was based on a correspondence game (Nielsen–Altshuler) which continued: 13 . . . ♘d4 14 ♕g4 ♗h6 (14 . . . e4 is premature – 15 ♕×f4 e×d3+ 16 ♕e3 etc.) 15 ♘h3 ♘6f5 (again 15 . . . e4 16 ♗×f4 e×d3+ 17 ♔f1 would leave Black unable to continue his attack) 16 ♘g5 ♗×g5 17 h×g5 f3 18 g3 e4 19 ♗e3 ♘×e3 20 f×e3 f2+ 21 ♔f1 (21 ♔×f2 ♖f8+ is too dangerous) and the attack has spent itself.

Once again we cannot go into much detail about the rights and wrongs of Black's play in this game, except to say that against a good defence it is far from easy to decide on the best placing of the pieces. The opening books suggest other moves with which he might experiment: 14 . . . ♗g7 instead of . . . ♗h6, for instance, or 15 . . . ♖f8 instead of . . .

♘6f5. On the whole Nunn's alternative seems to be at least as good as 13 . . . ♘d4

14 ♕g4?

Confronted by a new move, White immediately makes a fatal mistake. He is aware of Nielsen–Altshuler and is trying to transpose into it by 14 . . . ♘d4 15 ♘h3; but, perhaps not being thoroughly familiar with the type of position he is handling, he overlooks that the black knight can use e5 instead.

There are three other reasonable options, 14 ♗d5, 14 ♗d2 and 14 ♘e2, each of which appears to be quite playable. It is impossible to come to any definite conclusion about their relative merit, but the following analysis gives a good impression of some of the attacking methods at Black's disposal:

14 ♗d5 is a very natural move, trying to exploit Black's omission of . . . ♘d4, and was the one to which Nunn paid most attention when contemplating 13 . . . ♗h6. First of all, 14 . . . ♘d4 is no good because of 15 ♗×b7 ♘×f3+ 16 ♗×f3. Then Black can trap the knight at a8 by attacking at once: 16 . . . e4 17 d×e4 ♘×e4 18 ♘e2 d5, but in so doing he leaves his king fatally exposed: 19 0–0 ♕b7 20 ♗×f4 ♗×f4 21 ♘×f4 ♕×a8 22 ♘×d5! etc. Or he can play more slowly: 16 . . . ♘f5 17 c3 ♘×h4 18 ♗e4 ♗g5, but in that case White holds the knight secure until he can mount a rescue operation (playing c4 if need be, to prevent . . . d5) and thus preserves a substantial material advantage.

So Black will play 14 . . . ♗×a8, which wastes a tempo in a sense, as I remarked earlier; but things are different with the knight pinned by the bishop instead of the queen, and the threat of . . . ♘d4 is now renewed. We then have:

(a) 15 c3(?) ♖e8 and it appears that White can block the file by 16 ♗e4. But then comes 16 . . . ♘d4! 17 c×d4 ♘×e4 18 d×e4 e×d4 and the open file is deadly: 19 ♔f1 ♗×e4 20 ♕e2 ♗d3 and wins. White must therefore allow . . . e4: 16 ♘e2 e4 17 ♗×e4 (or 17 d×e4 ♘e5 18 ♕h3 ♗×d5 19 e×d5 with a lethal check on d3 to follow) ♘e5 18 ♕h3 ♘×e4 19 d×e4 ♗×e4 20 0–0 ♗f5 21 ♕h1 ♘f3+ 22 g×f3 ♕×e2, and he has a dismal position (. . . ♗d3 can follow, or . . . g5 and . . . ♖g8).

(b) 15 ♕g4 ♖f8 (A difficult point; 15 . . . e4 is less effective because 16 ♗×f4 e×d3+ 17 ♔f1 ♗×f4 18 ♕×f4 ♖f8 would produce the game position with the extra moves ♗d5 and . . . ♗×a8. Thus Black would not have the powerful move . . . ♘e4 available – see move 18 of the game –; instead, 15 . . . ♖f8 prepares . . . e4). Now 16 f3 might seem plausible, but on general principles it is undesirable to shut out the queen and 16 . . . ♘f5! introduces a new possibility for Black: the immediate threat is 17 . . . ♘g3 followed by . . . ♕c5, and if 17 ♘e2 ♘b4! 18 ♗×a8 (18 ♗b3 ♕c5) ♘×c2+ 19 ♔d1 ♘×a1, when the knight cannot easily be trapped on account of the . . . ♕c5 danger. If 17 ♗×c6 ♗×c6 18 ♘e2, then still 18 . . . ♕c5 19 ♘c3 ♘g3 and a winning check at g1. Therefore 16 ♘e2 is best and then: 16 . . . e4 17 ♗×f4 (17 d×e4? is a pattern we have seen already: 17 . . . ♘e5 18 ♕h3 ♗×d5 19 e×d5 f3 20 g×f3 ♘×f3+ 21 ♔f1 ♘e4, threatening . . . ♘fd2+ with a winning attack) ♗×f4 18 ♘×f4 ♕e5 (18 . . . e×d3+ 19 ♔f1 is not very helpful) 19 ♗×c6 ♗×c6 20 ♘e2 e×d3 21 c×d3 ♖e8, with two options for White: (1) 22 ♕g5+ ♕×g5 23 h×g5 ♗×g2 24 ♔d2! ♗×h1 25 ♖×h1 with a likely draw; (2) 22 ♔f1 ♕×b2 23 ♖e1 ♕×a2 24 ♖h3 ♘f5, which is probably about equal. White is still rather tangled up and Black will obtain counterplay with his a-pawn while the rooks are being activated.

(c) 15 ♘e2 ♘f5 (threatening 16 . . . ♘cd4) 16 c3 (or 16 ♕g4 ♕c5 17 ♗×c6 ♕×c6 18 c3 ♖e8, or here 17 ♗b3 d5 etc.) ♘×h4 17 ♕h3 ♗g5 18 g3 ♘f5, with an unclear position.

The second possibility, 14 ♗d2, is a Soviet suggestion aiming to bring the white king into safety on the queenside. The tempting 14 . . . e4 15 d×e4 leaves Black with an awkward choice since he has to commit his knight to e5 or d4; the former allows the white queen to settle at e2, while the latter permits ♕d3. Here are some specific lines: 15 . . . ♘d4 16 ♕d3 ♗×e4 17 ♕×d4 ♗g7 18 ♕b4 ♗×g2+19 ♘e2 ♗×h1 20 0–0–0 ♗×a8 21 ♗×f4 with advantage to White because of Black's exposed king; 15 . . . ♘e5 16 ♕e2 ♘×e4 17 ♘f3 ♘g4 18 ♘g5 (threat ♘f7+) ♗×g5 19 h×g5 ♘g×f2 20 0–0 and the attack collapses; or finally 15 . . . ♘×e4 16 0–0–0 ♘×d2 17 ♖×d2 ♘d4 18 ♖×d4 ♗×f3 19 ♘×f3 with too much material for the queen.

Thus Black should play 14 ♗d2 ♘d4 15 ♕g4 e4 16 0–0–0 e3 17 f×e3 ♘×b3+ 18 a×b3 f×e3 19 ♗e1 e2+ 20 ♖d2 ♗×a8 (this is a good moment to take time out for burying the knight, since White has no serious threats) 21 ♘×e2 ♖e8 22 ♘f4 ♕e3 23 ♗g3 (not 23 ♖f1 ♗×f4 and Black wins) ♘f5 24 ♗h2 ♘d4 when his active pieces provide sufficient compensation for White's extra material.

The third alternative, 14 ♘e2, concentrates on blocking the e-file, but Black has an effective reply in 14 . . . ♘d4 15 ♕h3 ♘×e2 16 ♔×e2 f3+ 17 g×f3 ♗×c1 18 ♖a×c1 (or 18 ♖h×c1 ♖f8 19 ♕g3 ♘f5 20 ♕g5 ♘d4+21 ♔f1 ♖f6 and again Black has a good position) ♖f8 19 ♔f1 ♖×f3 20 ♕g4 ♖f4! (not 20 . . . ♗×a8 21 ♕g5 ♖f6 22 ♖h3 when White can defend) 21 ♕h3 ♗×a8 with enough compensation for the material.

Despite the wide range of defensive plans available to him, White does not appear to have any way of gaining an advantage after 13 . . . ♗h6. In each case Black either regains the sacrificed material or preserves a strong initiative.

14 . . . e4!

15 ♗×f4 . . .

By now some of the tactical motifs are becoming familiar, and things which previously failed for Black are going to succeed, often by just one tempo. Compared to earlier variations, in other words, White's lack of development is proving disastrous. 15 d×e4 is out of the question: 15 . . . ♕×e4+ 16 ♘e2 (16 ♕e2 ♕×g2) ♘d4, with . . . ♖e8 or . . . ♗a6 to come; if 17 ♔d1 ♘×e2 18 ♕×e2 ♕×g2 wins. Nor can he repair the damage by 15 ♘e2, since 15 . . . e×d3 16 c×d3 ♘e5 17 ♕h3 f3 is devastating.

15 . . . e×d3+ *(2)*

16 ♔f1 . . .

Suddenly, everything has changed; Black has a winning attack and from now on the variations are all clear-cut. Not necessarily easy though! What happens after 16 ♔d1, for instance? Obviously only direct threats

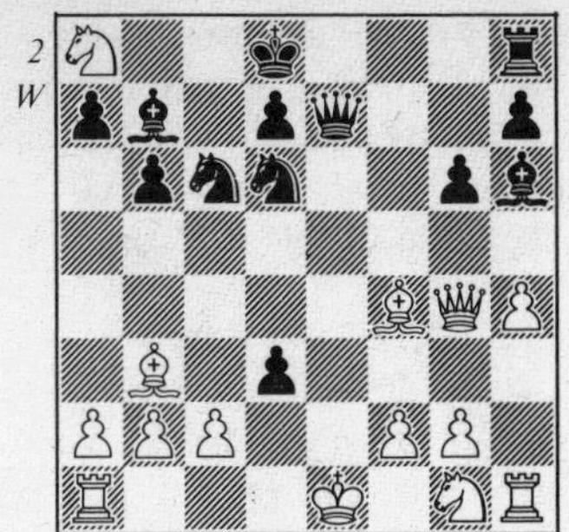

will do; and threats with some punch behind them too, not feeble things like 16 . . . ♗×f4 17 ♕×f4 ♖f8 18 ♕g5, or 16 . . . d×c2+ 17 ♗×c2, which would let White off the hook. If you examine the position, you will see that only the knights can act swiftly enough. In fact, Nunn's intended move during the game was 16 . . . ♘e5, which is essentially the right idea because it keeps the momentum going; it keeps harassing White with threats he cannot ignore: (a) 17 ♕g3 ♘f5; (b) 17 ♗g5 ♘×g4 winning a piece; (c) 17 ♗×h6 ♘×g4 18 ♗g5 ♘f6; or (d) 17 ♗×e5 ♕×e5 18 c3 (can't allow . . . ♕×b2) ♖e8 19 ♘h3 ♗×g2 and wins.

But he had overlooked something: 17 ♕g5!, which turns the tables in White's favour. The right way is to combine the two knights: 16 . . . ♘e4! 17 ♘h3 (if 17 ♗g3 ♘e5 18 ♕h3 d×c2+ 19 ♗×c2 ♕d6+ and wins) and only now 17 . . . ♘e5 18 ♗×e5 ♕×e5 19 c3 (still forced) ♘×f2+ 20 ♘×f2 ♕e3, winning the queen or mating.

16 . . . ♗×f4
17 ♕×f4 ♖f8

Of course, with the king at f1 this is much stronger. White's misfortune is that he has no decent square for his queen: 18 ♕g5 ♖×f2+ 19 ♔×f2 ♘e4+ 20 ♔f1 ♘×g5 21 h×g5 ♘e5! and White is unable to defend himself against the threat of . . . ♕f8+ and . . . ♗×g2. Other queen moves can also be disposed of, with the same tactical patterns tending to repeat themselves: 18 ♕c1 d2! 19 ♕×d2 ♘e4; 18 ♕d2 ♘e4; 18 ♕h6 ♘f5 and 19 . . . ♘e3+; 18 ♕h2 ♘e4 and then: (a) 19 ♘h3 ♘×f2; (b) 19 ♘f3 ♕c5; (c) 19 f3 ♕c5 20 ♘h3 ♕e3; (d) 19 ♕c7+ transposing into the game; 18 ♕g4 ♘e4 19 ♘f3 (or 19 ♘h3 ♘e5, or 19 f3 ♘e5) ♘e5 20 ♕h3 ♘×f3 21 g×f3 ♘d2+; 18 ♕a4 b5 etc.

There remains only:

18 ♕g3 ♘e4

Allowing the check looks perilous, but White is never able to exploit the position of the king and queen on the same file.

19 ♕c7+ ♔e8 *(3)*

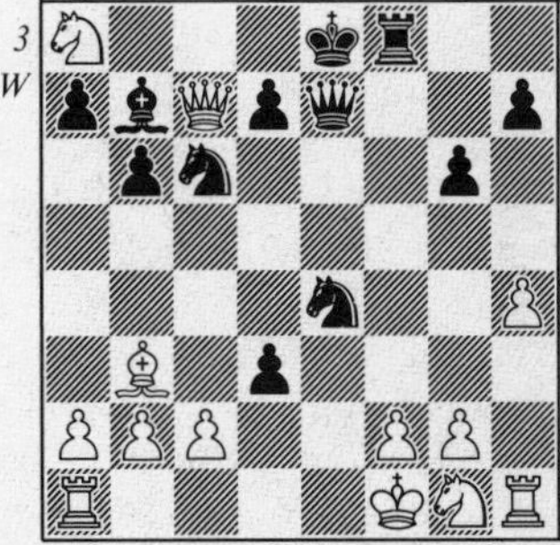

As early as move 14 Nunn will have seen the outline of the various attacks which might now unfold. After White's 18th move he will do some more detailed analysis along these lines: '18 . . . ♘e4, and 19 ♕c7+♔e8 is forced; then White has 20 f3, 20 ♘f3 or 20 ♘h3.' Now, just how quickly and efficiently he analyses these three moves depends on many factors; but a systematic approach vitally important. For instance, after 20 f3, ♘d2+ may be the first move that strikes him; but he will not make the mistake of analysing that one move at once. Many players would think along these lines: '20 . . . ♘d2+ 21 ♔f2 ♕c5+ 22 ♔g3. Then it gets difficult. Can I sacrifice by 22 . . . ♘e4+? No, that's no good. Perhaps I should play 22 . . . d×c2? Or just take the knight?' And much time is wasted, which could be saved by making a complete list of all the useful moves at the beginning. Then 20 . . . ♕c5! **cannot fail** to come to Black's attention, along with . . . ♘d2+ and anything else which might be appropriate; and by the same systematic process for the subsequent moves he will quickly exhaust the variation: 21 ♘h3 ♕e3! and wins.

20 ♘h3 is the game continuation and Black will soon see that 20 . . . ♘×f2 21 ♘×f2 ♕e2+ will give him at least perpetual check. 20 ♘f3 is altogether more complicated: 20 . . . ♕c5 21 ♔g1 and the play has to be exact. What might it be? 21 . . . ♕×f2+, 21 . . . ♖×f3, 21 . . . d×c2 – all kinds of things. In fact, 21 . . . ♕×f2+ is curiously feeble: 22 ♔h2 and then 22 . . . ♖×f3 23 ♖hf1 is unclear; Black cannot mate by 23 . . . ♖h3+ etc. because the white queen covers g3! Nunn's intention was 21 . . . ♖×f3! at once. Then White cannot capture either the rook or the bishop, and if 22 c×d3 ♕×f2+ 23 ♔h2 ♖f4! kills him. Beyond that he did not analyse during the game, judging that Black must win after . . . ♖×f3.

In fact, against the best defence there is still some work to do. The best try, 22 ♔h2, hoping for a transposition (22 . . . ♕×f2+ 23 ♖hf1 etc.), is met by the beautiful move 22 . . . d2!! Apart from the extra menace which the pawn itself represents, this forestalls the danger of a pin (♖he1) which would cripple the attack. We then have:

(a) 23 g×f3 ♕×f2+ 24 ♔h3 ♕×f3+ 25 ♔h2 ♕e2+! (psychologically difficult to spot, going away from the king, but an organised search for all possible checks will reveal the winning line) 26 ♔h3 ♘f2+ 27 ♔g3 (the king can never occupy the long diagonal because of . . . ♘a5+; so if 27 ♔h2 ♘×h1+) ♕e3+ 28 ♔h2 ♘g4+ and wins.

(b) 23 ♕×b7 ♕d6+ 24 ♔g1 d1/♕+ 25 ♖×d1 ♕×d1+ 26 ♔h2 ♕d6+ 27 ♔g1 ♖×f2, and after one check White will have no answer to the threats of . . . ♖f1+ and . . . ♖×g2+.

(c) 23 ♖hf1 ♖×f2 24 ♕×b7 ♕e5+ 25 ♔g1 ♕g3 26 ♖×f2 (26 ♕c8+ would not help, while 26 ♘c7+ ♔d8 would make things worse, as becomes clear in a moment) ♕×f2+ 27 ♔h2 ♕×h4+ 28 ♔g1 ♕e1+ 29 ♖×e1 d×e1/♕+ 30 ♔h2 ♕h4+ 31 ♔g1 ♕f2+ 32 ♔h2 ♕f4+ (had White played 26 ♘c7+, the knight would now be *en prise*!) 33 ♔g1 (or ♔h1) ♘e5! (threatening check at f2 and later at g4; also . . . ♘f3+; once White's checks run out he is doomed because his pieces are far away and his king is fatally exposed) 34 ♘c7+ ♔f8 35 ♕c8+ ♔g7 36 ♕g8+ (or ♘e8+) ♔h6 and wins.

(d) 23 ♖he1 d×e1/♕ 24 ♖×e1 ♕e5+! 25 ♔g1 (25 ♕×e5 ♘×e5 is no better) ♖×f2 and Black mates or remains a piece up: 26 ♖×e4 ♖×g2+ 27 ♔×g2 ♕×e4+ etc., or 26 ♕×b7 ♖×g2+ 27 ♔×g2 ♕g3+ 28 ♔h1 ♕×e1+ and mates.

20 ♘h3 ♘×f2

21 ♘×f2 . . .

There is no choice, since 21 ♔g1 ♕e3 forces White to capture and thus transpose.

21 . . . ♕e2+(?)

The presence of the pawn at d3 makes this check quite irresistible! Yet it is not the strongest. 21 . . . ♕e3! forces 22 ♔g1 anyway; then 22 . . . ♖×f2! Now, as an exercise you may like to analyse the position without moving the pieces. First of all establish precisely what Black is threatening (23 . . . ♖f4+ 24 ♔h2 ♖×h4 mate), because in that way you will eliminate 90 per cent of possible defences. Then you will see that White has only four attempts: (1) 23 ♖h2 ♖e2+ 24 ♔h1 ♖e1+ and mates; (2) 23 ♖h3 ♖f3+ 24 ♔h2 ♖×h3+ 25 g×h3 ♕f2+ 26 ♔h1 ♘a5+; (3) 23 g3 ♖e2+ and mate; (4) 23 ♔h2 ♘e5 with overwhelming threats of . . . ♘g4+ and . . . ♖×g2+.

22 ♔g1 ♕×f2+
23 ♔h2 ♕×h4+
24 ♔g1 ♕d4+
25 ♔h2 ♘e5! *(4)*

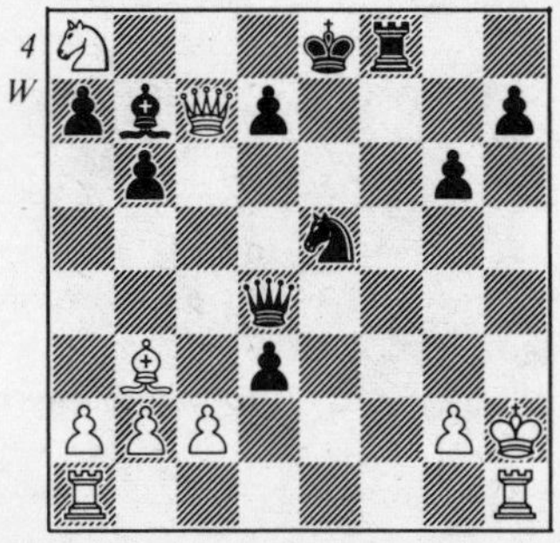

To continue the attack the knight and bishop must somehow be brought into play. Black's move is clearly stronger than any other attacking ideas which might occur to him (. . . ♖f4, . . . ♖f5) because he threatens mate in three (. . . ♕h4+, . . . ♕f2+ and . . . ♕×g2) and cuts out any checks on the e-file. Once again his analysis is simplified by being aware of the basic threat, and it goes as follows: (a) 26 ♕×b7 ♘g4+ 27 ♔h3 (27 ♔g3 ♕f4+ is quicker) ♘f2+ 28 ♔h2 ♕h4+ 29 ♔g1 ♕×h1 mate; (b) 26 ♖af1 (covering f2 is the only hope) ♕h4+ 27 ♔g1 ♖×f1+; (c) The game continuation 26 ♖hf1 ♘g4+, when the king must come out because 27 ♔h1 is defeated by 27 . . . ♗×g2+! 28 ♔×g2 ♘e3+ with mate at g2 after a couple of checks. This brings us back to the game.

26 ♖hf1 ♘g4+
27 ♔g3 . . .

27 ♔h3 ♗×g2+ 28 ♔×g2 is the same as above; or if 28 ♔g3 ♗×f1 29 ♖e1+ ♗e2, also with a mating attack.

27 . . . ♕e3+

If now 28 ♖f3, Black simply takes it; so the knight must be captured and we have an old-fashioned king hunt. Some king hunts are easy to play: this one is quite troublesome. The sheer number of alternative checks at each move is so confusing that even Nunn misses the quickest way on two occasions. What is more, White's pieces control several useful squares, and in the heat of battle (and short of time, as both players were by now) it would be easy to forget that Black cannot check, for example, on g8 or h2.

28 ♔×g4 *(5)* **. . .**

What about 28 ♔h4? Just follow the checking sequences, without any preconceived ideas about where you 'ought' to be driving the king. You can rarely deduce these things. For all you know at this stage, you may have to send him up the board or you may

5
B

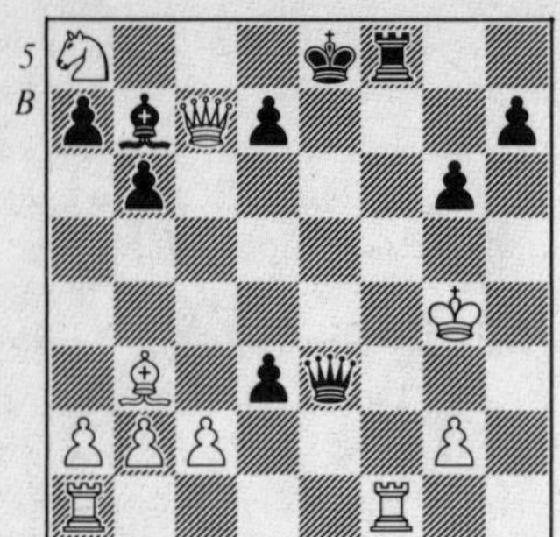

be able to drive him back and mate at g2: 28 ♔h4 ♕h6+ 29 ♔×g4 ♕h5+ 30 ♔g3 ♕g5+ 31 ♔h3 ♕×g2+ (back up the board now!) 32 ♔h4 g5+ 33 ♔h5 ♕h3+ 34 ♔×g5 h6+ 35 ♔g6 ♗e4+ 36 ♔g7 ♕g4+ 37 ♔×h6 ♕g6 mate. If here 29 ♔g3 ♕h2+ 30 ♔×g4 ♕h5+ transposes; 30 . . . ♕×g2+ also wins here, but it is a good idea to rely on transpositions: if you see the pattern repeating itself, it makes the mental work much easier.

28 . . . h5+

There is a quicker win here, but the calculation is more testing this time because there are three opening moves which all look attractive: . . . ♕e4+, . . . ♕e2+ and . . . h5+. After 28 . . . ♕e2+ 29 ♔h4 ♕h5+ Black transposes into the last note. 29 ♔g3 and 29 ♔h3 do the same, while 29 ♖f3 leads to 29 . . . ♗×f3+ 30 g×f3 ♕×f3+ 31 ♔h4 g5+ 32 ♔×g5 ♖f5+ 33 ♔h6 ♖h5+ 34 ♔g7 ♕f8 mate.

29 ♔h4 g5+

Again there is a quicker way: 29 . . . ♕e4+ 30 ♔g5 ♕e7+ 31 ♔×g6 ♗e4+ 32 ♔×h5 ♖h8+ 33 ♔g4 ♕h4 mate.

30 ♔×h5 ♖h8+

31 ♔g6 . . .

If 31 ♔g4 ♖h4+ 32 ♔f5 ♕e4+; then either 33 ♔f6 ♖h6+ 34 ♔×g5 ♖g6+ and mates, or 33 ♔×g5 ♖g4+ and mate.

31 . . . ♗e4+

The entry of Black's third piece has always been the decisive factor. If now 32 ♔f6 ♖f8+ 33 ♔g7 ♕d4+ and mates; or if 32 ♔g7 ♕d4+ 33 ♖f6 ♖h7+ 34 ♔g8 ♕×f6 (Black's only non-checking move in the entire ending!) and mates after White's harmless check.

32 ♖f5 ♗×f5+

33 ♔×f5 ♖f8+

34 ♔g6 . . .

34 ♔g4 ♕d4+ 35 ♔h5 ♕h8+ transposes into the game.

34 . . . ♕e4+

35 ♔g7 . . .

35 ♔×g5 ♖f5+, 35 ♔h6 ♖f6+ and 35 ♔h5 ♕h7+ are all quicker. Capturing the pawn always leaves the king wide open to mate on the two outer files.

35 . . . ♕e7+

36 ♔g6 ♕f6+

37 ♔h5 ♕h8+

38 ♔g4 . . .

If 38 ♔×g5 ♕g7+ and mates; if 38 ♔g6 ♖f6+ and mate in two more moves.

38 . . . ♕h4 mate.

Game 2

Pirc Defence
Groningen 1974–5
(European Junior Championship)

F. Borkowski v. J. Nunn

1	**e4**	**g6**
2	**d4**	**♗g7**
3	**♘c3**	**d6**
4	**f4**	**♘f6**
5	**♘f3**	**0–0**
6	**♗d3**	. . .

Generally regarded as stronger than 6 ♗e2, to which Black may reply 6 . . . c5 7 d×c5 (7 d5 b5! 8 ♗×b5 ♘×e4) ♕a5 8 0–0 ♕×c5+ etc. (8 c×d6 ♘×e4 is bad). After 6 ♗d3, on the other hand, 6 . . . c5 7 d×c5 d×c5 8 e5 ♘d5 9 ♘×d5 ♕×d5 10 ♕e2 favours White because the g7 bishop will be shut out of the game for some time; the move . . . f6 will require preparation, and even then White's e-pawn will be hard to dislodge.

6	. . .	**♘a6**

The purpose of this is to play . . . c5 and recapture with a piece. And, of course, 7 ♗×a6 b×a6 would be an unprofitable exchange because Black would put his bishop-pair and open b-file to good use long before the theoretical weakness of his a-pawns could be exploited (in some distant endgame). However, Nunn was experimenting here. 6 . . . ♘c6, preparing . . . e5, was the normal move in 1974; 6 . . . ♘a6 was considered dubious in view of the variation 7 e5 ♘e8 8 ♗e3 c5 9 d×c5 ♘×c5 10 ♗×c5 d×c5 11 ♕e2 f6 12 0–0–0 ♕a5 13 ♗c4+ ♔h8 14 h4, when Black's restricted bishop still gives him the worse of it, even though he has managed to exchange off one of White's bishops for a knight. In this line the knight's retreat to e8, rather than the more desirable square d7 (covering the important squares c5 and e5), was considered necessary because after . . . ♘d7 there is a danger of ♘g5 and e6; but some analysis of his own had convinced Nunn that the risks had been overestimated – hence his (successful) experiment. As a result of this and other games 6 . . . ♘a6 has now become quite respectable, and 7 0–0 is felt to be the soundest reply. Experience indicates that White does not have the centre under sufficient control to justify the sharper moves 7 e5 and especially 8 h4.

7	**e5**	**♘d7**
8	**h4** *(6)*	. . .

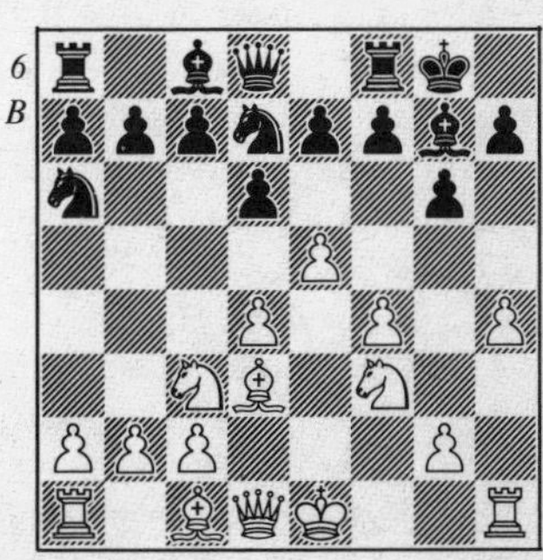

8 ♗e3 is nowadays reckoned to be the best move, and 8 ♘e4 is also

interesting, but lack of space unfortunately forbids any treatment of them here. Of course, 8 h4 is very dangerous in practice, even though it is not quite sound. This is one of the fiercest of all the anti-Pirc systems, and with his knight driven from f6 and his K-side weakened by . . . g6 Black is subject to all manner of attacks. In an earlier round of this tournament (against Bichsel) Nunn had faced another aggressive line: 8 ♘g5 ♘b6 (not 8 . . . h6? 9 ♘×f7 ♖×f7 10 e6) 9 ♗e3, but after 9 . . . ♘b4 10 0–0 ♘×d3 11 ♕×d3 ♗f5 12 ♕e2 f6 13 ♘ge4 ♕d7 he had a perfectly satisfactory position with pressure on White's centre and a potentially strong bishop-pair. As the main game proceeds we are reminded time and again what an important attacking piece White's K-bishop is; as a rule he needs a great deal of initiative to compensate him if it gets exchanged. But in the game just referred to 10 ♗e2 ♗f5 11 ♖c1 d×e5, followed by . . . ♘6d5, would have been altogether too awkward; or if 10 ♗e4 Black could happily choose between 10 . . . ♘c4 and 10 . . . d5 11 ♗f3 ♗f5. Bichsel could also have tried 9 h4, but again 9 . . . ♘b4 10 h5 (10 ♗e2 d×e5 11 f×e5 ♕×d4!) ♘×d3+ 11 ♕×d3 ♗f5 12 ♕e2 ♕d7 gives Black a grip on the white squares to offset the danger of attack.

8 . . . c5

Borkowski was evidently not satisfied that he had made the most of his chances in this game because he adopted the same line five years later (v. Balcerowski, Poland 1979). Alas, he met with an even worse fate! That game continued 8 . . . d×e5 (in one sense better than 8 . . . c5 because Black will shortly be in a position to take on e5 with a piece instead of a pawn; on the other hand, White's Q-bishop is now released) 9 f×e5 (if 9 d×e5 ♘dc5 is fine for Black, and better than 9 . . . ♘ac5 because either the K-bishop or the queens will be exchanged; . . . ♗f5 also becomes available) c5 10 h5 (10 e6 f×e6 11 h5 looks more promising, but Black has 11 . . . ♕c7, threatening check at g3, and nothing clear emerges; for example 12 ♘e4 c4 13 ♗e2 ♘f6 with a satisfactory game) c×d4 11 h×g6 h×g6 12 e6 d×c3! (12 . . . f×e6? 13 ♗×g6 d×c3 14 ♗h7+ wins) 13 e×f7+ ♖×f7 14 ♗×g6 (14 ♗c4 ♕e8 15 ♘g5 ♘e5 is not good enough) ♖×f3! 15 ♕d5+ e6! (to break the pin on the knight) 16 ♕×e6+ ♔f8 17 g×f3 ♘e5 18 ♖h8+ (desperate, but there is nothing else; the attack has misfired) ♗×h8 19 ♗h6+ ♗g7 20 ♕×e5 ♕d2+ 21 ♗×d2 c×d2+ 22 ♔×d2 and White resigned.

For sheer violence that takes some beating! Now we can use Borkowski–Balcerowski as a kind of introduction to the main game, firstly to examine some tactical points which are relevant to both, and indeed to the whole variation: (1) 11 . . . d×c3 is too dangerous on account of 12 ♘g5! ♘×e5 13 g×f7+ etc., or 12 . . . h×g6 13 ♗×g6, or 12 . . . h6 13 g×f7+. In the note to Black's tenth move you will find this attack analysed in more detail. 11 . . . f×g6? 12 ♗c4+ ♔h8 13 ♘g5 is naturally even worse. (2) On the other hand 12 . . . d×c3 is quite playable because 13 ♘g5 can safely be met by 13 . . . ♘e5 14 e×f7+ ♘×f7. (3) 14 . . . c×b2 15 ♗×f7+ ♔×f7 is bad because of 16 ♘g5+ ♔f8 17 ♕d5; but Black dare not waste time defending his rook and permitting ♘g5 and ♕h5

– hence his exchange sacrifice to eliminate one of the most dangerous pieces. (4) If 15 ♕×f3 ♘f6 stops everything, or if 15 g×f3 ♕b6 is the defence.

Secondly, some general questions arise concerning the art of defence, which is the main theme of both games. The crucial point for White is that as soon as he commits himself to 8 h4 his centre is bound to collapse, and he simply must keep the attack going full blast, or at least continue developing with threats. Any quick attack uses up resources out of your position (whether of material, time, pawn structure, king security or whatever) and if the attack fails you are left flat on your back, lacking the strength to meet the counter-attack in the centre which will inevitably hit you.

The defender, for his part, must take great care not to lose any time (obviously one tempo can make all the difference in such a sharp position), be on the look-out for a chance to return any sacrificed material, in order to grab the initiative for himself, and above all keep cool and examine **every one** of his opponent's aggressive possibilities. Defending for several hours is a wearying business and it is easy to lower your guard for a moment and miss something. Moreover, most people find their opponent's combinations much harder to spot than their own.

9 h5 . . .

This time 9 e6 f×e6 10 h5 c×d4 11 h×g6 h6 yields White very little on the K-side, and his centre has collapsed completely.

9 . . . c×d4

10 h×g6 . . .

Retracing our steps a bit, there is another theoretical line which has to be reckoned with here, namely 6 e5 ♘fd7 7 h4 c5 (7 . . . d×e5 8 d×e5 is open to the earlier objection – if 8 . . . ♘c5 9 ♕e2 and ♕f2) 8 h5 c×d4 9 h×g6, producing the game position, but without ♗d3 and . . . ♘a6. And the difference is very significant. In the 6 e5 line Black can and should take the knight at c3. If he plays 9 . . . h×g6 White gets a very dangerous attack by 10 ♕×d4 ♘c6 (or 10 . . . d×e5 11 d×e5 ♘×e5 12 ♕h4) 11 ♕f2 (11 . . . ♖e8 12 ♕h4 ♘f8 13 f5 ♗×f5 14 ♗h6, for instance); but after 9 . . . d×c3 Black gains the upper hand in some wild complications. Briefly (otherwise this would turn into a textbook on the Pirc!), these are as follows: 10 g×f7+ ♖×f7, and then (a) e6 c×b2 12 e×f7+ ♔f8 13 ♗×b2 ♗×b2 14 ♗c4 ♕a5+ 15 ♔f1 ♘f6 16 ♖b1 ♕c3 17 ♗b3 ♗f5, with a clear advantage (but not 17 . . . ♗g4? 18 ♘g5 ♗×d1 19 ♖×h7 1–0, Hessmer–Hafner, Correspondence 1983); (b) 11 ♘g5 c×b2 12 ♗c4! ♘×e5! 13 ♕h5 ♕a5+ 14 ♔f1 d5; (c) 11 ♗c4 e6! 12 ♘g5 (12 ♗×e6 ♘×e5 simplifies favourably, or if 12 f5 ♘×e5 13 f×e6 ♖e7 to Black's advantage) ♘f8! 13 ♘×f7 ♔×f7 14 ♕h5+ ♔g8 15 f5 ♕a5! and Black won easily (A. Schneider–Forgacs, Hungary 1975). One further point in this variation is that 9 ♕×d4 is refuted by 9 . . . d×e5 10 ♕f2 (10 f×e5 ♘×e5) e4! 11 ♘×e4 ♘f6 12 ♘×f6+ e×f6 13 h×g6 ♖e8+ 14 ♗e3, and Black gets a good game with either recapture. White is one move behind here compared with the earlier line and never gets a chance to do anything on the h-file.

But in Borkowski–Nunn (as in Borkowski–Balcerowski) the situation is reversed; the position of the bishop at d3 makes 10 . . . d×c3 too dangerous (see the next note), while 10 . . . h×g6 is good for Black because the queen cannot now reach h4 via d4 and f2!

10 . . . h×g6

10 . . . f×g6 is still bad, as you might expect: 11 ♗c4+ ♔h8 12 ♘g5 h6 13 ♕d3!, for instance, and if 13 . . . ♕e8 14 ♗f7 ♖×f7 15 ♕×g6 and wins. And if 10 . . . d×c3 White has a clear-cut win by 11 ♘g5! h×g6 (or 11 . . . h6 12 g×f7+ ♔h8 13 ♖×h6+ ♗×h6 14 ♕h5, or here 12 . . . ♖×f7 13 ♗h7+) 12 ♗×g6 ♘f6 (nothing better; if 12 . . . f×g6 13 ♕d5+; meanwhile 13 ♕h5 is threatened) 13 e×f6 f×g6 14 f×g7 ♔×g7 15 ♕d4+ e5 (or 15 . . . ♖f6 16 ♖h7+ ♔g8 17 ♖h8+) 16 ♖h7+ ♔f6 17 f×e5+ d×e5 18 ♕×d8+ ♖×d8 19 ♖f7 mate.

11 ♘g5 . . .

11 ♕e2 d×c3 12 ♕f2 would be unsound on account of 12 . . . d×e5 13 ♕h4 (if 13 f×e5 ♘f6 would be safest, transposing) ♘f6 14 f×e5 ♖e8! 15 e×f6 e×f6+ 16 ♔f1 ♗e6 17 ♕h7+ ♔f8 18 ♗h6 ♗×h6 19 ♕×h6+ ♔e7 etc. The text move stops 11 . . . d×c3 because of 12 ♗×g6, with the same variations as given above. At the same time ♕g4–h4, ♕f3–h3 and e6 are all in the air.

11 . . . d×e5

It is so natural to eliminate an important pawn and give his knight access to f6 that Nunn did not consider anything else at all; however, there were two other possible moves, 11 . . . ♘dc5 and 11 . . . ♘×e5:

The bishop at d3 is a dangerous attacking piece and if it can be exchanged the white squares (chiefly the diagonal h3–c8) will fall under Black's control and the attack will grind to a halt. And 11 . . . ♘dc5 is better than the more obvious 11 . . . ♘ac5 because the Q-bishop is released to take over these squares; at the same time the three dangers referred to above (♕f3–h3, ♕g4 and e6) are all eliminated.

Reducing this to concrete analysis gives us: 11 . . . ♘dc5 12 f5 (12 ♘ce4 ♘×e4 13 ♗×e4 ♘c5 is also fine for Black) ♘×d3+ 13 ♕×d3 ♗×f5 (still not 13 d×c3? 14 ♕h3 ♖e8 15 ♕h7+ ♔f8 16 ♘e6+ f×e6 17 ♗h6 and wins) 14 ♕×d4 ♕a5! (very instructive; not 14 . . . ♗×e5? 15 ♕h4, when 15 . . . ♖e8 is unplayable, nor 14 . . . d×e5 15 ♕h4 ♖e8 16 ♕h7+ ♔f8 17 ♘e6+ f×e6 18 ♗h6, with a very dangerous attack) 15 ♕h4 ♕×e5+ 16 ♘ce4 ♖fc8, and if 17 ♗f4 ♕×b2 18 ♕h7+ ♔f8 and the attack is exhausted. Notice how the centralised position of the black queen almost effortlessly frustrates the attack based on ♕h7+, ♘e6+ and ♗h6. There is a powerful kind of counter-attacking move which we shall encounter frequently in all the analysis which follows, and it would be as well to develop a feeling for it because it is most valuable in acquiring defensive skills. This is the move which combines defence with the generation of counter-threats. In this game it usually involves a centralising move by the queen, acting backwards along the long black diagonal for defensive purposes while at the same time preparing to exploit White's exposed king. Another move of this kind crops us in the next note.

We are not yet finished with 11 . . . ♘dc5, because White has one move to keep the attack going, namely, 12 ♔f2! with the powerful threat of 13 ♖h8+ ♗×h8 19 ♕h1 forcing mate. It would be very easy to overlook a sneaky move like ♔f2, but the open h-file near Black's king should make you alert to unusual tactical possibilities. Black's best reply is 12 . . . ♘xd3+ 13 cxd3 ♖e8, when White has two possible methods of continuing his attack. The immediate 14 ♖h8+ ♗xh8 15 ♕h1 ♗g7 16 ♕h7+ ♔f8 17 f5 seems to lead to a draw after 17 . . . ♗xf5 18 ♘e6+ fxe6 19 ♗h6 ♗xh6+ 20 ♕xh6+ ♔f7 (20 . . . ♔g8 21 ♖h1), but 14 ♘ce4 may be good for White, swinging another piece over to the K-side and reserving ♖h8+ for a more favourable moment.

The second alternative, 11 . . . ♘xe5, is based on the idea of breaking up White's pawn centre with gain of tempo. After 12 fxe5 dxc3 White's most dangerous move is still 13 ♔f2!. Then a game De Firmian–van der Wiel (Wijk aan Zee 1986) continued 13 . . . dxe5 14 ♗e3 (14 ♖h8+ ♗xh8 15 ♕h1 ♔g7 16 ♕h7+ ♔f6 17 ♘xf7 ♔e6 18 ♕xg6+ ♔d7 19 ♗f5+ ♔c7 20 ♘xd8 ♗xf5 wins for Black) ♕d6! (again the queen comes to the rescue, this time preparing to support the long diagonal with gain of tempo by . . . ♕f6+) 15 ♖h4 (15 ♖h8+ ♗xh8 16 ♕h1 ♕f6+ and 17 . . . ♕g7 defends) cxb2 16 ♖b1 ♖d8 17 ♕h1 ♕f6+ 18 ♔g1 ♖xd3 19 cxd3 ♗f5 20 ♘h7 ♕d6 21 ♘g5 ♕f6 22 ♘h7 ♕d6 23 ♘g5 with a draw by repetition. However, 13 . . . ♗xe5 would have been more dangerous for White. The sacrifice 14 ♖h8+ fails as before, so there would be nothing better than to play 14 ♗e3. Then 14 . . . e6 again prepares a possible . . . ♕f6+, so White would have to continue 15 ♔e2, with some attacking chances to compensate for the three-pawn deficit. Although this may well be good for Black, 11 . . . dxe5 is also promising, so 11 . . . ♘xe5 is not clearly better than the move played. It is worth noting that after 11 . . . dxe5 12 ♔f2 is completely ineffective because of 12 . . . ♘f6.

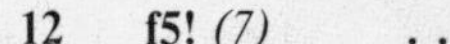

12 f5! *(7)* . . .

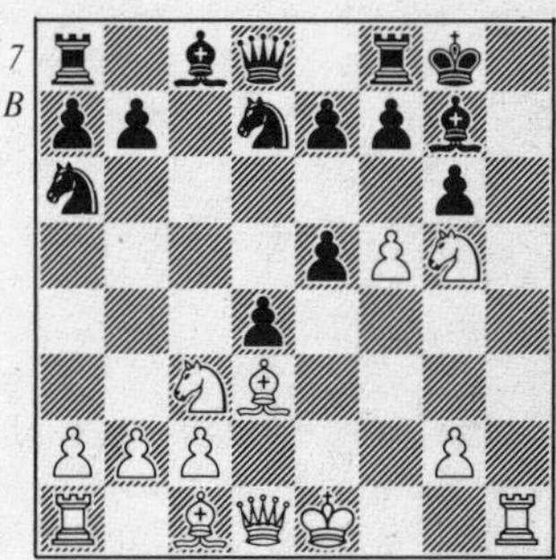

Much the best chance, which nevertheless cost White well over an hour on the clock. The alternatives fail dismally, as follows: (a) 12 fxe5 ♘xe5, and White is simply two pawns down for nothing; (b) 12 ♕f3 ♘f6 (12 . . . dxc3 13 ♗xa6 transposes; this way White is not allowed ♕h3) 13 ♗xa6 (or 13 fxe5 dxc3 14 exf6 exf6 and wins) dxc3 14 fxe5 ♗g4 and wins; (c) 12 ♕g4 ♘f6 13 ♕h4 dxc3 14 fxe5 (if 14 ♘e4 or ♘h7 ♖e8 15 ♘xf6+ exf6 16 ♕h7+ ♔f8 and White has nothing) ♘h5 15 g4 ♕d4! 16 gxh5 ♕xh4+ 17 ♖xh4 ♗xe5, with the decisive threats of . . . cxb2 and . . . ♗g3+.

Our typical counter-attacking move turns up again here (. . . ♕d4!). Some players positively relish this type of game (Korchnoi, for example, though not normally Nunn) and are at their most dangerous when defending, always provided they have some aggressive possibilities of their own and a chance to counter-attack.

Passive defence, with no real hope of more than a draw at the end of it, is a very different matter, a depressing experience for all but the toughest characters.

Now the strength of 12 f5 lies in its threat against g6, combined with the release of the Q-bishop. A further point is that the square e4 becomes available for the white knights and Black is left with a rather useless pawn at e5 which only obstructs his pieces. Just what constitutes a genuine attack and what doesn't is a hard thing to learn; it seems that against a perfect defence 12 f5 is still not quite good enough. In such a position the line between success and failure has become very fine indeed.

12 . . . ♘f6?

Here it was Nunn's turn to think for more than an hour. He has four options: (a) 12 . . . d×c3; (b) 12 . . . ♘dc5; (c) 12 . . . ♘f6 and (d) 12 . . . g×f5, and two of them lose rapidly, as follows: (a) 12 . . . d×c3 13 f×g6 ♘f6 (forced, because the threats are 14 g×f7+ and 14 ♕h5, and 13 . . . f6, . . . f5 and . . . f×g6 are all met by 14 ♗c4+) 14 g×f7+ ♖×f7 15 ♗h7+, winning the queen; (b) 12 . . . ♘dc5 13 f×g6 ♘×d3+ 14 ♕×d3 f×g6 (14 . . . f5 15 ♕c4+, or 14 . . . ♘c5 15 g×f7+ ♖×f7 16 ♕g6, threatening 17 ♖h8+ as well as the rook) 15 ♕c4+ e6 16 ♘×e6 ♗×e6 17 ♕×e6+ ♖f7 18 ♘e4, and White has a very strong attack with threats of ♘g5, ♘d6 and ♕×g6.

All that is straightforward enough, but deciding between 12 . . . ♘f6 and 12 . . . g×f5 is quite another matter; in fact it is impossible over the board because the position has become too complicated and finely balanced. Analysis indicates that Black should still win by 12 . . . g×f5 and that White should reach a favourable ending after the weaker move 12 . . . ♘f6.

But 12 . . . g×f5 looks suicidal, since among other things it allows ♕h5. Nunn actually gave it some thought during the game, but not surprisingly rejected it as too dangerous, even though he could not see a clear refutation.

Here then is the analysis to justify 12 . . . g×f5. White's choice lies among the obvious moves 13 ♕h5 and 13 ♗×f5 and the far from obvious 13 ♘ce4. The point of this peculiar idea is to keep the black knight out of f6, even at the cost of a piece; and if Black takes he gets into serious trouble, as follows: 13 . . . f×e4? 14 ♘×e4 and then: (a) . . . ♘f6 15 ♘×f6+ e×f6 16 ♗h7+ ♔h8 17 ♕h5 and wins; (b) 14 . . . ♕b6 15 ♕h5 ♕g6 (or 15 . . . ♖d8 16 ♕h7+ ♔f8 17 ♗h6 and wins – a theme which keeps recurring) 16 ♕×g6 f×g6 17 ♗c4+ ♖f7 18 ♘g5 with a clear advantage; (c) 14 . . . e6 (if 14 . . . f6 or . . . f5 at once 15 ♗c4+ is decisive) 15 ♕h5 f5 (if 15 . . . ♖e8 16 ♗h6! without the preliminary queen check this time) 16 ♕h7+ ♔f7 17 ♗g5! (clearer than 17 ♘g5+ ♔e7 18 ♕×g7+ ♔d6), and now: (i) 17 . . . f×e4 18 ♗×d8 e×d3 (or 18 . . . ♖×d8 19 0–0+ ♘f6 20 ♖×f6+ ♔×f6 21 ♖f1+ ♔e7 22 ♕×g7+ ♔d6 23 ♗×e4 and wins) 19 0–0+ ♔e8 20 ♖×f8+ ♗×f8 21 ♗g5 ♘dc5 22 ♖f1 and wins; (ii) 17 . . . ♕b6 (17 . . . ♕c7 is no improvement and 17 . . . ♕a5+ 18 ♔e2 only helps White to use his other rook) 18 ♕h5+ ♔g8 19 ♕g6 ♕×b2 (there are various threats, chiefly 20 ♖h7 ♖f7 21 ♗h6, and Black has few defences; 19 . . . f×e4 fails against 20 ♕h7+ ♔f7 21 ♖f1+ ♔e8 22 ♕g6, or if 19 . . . ♖f7

20 ♖h8+ ♔×h8 21 ♕×f7 ♘f8 – otherwise 0–0–0 – 22 ♘f6 and wins) 20 ♕×e6+ ♖f7 21 ♗c4 ♕b4+ (21 . . . ♕×a1+ 22 ♔f2 ♕×h1 23 ♕×f7+ ♔h7 24 ♕g8+ ♔g6 25 ♗f7 mate) 22 ♔e2 ♕f8 (or 22 . . . ♕×c4+ 23 ♕×c4 f×e4 24 ♖af1 and wins) 23 ♕g6 ♕e8 24 ♘d6 and wins.

But if Black declines the offer the . . . ♕b6 defence works, since h6 is now available for his queen, thus: 13 . . . ♕b6 14 ♕h5 ♕h6! (not 14 . . . ♕g6? 15 ♕×g6 f×g6 16 ♗c4+) 15 ♕×h6 ♗×h6 16 ♖×h6 f×e4 17 ♗×e4 ♘f6, and the bishop will be exchanged or driven off its aggressive diagonal; . . . ♗f5 then follows and White's compensation for his two-pawn deficit is quite inadequate.

The second of White's three options at move 13 can be disposed of readily enough. If 13 ♗×f5 ♘f6 (still not 13 . . . d×c3? 14 ♗h7+ ♔h8 15 ♗g6+ ♔g8 16 ♕h5) 14 ♗×c8 (or 14 ♗h7+ ♘×h7 15 ♖×h7 ♗f5 16 ♕h5 ♕d6, followed by . . . ♕g6) ♕×c8 15 ♘ce4 ♘×e4 16 ♘×e4 ♕f5, and again the arrival of the black queen signals the collapse of the attack.

That leaves only 13 ♕h5, the most natural move of all and the most dangerous for Black. After 13 . . . ♘f6 14 ♕h4 d×c3 the black knight obviously has to be driven from f6, whatever the cost, but both attempts just fail, as follows: (a) 15 ♘h7 ♘g4 16 ♘g5 (16 ♘f6+ ♘×f6 17 ♗h6 looks powerful, but again 17 . . . ♕d4! (–g4) and the attack disintegrates) ♘h6, and nothing will quite work; if 17 ♘e6 f×e6 18 ♗×h6 ♕d4, or 17 ♘e4 ♕b6, or 17 ♘×f7 ♖×f7 18 ♗c4 ♕d6, or 17 ♘h7 ♕d4 18 ♕×d4 e×d4 19 ♘×f8 ♔×f8 20 ♗×h6 ♗×h6 21 ♖×h6 ♔g7, with a clear advantage to Black in every case. (b) 15 ♘e4 f×e4, and now: (i) 16 ♗×e4 ♖e8! 17 ♗h7+ (17 ♗h6? ♕d4) ♔f8 18 ♗h6 ♕d2+! (nothing else will do because the king cannot escape via e7 or e8, but, as so often, the counter-sacrifice turns the tables completely) 19 ♗×d2 c×d2+ 20 ♔×d2 ♖d8+ and Black is winning, with both a material and a positional advantage. With the disappearance of one vital piece White's attack has dried up altogether, and his own king will soon be coming under fire. (ii) 16 ♗h6 c×b2 (another recurring motif; events in the a1 corner have a direct bearing on the K-side play; if now 17 ♗×g7 b×a1/♕+ and 18 . . . ♕×h1 wins, or if 17 ♕g5 b×a1/♕+ 18 ♔d2 ♕a5+ etc., and Black has . . . ♘e8 available, should he need it) 17 ♖d1 ♗f5! (the only move) 18 ♕g5 (or 18 ♗×g7 ♘h7 19 ♕g3 – 19 ♗×e5 ♕a5+ – ♕b6 20 ♗f6+ ♗g6 and wins) ♗g6 19 ♗×g7 ♘h7 20 ♖×h7 (anything else would be too slow) e×d3 21 ♗×e5 (the king escapes after 21 ♖h8+ ♔×g7 22 ♕h6+ ♔f6) ♕a5+ 22 ♔f1 ♕×e5 23 ♕×e5 ♗×h7 and Black wins.

Notice one hidden danger for Black in this line. 20 . . . ♗×h7 is a playable alternative to 20 . . . e×d3 because 21 ♗f6+ ♗g6 22 ♗c4 (threatening ♕×g6+) can be answered by 22 . . . ♕×d1+ 23 ♔×d1 b1/♕+ 24 ♔d2 ♖ad8+ 25 ♔e2 ♕×c2+ and 26 . . . ♕×c4. But 20 . . . ♕a5+ 21 ♔f1 ♗×h7 would be a blunder, permitting 22 ♗c4! e6 23 ♗f6+ ♗g6 24 ♕h6. Had the rook gone to b1 at move 17, 20 . . . e×d3 would certainly be the safest continuation, the alternative being the somewhat obscure 20 . . . ♗×h7 21 ♗c4 e6 22 ♗f6+ ♗g6 23 ♗×e6 ♕×f6 etc.

White may also play 14 ♕h3 or

♕h2 here. 14 ♕h3 has the advantage that the . . . ♕d4 resource is not at Black's disposal, but that is far outweighed by the handicap of placing the queen on the c8–h3 diagonal. For one thing any ideas based on ♘e4 are ruled out. In fact Black wins more easily here: 14 ♕h3 d×c3 15 ♘h7 ♘g4, and then: (a) 16 ♘f6+ ♘×f6 17 ♗h6 f4 18 ♕h4 c×b2 19 ♖d1 (or 19 ♖b1, which amounts to the same thing, but not 19 ♗×g7 b×a1/♕+ and 20 . . . ♕×h1, nor 19 ♕g5 b×a1/♕+, when Black mates or wins the queen) ♕a5+ 20 ♔f1 e4! 21 ♗×g7 ♕h5 22 ♕×h5 ♘×h5 and Black emerges a piece and several pawns up; (b) 16 ♘g5 ♘h6 17 ♘e6 c×b2! (17 . . . ♗×e6 18 ♗×h6 is too dangerous because there is now no . . . ♕d4!) 18 ♘×g7 b×a1/♕ 19 ♕×h6 ♕×c1+ 20 ♕×c1 f4 ♕d1 ♕a5+ 22 ♔f1 e4 23 ♗×e4 ♔×g7 and wins.

14 ♕h2 is weaker simply because . . . ♘g4 attacks the queen; 14 . . . d×c3 15 ♘e4 (15 ♘h7 ♘g4) f×e4 16 ♗×e4 ♖e8 17 ♗h7+ ♔f8 18 ♗h6 ♘g4, for example.

Returning to the game, White should gain some advantage after 12 . . . ♘f6 because the complete removal of the black king's pawn cover turns out to be more significant than the fact that ♕h5 (or anywhere else on the h-file) has been made more difficult.

13 f×g6 . . .

Not 13 ♘ce4? ♗×f5 14 ♘×f6+ e×f6 15 ♗×f5 f×g5, when Black just has three extra pawns.

13 . . . ♗g4

The intention of Black's previous move, of course; 13 . . . d×c3? 14 g×f7+ ♖×f7 15 ♗h7+ and 13 . . . f×g6? 14 ♗c4+ e6 15 ♘×e6 are still unplayable.

14 g×f7+ ♖×f7

15 ♘e2 . . .

White's choice is limited because his knight is under attack, but this is undoubtedly the best move. The other options all involve the exchange of queens in various ways, but in each case the resulting endgame position is unattractive. If 15 ♘×f7 ♔×f7 16 ♗e2 (16 ♘e2 ♕d5 transposes to the note to White's 16th) ♗f5 with tremendous pressure. If 15 ♗g6 ♗×d1 16 ♗×f7+ ♔f8 17 ♘e6+ (17 ♘×d1 ♘c7) ♔×f7 18 ♘×d8+ ♖×d8 19 ♘×d1 ♘b4 20 0–0 (20 ♔d2? ♘d4+ costs a rook) ♘×c2 21 ♖b1 e4 and Black is winning (two powerful passed pawns and White undeveloped). Finally, if 15 ♕×g4 ♘×g4 16 ♗h7+ ♔f8 17 ♘e6+ ♔e8 18 ♘×d8 ♖×d8 19 ♘e4 ♘b4 20 ♘g5 ♖f6, and Black's extra pawn, together with the possibility of playing . . . ♘d5–e3, would seem to outweigh slightly his bad bishop and White's blockade of the central white squares.

15 . . . ♕d5

Threatens g2 and prevents ♗c4. Here again we see one of the hazards of a quick attack – Black's willingness to surrender some material in order to seize the initiative. 15 . . . ♖f8 16 ♗c4+ ♘d5 might be playable, but after 17 ♕d3 ♗f5 18 ♕f3 ♘ab4 (or 18 . . . e6 19 ♘g3 ♗×c2 20 ♕g4, which looks dangerous) 19 ♘g3 he would certainly have an uphill defensive task ahead of him. Incidentally, there is another curious possibility here: 17 ♘c3 ♗×d1 18 ♗×d5+ ♕×d5 19 ♘×d5 (threatens mate) ♖fe8 20 ♔×d1 ♖ad8 and the knight is trapped. Then, after 21 ♘e3 d×e3+ 22 ♔e2 ♘b4!, or alternatively 21 ♘×e7+ ♖×e7 22 ♘e4 ♖c8, Black's lead in development is likely to be more significant that White's superior bishop.

And that raises an important point. In the sequel, by an odd reversal of the earlier state of affairs, it is White who will generally be in possession of the long-term advantages; and in several variations we shall have to judge whether Black's more advanced development amounts to sufficient compensation.

16 ♗g6 ...

16 ♘×f7 ♔×f7 is scarcely worth a second look: Black would have a huge lead in development, a mighty pawn centre and threats of . . . ♕×g2, . . . e4 and . . . ♘b4.

16 ... ♖ff8

17 ♕d3 ...

Threatening 18 ♗h7+ ♔h8 19 ♗e4+, the only possible way to follow up the attack. Against anything slower Black plays . . . ♕×g2 or . . . ♘c5 and White may as well give up.

17 ... e4 *(8)*

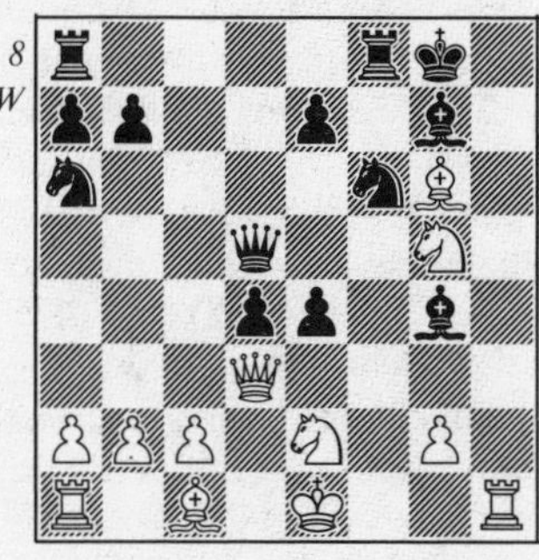

This too is forced, and the game has already reached its crisis. With his following move (18 ♕×d4) White misjudges (or misanalyses) the ensuing endgame and gets slightly the worse of it. But not all endings are bad, as we shall see; it depends how much initiative Black can obtain before White catches up in development.

Now both captures on e4 can be refuted quite easily: (a) 18 ♘×e4? ♘b4 19 ♘×f6+ ♖×f6 20 ♗h7+ (or 20 ♕e4 ♕×e4 21 ♗×e4 ♖e6 and wins) ♔f8 21 ♕g3 ♕e6 22 ♗d3 ♖c8 and Black has a winning advantage; and (b) 18 ♗×e4 ♘×e4 19 ♕×e4 ♕×e4 20 ♘×e4 ♘b4, winning at least a pawn and maintaining the attack.

Since White dare not play a passive move such as 18 ♕b3 while still a pawn down, his choice (apart from 18 ♕×d4) lies between 18 ♕g3 and 18 ♘c3! And 18 ♕g3 fails against 18 . . . ♘b4 19 ♕h4 ♘×c2+ 20 ♔d2 (20 ♔d1 ♘e3+ is worse) e3+ 21 ♔×c2 (21 ♔d1 ♗×e2+) ♗f5+ 22 ♗×f5 ♕×f5+ 23 ♔d1 ♘g4, with two pawns and a strong attack for the piece. Nor can White improve his play at move 19: if 19 ♕×g4 ♘×c2+ 20 ♔d1 ♘e3+ wins, since Black only needs to check on a black square with his queen to be able to play . . . ♘×g4; if 19 ♘f4? ♕×g5; if 19 ♗×e4 ♘×e4 20 ♕×g4 ♘×c2+ 21 ♔d1 ♘f2+; if 19 ♘×e4 ♘×c2+ 20 ♔d1 ♘e3+ and wins.

But 18 ♘c3! seems to guarantee some advantage because both captures are bad for Black, who therefore has to abandon his e-pawn: (a) 18 . . . d×c3? 19 ♗h7+; (b) 18 . . . e×d3 19 ♘×d5 ♖fd8 (19 . . . ♘×d5 20 ♗h7+ ♔h8 21 ♗e4+ ♔g8 22 ♗×d5+ e6 23 ♗×b7 and wins) 20 ♗f7+! ♔f8 21 ♘f4 ♗f5 22 ♗e6, and Black is obliged to surrender material – 22 . . . ♗×e6 23 ♘g×e6+ ♔g8 24 ♘×d8 ♘b4 25 ♘de6 etc., or 22 . . . ♗e4 23 c×d3 ♗c6 24 ♗f7. So Black has to move his queen. 18 . . . ♕a5 19 ♕×d4 ♖ad8 20 ♕c4+ e6 21 ♗e3 (not 21 ♘×e6 ♖d1+) gives White a solid centralised position with plenty of targets to attack; therefore the best square is e5, covering the d-pawn and keeping as aggressive and centralised as possible. We then have 18 . . . ♕e5 19 ♘c×e4 ♘c5 20 ♕g3! ♕×g3 21 ♘×g3 and it is now White who has time on his side. Some of his pressure against the castled position persists, and he has possibilities such as ♘f5, obliging Black to exchange, or ♗f4, 0–0 and ♖fe1, bringing the hanging pawns under fire. About the best Black can manage is 21 . . . ♘e6 22 ♘f5 ♗×f5 23 ♗×f5 ♘×g5 24 ♗×g5 ♔f7, with the two bishops and passed pawn certain to cause him problems in the endgame.

In this line 20 ♕c4+ might look more attractive, but actually achieves little: 20 . . . ♘e6 21 ♖h4 (or 21 g3, planning ♗f4, ♖ac8 22 ♕b3 ♖c6 and Black is safe enough) ♖ac8 22 ♕b3 ♖c6, and in this thoroughly confusing position it is probably Black who stands better. He can work to free himself by . . . ♗f5, and ♗f4 can be met by . . . ♕a5+.

18 ♕×d4(?) ♕×d4

19 ♘×d4 ♖ad8

The difference between 18 ♘c3 and 18 ♕×d4 boils down to the fact that Black is now operating aggressively along the d-file. Had White captured the e-pawn instead of the d-pawn that would not have been possible, and his own central position would have been more stable. Even as things stand, Black has to move fast before White consolidates and reaches a favourable ending. Players who are inclined to be casual about *tempi* should note that one extra move here could quite easily affect the result.

20 ♗e3 . . .

Everything else is bad. If 20 c3 e5 21 ♘e2 ♘c5, with the powerful threat of . . . ♘d3+; if 20 ♘e2 ♘b4; if 20 ♘ge6 ♖d6! 21 ♘×f8 ♖×d4 22 ♗e3 (otherwise . . . ♖d1+) ♖d6 23 ♘h7 ♘d5 and Black emerges with two pieces for a rook, or if here 23 ♗f4 ♖b6 24 ♗e3 ♖×b2 25 ♘h7 (25 ♗d4 ♖b4 26 ♗c3 ♖c4 wins) ♘d5 26 ♗d2 (or 26 ♗×a7 ♖×c2 27 ♗×e4 ♖e6 28 ♘g5 ♖×e4+ 29 ♘×e4 ♗×a1 with a winning advantage.

20 . . . ♘b4

Black's pieces are beginning to coordinate menacingly. The chief threat is 21 . . . ♖×d4 and the white king is caught most unhappily between the d- and f-files; moreover, several of his other pieces are suddenly in danger. For all that, though, his position is still holding together, and it is only his 21st move that wrecks everything. There is just one good continuation here, as we can see from the following analysis: (a) 21 c3 ♘d3+ 22 ♔d2 ♘e5, threatening both bishops; (b) 21 ♘×e4 ♖×d4 22 ♘×f6+ ♗×f6 23 ♗×d4 ♗×d4 and wins; (c) 21 0–0 ♘fd5! (using this knight because White has abandoned the h-file and because Black now controls f4) and White must lose material – 22 ♗f7+ (22 ♖×f8+ first is no improvement) ♖×f7 (definitely not 22 . . . ♔h8? 23 ♔f2) 23 ♘×f7 ♘×e3 24♘×d8 ♗×d4 25 c3 ♗b6 26 c×b4 ♘×f1+ 27 ♔×f1 ♗×d8 and wins; (d) 21 ♘ge6! and then: (i) 21 . . . ♘×c2+ 22 ♘×c2 ♗×e6 23 ♗×a7 ♖a8 (23 . . . ♖d5, threatening . . . ♖g5, is safely met by 24 ♗e3) 24 ♗d4 (24 ♗c5? ♖fc8) ♖×a2 25 ♖×a2 ♗×a2, and a draw is inevitable, Black's extra pawn being too weak to be of any significance; (ii) 21 . . .

♗×e6 22 ♘×e6 ♘×c2+ 23 ♔e2 ♘×e3 (or 23 . . . ♘×a1 24 ♖×a1, which is also very drawish) 24 ♘×d8 ♖×d8 25 ♔×e3 ♖d3+ 26 ♔e2 ♖g3 27 ♗f5 ♖×g2+ 28 ♔f1 ♖×b2 29 ♗e6+ ♔f8 30 ♖c1, and the position is unclear. White could also play 26 ♔f4 in this line, and in fact Black may be in some danger of overpressing by sacrificing the exchange.

21 ♖c1? ♘bd5

Black now wins material by force. This time, of course, he has to use the b4 knight or White would have 22 ♗h7+. If 21 . . . ♘×a2 22 ♖a1 ♘b4 White would have an opportunity to correct his error by 23 ♘ge6. Although he would have a pawn less, he would certainly stand a much better chance than in the game continuation.

22 ♗f2 . . .

If 22 ♔d2 ♘×e3 23 ♔×e3 ♘d5+ wins a piece, or if 22 ♗d2 e3 23 ♗a5 b6 24 ♗c3 ♘f4 25 ♗d3 (25 ♗f5 ♖×d4) ♘×g2+ 26 ♔f1 ♘e4+ and Black wins against any defence: (a) 27 ♔×g2 ♖f2+ 28 ♔g1 ♘×g5; (b) 27 ♔g1 ♘×g5; (c) 27 ♘gf3 ♗×d4 28 ♗×e4 ♗×f3 29 ♗×f3 ♖×f3+ 30 ♔×g2 ♖f2+ 31 ♔g3 ♗×c3 32 b×c3 ♖d6 (or 32 . . . ♖dd2) and wins; (d) 27 ♘df3 ♖×d3 28 c×d3 (or 28 ♔×g2 ♘×g5 29 ♘×g5 ♖d5) ♘×g5 and wins.

22 . . . ♘f4 *(9)*

23 ♗f5 . . .

Or 23 ♗h7+ ♘×h7, attacking the knight at d4.

9
W

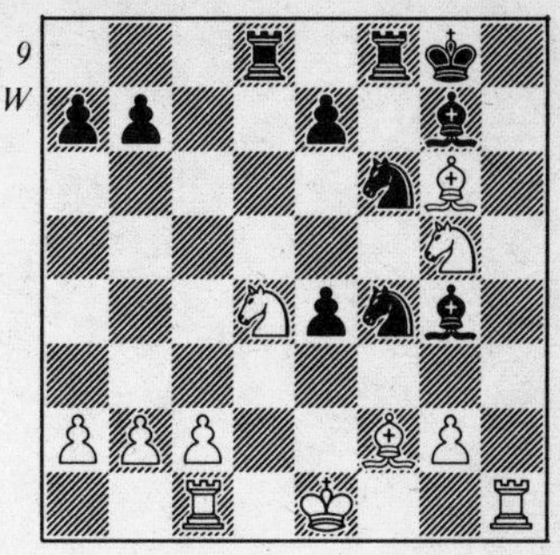

23 . . . ♖×d4

24 ♗×d4 . . .

Or 24 ♗×g4 ♘×g4, covering the rook.

24 . . . ♗×f5

25 g3 ♘e6

26 ♘×e6 ♗×e6

27 ♗×a7 ♘g4

28 ♗c5 . . .

Black has a decisive attack in addition to his extra material; if 28 c3 ♗e5 29 ♖g1 ♖f3 and wins.

28 . . . ♗×b2

0 – 1

Black either gets a mating attack or his pawn runs through. If, for instance, 29 ♖b1 ♗c3+ 30 ♔d1 ♖d8+ 31 ♔c1 e3 etc. There is also a trap which White could have tried: 29 ♗×e7, and if 29 . . . ♗×c1? 30 ♗×f8 ♔×f8 31 0–0+!, when Black would have technical difficulties in winning. The right way is 29 . . . ♗c3+ 30 ♔d1 (or 30 ♔e2 ♗c4+ 31 ♔d1 ♘f2 mate) ♘f2+ 31 ♔e2 ♗c4+ 32 ♔e3 ♖f3 mate.

Game 3

Two Knights Defence
Birmingham 1975
M. Corden v. J. Nunn

1	**e4**	**e5**
2	**♘f3**	**♘c6**
3	**d4**	**e×d4**
4	**♗c4**	**♘f6**
5	**e5**	**d5**

Almost always played, though 5 . . . ♘e4 is a simple and effective equaliser (6 ♕e2 ♘c5).

6	**♗b5**	**♘e4**
7	**♘×d4**	**♗c5** *(10)*

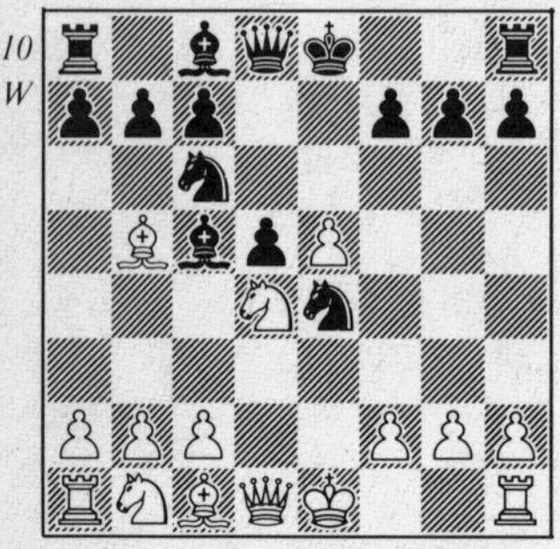

This is an ancient opening, going back to Steinitz and Morphy and beyond. The standard move is 7 . . . ♗d7, but 7 . . . ♗c5 has much to be said for it in that Black may be able to gain time by omitting . . . ♗d7 altogether. In reply 8 ♗e3 has the best reputation because it obliges him to transpose: 8 . . . ♗d7 9 ♗×c6 b×c6 10 0–0 etc. If Black tries a sacrifice by 8 . . . 0–0 9 ♘×c6 b×c6 10 ♗×c5 ♘×c5 11 ♗×c6 ♗a6, then 12 ♘c3! (rather than the dangerous 12 ♗×a8 ♕×a8) favours White: he has won a pawn, threatens the d-pawn and can organise castling by ♗b5 or ♘e2.

But against any other eighth move the aggressive potential of . . . ♗c5 manifests itself in all kinds of attacks and sacrifices. For example, 8 ♘×c6? ♗×f2+ 9 ♔f1 ♕h4! and then: (a) 10 ♕×d5 ♗e6 11 ♕d3 0–0 12 ♘b4 (or 12 ♘a5 ♗b6, or 12 ♘d4 ♗×d4) ♗c5, regaining the piece; if here 11 ♘d4+ ♔e7 12 ♘×e6 f×e6 13 ♕b3 ♗c5 and the attack is winning; (b) 10 ♘d4+ c6 11 ♘f3 (11 ♘×c6 0–0) ♘g3+ 12 ♔×f2 ♘e4+! 13 ♔e2 ♕f2+ 14 ♔d3 ♗f5 'with a decisive attack', says the book.

Decisive? Why? Such a claim might seem bewildering. Of course, it looks dangerous, but this is not a situation where White's next move is forced, and he is two pieces up: he might do anything. If you feel you simply can't cope with a muddled position like this, here are some hints:

First of all you may have one basic threat (as Black had . . . ♘g3+ after 9 . . . ♕h4 above, for example), or you may have a set of basic threats, so to speak, one of which is likely to operate against any particular defence. That is the state of affairs here; Black's threats are obviously his discovered checks together with . . . c×b5. Now the secret is **just to plunge in**: pick any reasonable move and work out the reply to it. You will often be surprised to see how easily much of the analysis falls into place. For example, 15 ♗a4 ♘d2+ 16 ♔c3 ♕e3+ 17 ♔b4 a5 mate! And straightaway you have learnt a lot about the position. You know that you can at least regain one piece whenever you wish, still keeping the white king exposed. What else might he do? Try all the minor piece moves, to be systematic: 15 ♘c3 ♘c5 mate; 15 ♗d2 or ♘d2 ♘×d2+ wins; 15 ♗e3 ♘d6+ wins, and so on. Against 15 ♗f4 c×b5 seems best, threatening to continue 16 . . . ♖c8, among other things, and White still cannot escape the discovered check. Again you may notice that 15 ♕e1 leaves c2 unprotected after 15 . . . ♘c5+; thus you eliminate any other queen move. If 15 ♘d4 ♗g6 keeps all the threats open. There does indeed seem to be no adequate defence.

Now after 8 0–0 nothing quite so drastic is going to happen, but still Black can happily part with a pawn at c6. Corden chooses 8 0–0 in this game because he wishes to test out a new idea at move ten.

8 0–0 0–0
9 ♗×c6 . . .

9 ♘×c6 b×c6 10 ♗×c6 ♗a6 exposes White's lack of development: 11 ♗×a8 ♗×f1 12 ♗e3 (12 ♗×d5? ♗c4, 12 ♕×d5? ♗c4, 12 ♕×f1 ♗×f2+ 13 ♔h1 ♕h4 and 12 ♔×f1 ♕h4 are all much worse) ♗×e3 13 f×e3 ♗×g2 14 ♕g4 (he can't stand . . . ♕g5, with or without check) ♗h3! 15 ♕×h3 (or 15 ♕h5 g6 16 ♕h6 ♕c8!) ♕g5+ 16 ♔f1 ♖×a8, with a winning positional advantage (Hermann–Keres, Correspondence 1936).

11 ♕×d5 is better, but after 11 . . . ♗×f1 12 ♕×e4 (forced) ♗b5! 13 ♘c3 ♗×c6 14 ♕×c6 ♗d4 15 ♗f4 ♖b8 16 ♖b1 (or 16 ♖d1 ♖b6 and . . . c5 is ready) ♕e8 White still falls short of equality. If he exchanges queens his e-pawn will be fatally weak, or if 17 ♕×c7 ♗×c3 18 ♕×c3 ♕a4 and Black will quickly regain at least one pawn (. . . ♖fc8) with much the more aggressive position.

9 . . . b×c6

There is a surprising positional point hidden in the theory of this variation, such as one might not expect to find in the old-fashioned open game. First of all 10 f3 is a bad move because of 10 f6! 11 f×e4 (11 e6 ♘g5 12 ♗×g5 f×g5 soon loses the e-pawn for nothing) f×e5 12 ♖×f8+ ♕×f8 13 ♗e3 e×d4 14 ♗×d4 ♗g4! with a clear plus for Black. Secondly, 10 ♗e3 is playable, but leaves Black with a very comfortable, aggressive position after, for example, 10 . . . ♕e8 11 c3 (11 f3 ♘d6, or 11 f4 f6) f6 12 e×f6 ♖×f6 13 ♘d2 ♖g6.

So 10 ♘×c6 is reckoned to be the test, after which Black can preserve a small advantage by 10 . . . ♕d7 11 ♘d4 ♗a6 12 ♖e1 ♕e7. For example, 13 ♗f4 ♕h4 14 g3 ♕h3 with strong white-square pressure and development problems for White, or 13 f4 ♕h4 14 ♗e3 ♗×d4 15 ♗×d4 ♕×f4 and . . . c5 to follow.

But Black should not play 10 . . . ♕h4. That is anything but obvious, but it amounts to a premature attack: 11 ♗e3! ♗×e3 12 f×e3 and suddenly White seizes the initiative by virtue of his two open files and threat to the d-pawn. Moreover, the weakness of his own pawns is something of an illusion: if 12 . . . ♕g5 13 ♖f4 ♗b7 14 ♕×d5 suits him very well (14 . . . ♖ad8 15 ♕×e4 ♖d1+ 16 ♔f2 ♗×c6 17

♕×c6 ♕×e5 18 ♕f3 ♖c1 19 ♖d4 (-d1) is insufficient).

If exchanging bishops is bad, Black has to keep things moving by 11 . . . ♗a6, but then comes 12 ♗×c5! ♗×f1 13 g3! (obviously he can't play 13 ♗×f8, and recapturing at f1 would give insufficient compensation for the exchange; 13 ♕d4 looks good, covering f2 and c5 and still hitting the bishop and the rook, but runs into trouble by 13 . . . ♕g5! 14 ♔×f1 ♕c1+ 15 ♔e2 ♕×c2+) ♕h3 14 ♕×f1 ♕×f1+ 15 ♔×f1 ♘×c5 16 ♘c3, and gradually it dawns that White has made a very good sacrifice. He will soon win a second pawn and Black will experience great difficulty in mobilising his rooks. All this depends on the advanced knight, of course; after 16 . . . d4 White would not capture and permit . . . ♖ad8, but play 17 ♘d5 (17 . . . ♘e6 18 f4 g6 19 g4 etc.); if 16 . . . f6 17 ♘×d5 f×e5 18 ♘×c7 regains the exchange. In both cases Black definitely stands worse.

Still there remains the problem of meeting 10 . . . ♕d7, though; that is what Corden is trying, unsuccessfully, to solve with his new move.

10 b4(?) ♗b6

Forced: 10 . . . ♗×b4 and 10 . . . ♗e7 both lose material to 11 ♘×c6, and 10 . . . ♗×d4 11 ♕×d4 ♘g5 12 ♗×g5! ♕×g5 13 f4 would present White with a large positional advantage. If Black once surrenders the initiative, his Q-side pawn weaknesses will certainly cost him the game.

11 ♘×c6 . . .

This is the point of the innovation: after 11 . . . ♕d7 12 ♕×d5 picks up a second pawn for insufficient compensation. For example, 12 . . . ♕×d5 13 ♘e7+ ♔h8 14 ♘×d5 ♗d4 15 c3 ♗×e5 16 ♖e1, followed by f3. Unfortunately the idea falls down because the . . . ♕h4 line is much better for Black this time!

11 . . . ♕h4

12 ♗e3 . . .

No choice whatever. After any other move Black, with his huge advantage in development, simply makes mincemeat of his opponent: (a) 12 g3 ♘×g3 13 h×g3 ♕×g3+ 14 ♔h1 ♕h3+ 15 ♔g1 ♗g4; (b) 12 ♘d4 ♘×f2; (c) 12 ♕f3 ♗g4! 13 ♕f4 g5 14 ♘e7+ ♔h8 15 ♘f5 ♕h5; (d) 12 ♕e1 ♗a6.

12 . . . ♗a6

13 g3 . . .

Forced again: if 13 ♖e1 ♘×f2, or if 13 ♗×b6 ♗×f1 14 g3 ♕h6 15 ♘e7+ (15 ♕×d5 a×b6 16 ♕×e4 ♕c1 is worse) ♔h8 16 ♗e3 ♕e6 17 ♔×f1 ♕×e7 18 ♕×d5 ♕×b4, and White has nothing like enough for the exchange.

13 . . . ♕h3

14 ♖e1? . . .

This is a decisive error. Probably White recoiled from the idea of accepting what is now a doubtful ending so soon after his innovation, but that was objectively his best chance, i.e. 14 ♗×b6 ♗×f1 15 ♕×f1 ♕×f1+ 16 ♔×f1 a×b6 17 f3 ♘g5 18 ♔g2. Notice the difference: White's pawn structure is weaker, Black's is stronger and one black rook is already in action. All the same, progress would not be easy.

14 . . . ♗×e3

15 ♖×e3 *(11)* **. . .**

You will recall that previously f×e3 was quite acceptable: here the absence of White's rook from f1 and the extra weakness (g3) in his position would make all the difference and the initiative would be transferred to Black: 15 f×e3 ♖ae8! (the

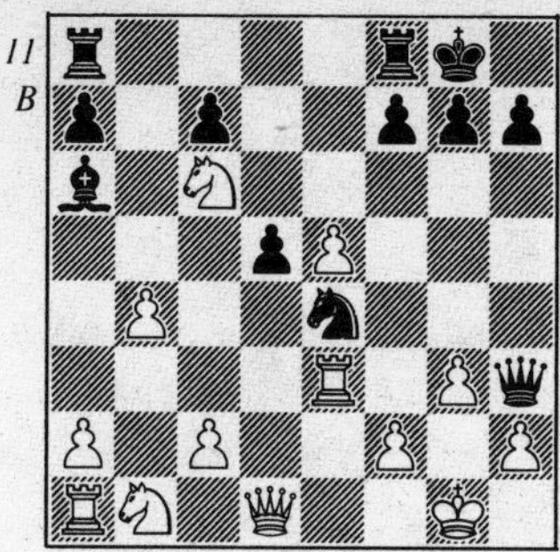

sacrifice at g3 would be premature, but now we have a basic threat of . . . ♖e6 followed by sacrificing) and now: (a) 16 ♕×d5 ♕f5! 17 ♘a3 ♕f2+ 18 ♔h1 ♘×g3+ 19 h×g3 ♖e6 and wins; or (b) 16 ♘d2 ♘×g3 17 ♕f3 ♖e6! (17 . . . ♘e2+ 18 ♔h1 is no good) and White must either accept a terrible endgame position by 18 ♕×g3 ♕×g3+ 19 h×g3 ♖×c6, or suffer a mating attack: 18 ♕×d5 ♘e2+ 19 ♔h1 ♘c3! 20 ♕c5 ♖h6 21 ♘e7+ ♔h8 22 ♘g6+ h×g6 23 ♕×f8+ ♔h7 and wins, or 18 b5 ♗×b5 19 ♘d4 ♖g6 20 ♘×b5 ♘e4+ 21 ♔h1 ♕×f3+ 22 ♘×f3 ♘f2 mate.

15 . . . ♘×f2!

This initiates the main attack, which Nunn has calculated as far as the 24th move. Quite a long way; but he is using two guidelines to assist him. Positionally he knows that the queen and bishop cannot win the game alone; therefore he must at some point open a line for his rooks, preferably with gain of tempo. This will be the d-file, or in one variation the f-file. Tactically he knows that the undefended knight at c6, at one time such an excellent piece, is now nothing but a millstone around White's neck. In one variation after another Black is able to exploit this; ideally he is seeking to open a file by playing . . . d4 at a moment when the knight is obliged to take. In what follows notice too how White has cause to regret the holes created by 10 b4, once he is thrown onto the defensive.

16 ♔×f2 ♕×h2+
17 ♔f3 . . .

During the game Nunn did not spend a great deal of time analysing 17 ♔e1; he saw that he would have a happy choice between 17 . . . d4!, transposing into the game after 18 ♘×d4 (18 ♕×d4 ♕h1+, or 18 ♖f3 ♕h1+ 19 ♔d2 ♕h6+, still winning the knight) ♕g1+ 19 ♔d2 ♕f2+, and 17 . . . ♕g1+ 18 ♔d2 ♕f2+ 19 ♖e2 ♕b6 20 ♘e7+ ♔h8, when he wins his material back because there are so many threats: 21 . . . ♕×b4+, . . . ♕e6, . . . ♕d4+ and . . . ♗×e2. In fact it seems to be almost a matter of taste. Analysing the 17 . . . ♕g1+ line a bit further gives us 21 ♘f5 g6; then . . . ♕d4+ if the knight moves, or if 22 ♖h2 g×f5 23 ♕h5 ♕g6 with a comfortably won endgame. If 21 ♖h2 ♕×b4+ 22 ♘c3 ♕×e7 23 ♕h5 (23 ♖×h7+ ♔×h7 24 ♕h5+ ♔g8 25 ♖h1 f5 is no good), Black defends without any trouble by 23 . . . h6 24 ♖ah1 ♔g8.

17 . . . ♕h5+

Luring the pawn to g4 for a definite purpose.

18 g4 ♕h3+
19 ♔f2 ♕h2+
20 ♔e1 . . .

No choice now, since 20 ♔f3 f5! would force open either the f-file or the h5–d1 diagonal, with catastrophic results (21 ♘e7+ ♔h8 22 ♘×f5 ♖×f5 23 g×f5 ♕h5+).

20 . . . ♕h4+

21 **♔d2** *(12)* ...

21 ... **d4!**
22 **♘×d4** ...

Forced again, or . . . ♕h6+ wins the knight.

22 ... **♕f2+**
23 **♘e2** **♖ad8+**
24 **♖d3** ...

Black can now liquidate the position in two similar ways: 24 . . . ♗×d3 25 c×d3 ♖×d3+ 26 ♔×d3 ♖d8+ 27 ♔c2 ♖×d1 28 ♔×d1 ♕f1+ 29 ♔d2; or 24 . . . ♖×d3+ 25 c×d3 ♖d8 26 ♕b3 ♖×d3+ 27 ♕×d3 ♗×d3 28 ♔×d3 ♕f1. In each case White will have to spend several moves unscrambling his pieces, while the g- and h-pawns advance, costing him at least a knight. The ending should certainly be won, but Nunn is looking for something even more conclusive; in any case there is no reason to hurry.

24 ... **♕f3!**

A bit of extra tension on the position makes the defender's task all the harder. Black is not looking for mate; he will simply take the exchange and then bring his rooks to bear on the ragged pawns, knowing that he can be almost certain of winning any end-game that may arise.

25 **♔c3** ...

If 25 ♘c1 ♕f4+ 26 ♔c3 ♕×e5+ 27 ♖d4 c5 and wins, or if 25 ♘ec3 ♕f4+ 26 ♔e1 ♗×d3 27 c×d3 ♖fe8 and wins. All very convincing.

25 ... **♗×d3**
26 **c×d3** **♖fe8** *(13)*

At the very least two pawns will now disappear; and then, even if White manages to get developed, he will never be able to organise his position. His king will be permanently exposed and his knights will be quite unable to find any decent squares. All he can try to do is hang on to the d- and g-pawns: if one of them goes, either the black rooks will annihilate him down the central files or he will face three united passed pawns on the K-side.

27 **♔c2** ...

27 ♘a3 ♖×e5 28 ♘g1 (28 ♘d4? ♕f6 29 ♘ac2 c5 30 b×c5 ♖×c5+ and wins) is the only way to make a fight of it, because White is at least attempting to hold his two vital pawns. Even so he gets a lost ending: 28 . . . ♕f6 29 ♔c2 ♖e3 30 ♕f1 (there is no other way to meet the threat of 30 . . . either ♖×d3; if 30 ♖c1, simply 30 . . . ♕g6; or if 30 ♖b1, there is the neat variation 30 . . . ♖e×d3 31 ♕×d3 ♖×d3 32 ♔×d3 ♕a6+ 33 ♘c4 ♕g6+) and now Black can choose:

(a) 30 . . . ♕c6+ 31 ♘c4 ♖e×d3 32

♕×d3 ♖×d3 33 ♔×d3 ♕g6+ 34 ♔d2 ♕×g4 35 ♖c1 h5, and his pawn mass should ensure a winning endgame because White lacks counterplay: no threats against the king and no passed pawn of his own.

or (b) 30 . . . ♕×f1 31 ♖×f1 ♖d×d3 32 ♘c4 (32 ♘b1 ♖d4 wins a pawn, or if 32 ♘b5 a6 33 ♘×c7 ♖c3+ 34 ♔d2 ♖ed3+ 35 ♔e2 ♖d6 and the knight is trapped) ♖c3+ 33 ♔d2 ♖ed3+ 34 ♔e2 ♖g3, and rook + three united passed pawns should not have much trouble winning against two knights.

27	**. . .**	**♖×e5**
28	**♘ec3**	**. . .**

If 28 ♘bc3, Black simply takes at g4; if 28 ♘c1 ♕×d1+ 29 ♔×d1 ♖d4 also wins another pawn at once. After the next move the d-pawn cannot be saved.

28	**. . .**	**♕g3**
29	**♘a3**	**♖e3**
30	**♕g1**	**♖d×d3**
	0 - 1	

Game 4

Hungarian Defence
Surrey Weekend Open 1976

J. Nunn v. J. Cooper

1	**e4**	**e5**
2	**♘f3**	**♘c6**
3	**♗c4**	**♗e7**

This is the unusual Hungarian Defence in which Black accepts a solid, passive position, hoping to develop counterplay later. In that respect it is similar to Philidor's Defence (2 . . . d6). In reply an immediate 4 d4 is theoretically the best way to maintain the initiative, because after 4 . . . e×d4 5 ♘×d4 Black cannot readily achieve the equalising move . . . d5, as in, for example, the Scotch Game.

4	**d4**	**d6**
5	**d5**	**. . .**

White has three options here, all about equal, the choice depending on personal preference. The alternative are: (a) Simple development to keep a space advantage: 5 ♘c3 ♘f6 6 h3 (the consistent move here because it helps to restrict Black and because . . . ♗g4 would force White to switch plans by d5 or d×e5) 0–0 7 0–0 e×d4 8 ♘×d4 ♘×d4 9 ♕×d4 c6 10 a4 (Spassky–Hort, match 1977), with a slight plus to White; (b) Liquidation to an endgame: 5 d×e5 d×e5 6 ♕×d8+ ♗×d8 7 ♘c3 f6 (alternatively 7 . . . ♘f6 8 ♗e3 ♗e7 9 ♘d5 ♗d6 10 ♘×f6+ g×f6 11 ♘h4, with a slight advantage – van der Wiel–Nikolić, Malta 1980) 8 a3 (because ♗a2, preventing . . . ♗e6 and subsequently . . . ♘c4, is better than ♗d3 after Black's anticipated . . . ♘a5) ♘ge7 9 ♗e3 ♗g4 10 0–0–0 ♘c8, followed by . . . ♘d6, and White stands just a little better.

The text move gains space and creates a blocked position, a comparatively rare occurrence in openings beginning 1 e4 e5. Only in the Ruy Lopez is it likely to happen, and much later there because White normally delays d4 and d5 for a long time. In most of the other openings in this group Black strives for . . . d5 rather than . . . d6. In the Philidor Black's knight goes to d7, not c6; therefore d5 is less attractive and White prefers to maintain his pressure against the e-pawn.

5	**. . .**	**♘a5?**

With the centre blocked it is becoming more appropriate to compare this position with the King's Indian or Czech Benoni Defences, rather than with the Philidor or any K-side opening. The book line is 5 . . . ♘b8 6 ♗d3 (aiming ultimately for b4 and c5) ♘f6 (if 6 . . . c5, the white knight would settle on c4, supported by a4, and White would prepare f4 and e5 with a very favourable game) 7 c4 0–0 8 h3 ♘bd7 9 ♘c3 ♘e8 (Black must try for . . . f5) 10 0–0 g6 11 ♗h6 ♘g7 12 ♕d2, with a small advantage (Fuchs–Kholmov, Leningrad 1967), this position resembling a Czech Benoni except that Black's pawn is still at c7 instead of c5.

5 . . . ♘a5, on the other hand, appears not to be considered at all by any theoretical books, and indeed the knight turns out to be badly placed on the edge of the board. Black was aware of the danger, of course, but was no doubt anticipating c4 and thinking in terms of certain King's Indian variations where the knight exerts useful pressure on White's c-pawn (for example, 1 d4 ♘f6 2 c4 g6 3 ♘c3 ♗g7 4 ♘f3 d6 5 g3 0–0 ♗g2 c5 7 0–0♘c6 8 d5 ♘a5). Even there, though, it is far from easy for him to justify . . . ♘a5, and in the present game the c-pawn is going to be more solidly defended than it would be after a K-side fianchetto. The result is that Black is handicapped from the start.

6	**♗d3**	**c5**
7	**c4**	. . .

This time 7 ♘bd2 and ♘c4 would only exchange the knight and solve Black's main problem.

7	. . .	**♘f6**
8	**♘c3**	**0–0** *(14)*

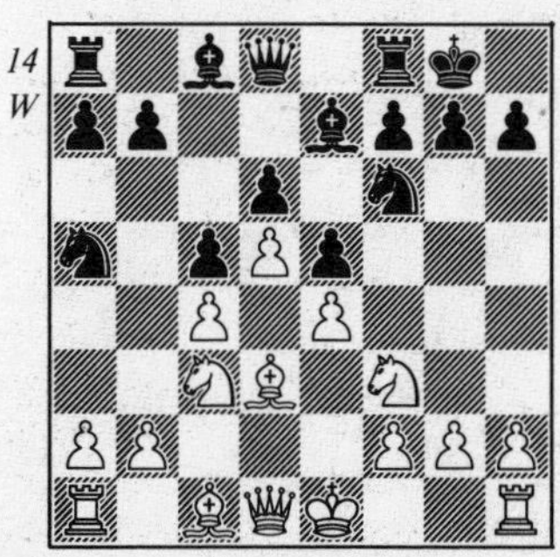

14
W

The opening has settled down into something like a Czech Benoni, except that the black knight should be on d7; from a5 he can only return to civilisation via b7 and d8, and even then further active play is difficult to find. Given the blocked nature of the position, of course, White can only exploit this weakness slowly.

Now let us tackle the problem by summarising White's possible plans against a Czech Benoni, imagining that the knight is on d7 (These plans are all based on pawn advances to open up lines; Black's position is too tough to be broken down by piece action alone. A continuation such as ♗g5, ♘h4–f5, and ♕f3, even if it were tactically possible, would get nowhere):

(a) A K-side attack beginning h3 and g4; then 0–0–0, ♖dg1, ♘e2–g3–f5 etc. (or ♘d1–e3–f5).

(b) The same attack, but castling on the K-side, so that any Q-side counterplay will be much less significant. With the centre blocked, Black will have very few chances to harass the king after the pawns' advance, but the attack will develop more slowly and the king himself is likely to get in the way.

(c) K-side castling and a Q-side advance by a3 and b4.

Notice that the fourth possibility, 0–0 and an attack based on f4, is not appropriate in this exact position because Black would exchange pawns and arrange his pieces conveniently by . . . ♘d7–e5 and . . . ♗f6; and the occupation of this outpost at e5 would as a rule count for more than White's pressure along the f-file. But I stress 'exact' here because you will see from the note to White's 11th move that the black knight may well wish to go to e8 (in order to prepare . . . f5 thoroughly after . . . g6 and

. . . ♘g7). In that event his route to e5 would take longer and White could well react with a quick f4, perhaps even following with e5 if Black captures. In other words, we have here an example of a theme which recurs throughout this book – that pieces must come before pawns. The pawn structure only matter in so far as it affects the power or scope of the pieces.

Now how does Nunn choose between the three plans, and does the position of the knight at a5 instead of d7 make any difference? Yes, it does. He rejects a3 and b4 because . . . b6 and . . . ♘b7 is a very solid defence, hard to break down; in that case it would even be preferable to have the knight at b7, rather than d7, because no other pieces would be obstructed. He also feels a little uneasy about Q-side castling because the knight would be ready to help with Black's counter-attack and its position on the edge might be justified. Therefore plan (b) is the favourite for the moment, but by adopting the right move order he can still avoid committing himself to it, at least for a move or two.

9 h3 a6

We are concerned here with the delicate question of keeping options open, and the positional play is tricky, especially for Black. He would like to prepare . . . f5 at once, but if 9 . . . ♘e8 10 g4 g6 White can still castle Q-side and a subsequent . . . f5 will expose Black's own king very dangerously; for example 11 ♗h6 ♘g7 12 ♕e2, and if 12 . . . f5 13 g×f5 g×f5 14 0–0–0, followed by ♖dg1. If he avoids an early . . . f5, the voluntary weakness created by . . . g6 will nevertheless argue in favour of White's attack breaking through first. Black therefore spends a couple of moves discouraging 0–0–0; but keeping your options open is first cousin to time-wasting, and he comes up against other problems as a direct result.

10 ♕e2 . . .

Finally abandoning any idea of a3 and b4, which would now be met by . . . ♘b3–d4, but developing another piece and hinting that his intention may still be to castle long, which is indeed still possible after 10 . . . ♘e8 11 g4 g6 etc. Black's next move is again designed to discourage this.

10 . . . ♖b8

11 0–0 . . .

Much more than just an obvious developing move, this has the effect of revealing . . . a6 and . . . ♖b8 as loss of time; and if now 11 . . . ♘e8 **the plan of f4 is suddenly very effective.** On the other hand, 11 . . . ♘d7, forestalling f4, in no way contributes to . . . f5 and Black will be in grave danger of getting a totally passive position. Now here is the analysis of 11 . . . ♘e8. Notice how White is basing his play entirely on the **opening of the position**, which suits his generally superior development and especially the bad placing of the knight at a5. It is most important to grasp the significance of the exact location of the pieces; if either of Black's knights could settle on e5, these variations would be tolerable for him:

(a) 11 . . . ♘e8 12 ♘h2 g6 (or 12 . . . f5 13 f4, opening everything up at once) 13 f4 e×f4 (If 13 . . . f6 14 f5! g5 15 h4, or 15 ♘g4 first, and although White is now attacking on a narrow front,

Black's chronic lack of space is the decisive factor. White will continue ♔f2, ♗d2, then double rooks on the h-file, and Black is most unlikely to be able to find an adequate defence) 14 ♗×f4 ♗f6 (or 14 . . . f6, as in b) 15 ♘f3, followed by e5, and the white pieces come pouring in long before Black completes his development.

(b) 11 . . . ♘e8 12 ♘h2 ♗g5 13 f4 ♗×f4 14 ♗×f4 e×f4 15 ♖×f4, and now Black faces a dilemma: 15 . . . f6 stops e5, but blocks his pieces and leaves his position altogether too passive; White could take his time building up the attack here – if necessary by an eventual g4, h4 and g5. On the other hand, 15 . . . ♘f6 (15 . . . ♕e7 16 ♖e1 and the opening of the centre will still favour White, even if the queens disappear) is met by 16 ♖af1 (16 e5 ♖e8 would be premature) and if 16 . . . ♘d7 17 e5! with a winning attack, thus: (a) 17 . . . d×e5 18 ♗×h7+ ♔×h7 19 ♕h5+ ♔g8 20 ♖×f7 (threatening 21 ♕g6, among other things) and Black can play neither 20 . . . ♕e8 nor 20 . . .♘f6 (21 ♖1×f6); or if 20 . . . ♖×f7 21 ♕×f7+ ♔h8 22 ♕h5+ ♔g8 23 ♘e4 and wins by the threat of ♘g5 or ♕f7+ and ♖f5 (if 23 . . . ♕e7 24 d6); (b) 17 . . . ♘×e5 18 ♗×h7+ ♔×h7 19 ♕h5+ ♔g8 20 ♖h4, and then (i) 20 . . . f6 21 ♘e4 with ♘g5 to follow; (ii) 20 . . .f5 21 ♘e4! ♕×h4 (otherwise 22 ♘g5, or if 21 . . . ♕e8 22 ♘f6+) 22 ♕×h4 f×e4 23 ♖×f8+ ♔×f8 24 ♕d8+ ♔f7 25 ♕c7+ and wins; (iii) 20 . . . ♕×h4 21 ♕×h4 ♘a×c4, and Black's position remains too passive for comfort, even though he has approximate material equality.

Finally, 16 . . . ♖e8 prevents e5, but after 17 ♖af1 the knight remains permanently pinned against f7 (White can triple if need be) and Black faces a long and unpleasant defence with the constant threat of an exchange sacrifice at f6 hanging over him.

11 . . . ♘d7

Black reckons that passive defence is the best chance. One more possibility here is 11 . . . ♗d7, followed by . . . ♕e8 and . . . b5; but White replies b3 and the b-file simply cannot be used by Black to any effect. Even if he managed to treble on the file, the entry would be barred by the opposing minor pieces, and Black's own bishops and knights are too badly restricted to be able to help clear the way by exchanges, at any rate within a reasonable time.

12 b3 . . .

A semi-waiting move. Whether the bishop should go to b2 is not yet clear.

12 . . . b6

13 ♘d1 . . .

White is still ready to react to . . . g6 by g4; meanwhile the knight, who has no future at c3, heads for a nice aggressive post at f5.

13 . . . ♔h8

Passive defence is a tedious affair. Black has to try to anticipate his opponent's likely attacking formation and prepare for it well in advance. The trouble is that White can adjust his own plans in such a way as to exploit whatever arrangement of pieces Black chooses; moreover, his manoeuvring is bound to be swifter. With 13 . . . ♔h8 Black intends to meet ♘e3 by . . . g6 (risking the weakness rather than allowing the knight to settle on f5) and has probably foreseen the subsequent g4 and standard knight sacrifice at f5. That will lead to problems on the g-file (imagine ♔h2, ♖g1, ♖g3 and ♖ag1 having also been played); so the king side-steps it. The disadvantage, of course, is that he may run into fresh trouble on the long diagonal.

14	**♘e3**	**g6**
15	**g4**	**♕e8**
16	**♔h2**	**♘b7**
17	**♖g1**	**♘d8**
18	**h4(?)**	**. . .**

It may seem strange to talk about White creating a weak point in his position by this move, given that he is very definitely the one who holds the initiative; but you have to be careful when handling an attack of this kind. Obviously you are leaving potential holes behind by advancing pawns at all, and there is a danger of getting the pawns locked in an unfavourable formation, if you are not alert. In this case White should have prepared more thoroughly before committing himself to h4, i.e. ♗b2, ♖g3 and ♖ag1 should have come first. After 18 h4 a weakness is created at g4, which Black can try to exploit by a combination of . . . ♘f6 and . . . h5. If White replies g5 either before or after . . . h5, the black knight will go to h5 or g4 respectively; then the advancing pawns are locked and Black may prepare the counter-attack . . . f6 at his leisure. If White answers . . . h5 by g×h5, then . . . ♘×h5 and the square f4 is a serious weakness. Nor can White sacrifice a pawn: after . . . ♘f6 Black can quite safely take twice.

It happens that White can forestall this danger by tactical means, as we shall see, and he is still guaranteed a very good position. Nevertheless, his premature h4 has complicated his task. Whatever may happen in the sequel, the extra preparatory moves could only have improved his chances.

Now after 18 . . . ♘f6 White has 19 ♗b2, refuting 19 . . . h5 by 20 ♘×e5 d×e5 21 ♗×e5, with threats of ♗×b8, g5, ♕b2 and even d6. Obviously Black cannot allow that; so he will play 19 . . . ♖b7, which makes the combination unsound: 20 ♘×e5? d×e5 21 ♗×e5 ♔g8! 22 d6 (or 22 ♕b2 ♘d7) ♘c6 23 d×e7 ♕×e7, and he suddenly has a very dangerous counter-attack in return for a pawn (g4 is threatened and h4 is also weak).

But White can do better, and 19 . . . ♖b7 is met by 20 ♘f5! It will make the game easier to understand if we defer the analysis of this knight sacrifice until it actually occurs in the game in almost identical circumstances (see the note to Black's 21st move). Suffice to say here that although 20 ♘f5 does not carry an immediate threat, Black would not improve his chances by declining the offer because he has no really constructive moves; 20 . . . h5? would be met by 21 ♕e3 and 20 . . . ♖g8 by 21 ♘h6.

In fact Black decides to play the rook move first, which makes no objective difference. It is the placing of White's Q-bishop which is the significant point.

18	**. . .**	**♖b7** *(15)*
19	**♗d2?**	**. . .**

Surprisingly, this is an error. White is still not certain which diagonal will suit his bishop better, and the later analysis (note to Black's 21st again!) demonstrates that b2 was right. But why should the decision be so critical? Surely White can go on manoeuvring for as long as he wishes? The answer goes back to the

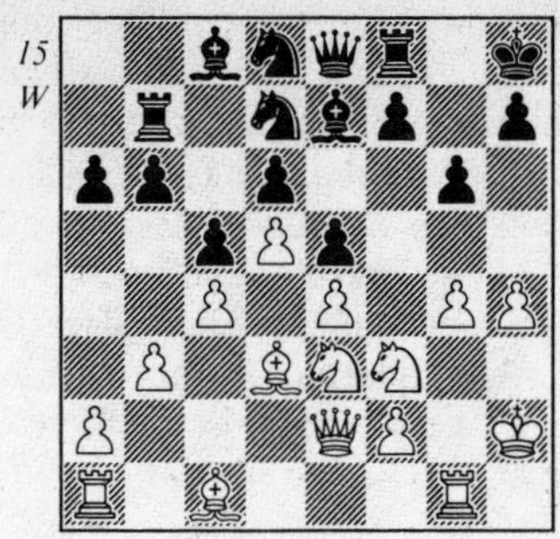

15
W

inexact 18 h4. As a result of that Black can force events by his following move . . . ♘f6, and oblige White to offer his knight at once (or suffer the locked pawn structure explained above). And for the sacrifice to work properly the bishop should be on b2.

Here another factor enters. Against either 19 ♗b2 or ♗d2 Black has an alternative defence, 19 . . .f6 (which is really what influenced White's choice of 19 ♗d2). Nunn's intention then was a complete change of theme, i.e. ♖g3, ♖ag1 and h5, while Black is making purely passive moves. At that point . . . g5 will be forced, in the face of the terrible threat of breaking through by h×g6 and g5; and with the K-side now permanently closed White will switch his rooks back to the other flank and work for a3 and b4. Anyone familiar with the King's Indian Defence (Averbach's variation in particular) will probably have seen this plan before. Apart from his big space advantage, White can increase the pressure considerably by occupying f5 with his knight, a manoeuvre impossible for Black to imitate. If the knight is captured the square e4 opens for the other knight. Whether these advantages would suffice for a win is unclear, since White would be conducting his attack over a very narrow front. Certainly Black would have a thoroughly miserable time of it.

19 . . . ♘f6!

Definitely the best move against 19 ♗d2, though Black fails to find his way through the jungle of complications at move 21.

20 ♘f5 . . .

White is being pushed into this, otherwise comes 20. . . h5; but in any case it is a standard kind of breakthrough sacrifice (of two pieces here, not just one) to resolve a blocked position. White would probably have played it eventually anyway. Technically it is the defender's restricted position which justifies it. His pieces are bound to exhibit an unfortunate tendency to get in each other's way, especially since all eight of them remain on the board; and any attempt to transfer one of them to the K-side is like trying to solve a sliding-block puzzle! Notice in the following variations what terrible trouble he has in stopping the simplest threats, and how the infiltration of one or two enemy pieces leaves him unable to defend himself.

But another question arises here, one which seems to worry many players, i.e. 'How much are you supposed to analyse before making this kind of sacrifice?' And the answer is that you analyse as much as you reasonably can within the time allowed; and if that analysis does not prove the validity or otherwise of the idea, you rely on your judgement. That means that you treat the position as coldly and objectively as you can; you look down on it, so to speak, as if it were someone else's game, and say something like: 'On the basis of all my experience of the game and all that I've discovered by analysing (even though the analysis is not complete), do I really think it's right to sacrifice?' **Not** 'Can I get away with it?', which in the long run is a disastrous way of thinking, but 'Is it right?' Easier advice to give than to follow, perhaps! But that kind of balance is really the only answer. Weaker players are likely to fall into the trap either of refusing to sacrifice because they cannot see the outcome with complete clarity, or of sacrificing without any analysis at all, which amounts to mere guesswork. Since this game was played in a weekend tournament with a fast time-limit, Nunn has relied more on judgement than he might otherwise have done, paying most attention to the sharpest move 21 . . . e4 (after 20 . . . g×f5 21 e×f5). This point is taken up again in the note to Black's 21st move.

20 . . . g×f5

Although 20 ♘f5 does not threaten anything directly (21 ♘×e7 ♕×e7 22 ♗g5? could be met by 22 . . . h6! 23 ♗×h6 ♘×g4+ 24 ♖×g4 ♗×g4 25 ♗×f8 ♕×f8, to Black's considerable advantage), the attack will only increase in power, the longer Black refuses to take the knight. For example, 20 . . . ♘g8 could produce 21 g5 f6 22 h5! and then: (a) 22 . . . g×f5 23 g6 ♖f7 (As I said, simple threats are hard to stop! If 23 . . . h×g6 24 h×g6 ♔g7 25 ♘h4 f×e4 26 ♕h5 and wins, or if here 25 . . . ♘h6 26 ♗×h6+ ♔×h6 27 g7 ♖g8 28 e×f5 and wins by ♖g6+) 24 e×f5 and White wins at least the exchange; (b) 22 . . . f×g5 23 h×g6 h×g6 24 ♘×e7 ♖×e7 25 ♘×g5 and White's attack is breaking through without any sacrifice; moreover, his black-square bishop is bound to become very dangerous in the next few moves; (c) 22 . . . g×h5 23 g6! (a remarkable variation, which again shows how helpless Black is, once the position opens up) h×g6 24 ♖×g6! ♕×g6 25 ♖g1 ♗×f5 (forced soon anyway) 26 e×f5, and then: (i) 26 . . . ♕f7 27 ♘h4 and Black must lose a lot of material after 27 . . . ♔h7 28 ♘g6 ♘h6 29 ♕×h5 ♕g7 30 ♘×f8+ ♕×f8 31 ♖g6; (ii) 26 . . . ♕h7 27 ♘h4 ♘f7 28 ♘g6+ ♔g7 29 ♘×e7+ ♘g5 (or 29 . . . ♔h8 30 ♘g6+ ♔g7 31 ♘×e5+ etc., and White can even regain the exchange at f8 if he wishes) 30 ♗×g5 f×g5 (30 . . . ♖×e7 31 ♗h6+!) 31 f6+ and wins; (iii) 26 . . . ♕×g1+ 27 ♔×g1 ♖f7 (otherwise ♘h4 wins the h-pawn) 28 ♘h4 ♖h7 29 f4! (threatening ♕g2 and ♘g6+) ♔g7 30 ♕g2+ ♔f8 31 f×e5 d×e5 (or 31 . . . f×e5 32 ♘g6+ ♔f7 33 ♘×e5+, or here 32 . . . ♔e8 33 ♘×e7 ♘×e7 34 f6) 32 ♘g6+ ♔e8 33 ♘×e7 ♘×e7 34 d6, winning a piece with more to follow.

21 e×f5 *(16)* **. . .**

16
B

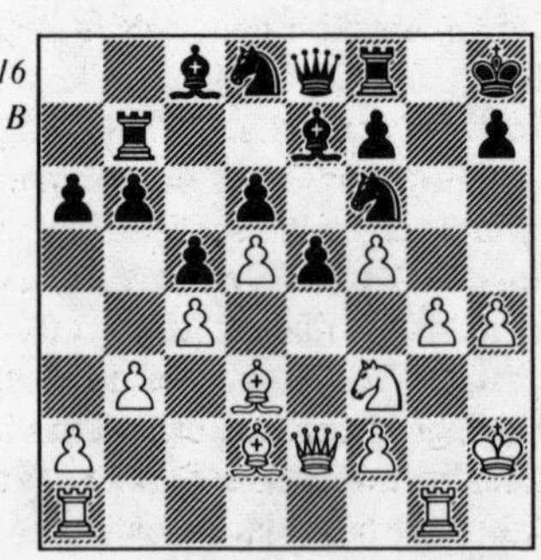

Not 21 g×f5. In this type of attack it is usually the momentum of the pawn roller which justifies the sacrifice, rather than the open g-file. White also extends the range of his K-bishop by this recapture, and his threats to sacrifice at e5 are intensified. Meanwhile, the immediate danger is g5 and f6.

21 . . . e4?

Black slips up at the critical moment. Although this move wins a second piece, the opening of the long diagonal proves to be more than his position can stand. It is worth mentioning here that Black's extreme shortage of useful moves is one of the things which makes White's task of analysing easier. Given his basic threat of g5 and f6, only 21 . . . e4, 21 . . . ♘g8 and 21 . . . ♖g8 really need to be examined.

Now 21 . . . ♘g8? can be refuted as follows: 22 g5 f6 (otherwise the bishop goes; 22 . . . ♕d7 23 ♖g3 does not help, though White has to watch out for this nasty little counter-attack in some lines) 23 g6 h×g6 (if 23 . . . ♔g7 24 g×h7+ ♔×h7 25 ♖g6 and the threat of ♘g5+ is decisive) 24 f×g6 ♔g7 25 ♘d4! f5 (otherwise ♕h5 wins at once) 26 ♕h5 ♘f6 (the only reasonable way to stop 27 ♕h7+ ♔f6 28 ♕h8 mate) 27 ♕h6+ ♔g8 28 g7 and wins.

The right defence is 21 . . . ♖g8! Then White cannot do better than 22 g5, since the slower line 22 ♗c3 ♘×g4+ 23 ♖×g4 ♖×g4 24 ♘×e5 fails against 24 . . . ♖×h4+ 25 ♔g3 f6. So 22 g5 ♘h5, and now it has to be the sacrifice at e5 because other tries fail as follows: (a) 23 ♗c3 ♘f4 24 ♘×e5! f6! 25 ♘g6+ (can't stop now) h×g6 26 ♕f3 (or 26 ♕e3 ♘h5, so that 27 g×f6 can be met by . . . ♗×f6, stopping the mate at h6; 26 . . . ♘×d3 would be too dangerous here) ♘×d3 27 g×f6 ♘e5 28 ♗×e5 d×e5 29 f×g6 ♗×f6, and the attack is insufficient; (b) 23 f6? ♕d7; (c) 23 ♘e1 f6 24 g6 ♘f4 25 ♗×f4 e×f4 26 ♕h5 (or 26 ♘f3 ♕f8–h6 to unscramble his position) ♖g7 (26 . . . ♗f8? 27 g×h7!) 27 ♘f3 ♕g8, and Black will unwind himself (admittedly very slowly!) along the lines of . . . ♖c7, . . . ♘b7, . . . ♗d8, . . . ♖ce7, taking care not to permit the sacrifice ♘g5, . . . f×g5, f6. If all else fails, he could return the piece by 27 . . . ♘f7, to give himself some air.

Therefore White plays 23 ♘×e5, and again the choice of reply is critical. First of all, 23 . . . d×e5 leads to 24 ♕×h5 f6 25 g6 ♗d6 (25 . . . ♗f8? 26 g×h7) 26 ♗e4, when White has two pawns and a dangerous attack for the knight, with every chance of winning. He can build up by doubling rooks on the g-file and he can play ♗h6; meanwhile, there seems no hope at all of ever disentangling the black minor pieces. Secondly, any attempt to protect the h5 knight, or retreat it, is futile: (a) 23 . . . f6 24 ♘g4 ♘f7 25 f4 when Black is virtually paralysed; (b) 23 . . . ♘g7 24 ♘g4! (threatening ♗c3 etc., as well as f6) ♗×f5 (24 . . . ♘×f5 25 ♗×f5 ♗×f5 26 ♗c3+ ♖g7 27 ♗×g7+ ♔×g7 28 ♕b2+ ♔g6 29 ♘f6 ♕h8 30 h5+ ♔g7 31 ♘g4+ and wins) 25 ♗c3, and here White can take his time, increasing the pressure more gradually; for example 25 . . . ♕d7 26 ♖ae1 ♗g6 (or 26 . . . ♗×d3 27 ♕×d3 with the crushing threat of ♖×e7 and ♘f6, or 26 . . . ♗×g4 27 ♖×g4, threatening 28 ♕e4) 27 ♘h6 ♗f8 (or 27 . . . ♖e8 28 ♗×g7+ ♔×g7 29 ♕b2+ f6 30 ♖×e7+ ♕×e7 31 ♘f5+ ♗×f5 32 g×f6+ and wins) 28 h5 ♗×d3 29 ♕×d3 and Black has no decent moves: a subsequent ♘g4 followed by h6 or ♘f6 will finish him off; (c) 23 . . . ♘f6

24 ♘f3, and if 24 . . . ♘h5 25 f6 ♘×f6 26 ♗c3, threatening above all 27 ♕e4 ♖g7 28 g×f6. Once again White's attack is overwhelming.

Finally, Black can try to engineer a queen exchange at e5 – the only satisfactory defence. Not by 23 . . . ♗×g5 24 ♖×g5! ♕×e5+ (24 . . . ♖×g5? 25 ♘g6+) 25 ♕×e5+ f×e5 26 ♖×h5 f6, because the white rook escapes after, for example, 27 f4 ♘f7 (or 27 . . . e×f4 28 ♗c3 and 29 ♖g5) 28 ♗c3 ♖e8 29 ♖e1 ♖be7 30 d6. Sooner or later Black can be forced to re-capture with his pawn on e5, allowing ♖g5 or f6. In each case White emerges with a won endgame. The only move is 23 . . . ♗f6! 24 g×f6 ♕×e5+ 25 ♕×e5 d×e5 26 ♖×g8+ ♔×g8 27 ♗h6, and the game suddenly fizzles out into perpetual check; for example 27 . . . ♖d7 28 ♖g1+ ♔h8 29 ♗e2 ♘f4 30 ♗g7+ etc. Neither side can improve on this, nor can White do better at move 25: if 25 ♔h1? ♘×f6 26 ♖×g8+ ♘×g8 and he has no attack to speak of, or if 25 f4? ♘×f4 (not 25 . . . ♕×e2+? 26 ♗×e2 ♘×f6 27 ♗c3) 26 ♖×g8+ ♔×g8 27 ♖g1+ (or 27 ♕g4+ ♘g6+ and 28 . . . ♕×a1) ♔f8 and again there is no good continu-ation.

If you transfer the white bishop from d2 to b2 you will see why it should have gone there at move 19 – 23 . . . ♗f6 is now unplayable (24 g×f6 ♘×f6 25 ♘g4), and all the other variations work at least as well for White.

22 ♗c3! . . .

Not 22 ♗×e4? ♘×e4 23 ♕×e4 ♗f6 and Black wins. But can White really generate enough attack to make up for two pieces? If the sacrifice seems rather heavy, bear in mind that it is essentially the advance of the g-pawn which is going to destroy Black. With his whole army immobilised by the pin on the long diagonal, and with his king trapped in the corner, he is actually quite helpless against this thrust. If he now refuses to take a second piece, the threats of 23 g5 and 23 ♗×e4 will be unanswerable (22 . . . ♔g8 23 g5 ♘h5 24 ♕×e4 and he cannot play 24 . . . f6). If he takes the bishop, we have 22 . . . e×d3 23 ♕e3 with a basic threat of ♕h6, ♘g5 and ♗×f6, and then: (a) 23 . . . ♖g8 24 g5 and wins because the bishop cannot escape any more than the knight – 24 . . . ♗d7 25 g×f6 ♗f8 26 ♖×g8+ ♔×g8 27 ♕g5+ ♔h8 28 ♖g1; (b) 23 . . . ♔g8 24 ♕h6 etc.; (c) 23 . . . ♘e6 (best hope, trying to get some air) 24 ♕h6! ♘d4 25 ♘×d4 c×d4 26 ♗×d4 d2 (clutching at straws to stop ♖ae1 and ♖×e7!) 27 g5 ♖g8 28 g×f6 ♗d8 (28 . . . ♗f8 29 ♖×g8+ as before) 29 ♖g7 ♗×f5 30 ♖ag1 ♗g6 (otherwise ♖×g8+) 31 ♖1×g6 and mates. Therefore . . .

22 . . . e×f3

23 ♕e3! . . .

Apparently Black had missed this move when he decided on 21 . . . e4 (so had Nunn, to tell the truth, when he sacrificed his knight!). He reckoned only on 23 ♕b2, which is insufficient: 23 ♕b2? ♔g8 24 g5 (or 24 ♗×f6 ♗×f6 25 ♕×f6 ♕e5+) ♘h5. If then 25 g6 f6 and Black is safe, or if 25 f6, ♕d7 pops up again. But after 23 ♕e3! ♔g8 loses promptly by 24 ♕g5+ ♔h8 25 ♗×f6+ ♗×f6 26 ♕×f6+ ♔g8 27 ♖ae1 ♕d7 28 ♕g5+ ♔h8 29 f6 ♖g8 30 ♕h6 ♖g6 31 ♗×g6 f×g6 32 ♕f8 mate.

That leaves only the counter-sacrifice 23 . . . ♘e6, which is relatively the best chance, and 23 . . . ♖g8, which is dealt with by a now familiar attack: 24 g5 ♗d7 (preparing . . . ♗f8) 25 g×f6 ♗f8 26 ♖×g8+ ♔×g8 27 ♖g1+ ♔h8 28 ♕g5 and wins.

23 . . . ♘e6

24 f×e6 f×e6

25 d×e6 . . .

This is another opportunity to go astray. If 25 g5? e5! 26 g×f6 ♖×f6 and Black's pieces have miraculously come to life, with White's attack a thing of the past. The right plan is to hold the pawn on e6, at least for a few moves, and concentrate on exploiting the newly-opened d3-h7 diagonal. For the moment White is working with the two basic threats of ♕h6 and g5; regaining the second sacrificed piece can wait.

25 . . . ♗d8 *(17)*

17
W

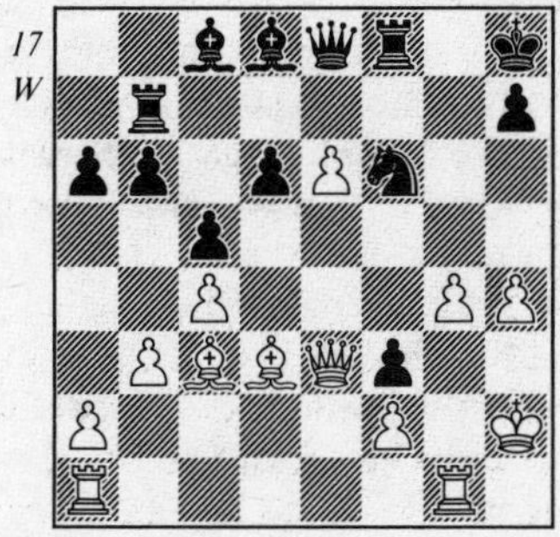

Other tries are: (a) 25 . . . ♔g8 26 g5, which is the game continuation without . . . ♗d8 and ♖ae1, and which would most likely transpose, and (b) 25 . . . ♖g8 26 ♕h6 ♖g7 27 g5 and wins. Or Black could attempt a counter-attack in the centre, which gives us: 25 . . . d5 26 c×d5 ♗d6+ 27 ♔h1 (not 27 ♗e5 ♕e7 28 g5 ♕c7!) ♔g8 28 ♕h6 (not 28 g5 ♘×d5, but now 28 . . . ♘×d5 is met by 29 ♕g5+) ♕e7 29 g5! ♘×d5 30 g6 ♘×c3 31 g7 ♕×g7 32 ♕×h7 mate.

26 ♖ae1 . . .

Still the e-pawn is important; 26 g5? ♕×e6 would allow Black to escape. But White can afford to pause for a moment: g5 is now threatened again, 26 . . . ♖e7 is met by 27 ♕h6 (27 . . . ♗×e6 28 ♖×e6), and 26 . . . ♖g7 loses to 27 g5 ♘h5 28 ♕e4 ♕g6 29 ♕×g6 h×g6 30 e7. Nor can Black counter-sacrifice at e6, because the force of the attack is undiminished: 26 . . . ♗×e6 27 ♕×e6 ♕×e6 28 ♖×e6 ♔g8 29 g5 ♘h5 (or ♘ anywhere else) 30 g6 h6 31 ♗e4 (-d5) and wins; alternatively 31 g7 ♘×g7 32 ♖×h6 with a crushing attack. Black therefore breaks the pin.

26 . . . ♔g8

27 g5 ♘d7

Black does not survive for long by returning the second piece, but he has nothing better; if 27 . . . ♘h5 28 g6 h6 29 ♕×h6 ♗f6 (or 29 . . . ♘f6 30 g7) 30 g7 and mates.

28 e×d7 ♕×d7

Threatens mate. If 28 . . . ♕×e3 29 ♖×e3 ♖×d7 (29 . . . ♗×d7 30 ♗e4) 30 g6 h6 31 g7 and wins.

29 ♖g3 d5

Otherwise comes g6, but now more diagonals open up for the white pieces.

30 c×d5 ♗c7

31 d6 ♗×d6

32 ♗c4+ ♖f7

33 ♕e8+ ♗f8

34 ♗×f7+ ♕×f7

35 ♕×c8 1 – 0

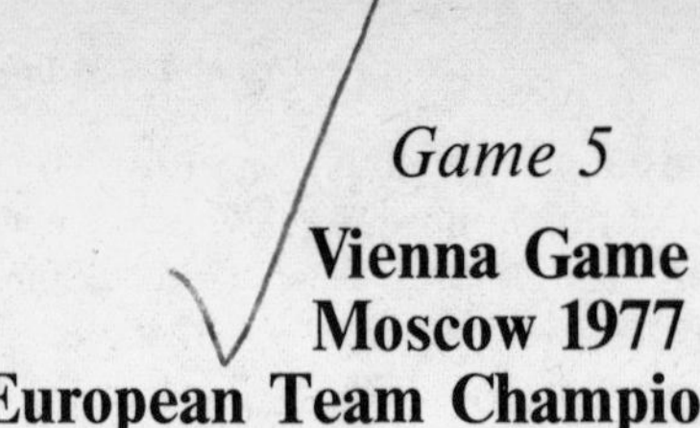

Game 5

Vienna Game
Moscow 1977
(European Team Championship Final)

J. Augustin v. J. Nunn

1	**e4**	**e5**
2	**♘c3**	**♘f6**
3	**g3**	**. . .**

A variation favoured by Spassky, who adopted it in his Candidates' Final match with Korchnoi in 1977. The intention is partly to strengthen his control of d5 and partly to prepare f4 after ♗g2 and ♘ge2; White also side-steps the variations arising after 3 ♗c4 ♘×e4 etc! (See Game 1.) In reply, the immediate opening of the centre (3 . . . d5), as played by Korchnoi, is acceptable because White will take one more move to attack the e-pawn than in the Bishop's Opening, 2 ♗c4. (Compare the notes on Game 18.) Simple piece development, as used here, is also quite satisfactory.

3	**. . .**	**♗c5**
4	**♗g2**	**d6**

4 . . . ♘c6 is more flexible, and if 5 d3 a6, preserving the bishop from exchange against a knight; the text move gives White an opportunity to gain the two bishops by 5 ♘a4. Nunn was aware of this, and the reason for his inexact move brings to light an interesting positional point. His intention was to permit the exchange at c5 and reach a position similar to a game Larsen–Portisch (Candidates' match 1968), with colours reversed. That game had begun 1 e4 e5 2 ♘c3 ♘c6 3 ♗c4 ♘f6 4 d3 ♘a5 5 ♘ge2 ♘×c4 6 d×c4 ♗e7 7 0–0 d6, with White holding some advantage thanks to his half-open d-file and outpost at d5, and **because Black could not readily prepare . . . f5** (the only plausible plan) **to open up the game for his bishop-pair.** Moreover, White still retained the option of ♘g3, making . . . f5 even harder to achieve. Notice too that the capture at c4 has not weakened White's pawn formation at all, in spite of one's immediate impressions.

But if you compare this with the present game you will see that Augustin could have gained some advantage by ♘a4 and ♘×c5, because, unlike Portisch, he could have continued ♘e2, d3 etc., quickly preparing f4. The opening of the game for his bishops by this natural plan would have counted for more than Black's d-file. There lies the subtle difference; a striking illustration of one of the major positional themes of this book: that pawn structures cannot be judged in isolation from the arrangement of the pieces.

After 5 ♘a4 Black's best scheme of development would be . . . h6, . . . ♗e6, . . . ♘c6 and . . . ♕d7, reserving the option of . . . 0–0–0, to move the king to safer spot, in case White aims for f4. In that way he would keep his opponent's advantage within reasonable bounds.

5 ♘ge2 ♘c6
6 0-0(?) *(18)* **. . .**

18
B

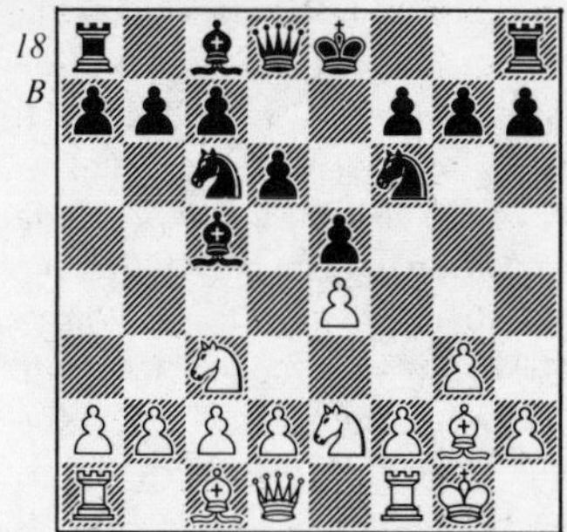

One of those occasions when early castling in inadvisable, for two reasons: (1) The pawn at g3 and the knight at e2 (rather than f3) encourage Black's following pawn thrust; (2) Black can safely leave his king in the centre for a while, to concentrate on this attack, because quick counterplay in the centre (by c3 and d4) will not be readily available. If White's Q-knight were not obstructing his c-pawn, Black might have had second thoughts about 6 . . . h5.

The best move would still be 6 ♘a4, or even 6 d3, which would be met by 6 . . . a6.

6 . . . h5!

Quite a natural move really, yet strangely enough the theory of 1977 recommended the insipid 6 . . . ♘d4; fortunately Nunn was unaware of this fact!

Now how are you supposed to meet such a thrust? Here are some of White's options:

(a) 7 h4, which is not to be recommended; it cannot be refuted directly, but it weakens the square g4 and means that White will not seriously be able to contemplate playing f4 in the near future. Meanwhile, Black will play 7 . . . a6, then . . . ♗g4, . . . ♕d7 etc.

(b) 7 h3 ♗e6 8 d3 (8 ♘d5 ♗×d5 9 e×d5 ♘e7 10 ♘c3 h4 11 g4 ♘g6 is fine for Black) ♕d7 9 ♔h2 0-0-0 and Black has completed his development with a comfortable position. Moreover, any attempt at immediate action by White would lead to trouble: 10 f4? ♘g4+ or 10 ♗g5 ♖dg8, followed by . . . ♘h7 and . . . g5. There is also a tempting sacrifice here, unfortunately not quite sound, but worth a brief look: 7 h3 h4 8 g4 ♘×g4 9 h×g4 h3 10 ♗f3 ♕h4 11 ♔h1! (avoiding a nasty check on g3 at move 14), and now 11 . . . ♗×g4 12 ♗×g4 ♕×g4 13 ♘g3 stops the attack dead; so it has to be 11 . . . ♗×f2 12 d3 ♗b6 (12 . . . ♘d4 13 ♘×d4 c×d4 14 ♘d5 wins for White because 14 . . . ♕g3, threatening . . . ♗g4, is countered by 15 ♗f4 – the difference between 11 ♔h1 and 11 ♔h2) 13 ♕e1 ♗×g4 14 ♕×h4 ♖×h4 15 ♗g5 ♗×f3+ 16 ♖×f3, but here the three pawns are quite unequal to White's extra piece.

(c) 7 ♘a4 h4 8 ♘×c5 d×c5 9 d3 h×g3 and each recapture has its own drawback: (i) 10 h×g3 ♗e6, then . . . ♕d7 and . . . 0-0-0 and Black will soon put the h-file to good use; (ii) 10 f×g3 ♗g4 11 ♗e3 ♘d4 12 ♗×d4 c×d4 favouring Black because his bishop is superior (Majerić–Velimirović, Yugoslav Championship 1980); (iii) 10 ♘×g3 ♘g4 11 h3 ♕h4 with good play; for example 12 ♘f5 ♗×f5 13 e×f5 ♘h6 (13 . . . ♘d4? 14 c3!) and if 14 ♗×c6+ b×c6 15 ♕f3 0-0-0! with an unclear position, though Black's aggressive development should guarantee him at least equality.

It is far from certain which line

White should adopt, but 6 . . . h5 would at any rate appear to be fully justified. In the event he simply ignores the h-pawn.

7 d3 h4

8 ♗g5 . . .

This position had been reached before (Smyslov–Kots, USSR Championship 1961), with the plausible if rather routine continuation 8 . . . ♗g4 9 ♕d2 (9 ♗×h4 ♘d4 is too strong) h×g3 10 ♘×g3 ♕d7 and White came out on top by 11 ♗×f6 g×f6 12 ♘d5 0–0–0 13 ♘×f6 ♕e7 (13 . . . ♕e6 14 ♕g5!) 14 ♘×g4 ♕h4 15 ♕d1 ♖dg8 16 ♘f5 ♕×g4 17 ♕×g4 ♖×g4 18 c3 and White came out on top. Positionally, the point is that White will most likely have to play ♕d2 anyway, whereas . . . ♗g4 will not necessarily be useful for Black. So instead of these formal developing moves Nunn first exchanges at g3, to see which pawn structure his opponent will choose, and then reacts accordingly. There is a tactical difference too, as the next note indicates.

8 . . . h×g3

9 ♘×g3 . . .

9 h×g3 would be too dangerous, because this time 9 . . . ♗g4 would be in order: 10 ♕d2 ♕d7, and if 11 ♗×f6 g×f6 12 ♘d5 0–0–0 13 ♘×f6 ♕e6, when 14 ♕g5 is not available. He would therefore have to settle for 14 ♘×g4 ♕×g4, yielding Black a very strong attack. 11 ♘a4 is another way, but Black would still come out very well: 11 . . . ♗h3 12 ♘×c5 d×c5 13 f3 ♗×g2 14 ♔×g2 ♕h3+ 15 ♔f2 ♕h2+ 16 ♔e1 ♘d4, winning at least a pawn. The position is full of traps, though, as you might expect, and witty moves which are not quite sound. For instance: 11 . . . ♗f3? (hoping for 12 ♘×c5? ♕h3) fails against 12 ♗×f3 ♕h3 13 ♗h4 ♖×h4 14 g×h4 ♕×f3 15 ♘×c5 ♘g4 16 ♘g3 and the attack fizzles out.

9 . . . ♘d4!

This is a precise response to the knight's recaputure at g3. (In fact Kots would still have kept a satisfactory position, had he played this at his tenth move; 10 . . . ♕d7 was his real error.) By threatening to seize control of the weak point at f4 (. . . ♘e6) Black forces his opponent to take some immediate action, before the grip tightens. Of course, 9 . . . ♗g4? 10 ♗×f6 would be a blunder.

10 ♘h5 . . .

No doubt having the ensuing combination in mind; but he is stirring up a hornet's nest. Had White foreseen all the consequences of this move, he would certainly have preferred 10 ♘d5, which still guarantees him a roughly equal game: 10 . . . c6 (or 10 . . . ♘e6 11 ♘×f6+ g×f6 12 ♗e3 with approximate equality) 11 ♘×f6+ g×f6 12 ♗e3, and Black cannot transfer his queen with any effect to the h-file (12 . . . f5 13 e×f5 ♕h4 14 h3 ♘×f5 15 ♗×c5 d×c5 16 ♕e2 f6 17 ♕e4 ♘×g3 18 ♕g6+ is no good). He would thus prefer 12 . . . ♖h4, intending . . . ♗g4, with about even chances.

10 . . . ♘e6

11 ♘×g7+ . . .

Nunn confesses that he had completely overlooked this move! In a sense it doesn't matter because the game continuation favours Black and he could not have improved on his tenth move in any case. The chief point of interest in the remainder is a comparison of Black's positional advantage with White's extra material after the coming queen sacrifice.

First, we can examine White's alternatives:

(a) 11 ♘×f6+ g×f6 12 ♗e3 f5! (favourable this time because the white knight is out of play instead of helping with the defence at g3) 13 e×f5 (13 ♗×c5 is no better) ♛h4 14 h3 ♖g8 15 ♔h1 (15 ♕f3 ♘g5 and the knight has to be captured) ♘d4, followed by . . . ♗×f5 with a tremendous attack.

(b) 11 ♗×f6 g×f6 12 ♘d5 ♖h6, and now White has three options: (i) 13 ♕f3, which fails after some delightful twists: 13 . . . ♘d4! and White must retreat because 14 ♘h×f6+ (or the other knight) loses to 14 . . . ♔f8 15 ♕e3 (no choice) ♖×f6 16 ♕g5 ♘f3+! 17 ♗×f3 ♖g6; (ii) 13 b4 ♗b6 14 ♘×b6 (14 ♕g4 is met by 14. . . ♔f8 15 ♘×b6 a×b6 16 f4 e×f4 17 ♘×f4 ♘×f4 18 ♕×f4 ♖g6 19 ♔h1 ♔g7 with a roughly level position) a×b6 15 f4 ♔e7, followed by . . . ♛h8; (iii) 13 ♘e3 (trying to control f5; 13 c3 c6 14 ♘e3 amounts to the same thing) ♗×e3! Positionally the most instructive variation of all. Black surrenders his strong bishop, opens the f-file for White and deprives his own knight of f4 and d4! And still it is the right move because after the further 14 f×e3 ♔e7! 15 ♘g3 ♘g5 White cannot use the f-file in any effective way, yet Black can use the g-and h-files. Furthermore, Black's king is quite secure at e7, while White's is not, and Black is well on the way to exchanging all his opponent's minor pieces except the inferior bishop – often a winning plan in itself. If White continues 16 ♘f5+ ♗×f5 17 ♖×f5, that part of the plan is complete, and in any case the h-pawn would fall after 17 . . . ♛h8. Against other moves Black develops the same kind of automatic attack (and rapidly too) by . . . ♛h8, . . . ♗h3 and . . . ♖g8.

Does it still seem unfair that White can't use his f-file? Sometimes establishing an outpost (♘f5) is the only way to break down your opponent's resistance in a file. If you can't do that, for whatever reason, the file may be useless to you because you can't clear the way, so to speak, for the heavy pieces. That is what we have here: White can't treble against the f-pawn; he can't use pawns to break down the resistance; he can't do anything.

From all this it follows that 11 ♘×g7+ is decidedly the best chance.

11	. . .	♘×**g7**
12	♘**d5** *(19)*	. . .

19
B

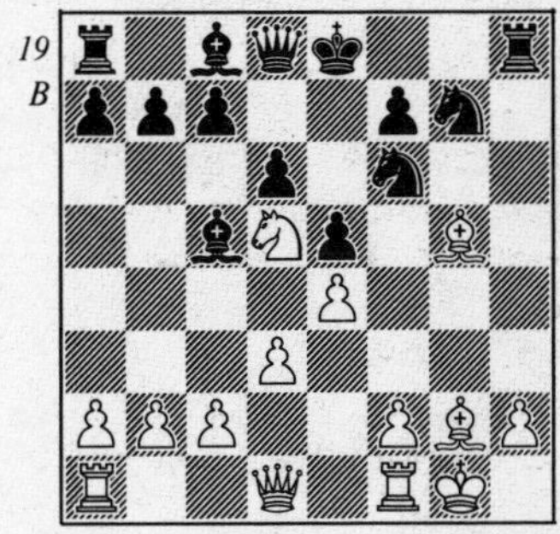

Regaining the piece, because after the obvious 12 . . . ♘gh5 he has 13 ♘×f6+ ♘×f6 14 ♕f3. Then 14 . . . ♗g4 15 ♕×f6 ♛×f6 16 ♗×f6 ♖h5 leaves a delicate situation in which White has to act quickly to rescue his bishop from the menace of . . . ♔d7 – e6. The only way appears to be 17 ♔h1 (17 c3, hoping for d4, fails against . . . ♗e2, while 17 h4 ♔d7 loses at least the h-pawn), meeting 17 . . . ♔d7 by 18 f3! ♗e6 (18 . . . ♗h3 19

♗×h3 ♖×h3 20 f4 ♔e6 21 f×e5 d×e5 22 ♖f5 suits White very well) 19 f4, thus maintaining his bishop in a strong position. Looking for improvements for Black, we find that he cannot do better than a repetition after 17 . . . ♗e2! 18 ♖e1 ♗g4 19 ♖f1 etc; but neither can White: if he tries 19 f3 ♗e6, he suddenly faces the threat of . . . ♗f2–g3 and both 20 ♖f1 ♗e3 (–f4) and 20 ♖e2 ♔d7 21 c3 ♖g8 22 d4 ♗b6 leave him in trouble.

So after what appears to be the forced move 12 . . . ♘gh5 a draw is likely with correct play. Instead Nunn sets his opponent some far more testing problems with a positional queen sacrifice.

12	**. . .**	**♘×d5!**
13	**♗×d8**	**♘f4**
14	**♗g5**	**. . .**

The bishop has to be exchanged because 14 ♗f6? (or 14 ♗×c7? ♘e6 and . . . ♖g8) loses another piece after 14 . . . ♖g8 15 ♔h1 ♘gh5, or 15 ♗h4 ♘gh5 16 ♗g3 ♘×g3 17 h×g3 ♖×g3.

14	**. . .**	**♘ge6**
15	**♗×f4** *(20)*	**♘×f4**

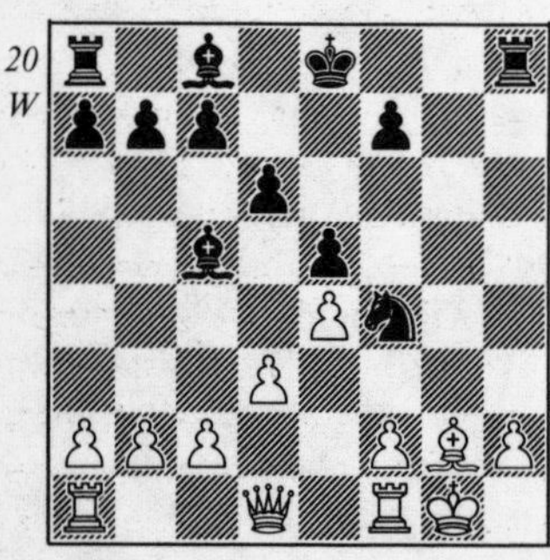
20
W

On what grounds can we justify Black's play? The obvious factors are the two open files leading to White's king and the tremendous outpost at f4; add to that the generally passive nature of White's position and the fact that his bishop in particular is a useless piece, a liability to its owner, and you are building up quite a good case for the substantial material investment. But still not enough: it is the power of the queen which concerns us most. Can she do anything really useful? Does she have any targets? Sometimes an extremely simple question may hit the nail on the head: "Will the queen be able to take anything or threaten the king in the foreseeable future?," for example. Because if she won't, and provided Black does not exchange pieces too readily, White may abandon all hope of even a draw in this position.

If you look around, you will see that Black's positon is very solid and presents hardly any targets to the queen. Therefore White's only chance is to open the game and try to give her more scope; and the only way to do that is by the pawn break c3 and d4. If you think along these lines, the queen's power will be brought into proper perspective. She must have wide open spaces or weaknesses to attack; lacking these she is anything but omnipotent.

Now in our position analysis indicates that an accurate defence, together with a willingness to return some of the material, will just save White – desperately difficult in practice, though; without the help of c3 and d4 he would have no chance at all. What follows will be easier to understand if we set aside the best move 16 ♗f3! for the moment, and concentrate on the game continuation, in which White chose the inferior way to meet the threat of

16 . . . ♖g8.

16 ♔h1? ♗e6

Not 16 . . . ♗h3; Black does not want to commit himself to such an early exchange; besides, the queen would come into action after 17 ♗×h3 ♖×h3 18 ♕g4. His correct plan is simply to win the h-pawn and develop a mating attack. There are three reasonable defences: (a) 17 c3 and d4; (b) 17 ♕f3, to get the queen involved; (c) 17 ♗f3 (the game continuation), to use the rook on the g-file.

(a) 17 c3 0–0–0 (in most cases . . . ♔e7 is better, to avoid check at g4, but here it makes no difference) 18 d4 ♖h4! 19 d×c5 ♖dh8 20 ♗f3 (20 ♕f3 ♖×h2+ 21 ♔g1 ♖×g2+ 22 ♕×g2 ♘e2 mate) ♖×h2+ 21 ♔g1 ♖2h4 22 ♖e1 ♖g8+ 23 ♔f1 ♗h3+ and wins.

(b) 17 ♕f3 (using the queen obviously strengthens the defence; the danger is that, with so little room to manoeuvre, she may get trapped) ♔e7 18 ♖g1 ♖h6 19 ♗f1 ♖ah8, and now 20 ♖g2 is one defence. In some of these variations the counter-sacrifice of an exchange permits a successful defence, in others it does not; it depends how much initiative Black retains. Here two very aggressive rooks and bishops are bound to be too much of an attacking force for White to cope with: 20 . . . ♘×g2 21 ♕×g2 (or 21 ♗×g2 ♖×h2+ 22 ♔g1 ♖2h4, then . . . ♖f4 or double on the g-file) ♖g6 22 ♕f3 ♖h4! (f2 naturally becomes the new target with the disappearance of the rook, and this is even better than 22 . . . ♖f6, which might permit a little activity by ♕g3–g7) and White simply has no constructive moves: 23 ♗g2 ♖f4 24 ♕d1 ♖×f2 25 ♗f3 ♖h6; or 23 c3 ♖f6 24 ♕d1 (24 ♕g3 ♖g4 25 ♕h3 ♗×f2 26 ♗g2 ♖h4) ♗g4 25 ♗e2 ♗×e2 26 ♕×e2 ♖×f2 and wins.

The other defence at move 20 is ♕g3, which produces: 20 ♕g3 ♗g4! (impossible after 17 . . . 0–0–0!) and in face of the terrible threat of 21 . . . ♗×f2+! 22 ♕×f2 ♗f3+ and mate (which is stronger than 21 . . . ♗f3+ 22 ♖g2) White again has to throw the exchange back: 21 ♖g2 ♘×g2. If then 22 ♕×g2 (22 ♔×g2 ♖g6 is just as bad) ♖g6 and Black threatens 23 . . . ♗h5 24 ♕h3 ♗e2! 25 ♕×h8 (25 ♕f5 ♗g4) ♗f3+ 26 ♗g2 ♖×g2 and wins. Therefore 23 ♕g3 (23 f3 ♗×f3) ♗e6 24 ♕f3 ♖h4, and this is the winning position we reached in an earlier line.

22 ♗×g2 is a bit better, but still insufficient in the long run: 22 . . . ♖g6 threatens . . . ♗e2 and 23 f3 ♗e6 24 ♕e1 ♖hg8 gives Black a decisive attack; so does the longer variation 23 ♖e1 ♗e6 24 ♕f3 ♖f6 25 ♕d1 ♖fh6 (threat . . . ♗×f2) 26 ♔g1 (or 26 ♖f1 ♖×h2+ 27 ♔g1 ♖2h6 28 ♖e1 ♖g6 29 ♔f1 ♖h2) ♖g6 27 ♔h1 ♗×f2 28 ♖f1 ♗g3. In this line the queen has to use the emergency exit: 23 d4; but after 23 . . . ♗×d4 Black will win at least one more pawn, guaranteeing himself approximate material equality, and his attack will continue undiminished.

In the game, you will recall, White played his third option 17 ♗f3. But before turning to that we need to see why 16 ♗f3 would have been stronger than 16 ♔h1. Essentially it amounts to a difference of one (vital) tempo, because if the king is at h1 Black will capture the pawn at h2 with check. If we try variation (a) above after 16 ♗f3, we get: 16 . . . ♗e6 17 c3 ♔e7 18 d4 ♖h4 19 d×c5 ♖g8+ (three moves instead of two to get doubled and take with check; 19 . . . ♖ah8 would be even slower) 20 ♔h1 ♖gh8 21 c×d6+ c×d6 22 ♖e1! ♖×h2+ 23 ♔g1 ♖2h4 24 ♖e3, and with e1 and d2 vacant for the king, and the rook ready to interpose at g3 in some lines, Black cannot win: 24 . . . ♗h3 25 ♗h1 ♗f1! 26 ♗f3 ♗c4 27 ♗g2, for instance, going round in circles. The best try seems to be 24 . . . ♗h3 25 ♗h1 ♗g4 26 ♗f3, since White is then reduced to moving his a1 rook or a pawn. But still there is no way to improve Black's position, and White can save himself by returning the queen. 26 . . . ♖h3 doesn't threaten . . . ♗×f3 because the queen can recapture; nor does 26 . . . ♖h2 followed by ♖8h3 carry any threat. The only other attempt is 26 . . . ♖8h6, which gives us: 27 ♖c1 ♗h3 28 ♗h1 ♗f1 29 ♗f3 ♗c4 30 ♗g2 ♖g6 31 ♖g3 ♘e2+ 32 ♕×e2 ♗×e2 33 ♖×g6 f×g6, and again White slips away into an equal ending!

There is one more point to make. No doubt Augustin avoided 16 ♗f3 because it allows the black pieces easy access to h3, and indeed White has to defend very carefully after 16 . . . ♗h3; but with best play there seems to be only a draw. Incidentally, 16 . . . ♘h3+ 17 ♔h1 would be a waste of time, since Black dare not win the exchange this time: 17 . . . ♘×f2+ 18 ♖×f2 ♗×f2 19 ♗g4 favours White strongly.

So 16 ♗f3 ♗h3 17 c3 (he must prepare d4 at once : 17 ♔h1? ♗×f1 18 ♕×f1 ♘h3 is bad; or if 17 ♖e1 ♔e7 18 ♔h1 ♖h4 19 c3 – too late – ♖ah8 20 ♖g1 ♗e6 and wins) ♔e7 18 ♔h1. This is forced because Black was threatening 18 . . . ♖ag8+ 19 ♔h1 ♗g2+ 20 ♗×g2 ♖×g2, but now, for all its useful work, the bishop is obstructing its rooks on the h-file! 18 . . . ♖ag8 19 ♖g1 ♖×g1+ 20 ♔×g1 is no use, nor is 18 . . . ♗×f1 19 ♕×f1 ♘h3 20 d4 e×d4 21 ♗g4! Still Black has a comfortable draw, though, by concentrating on his main target: 18 . . . ♖h4! 19 d4 ♖ah8 (threat 20 . . . ♗g2+) 20 ♖g1 ♗f1! (20 . . . ♗e6 21 ♖g3 leaves him struggling) 21 ♖×f1 (21 ♖g3? ♖×h2+ 22 ♔g1 ♗e2 wins) ♖×h2+ 22 ♔g1 ♖2h4 23 d×c5 (or 23 ♖e1 ♖g8+ 24 ♔f1 ♖gh8 with a draw) ♘h3+ 24 ♔h2 ♘f4+ and perpetual check (25 ♔g3? ♖h3+ 26 ♔g4 ♔f6! and mate).

Summing up this difficult section, then: after 16 ♗f3 neither 16 . . . ♗e6 nor 16 . . . ♗h3 quite wins; after 16 ♔h1 ♗e6 wins, but not 16 . . . ♗h3. I need hardly add that only the outline of these variations could possibly be seen over the board. In practice no-one could be expected to perceive the difference between the two defences; even after analysis it is far from easy to understand.

17 ♗f3? . . .

Ironically this is now probably the weakest defence, because the threat of 18 ♗g4 can be met by a move which Black wants to play in any case.

17 . . . ♖h4

Now 18 c3 leads to variation (a) above; so White sacrifices the exchange, as in variation (b), but this time his queen is out of play.

18 ♖g1 ♔e7

19 ♖g2 . . .

19 ♖g3 ♗×f2 only makes matters worse, because the king will be trapped at h1.

19 . . . ♘×g2

20 ♗×g2 ♖ah8

21 ♕d2 . . .

If 21 ♕g1 ♖f4 22 ♖f1 ♗g4, followed by . . . ♗e2.

21 ... **♖×h2+**
22 ♔g1 ♖2h4 *(21)*

21
W

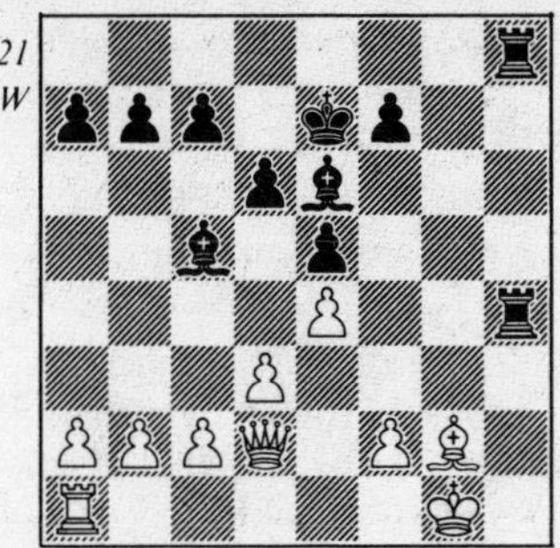

Henceforth the g-file and the bishop are Black's targets. He threatens simply to double rooks, and if 23 ♔f1 ♖g8 (even better than 23 ... ♖h1+) 24 ♗f3 ♖h2, followed by ... ♗h3+, wins easily. If 23 ♕g5+ f6 24 ♕g7+ ♗f7, and ... ♖g8 is threatened; therefore 25 ♕g3 ♖4h7! and the g-file is seized: 26 ♔f1 ♖g8 27 ♕f3 ♖h2 28 ♗h3 ♗h5!, mating or picking up the queen.

23 ♖e1 ...

White returns the material with interest.

23 ... **♖g8**
24 ♖e3 ...

Or 24 ♔f1 ♖h2 25 ♗f3 ♗h3+

24 ... **♗×e3**
25 ♕×e3 ♗h3
26 ♔f1 ♗×g2+

26 ... ♖×g2 27 ♔e1 ♗e6 is quicker because the rooks can seize f2 almost at once, but Black has more than enough material in any case.

27 ♔e2 c5
28 ♕d2 b6
29 ♕c3 ♖f4
30 ♕a3 a5
31 ♕b3 ♗h3

To stop the checks, if necessary, by ... ♗d7.

32 f3 ♖g2+
33 ♔e3 ♗g4!

And mates after 34 f×g4 ♖gf2.

0 – 1

Game 6

Modern Defence
Islington Open 1978
R. Britton v. J. Nunn

1	e4	g6
2	d4	♗g7
3	♘c3	d6
4	♘f3	a6 *(22)*

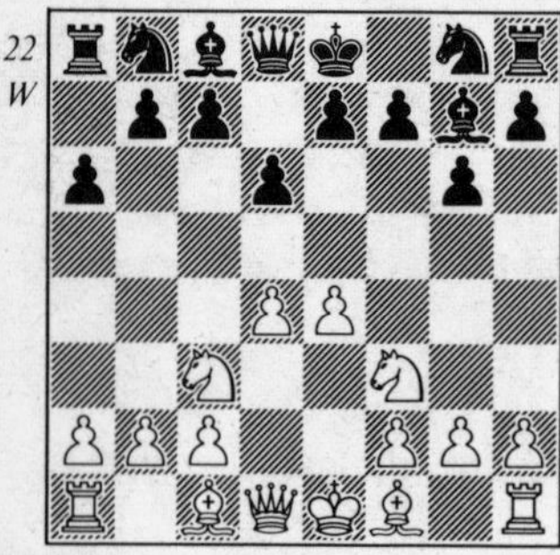

22
W

The intention of this somewhat eccentric move is to expand immediately on the Q-side (. . . b5, . . . ♗b7, . . . ♘d7 and . . . c5) at the expense of more conventional development. A double-edged procedure, to be sure, but this game was played in a weekend tournament where a string of wins (typically 5/6) is likely to be needed for first prize. Nunn is therefore prepared to take a few (reasonable) risks with his opening. If the plan succeeds, he will eliminate White's d-pawn by . . . c5. That will permit the development of his knight at f6 (without worrying about the e5 thrust) and he should end up with a favourable type of Sicilian Dragon formation.

There are two dangers: one is that Black's king will have to remain in the centre for some time; the other is that White may strike at the advanced b-pawn by a4 and obtain a positional advantage by breaking up or fixing the Q-side pawn structure.

5 ♗e2 . . .

An obvious alternative is to restrain the Q-side advance by 5 a4, but then Black can comfortably switch plans: 5 . . . ♗g4 6 ♗e3 ♘c6, still exerting pressure on White's centre. Without the moves a4 and . . . a6 White could now continue 7 ♗b5 and gain some advantage, but here he would have to be content with 7 ♗e2 ♗×f3 8 ♗×f3 e5. In other words, Black has safeguarded his knight by . . . a6 **without tempo loss**. Naturally, if he tried any such change of plan in the absence of White's a4, the loss of time caused by . . . a6 would be a serious matter.

5 ♗e2 is sound enough, but altogether more aggressive is 5 ♗c4, which interferes with Black's plan: 5 . . . ♘d7? would be met by 6 ♗×f7+ ♔×f7 7 ♘g5+, and 5 . . . ♗g4? also by 6 ♗×f7+. The best antidote is probably 5 . . . b5 6 ♗b3; but now, although Black could get away with 6 . . . ♗b7 (7 ♗×f7+ ♔×f7 8 ♘g5+ ♔e8 9 ♘e6 ♕d7 10 ♘×g7+ ♔f7, trapping the knight) he still could not play 7 . . . ♘d7 (after 7 0–0, say) because 8 ♗×f7+ would again work.

So he would have to switch plans: 6 . . . ♘c6 7 0–0 ♘a5 8 h3 ♘×b3 9 a×b3 c6; but here White has an ominous lead in development to compensate for the bishop-pair.

Two points about this last variation which might be puzzling: (1) White has to play 8 h3, even though he is trying to exploit his lead in development (time advantage) and would therefore prefer to make a more aggressive move. Without it Black would develop conveniently and put pressure on the d-pawn by . . . ♗g4; (2) Black in turn would prefer 9 . . . ♗b7 to another pawn move, but then comes 10 ♕e2 (threatens ♘×b5) and if 10 . . . b4 11 ♘d5 ♗×d5 (or 11 . . . c5 12 d×c5 d×c5 13 ♖d1, then ♘d2-c4) 12 e×d5, when his Q-side position is already past praying for.

5	**. . .**	**b5**
6	**0–0**	**♘d7**

6 . . .b4 would be bad because Black does not have the development to back it up: 7 ♘d5 a5 8 a3! b×a3 9 ♖×a3 yields him nothing but weaknesses; or even worse 7 . . .c5 8 d×c5 d×c5 9 ♗f4. So the choice lies between 6 . . . ♗b7 and 6 . . . ♘d7. These **may** transpose or they may lead to very different situations. For example, after 6 . . . ♗b7 the e-pawn is under fire and . . . b4 becomes a serious possibility. Or after 6 . . . ♘d7 Black may postpone . . . ♗b7 (as in the game) and hit the centre at once by an early . . . c5.

Before we reduce these ideas to some variations, it may be profitable to consider the position for a moment from White's point of view. Black is playing a dangerous game, as we have indicated, but at least his plan of development is fairly well defined. For White the plan is less apparent, since Black has not committed himself in the centre. Where is he supposed to hit Black? The king is in the centre, so presumably by e5; but how should he prepare it? Should f4 come into it? In outline the answers are: (1) He should base his play on trying to achieve e5; (2) He will prepare it by ♖e1 and ♗f1; also ♗g5 which usefully pins and attacks the e-pawn. In reply . . . h6 weakens Black (more than you might think – see one of the variations below), while . . . f6 blocks all his pieces and leaves a serious hole at e6; (3) ♘e1 and f4 would not be appropriate because of the time factor: Black would play . . . c5 and then complete his development without any problems; (4) . . . c5 should not generally be met by d5. White wants to keep the central position more fluid because of his lead in development. In normal Benoni-type positions this move is more fitting because a subsequent . . . a6 can be met by a4, cramping Black on the Q-side. Here . . . a6 and . . . b5 have already appeared and Black has room to develop (. . . ♗b7 is possible, for instance).

Now for some variations: suppose Black plays 6 . . . ♗b7 7 ♖e1 ♘d7 (or 6 . . . ♘d7 7 ♖e1 ♗b7). We then have: (1) 8 ♗g5 h6 9 ♗h4 ♘b6(?) (out of place, even though it forces White's next move; the knight is needed to defend the points e5 and c5) 10 a3 (otherwise . . . b4, since ♘d5 now costs a pawn) c5 11 e5! c×d4 (11 . . . d×e5 12 d×c5 favours White) 12 ♕×d4 d×e5 13 ♕e3 ♕c7 14 ♗g3 f6 15 ♘h4, leading to a decisive attack (Grunfeld–Soltis, Lone Pine 1979).

Even without the weakening move . . . h6 this would be an unhappy line for Black. (2) 8 ♗g5 c5 (8 . . . ♘gf6 is strongly met by 9 e5) 9 ♗f1 (9 d5 is like the main game: 9 . . . ♘gf6 10 ♗f1 0–0 etc., with equality) c×d4 10 ♘×d4 ♘gf6 11 ♕d2 h6 12 ♗h4 0–0, with perhaps a very slight advantage to White (Bennett–Nunn, Islington Open 1975). (3) 8 ♗f1 c5 9 a4 b4 10 ♘d5, and now an exchange would be most unwise, not only on account of the open file, but because his white squares would be seriously exposed. But 10 . . . e6 also leads to trouble: 11 ♗f4! e5 (11 . . . e×d5 12 e×d5+ ♘e7 13 ♗×d6 ♗f6 14 ♗×e7 ♗×e7 15 d6) 12 d×e5 d×e5 13 ♗g5 f6 (Honfi–Vadasz, Kecskemét 1975) and Black lost because of his Q-side pawn weaknesses. The best way is: 10 . . . ♘gf6! 11 ♘×f6+ ♘×f6 12 d5 0–0 13 ♗c4 a5 14 ♕d3 ♘d7 with equality (Geller–Hort, Linares 1983).

These lines demonstrate how White should be thinking about his attack; but they may be short-circuited by the fact that Black can begin with 6 . . . ♗b7 and answer 7 ♖e1 by 7 . . . b4. Then 8 ♘a4 is unsound: 8 . . . ♗×e4 9 ♗c4 d5, or 9 ♘g5 ♗c6 10 ♗c4 d5, with little or no compensation for the lost pawn. So 8 ♘d5 is necessary. Then 8 . . . e6 again leads to a bad position (9 ♘×b4 ♗×e4 10 d5! etc.), but 8 . . . a5 is unclear: the knight will shortly be driven back, leaving Black to complete his development satisfactorily, unless White can find a sacrifice, 9 ♗c4 e6 10 ♗g5 f6 11 ♘f4, for example.

This line is the critical one, then. If 6 . . . ♗b7 is playable, it seems that White cannot expect any advantage from the 5 ♗e2 variation. Nunn's choice is to delay the development of the bishop for several moves.

7	**♖e1**	**c5**
8	**d5**	**. . .**

As we explained, this is unlikely to yield any advantage. 8 ♗f1 or 8 ♗g5 would offer a more serious test of Black's unusual opening.

8	**. . .**	**♘gf6**
9	**♗f1**	**0–0**
10	**h3**	**. . .**

Black must now break up the centre by . . . e6; without that he cannot expect to get any decent scope for his rooks. So his scheme of development has to be . . . ♕c7, . . . ♗b7 and . . . ♖ad8, backing up the weak d-pawn; then . . . e6. White in turn will seek to prevent this operation by ♗f4, ♕d2 and ♖ad1, and only then consider more aggressive plans. The purpose of 10 h3 is to secure the bishop against a later . . . ♘h5.

The square c4 deserves a special mention. Black must never be tempted into playing . . . b4 without a good reason, because it allows ♘d2–c4, or ♘b1–d2–c4, a superb outpost from which the knight attacks the crucial d6 square. White may, of course, force the advance at any moment by playing a4, but that will cost him a tempo. At the moment his lack of development would in any case veto the idea: 10 a4 b4 11 ♘b1 ♕c7 12 ♘bd2 e6 and then: (a) 13 ♘c4 e×d5 14 e×d5 ♗b7, when his d-pawn disappears; (b) 13 d×e6 f×e6 14 ♘c4 d5 with a strong centre which can be supported by the black pieces. Sometimes this pawn structure is weak and unwieldy, but not here: Black can develop comfortably by . . . ♗b7, . . . ♖ad8 etc.

The possibility of a4, seizing

control of c4, nevertheless remains a point of supreme importance for the next dozen moves.

10 . . . ♕c7 *(23)*

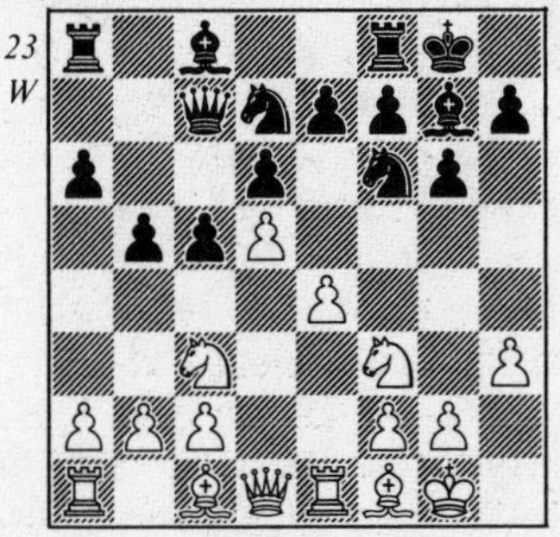

11 a3(?) . . .

Since . . . b4 is not really threatened, this is a tempo loss: not a fatal one, but enough to make the game that little bit less comfortable to handle. The mistake is very understandable, though: after the correct move 11 ♗f4 White has to meet 11 . . . b4 by 12 ♘a4 (12 ♘b1? ♘h5). Then he has to appreciate three points: (1) That 12 . . . ♕a5 13 c3 is favourable to him because the queen will soon be expelled by ♘d2–c4; (2) That 12 . . . c4 is too rash (13 ♘d4 ♗b7 14 c3 would be very good for White); (3) That after 12 . . . ♗b7 his control of c4 counts for more than the difficulties he will experience in recentralising his knight. This does indeed seem to be the case, though he must take care to restrain Black's play in the centre before attending to the knight. Best seems to be: 13 ♕d2 ♖ad8 14 ♕e3! (stops . . . ♘e5) and then: (a) 14 . . . e6 15 d×e6 f×e6 16 ♘g5 ♖fe8 17 ♗c4 ♘f8 18 ♕b3, followed perhaps by e5, favouring White; (b) 14 . . . ♗×d5 15 e×d5 ♘×d5 16 ♕d2 ♘×f4 17 ♕×f4 ♕c6 18 b3 (or 18 ♖×e7 ♕×a4 19 ♗c4 with an attack), which is also at least a little better for White; (c) 14 . . . ♕a5 15 ♕b3 followed by a3, with a promising position. If Black plays more slowly (say 14 . . . ♖fe8), White keeps developing by ♗c4 and ♖ad1, making . . . e6 more and more difficult to achieve, and eventually plays b3 and ♘b2.

11 . . . ♗b7
12 ♗f4 ♖ad8
13 ♕d2? . . .

This is a more serious mistake and leads to real trouble. White is still planning ♖ad1, but **because of the tempo loss** at move 11 he never gets a chance to play it. The queen should leave the dangerous d-file at once: 13 ♕c1 ♘e5 14 ♘×e5 d×e5 15 ♗h6, when Black keeps only a tiny advantage.

13 . . . ♘e5!

"Achieving . . . e6 is everything", says Nunn. Making his pieces work is his sole concern, and the centre pawns have to go along with that, whatever shape they may be required to assume. In a moment they will be doubled and isolated, but that goes almost unnoticed.

14 ♕e3 . . .

What else? If 14 ♗×e5 d×e5 with transposition into the game, since the queen will have to leave the d-file anyway. If 14 ♗e2, Black can pick up the e-pawn by 14 . . . b4. If 14 ♘×e5 d×e5 15 ♗h2 e6 is very unpleasant; and here is where the tempo loss comes into the picture: with the white rook at d1 instead of the pawn at a3 White would have the strong reply 16 d6.

14 . . . e6
15 ♗×e5 . . .

Since everything else loses material,

White reluctantly exchanges his important black-square bishop. The d-pawn cannot be held in place by 15 ♖ad1 because Black still has . . . b4; or if 15 d×e6 ♘×f3+ 16 ♕×f3 f×e6 and his pieces are in a sorry plight on the f-file: 17 ♕e3 ♘h5, with . . . ♗d4 coming.

15 . . . d×e5

16 d×e6 f×e6 *(24)*

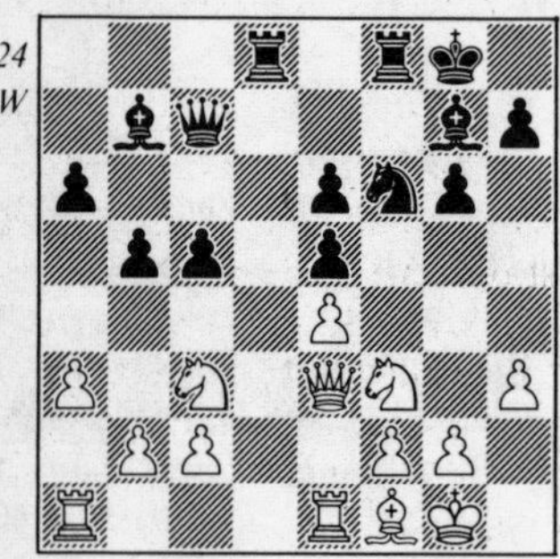

24 W

The aggressive appearance of Black's pieces, especially his rooks, presents a striking contast with the position of three or four moves ago. Also his pawns are controlling some important squares, keeping the white knight out of d5 for example.

But perhaps you still feel a bit suspicious about those e-pawns? Why should they not be weak here? Well, there are two technical reasons: (1) They are not standing on an open file; and (2) The square e4 is blocked by a pawn. In similar situations (with the white pawn at d3 or e3, for instance) ♘g5–e4 would be a most desirable blockade manoeuvre for White. But in both these cases, with the file open or with e4 vacant, we would be saying no more than that White's pieces had more scope than in the present game. You see how it always comes back to that? Black stands better here because he has the initiative; because his pieces are more active. **Therefore, his pawns are not weak. It is the white ones which are weak!** Even now one of them is threatened, by 17 . . . b4; hence White's next move.

17 ♘d2 . . .

17 ♕g5 would be met by 17 . . . b4, all the same; or if 17 ♗d3, Black would continue . . . ♖d4, as in the game, rather than with an immediate . . . c4 or . . . b4.

A crucial aspect of Black's plan for the next few moves will be to emphasise his domination of the dark squares, which the disappearance of White's Q-bishop has given him. Thus . . . ♘h5, . . . ♘f4 and . . . ♗h6 will be coming shortly. But he hasn't won yet; he must take care not to release the white pieces from their bind. Specifically, the danger lies in a4, dislodging the b-pawn and following up with ♗c4. And that is where a weaker player might well have stumbled. Lacking the sense of urgency to which I have referred elsewhere, he might easily have permitted White to achieve that. So we must observe the energy with which Nunn tackles the problem. He controls the tactics in such a way that White never gets a free tempo to play a4.

17 . . . ♖d4!

Intending to refute 18 a4 by 18 . . . b4 19 ♘e2 ♘×e4 20 ♘×d4 e×d4 21 ♕d3 (or 21 ♕e2 ♖×f2) ♘×f2. This is as far as Nunn calculated during the game, though surprisingly White is not quite dead. He can keep the game going by 22 ♕b3 ♗d5 23 ♗c4 ♗×c4 24 ♕×c4 (if 24 ♘×c4 d3! is good: 25 c×d3 ♘×h3+ 26 ♔h1 ♘f2+ 27 ♔g1 ♗d4 28

♘e3 ♕e5) ♘×h3+ 25 g×h3 (25 ♔h1 ♘f4) ♕g3+ 26 ♔h1 ♕×h3+ 27 ♔g1 ♕g3+ 28 ♔h1. At this point Black cannot do better than to regain some of his material; he has no mate because the threat against e6 is too strong. But after 28 . . . ♕h4+ 29 ♔g1 ♕g5+ 30 ♔h1 ♕h6+ 31 ♔g1 ♕×d2 32 ♕×e6+ ♔h8 33 ♖f1 ♖g8 (or perhaps 33 . . . ♖×f1+ 34 ♖×f1 ♕e3+) he still keeps the advantage with his threats of . . . ♕×c2 and . . . d3.

If 18 ♘b3, still 18 . . . ♘×e4 etc.; so White settles for the text move, further weakening his black squares.

18 f3 ♘h5

This time, if 19 a4, Black is ready with 19 . . . ♖fd8! 20 ♖ad1 (20 ♘b3 c4) ♘f4 21 a×b5 ♗h6 22 ♔h1 ♕g7 23 ♕f2 ♘×h3 24 g×h3 ♗×d2, winning either a piece by 25 ♖e2 ♗×c3 or the exchange by 25 b×a6 ♗×e1 etc. In the latter case a lot of technical problems remain, but Black should win. Since he has no other possibility of active play, White decides to attack the intruding rook.

19 ♘e2 ♘f4! *(25)*

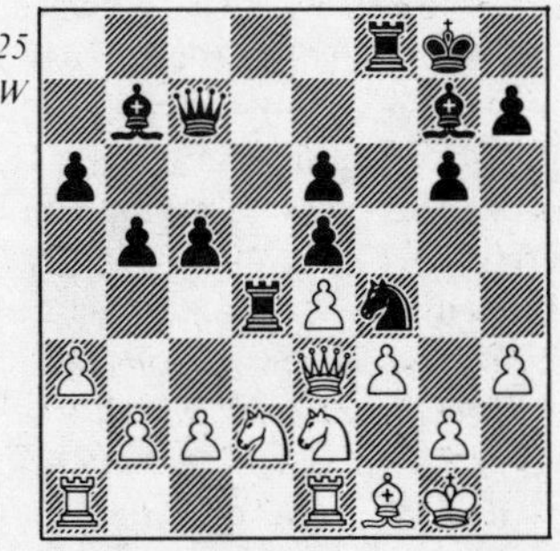

25
W

And here is the kind of positional sacrifice which seems so natural and logical when played by a Grandmaster. We can all appreciate that Black is getting plenty of compensation for the exchange, yet we hesitate to take such decisions ourselves. Why? For two reasons, it seems. The first is that although material is only one element in chess (the others being time, space, development, pawn structure etc.) it is the tangible one; and the same player who will throw tempi around with appalling abandon, or neglect his development, will shrink from sacrificing even a pawn unless he can see the consequences with absolute clarity. But Grandmasters have a highly developed sense that material is just one factor in the equation; so in their games it is constantly being interchanged with the other elements. It is not a question of their being more daring than other players, or more prepared to risk losing. To a GM there is no danger whatever in this type of sacrifice; it is simply a matter of technique, a transaction. In this connection I might add that players who are generally regarded as extremely hard to beat tend to specialise in the art of positional sacrifice (Petrosian and Andersson spring to mind).

The second reason is what Dr Lasker calls 'the certainty of having to apply yourself vigorously' (after sacrificing, that is). In other words: "It's all very well for Nunn to do that, but if I tried it I would soon go wrong and then lose the endgame". Well, it's true that after sacrificing you have to play with a certain amount of vigour. But you have to do that anyway! If you want to stand up to really strong opponents, that is. Look at it this way: in allowing his pawns to be doubled at move 14 Nunn has already made a sacrifice of a kind (his pawn structure), and without vigorous play to follow it up he would have let the white bishop into c4. He also sacrificed at move four (development) and any hesitation after that would have let to trouble. He is always 'sacrificing'; you cannot play this game without doing it.

White has to accept the offer, otherwise . . . ♗h6 comes anyway.

20	**♘×d4**	**e×d4**
21	**♕f2**	**♗e5**

Now we shall see how Nunn 'applies himself vigorously'. In return for the exchange he has total control of the black squares and has also improved his pawn structure by the capture at d4. He has seen that there are two equally good continuations here: 21 . . . ♗e5 and 21 . . . d3 which guarantees a protected passed pawn by threatening . . . ♗d4 (22 c3 c4 etc.) With 21 . . . ♗e5 he is preparing . . . ♘h5, and if 22 g3, still 22 . . . ♘h5. This is what we shall now analyse, but during play it would not have been necessary to see beyond that outline.

The knight move will threaten both . . . ♗g3 and . . . ♗h2+, ♔h1 ♘g3+ winning the queen; so at this point White has three options: he can move his rook away from e1, he can return the exchange, or he can try to fight back by 22 g3 and 23 f4.

The rook move will not really stand up to examination: if 22 ♖ec1 ♘h5 and he must compromise his pawn structure even more, to make air for the king: 23 g4 ♗g3 24 ♕e2 (24 ♕g2 ♘f4!) ♘f4 25 ♕d1 and Black now wins by attacking in two places, i.e. 25 . . . ♕e7 26 ♗g2 ♕h4 27 ♕f1 c4! and the continuation . . . d3 and . . . ♘e2+ is altogether too much. At the outset White could also try ♕e1, since he can just stand the discovered check after 23 . . . ♗h2+ 24 ♔h1 ♘g3+ 25 ♔×h2 etc.; but Black forces g4 anyway by beginning with 23 . . . ♗f4.

Definitely the best fighting chance is 22 g3, in spite of the awful danger of loosening his pawn cover. That way at least his pieces can move more freely and any uncertainty by Black might permit a recovery. Nevertheless, Black has two very good lines after 22 g3 ♘h5 23 f4:

(a) 23 . . . g5 24 ♕f3 (24 ♕g2 g×f4 25 g×f4+ ♗g7 wins the f-pawn under much more favourable circumstances) ♘g7 25 ♕g2 g×f4 26 g4, when, at the cost of a pawn, White has driven back the knight and managed to find a good defensive square for his knight at f3. Still Black has a clear advantage, though: the white rooks are almost useless and the e-pawn is a permanent target. This in addition to his extra space and strong centre pawns.

(b) 23 . . . ♘×g3 24 ♕×g3 ♗×f4 and then: (1) 25 ♕g2 ♗e3+ 26 ♖×e3 d×e3 27 ♘f3 ♗×e4 28 ♗e2, when Black has three pawns for a piece (or four pawns after . . . ♗×c2, but the pin on the knight is very unpleasant). He also has chances of winning more material by attacking the Q-side pawns with his queen. The only problem here is the rather exposed state of the black king, which might conceivably allow perpetual check. (2) 25 ♕d3 c4! 26 ♕×d4 ♖d8 27 ♕f6 ♖×d2 28 ♗g2! (not 28 ♕×e6+ which loses in a curious fashion: 28 . . . ♔g7 and however White meets the threat of 29 . . . ♗e3+ – say 29 ♗g2 – his queen is trapped by 29 . . . ♗c8 30 ♕e8 ♖d8) and Black again has a very promising position, but no forced win.

This brings us back to the game. White's chosen move leaves him no chance at all because he is obliged to play the suicidal move g4, as well as returning the exchange.

22 a4(?) ♘h5

Threatens the queen in two ways: 23 . . . ♗g3 24 ♕e2 ♗h2+ and 23 . . . ♗h2+ 24 ♔h1 ♘g3+. If 23 ♔h1 ♗h2 forces 24 g4.

23 g4 ♗g3

24 ♕e2 . . .

Or 24 ♕g2 ♘f4, forcing 25 ♕h1.

24 . . . ♘f4

25 ♕d1 c4

Black is still thinking in terms of restricting the enemy pieces as much as possible. With this move he meets the attack on b5 without yielding the square c4.

26 a×b5 a×b5

27 ♗g2 ♗×e1

28 ♕×e1 e5 *(26)*

26
W

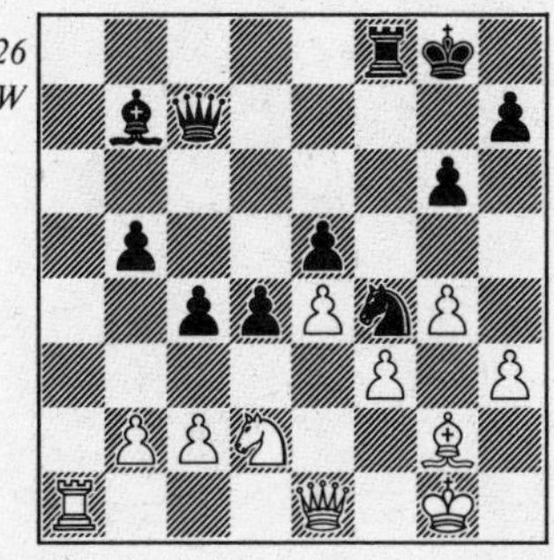

With admirable timing this move immediately follows the disappearance of his own black-square bishop! Now, how to finish off? Obviously Black's game is overwhelming: just compare each piece with its white counterpart. The pawn majority on the Q-side would normally bring about the decision, though as things turn out Black gets the opportunity to finish quickly with a mating attack. But still the pieces must come before the pawns! First, the queen's position is improved, incidentally keeping the white rook out of a7.

29 ♘f1 ♕c5

30 ♔h2 . . .

30 ♕f2 is possible; then . . . b4–b3 would be strong.

30 . . . d3

31 c×d3 ♘×d3

Of course, 31 . . . c×d3 is playable, but again the pieces are given priority over the creation of a passed pawn. The knight is even stronger at d3 than f4, the queen will be immensely powerful at d4, and White's queen and rook will be tied to the defence of the b-pawn.

32 ♕d2 ♕d4

33 ♖b1 ♗×e4!

And the result is an attractive combination; a quick knock-out to end the game.

Since Black could also win by 33 . . . b4 etc., a tactical finish of this kind is only appropriate if it works perfectly. If there were any doubt about the outcome, the slower method would be preferable.

34 f×e4 ♖f2

35 ♕g5 . . .

Moving the queen to d1, e3 or h6 allows . . . ♘f4, winning the bishop or the knight. If 35 ♕c3 ♕×e4 etc. After 35 ♕g5 or ♕a5 White can meet 35 . . . ♘f4 by 36 ♘e3, with perpetual check if Black captures. However . . .

35 . . . ♖×g2+

Seeing the second sacrifice at the outset is often the difficult part. Curious, too, how frequently this pattern repeats itself: the very bad bishop is the piece which is holding White's position together; hence it is the one which has to be removed by violent means.

36 ♔×g2 ♘f4+
0 - 1

If 37 ♔f3 (37 ♔g3 ♕g1+ 38 ♔h4 is one move shorter, or if 38 ♔f3 ♕g2+ and mate) ♕d3+ 38 ♔f2 ♕e2+ 39 ♔g3 ♕g2+ 40 ♔h4 ♕f2+ 41 ♘g3 ♘g2 mate. Quite an unusual mate. With the queen at a5 instead of g5 one more move would be needed: 42 ♔g5 ♕f4 mate.

Game 7

Queen's Gambit Declined, Tarrasch Defence Dortmund 1979

J. Nikolac v. J. Nunn

1	**♘f3**	**d5**
2	**c4**	**e6**
3	**g3**	**c5**
4	**♗g2**	**♘c6**
5	**0–0**	**♘f6**
6	**c×d5**	**e×d5**
7	**d4**	**♗e7**
8	**♘c3**	**. . .**

8 d×c5 ♗×c5 would gain a tempo by making Black's bishop move twice, but would allow the d-pawn too much freedom; after 9 ♗g5 d4 it would restrict White seriously. If 9 e3 Black could castle and play . . . d4, eliminating his only weakness, with easy equality.

8	**. . .**	**0–0**
9	**♗g5**	**c×d4**

Here Black does best to make the exchange (or he can play 9 . . . ♗e6) because of the increasing pressure on his centre pawns: if 9 . . . h6? 10 ♗×f6 ♗×f6 11 d×c5, and he is in trouble.

10	**♘×d4**	**h6**
11	**♗e3**	**♖e8**

These eleven moves are nowadays regarded as the main line of the Tarrasch, a defence which has always been considered an uphill struggle for Black, but which becomes fashionable for short periods when some great player attempts to revive and improve it. Spassky used it for a while in the 1960's, and more recently Kasparov adopted it twice in his first match with Karpov. Unfortunately, he lost on both occasions and abandoned it altogether in the second match! Nunn played it from time to time in the 1970's but gave it up after some poor results, one reason being that Black's winning chances are slim, at any rate in international play. It seems to be the kind of opening in which White has quite a wide margin of error: he can often play indifferently and still hold the draw.

Technically we have a standard type of IQP position in which Black will look for K-side counterplay by occupying the half-open e-file and perhaps the outpost at e4. White for his part has a choice of two plans: he may continue to blockade d4 and build up pressure on the weak pawn, or he may exchange knights and transfer his attack to the backward c-pawn and the blockade point c5. In the present game White makes this exchange almost at once; so we are concerned here exclusively with the second plan.

12	**♖c1**	**. . .**

The usual move at the time this game was played. Karpov played 12 ♕b3 in his two defeats of Kasparov.

12	**. . .**	**♗f8**
13	**♘×c6**	**b×c6** *(27)*

White players have experimented with many different 13th moves to try to keep the initiative; 13 ♘b3, ♘a4, ♘cb5, ♕c2, ♕b3 and ♕a4 have all

27
W

been tested. Here we have to restrict our comments to the exchange of knights and the fundamentally different pawn structure which it brings about. In substance White's strategy is based on two things: **fixing and simplifying**. He wishes to immobilise the black pawns and specifically to fix the c-pawn by blockading c5. After that he may think about how best to threaten it directly. Notice that the g2 bishop is assisting admirably in this process by pinning down the pawns. White also wishes to simplify by exchanging minor pieces, because the process of attacking the pawn weaknesses would be so much easier without the nuisance of having his major pieces harassed by bishops and knights. To understand this more clearly, imagine White's ideal position: something like rooks on c5 and d4, queen on c3 and pawn on e3. A real nightmare for Black! His c-pawn and a-pawn are exposed, his pieces are certain to be passive and he lacks the necessary punch for any effective K-side counter – unless he has managed to weaken White's castled position in the meantime.

That brings us to Black's strategy, which is a bit more complicated to put into action. He cannot very well use the b-file because his a8 rook is temporarily tied to the defence of the a-pawn; so he will concentrate on developing play along the e-file and on the K-side generally. The earlier remarks about exchanging need to be modified slightly inasmuch as Black will be pleased to exchange the white-square bishops. In that way he will weaken White's position and eliminate his own inferior bishop. Indeed, without that element in his plan he cannot hope to make much of a dent in his opponent's fortress.

14 ♗d4 . . .

One reason why the Tarrasch Defence is under a cloud is that White is thought to have a more accurate move than ♗d4 at this point, and it is hard to see how to equalise against it. 14 ♘a4 is the direct and obvious attempt to blockade c5 and to exchange Black's better bishop (♗c5), but in 1979 its strength was not appreciated because the reply 14 . . . ♕a5 was considered good.

It appears that the queen move is playable because 15 ♖×c6 can be met by 15 . . . ♗d7, and Black therefore seems to have time to settle his queen on the nice active square b5, hitting e2 and conveniently covering c6. For example: 14 ♘a4 ♕a5 15 b3 ♕b5 16 ♕c2 ♗d7 17 ♘c3 (can't occupy c5) ♕b4 18 ♖cd1 ♕g4 19 ♗d4 (19 h3 ♕h5, or 19 ♗f3 ♕h3, or 19 ♖d4 ♕e6, threatening . . . c5) ♗f5 20 ♕c1 ♕g6 21 ♖fe1 ♘e4 22 ♘×e4 ♗×e4 23 ♗×e4 ♖×e4 24 ♗c5, ½ – ½ (Timman – Gligorić, Buenos Aires 1978). By keeping his pieces active and by playing this difficult kind of manoeuvring game, Black manages to hold the balance. In the final position he would continue 24 . . . a5 25 ♗×f8 ♖×f8; then follows . . . a4 (or if 26 a4 ♖b4 etc.) and instead of Black's having two weak pawns to defend, the players will have one each. An instructive point: if Black's pieces had been a little less lively he might have been unable to liquidate in this manner, and would have been in trouble.

However, all this is invalidated by the fact that White can, after all, play 15 ♖×c6! If then 15 . . . ♗d7 16 ♗d2, and now: (a) 16 . . . ♕b5 17 ♖×f6 g×f6 (or 17 . . . ♕×a4 18 ♕×a4 ♗×a4 19 ♖f4! ♗c6 20 ♗e3 ♗d6 21 ♖g4, and White keeps both his extra pawn and his positional advantage – Sosonko – Salazar, Lugano 1985) 18 ♘c3 ♕×b2 19 ♘×d5, with a winning attack; for example 19 . . . ♖ac8 20 ♗c3! ♖×c3 21 ♘×f6+ ♔h8 22 ♕×d7 ♖e7 23 ♕f5 ♔g7 24 ♘h5+ ♔g8 (if 24 . . . ♔h8 25 ♗e4 ♖×e4 26 ♕×e4 and wins) 25 ♕g4+ ♔h8 26 ♘f6 ♗g7 1 – 0 (27 ♕f5 wins a rook – Strauss–King, British Championship 1984); or (b) 16 . . . ♗b4 17 ♖c5, and Black gets the worse of it every time, finishing up either a pawn down or with a bad ending: (i) 17 . . . ♗b5 18 ♕b3; (ii) 17 . . . ♗×a4 18 ♖×a5 ♗×d1 19 ♗×b4 ♗×e2 20 ♖c1; (iii) 17 . . . ♕×a4 (best hope) 18 ♕×a4 ♗×a4 19 ♗×b4 ♖×e2 20 b3 ♗d7 21 ♖a1 ♖c8 22 ♖×c8+ ♗×c8 23 ♗f1 (Black's rook can eventually be forced off the seventh, when he will be left with weak pawns and facing the two bishops) ♖b2 24 ♗a3 ♖d2 25 ♗c5 a6 26 ♗e3 ♖b2 (Ribli–Barle, Portorož/Ljubljana 1985) 27 h3!, followed by ♗d3 and ♗c1, and White should be winning.

If 14 . . . ♕a5 is bad, what should Black do against 14 ♘a4? On the whole his outlook is rather gloomy because his f8 bishop is bound to be exchanged. Here are a few examples: (1) 14 . . . ♗d7 15 ♗c5 ♗×c5 (or 15 . . . ♘e4 16 ♗×f8 ♔×f8 17 ♖e1, Tukmakov–Balashov, USSR 1972) 16 ♘×c5 ♗g4 17 ♖e1 ♕b6 18 ♕c2 ♖ad8 19 h3 ♗c8 20 b3 ♕b8 21 e3 ♖e7 22 ♖ed1 (Ljubojević–Gligorić, Bugojno 1978); (2) 14 . . . ♘g4 15 ♗c5 ♗×c5 16 ♘×c5 ♕f6 17 h3 ♘e5 18 e4 ♖b8 19 b3 ♖b5 20 e×d5 c×d5 21 ♖e1 (not 21 ♕×d5? ♗b7) – Timman–Gligorić, Niksić 1978. In every case Black gets a passive position or (usually after e4) an unpleasant pawn weakness.

At the time this game was played 14 ♗d4 was considered necessary, to prevent . . . ♕a5, but since the queen move is unplayable anyway it amounts to a loss of tempo.

14 . . . ♘h7

Quite a vigorous and ambitious move, and a bit of a shock if you were expecting the more routine . . . ♘e4. The plan, of course, is . . . ♘g5, then . . . ♘h3+ or . . . ♗h3; from g5 the knight might also drop back to e6 to help with the defence of the blockade points d4 and c5. Hereabouts the analysis is far from clear-cut and it is anyone's guess what the very best move is. One thing is certain, though: Black should avoid at any price the kind of defensive position which arises after, for example, 14 . . . ♗d7 15 ♖e1 ♘h7 16 ♘a4 ♘g5 17 ♗c5 ♘e6 18 ♗×f8 ♖×f8 19 e4 (Stein–Tarve, Parnu 1971). Here his pawns are beginning to come under fire and he has no counterplay to speak of. In the main game Nunn delays the development of his Q-bishop for one move; in that way he can meet 15 ♘a4 by the more aggressive 15 . . . ♗g4, followed comfortably by . . . ♕d7. One more possible move-order is an immediate 14 . . . ♗g4, since White will wish to avoid blocking his bishop and weakening e2 and e3 by playing 15 f3 (this important point is taken up again in the note to Black's 19th move), and 15 h3 ♗h5 16 g4 ♗g6 is also fine for Black. The fly in the ointment here is 15 ♕a4, which threatens ♗×f6 as well as the c-pawn; and after 15 . . . ♗d7 16 ♕c2 White has the advantage because e4 can follow (16 . . . ♕e7 17 e4 f×e4 18 ♖fe1 ♗f5 19 ♗×f6 etc.). Incidentally, 16 ♗×f6 ♕×f6 17 ♗×d5 would be a premature liquidation, allowing Black counter-chances – 17 . . . c×d5 18 ♕×d7 ♖ad8 (Stein–Damjanović, Vrnjačka Banja 1971, which ended in a draw).

One other move is worth mentioning – 14 . . . ♗f5, a sound and sensible continuation, possibly the best, which controls e4 and keeps the queen out of c2. Unfortunately this has not been tested very severely, the only available reference being Adorján–Gligorić, Vrsac 1983, which concluded 15 ♕d2 ♕d6 16 ♖fe1 ½–½!

15 ♘a4 ♗g4

16 ♖e1 ♕d7

17 ♗c5 . . .

A knight tends to be more useful on this kind of outpost square; so White avoids 17 ♘c5 ♗×c5 18 ♗×c5 ♘g5. A continuation such as 19 ♕d2 ♗h3 20 ♗h1 ♘e4 would be quite satisfactory for Black.

17 . . . ♘g5

18 ♗×f8 ♔×f8

One would normally prefer to retake with a piece other than the king, in order to avoid later checks and to prevent the queen from penetrating to h7, but here Nunn wishes to keep his rook trained on the e-pawn. He may play . . . ♔g8 soon, when it will simply come to the same thing, or the king's position at f8 may provoke additional complications.

19 ♘c5 . . .

A later game (Adorján–Lobron, Indonesia 1983) shows how Black's aggressive distribution of pieces typically yields him sufficient tactical resources to keep the balance. That game continued 19 ♕c2 (probably not quite as strong as Nikolac's ♘c5) ♔g8 (19 . . . ♖ac8 20 ♘c5 ♕d6 21 h4 ♘e6 22 ♘×e6+ followed by ♕h7 would be dangerous; Black could also play 20 . . . ♕f5 here, but the exchange of queens is not in his interests – his K-side play would be reduced to nothing and he would face a long and difficult defensive endgame) 20 ♘c5 (or 20 ♕×c6 ♕×c6 21 ♖×c6 ♗×e2, meeting 22 ♗×d5 by . . . ♗b5; or 20 h4 ♘h3+ 21 ♗×h3 ♗×h3 22 ♕×c6 ♕×c6 23 ♖×c6 ♗d7 24 ♖a6 ♗b5 25 ♖a5 ♗×e2, and if 26 ♖×d5? ♗f3 wins) ♕e7 21 ♘d3 ♗f5 22 ♕c5 ♗×d3 23 ♕×e7 ♖×e7 24 e×d3 ♖×e1+ 25 ♖×e1 ♖b8 26 ♖c1 ♖b6 (better than opening the position for the bishop's benefit by 26 . . . ♖×b2 etc.) 27 b3 ♘e6 28 ♖c2 ♘d4, with a very slight plus for Black. The game was eventually drawn.

19 . . . ♕f5

More aggressive than 19 . . . ♕e7, which carries no threat to the e-pawn, e.g. 20 ♕a4 ♗×e2? 21 h4 ♘e6 22 ♘×e6+ ♕×e6 23 ♗f3, and Black is forced into 23 . . . ♗×f3 24 ♖×e6 ♖×e6, which is inadequate. The mating danger can be dispelled, if need be, by 25 ♕f4 ♖f6 26 ♕b4+ ♔g8 27 ♖e1, and the queen will use the black squares to great effect.

Notice that in building up his K-side play Black is relying on the fact that the move f3 can hardly be avoided for much longer. If White does refuse to play it, his own forces will remain too much tied down to the defence of e2 to be able to attack the Q-side profitably. If he plays f3, Black will seize his chance to hit the new weaknesses at e2 and e3. In an endgame the white king could sit at f2 and Black's play against these squares would not amount to much; but in the middle-game it will provide a genuine counterweight to his own pawn weaknesses.

In a moment White resigns himself to having to make this pawn move, but first he manoeuvres his knight to a more appropriate square. He feels that his control of c5 is adequate, and that with most of the enemy forces (especially the bishop) committed to the other flank the time is right to threaten the c-pawn directly. This certainly seems to be the strongest idea, sufficient to guarantee a slight advantage with accurate play. If he tries the less precise 20 ♕c2 ♕f6, he finds that 21 f3 ♕d4+ 22 ♔h1 ♘h3 (threatening . . . ♕g1+) 23 ♗×h3 ♗×h3 produces only approximate equality, with the two sets of weak pawns balancing each other, and that anything slower also results in the loss of his good bishop; for example 21 ♘b3 ♘h3+ 22 ♗×h3 ♗×h3 23 ♕×c6 ♕×b2, and again there is no advantage.

It might be opportune here to mention the circumstances in which this game was played. Nikolac wanted three points from his last four games in the tournament to obtain the Grandmaster title (this being the first of the four). He was therefore thinking in terms of winning his white games against Nunn and Böhmfeldt and drawing the black ones against Miles and Jansa. That may explain his surprising choice of moves in one or two places, where he adopts a more risky or complicated continuation than he might otherwise have done. In the end things turned out very differently from his expectations, as they always seem to in such cases. After losing against Nunn he had to revise his plans radically and try to win the remaining three games. It says much for his resilience and determination that he did just that!

20 ♘b3 ♖ac8

21 f3 . . .

White can hardly hope to make progress any other way. If 21 ♘d4? ♕f6 threatens . . . c5, and if then 22 b4 ♖e4! 23 ♗×e4 ♘h3+ 24 ♔g2 ♕×f2+ 25 ♔h1 ♕e3! favours Black strongly. But 21 f3 stops the knight check, which can now be answered by ♔f1, and Black gets tangled up, thus: 21 . . . ♘h3+? 22 ♔f1 ♖e3 (the only try; if 22 . . . ♗h5 23 ♘d4 ♕d7 24 g4 wins – 24 . . . ♗×g4 25 f×g4 ♕×g4 26 ♖c3, for example) 23 ♕d4 ♖×f3+ (23 . . . ♗×f3 24 ♕×e3 ♗×e2+ 25 ♔×e2 ♖e8 26 ♕×e8+ also fails) 24 e×f3 ♗×f3 25 ♖e5 ♕f6 (double checks are useless) 26 ♗×h3 and wins.

21 . . . ♗h3

22 ♕c2 ♕e6

For the next few moves the position of the king at f8 gives rise to some tactical points. For instance, if 23 ♘c5(?) ♕e3+ White would have to play the awkward 24 ♔f1, 24 ♔h1? being refuted by 24 . . . ♕f2 25 ♗×h3 ♘×f3! But Black is not threatening this at present because . . . ♕e3+ ♔h1 ♕f2 could be countered by ♕c5+. However, there is no way in which White can improve on his following exchange at h3: 23 ♕c5+ ♔g8 24 ♕×a7 is met by 24 . . . ♖a8, as in several subsequent variations, while against quiet moves Black plays . . . ♔g8 anyway.

23 ♗×h3 ♕×h3? *(28)*

28
W

The wrong recapture, which should have led to the loss of a pawn. It takes the queen a long time to develop any threats against the castled position; so for the moment she ought to remain in the centre to oppose White's invasion. Best play would be 23 . . . ♘×h3+ 24 ♔g2 (hitting the knight; if 24 ♔h1 ♔g8, but now 24 . . . ♔g8? loses to 25 ♘c5) ♘g5 25 ♕c5+ ♔g8 26 ♕×a7 (if 26 ♘d4 Black can take advantage of the king's placing on g2: 26 . . . ♕h3+ 27 ♔g1 ♘e6 28 ♘×e6 – 28 ♕×a7? ♖a8 29 ♕b6 ♖eb8 – ♕×e6 29 ♕×a7 ♖a8, with much the same effect as the main line) ♖a8 27 ♕c5 ♖×a2, when White has a slight advantage, but no hope of winning against accurate play.

But after the text move White could successfully play 24 ♕c5+ ♔g8 (24 . . . ♖e7 25 ♘a5 ♘e6 26 ♕d6 is very unpleasant) 25 ♕×a7 (not 25 ♘d4 ♘e6, leading into the previous note) ♖a8 26 ♕c5, because this time the defending queen is not on hand to cover the d-pawn. After 26 . . . ♖×a2 27 ♕×c6 the best Black could hope for would be a laborious endgame with 3 pawns v. 4 pawns on the same side, and with two or three pieces remaining (the more pieces, the more dangerous this type of ending is for the defender).

Nikolac must have been aware of this variation but chooses instead a more risky and adventurous tactical line, which ultimately fails and allows Black at least equality. Almost certainly he feared that the endgame advantage would be insufficient, and his desire to win at any price distorted his judgement.

24 ♘d4? c5
25 ♘f5 . . .

Part of White's purpose in making this knight manoeuvre is to shut the black queen out of the game and try to exploit her absence. But although Black's next move represents the most forcing continuation, it is by no means obligatory; he could play 25 . . . ♖c6, for example, and meet 26 b4 comfortably by 26 . . . c4. In that event it is not clear what White intended.

25 . . . ♖e5
26 ♘d6 ♖c6
27 f4 . . .

27 ♘b5 or ♘b7 would be pointless and would only encourage Black's attack: 27 ♘b7 ♘e6, for instance, threatening . . . ♘d4 and . . . ♖h5; the latter move is also the reply to 28 ♕h7. That, of course, was not White's intention; in playing 24 ♘d4 he analysed the forcing line up to 27

f4 and planned to refute 27 . . . ♖e3 (threatening perpetual check by . . . ♖×g3+) by 28 ♘f5. He overlooked the following simple reply because he assumed that Black could not allow the queen into h7.

27 . . . ♖e6

28 f×g5 . . .

Forced; if 28 ♘b7 ♘e4 and Black's attack is too strong (29 ♘d8 ♖g6).

28 . . . ♖e×d6

29 ♕h7 . . .

White has to persist with his idea. If he plays 29 g×h6 ♖×h6 the position simplifies to Black's considerable benefit because the e-pawn, now the weakest on the board, becomes a target.

29 . . . ♖g6

Obviously Black must cover his g-pawn against the danger of ♕h8+ and ♕×g7, otherwise his king would have no more shelter. White in turn must now abandon his g-pawn (30 g×h6? ♖×h6) and regain the material on the other wing; more than that the queen cannot accomplish on her own.

30 ♕h8+ ♔e7

31 ♕b8 ♖×g5

31 . . . ♕d7 would be too passive, permitting 32 e4 d4 33 g×h6 ♖×h6 34 ♕e5+.

32 ♕×a7+ ♔f8

32 . . . ♕d7 is now a perfectly good alternative. The exchange of queens would seem to yield Black a favourable ending: slightly stronger pawns (3 islands v.2), a useful pawn centre backed up by the king, which would tend to restrict White, and a tendency for the white king to be harassed by the rooks if he tried to become active. On the other hand, the whole thing seems to dissolve into a draw quite quickly, if White attacks at once: 33 ♕×d7+ ♔×d7 34 e4 d4 35 ♖c4 ♖b6 36 b4! ♖×b4 37 ♖×b4 c×b4 38 ♖d1 etc. After 32 . . . ♔f8 the game should also be drawn, and the choice is merely a matter of personal taste.

33 ♕b8+ . . .

Not 33 ♖×c5? ♖×g3+ 34 h×g3 ♕×g3+ 35 ♔h1 ♕h3+ and Black wins.

33 . . . ♖c8

34 ♕d6+ ♔g8 *(29)*

White can draw comfortably enough on two occasions during the next few moves, beginning here with 35 ♖×c5. But he is still hoping to win, for reasons already explained; and, being short of time, it is also more than likely that he was worried by Black's sacrifice 35 ♖×c5 ♖h5. That turns out to be unsound, but after 36 ♖×c8+ ♔h7 there is only one move to refute it, as follows: (a) 37 g4 ♕×g4+, followed by . . . ♕×c8, and White stands worse because his king is more exposed; (b) 37 ♕f4 ♕×h2+ 38 ♔f1 ♕h3+ and . . . ♕×c8 with the same result; (c) 37 ♖cc1 ♕×h2+ 38 ♔f1 ♖f5+ (had the c8 rook moved anywhere except c1, Black could do even better with 38 . . . ♕h1+ 39 ♔f2 ♖h2+) 39 ♕f4 ♖×f4+ 40 g×f4 h5!, with advantage because the rooks are passive and it is very awkward to stop

. . . h4–h3 without losing too many pawns; (d) 37 ♖ec1 ♕×h2+ 38 ♔f1 ♕h1+ 39 ♔f2 ♖h2+ 40 ♔e3 ♕e4+ 41 ♔d2 ♖×e2+ 42 ♔c3 ♖e3+ 43 ♔d2 ♕d3 mate. So far White has not had much luck, but the solution is surprisingly simple – the king just walks away. After 37 ♔f2! ♕×c8 (37 . . . ♖f5+ 38 ♔e3 and 37 . . . ♕×h2+ 38 ♔e3 are useless) 38 h4 ♕c2 39 ♕b4 Black will have to admit that he does not have sufficient compensation for the pawn. It follows that Black should exchange rooks at c5, which gives us: 35 ♖×c5 ♖×c5 36 ♕×c5 ♖×g3+ 37 h×g3 ♕×g3+ 38 ♔f1 ♕h3+, and one side or the other will give perpetual check (39 ♔f2 ♕h4+ 40 ♔e3 ♕×e1 41 ♕c8+ ♔h7 42 ♕f5+, for example).

With his next move White opens the second rank, enabling him to defend h2, and avoids the blockade of his pawn at e2 (otherwise Black might play . . . d4, . . . ♖e8, . . . ♖ge5 etc.). At the same time, though, he concedes Black a dangerous passed pawn.

A few general comments might be useful here about what to exchange and what to retain in this type of heavy piece ending: (1) Obviously king safety is paramount, at least until the queens or all the rooks disappear; (2) White's outside passed pawn (or two united pawns if he takes the c-pawn) is likely to be a more relevant factor in a rook ending; if the queens and one pair of rooks remain, threats against the king are liable to be much more significant; and throughout this phase White's king is always the more exposed; (3) After the following moves (35 e4 d4) even a pure queen ending may well favour Black because the queen is always so effective in supporting one strong passed pawn. In the face of that even two united passed pawns, if they are far back, may not provide an adequate counter.

35 e4 d4
36 ♖f1 . . .

If 36 e5 Black could draw at once by 35 . . . ♖×g3+. Against slower moves . . . h5–h4 promises to be dangerous. White therefore aims for play against f7 (36 . . . h5? 37 ♕f4).

36 . . . ♖e8
37 ♕c7(?) . . .

Until now White was quite justified in seeking complications, but here he overdoes it and gets into trouble. With . . . ♖e8 Black is preparing to consolidate and bring the e-pawn under pressure (by . . . f6, . . . ♖ge5 and possibly . . . ♕e6); and once he achieves that he holds the initiative, since the loss of the pawn would put the white king in danger. White should therefore have taken his last chance for a comfortable draw by playing 37 ♖×c5 ♖×c5 38 ♕×c5 ♖×e4 39 ♕d5 (if 39 ♕c4 ♕d7, and . . . h5–h4 may follow; 39 ♕d5 is more forcing because the rook ending after 39 . . . ♕e6 – 39 . . . ♖e7? 40 ♕d8+ – favours White for reasons already given) ♖e2 40 ♕×f7+ ♔h7 41 ♕f5+ ♕×f5 42 ♖×f5 d3 43 ♔f1 (forced) ♖×b2 44 ♖d5 ♖×h2 45 ♖×d3 ♖×a2 46 ♖d6 etc.

37 . . . ♕h5

Defending f7 and c5. Now White must pay attention to his e-pawn; he cannot just abandon it and make a quick dash with the a-pawn because Black's threats would become too serious. If 38 a4 ♖×e4 39 a5 ♖e2 wins, or if here 39 ♖f2 (39 ♖c2 ♖d5 40 a5 d3 is even worse) ♖d5 40 a5 d3 41 ♖d2 ♖e2 42 ♖×e2 ♕×e2, threatening . . .

d2 and . . . ♕e3+. If 38 a4 ♖×e4 39 ♖fe1 ♖ge5 40 ♖×e4 ♖×e4, and White has no good move: (a) 41 ♕×c5 ♖e1+ 42 ♔g2 ♖e2+; (b) 41 ♖×c5 ♖e1+; (c) 41 a5 ♖e2; (d) 41 ♖f1 ♖e2 42 h4 ♕d5 (or . . . ♖×b2); (e) 41 ♕c6 ♖e2 42 h4 ♕e5.

38	**♖f4**	**♖ge5**
39	**♖cf1**	**f6**
40	**♕c6** *(30)*	

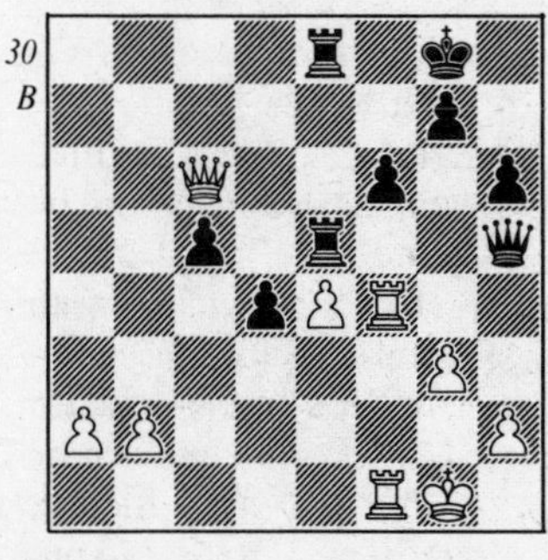

40	**. . .**	**♕e2?**

Black's timing is inaccurate here, in that he allows his opponent one extra counter-attacking chance at move 43. But this was the last move before the time-control and major piece endings are in any case notoriously difficult to analyse. The sheer power of the pieces and the large number of possible moves means that even the strongest players tend to miss quite a lot. Black's overall plan is straightforward enough: to combine attacks on the e-pawn with the advance of the d-pawn. But the right move-order is 40 . . . d3 41 ♕d7 ♕e2 42 ♖1f2 ♕e1+ 43 ♔g2 (43 ♖f1 ♕e3+ helps Black, if anything) c4, transposing into the game position after 43 moves, which is highly favourable to Black, even if not quite a certain win. The extra possibility which the inexact move-order grants White is made clear in the next note.

If, after 40 . . . d3, White changes his own move-order by 41 ♖1f2, then Black, instead of transposing into the inferior game continuation by 41 . . . ♕d1+ 42 ♔g2 ♕e1 etc., can introduce a new idea – 41 . . . ♕f7!, which hits the a-pawn, reduces the scope of the white queen, and generally prepares a regrouping of his forces. If then 42 ♕d6 c4 43 ♕d4 (the e-pawn needs protection) ♕c7, followed by . . . ♖d8, and the placing of his rook behind the passed pawn guarantees Black a big advantage.

Apart from 42 ♕d6 White's choice is limited. 42 ♖d2 c4 is very similar, while 42 b3 ♖d8 43 ♖d2 ♕a7! prepares a quick invasion of the other side by the queen; for example 44 ♔g2 ♕a5 45 ♖ff2 ♕b4, with a very awkward threat against the e-pawn. If here 44 ♕b5? c4+, or if 44 ♖f3 ♕a5! and the pawn cannot be taken. Strategically, the point to bear in mind here is that the d-pawn acts as a wedge and cuts White's position in two. That is why he finds it so difficult to transfer his forces from one wing to the other, and why he cannot keep pace with the black queen's lightning manoeuvres!

This . . . ♕f7–a7 and . . . ♖d8 plan is so appealing once its power is appreciated that one wonders whether it might be good on the previous move. And sure enough, it seems to be just as strong as 40 . . . d3, provided Black takes care not to allow the sacrifice ♖×f6. For example, 40 . . . ♕f7 41 b3 (41 ♖×f6? g×f6 42 ♖×f6 ♖5e6!) ♕a7 (not 41 . . . ♖d8 because 42 ♖×f6 g×f6 43 ♖×f6 would now be dangerous: White gets at least perpetual check, either immediately or after 43 . . . ♕×f6 44 ♕×f6 etc.) 42 ♖1f2 (not 42 ♖×f6 g×f6 43 ♖×f6 ♖8e7, when White has no attack: 44 ♖g6+ ♖g7, or 44 ♕c8+ ♔h7 45 ♕f8 – 45 ♕h3 h5 – ♖g7) ♖d8, and Black gets the same advantageous type of position as before.

41	**♖1f2**	**♕e1+**
42	**♔g2**	**d3** *(31)*

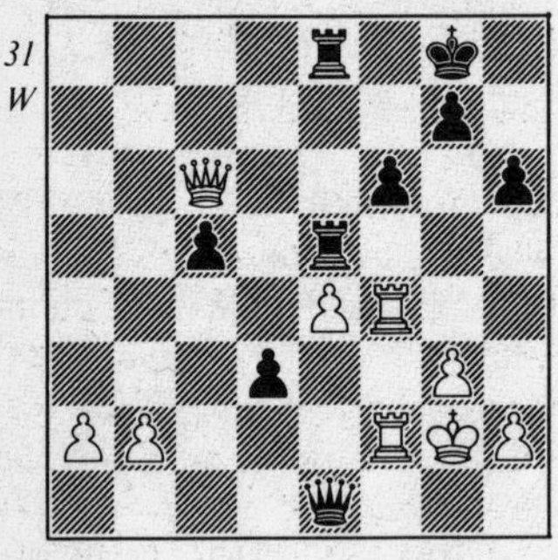

31
W

After 42 . . . ♖×e4 43 ♕×c5 ♖×f4 44 ♕d5+ ♔h8 45 g×f4 Black has much less advantage. Although the enemy king is exposed a little more, it is quite difficult to advance the d-pawn; and we mustn't forget that White possesses the weapon of being able to offer a queen exchange. Therefore 45 . . . ♕e3, for instance, could be countered by 46 ♕f3.

White's best line now is 43 ♖g4!, threatening ♖×g7+. If, for example, 43 . . . d2 44 ♖×g7+ (not 44 ♕×f6 ♕g1+! 45 ♔h3 ♖h5+) ♔h8 (or 44 . . . ♔×g7 45 ♕×f6+ with perpetual), he has a draw by 45 ♕b7! ♕×e4+ 46 ♕×e4 ♖×e4 47 ♖d7, though probably not by 45 ♕×f6 ♕×e4+ 46 ♖f3 (forced) ♕×f3+ 47 ♕×f3 ♔×g7; at any rate that position is dangerous for him. All this is typical of the kind of counterplay which is bound to prevail in the presence of such powerful pieces. And there is more to come. Black cannot stop the threat by 43 . . . ♖5e7? 44 ♕d5+; so the critical line is 43 . . . ♖8e7 44 ♕c8+ (44 ♕×f6 d2 is bad again) and then: (a) 44 . . . ♔h7 45 ♖×f6 ♕e2+ (45 . . . d2? 46 ♖×h6+ and mate) 46 ♖f2 (forced; if 46 ♔h3 ♖h5+, or 46 ♔h1 ♖h5, or 46 ♔g1 ♕e3+ 47 ♔g2 d2 etc.) ♖f7! 47 ♖×e2 d×e2 48 ♖f4 (forced again) e1/Q (48 . . . ♖×f4 49 g×f4 e1/Q is no more than a draw) 49 ♖×f7 ♕×e4+ 50 ♖f3, and despite appearances there is only a slight plus for Black after 50 . . . ♖d5 51 ♕f8 ♖d2+ 52 ♔h3; (b) 44 . . . ♔f7 45 ♕h8 ♖g5 46 ♖gf4 (threatening ♖×f6+) ♖e6 47 ♕d8 ♖×e4 48 ♕×d3 ♖×f4 49 ♖×f4 and the game is equal. If Black tries for more here he will regret it because his own king is exposed: 47 . . . c4? 48 ♕c7+ ♔f8 49 ♕×c4 d2 50 ♕×e6! d1/Q 51 ♖×f6+ and mates.

43	**♕d7(?)**	**c4**
44	**b3**	**. . .**

The only thing he can do is try to break up the pawns. With the d-pawn covered it is too late for 44 ♖g4 ♖5e7! 45 ♕d5+ ♔h8, when there is no further danger to Black's solidly defended K-side.

44	**. . .**	**♖×e4**
45	**b×c4**	**♖×f4**
46	**♕d5+?**	**. . .**

A natural enough check, supporting the advance of the c-pawn and preventing . . . ♕e4+, but it looks like the losing move. It seems that after 46 g×f4 White can stand 46 . . . ♕e4+ provided he replies 47 ♖f3. Nothing else will suffice: if 47 ♔g3 ♕g6+ 48 ♔h3 ♖e3+ 49 ♔h4 f5, or if here 48 ♕g4 ♖e3+ 49 ♔h4 ♕e4 50 f5 ♕e5 etc., or if 48 ♔f3 f5 49 h3 ♕h5+ 50 ♔g2 ♖e3. If 47 ♔h3 ♕g6, trapping the king on the edge and threatening

48 . . . ♖e3+ 49 ♔h4 f5, leads to similar play, or if 47 ♔g1 ♕g6+ 48 ♔f1 ♖b8 with decisive threats. But at f3 the rook is more efficient, attacking the d-pawn and ready to interpose at g3 against a check. And since 47 . . . ♕e2+ 48 ♖f2 and 47 . . . ♕g6+ 48 ♖g3 lead nowhere, Black cannot do better than 47 . . . d2 48 ♕×d2 ♕×c4. He maintains a small advantage here, but nothing is forced. If Black meets 46 g×f4 by 46 . . . ♕e3, the answer is still 47 ♖f3; but the crucial difference after 46 ♕d5+ is that White no longer covers g4, which brings us back to the game.

46	**. . .**	**♔h8**
47	**g×f4**	**♕e3!**

The difference between this position and the one referred to in the note to Black's 42nd move (42 . . . ♖×e4 etc.) is that the pawn is one square further forward; and that limits White's defensive scope considerably. 48 ♖f3 ♕e2+ 49 ♖f2 ♕g4+ 50 ♔f1 ♕d1+ 51 ♔g2 ♖e1 would now concede another winning attack, or if here 49 ♔g3 d2 50 ♖d3 ♖e3+ and wins. With his strong, centralising queen move, Black is able to secure his pawn and generally consolidate things in preparation for fresh attacks. Centralisation is a principle which we can hardly stress too much, and the rest of this game (especially after move 49) is an excellent illustration of its power. And yet . . . even the most reliable of maxims can be overworked; in the end concrete tactical lines have to take precedence over **everything**. As an antidote to too much reliance on general thinking, I cannot resist pointing out again that the centralising 46 ♕d5+ is the move which finally costs White this game!

48	**c5**	**f5** *(32)*

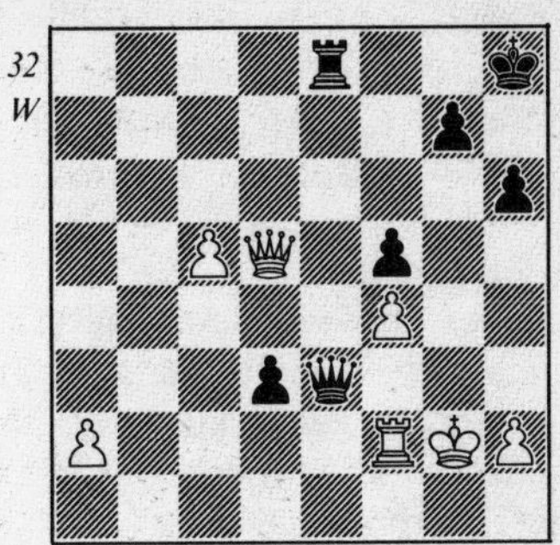

32
W

Partly with the idea of . . . ♖e6–g6+, partly planning . . . ♕e4+ if the circumstances are right; but Black still has to be wary of this queen exchange, as we shall see.

49	**♕f3**	**. . .**

Not 49 ♕×f5 ♖d8 50 c6 d2 51 c7 d1/Q 52 c8/Q, because the checks run out: 52 . . . ♖×c8 53 ♕×c8+ ♔h7 54 ♕f5+ ♔g8 55 ♕c8+ ♔f7 etc. 49 c6 puts up more resistance, though not enough to save the game against correct play. Nikolac was understandably worried about 49 c6 ♕e4+ (not 49 . . . ♖e6 50 ♕×f5), but the passed pawns are not as formidable as they look – 50 ♕×e4 f×e4 51 ♖b2! ♖c8 (51 . . . e3 52 ♔f1 only weakens the pawns; the black rook needs to be more mobile for this formation to win, but if 52 . . . ♖c8 53 ♖b3, or if 52 . . . ♖e6 53 c7 ♖c6 54 ♖b8+ and wins) 52 ♔f2 ♖×c6 53 ♔e3, and the win is very uncertain.

The right way is 49 . . . ♖c8 (now threatening . . . ♕e4+ and meeting 50 ♕×f5 ♖×c6 51 ♕f8+ ♔h7 52 ♕f5+ by 52 . . . ♖g6+) 50 ♕f3 (or 50 ♖b2 ♕×f4 51 ♕×d3 ♖×c6 and wins, or 50 ♖f3 ♕e2+ 51 ♖f2 ♕e4+, or here 51 ♔g3 d2 52 ♕d7 – 52 ♖d3 ♖×c6 – ♖×c6 53 ♕×c6 d1/Q, stopping the checks by playing the king to f7) ♕e4

51 ♖d2 ♖×c6 52 ♖×d3 ♖g6+ 53 ♔f2 (53 ♔h3 ♕c4 is similar: Black threatens . . . ♕×a2 and . . . ♖g4, followed by . . . ♕f7–h5 mate) ♕c4, and White faces too many threats to survive: . . . ♕×a2+, . . . ♕c2+ and . . . ♖g4.

The text move presents the black queen with another dominating central square, which, along with the advantages of a safer king, more aggressive rook and more advanced passed pawn, is altogether too much.

49	**. . .**	**♕d4**
50	**c6**	**. . .**

If ♖d2 ♖e3 51 ♕f2 ♕e4+ and wins, or if here 51 ♕c6 ♕×f4; but now 50 . . . ♖e3 can be answered by 51 c7.

50	**. . .**	**d2**
51	**♖f1**	**♔h7!**

Genuinely threatening the decisive . . . ♖e3 because the c-pawn will not now queen with check. White is therefore obliged to advance it again, but it is too weak to survive.

52	**c7**	**♖c8**
53	**♕b7**	**♕d7**
54	**♖d1**	**♖×c7**
55	**♕b2**	**. . .**

To finish the game Black now re-centralises, secures the d-pawn and starts attacking the K-side again (and also the a-pawn). Notice how he still relies heavily on the power of his queen to make the win as swift and certain as possible. He will on no account permit an exchange of queens until he has won at least one more pawn; by doing so he would renounce all his attacking prospects and most likely lose the d-pawn as well.

55	**. . .**	**♕d5+**
56	**♔f2**	**♖d7**
57	**♕e5**	**♕d3**

Threatens 58 . . . ♕h3, and if 59 ♔g1 ♕g4+.

58	**♕e3**	**♕c2**
59	**♕b3**	**. . .**

Or 59 ♔e2 ♕c4+ and . . . ♕×a2.

59	**. . .**	**♕c5+**

0 – 1

The f-pawn is inevitably lost because of the threat of a pin on White's third rank: 60 ♕e3 ♖d4 61 ♔f3 ♕d5+ 62 ♔f2 ♕d6, for example. Other 60th moves have the same result.

Game 8

Modern Benoni Defence
Skara 1980

L. Polugaevsky v. J. Nunn

1	**d4**	**♘f6**
2	**♘f3**	**c5**
3	**d5**	**e6**
4	**c4**	**e×d5**
5	**c×d5**	**d6**
6	**♘c3**	**g6**
7	**e4**	**♗g7**
8	**♗e2**	**0–0**
9	**0–0**	**♖e8**
10	**♘d2**	**. . .**

Played here because White wishes to advance his f-pawn and in many variations to post the knight at c4. From there it will hit the d-pawn and support the thrust e5. Black in turn must try to restrain White's pawn centre, or dissolve it if it comes on too quickly. Meanwhile, he will be seeking counterplay, either by advancing his Q-side pawn majority (. . . a6 and . . . b5) or, as in this game, by creating threats on the other wing.

10	**. . .**	**♘bd7**
11	**♕c2** *(33)*	**. . .**

33
B

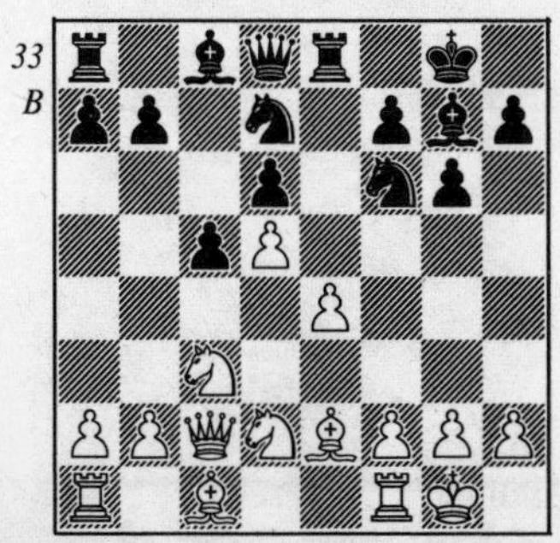

We have an opportunity here to observe now opening ideas evolve among Grandmasters. Until about 1972 the development plan of . . . ♘a6–c7 was generally adopted, because in that way Black can bring more force to bear on b5 in furtherance of his Q-side plans. The alternative scheme of . . . ♘bd7–e5 was judged inferior because it seemed that Black could not maintain his knight at e5 and was only encouraging White's central pawn push.

It required a strong, imaginative player (in this case Fischer) to throw doubt on that theory and ask: 'Is this true? Can we really make nothing of it for Black?' And the result of his investigations was 11 . . . ♘h5 (Spassky–Fischer, 3rd Game 1972), the kind of move to make an average player's heart sink! But White's castled position is none too well defended, and in return for the shattering of his pawn structure after 12 ♗×h5 g×h5 Black gets good aggressive play for his remaining forces (. . . ♘e5 and beyond, . . . ♕h4, . . . ♗d4; and perhaps even the g-file might be used). The game with Spassky continued: 13 ♘c4? ♘e5 14 ♘e3 ♕h4 15 ♗d2 ♘g4 16 ♘×g4 h×g4 17 ♗f4 ♕f6 with a comfortable position for Black, who went on to win.

Of course, after this game everybody started playing . . . ♘h5 in the

Benoni! But when the shock wore off and when others started asking the same question: 'Do we believe all this?', some conspicuous improvements for White were discovered. For example, 13 a4 is much better: 13 . . . ♘e5 14 ♘d1 b6 15 ♖a3 ♗a6 16 ♖h3 ♗×f1 17 ♘×f1 b5 18 ♘de3 led to a beautiful win for White in the game Petrosian–Rashkovsky, USSR Championship 1976. Another line is: 13 a4 ♘e5 14 ♘d1 ♕h4 15 ♘e3 ♘g4 16 ♘×g4 h×g4 17 ♘c4, favouring White (Gligorić–Kavalek, Skopje 1972). The key points here are the operation of the rook on the third rank and the manoeuvre ♘d1–e3, aiming at the weakened square f5, which in the first example more than justified Petrosian's exchange sacrifice.

These ideas have put 11 . . . ♘h5 out of business, and in the present game Nunn is trying to improve the idea by delaying it for a move.

11 . . . ♘e5

12 b3 . . .

This is Polugaevsky's pet line, the standard move being 12 a4. It is not good to drive the knight from e5 at once because Black develops a dangerous initiative: 12 f4? ♘eg4 13 ♘f3 ♘h5 14 h3 (otherwise . . . f5 comes anyway) ♘h6 15 ♔h2 f5! (Toynt–Shamkovich, USA 1976) and if 16 e5 d×e5 17 f×e5 (17 ♘×e5 ♘×f4) f4 etc.

The positional principle operating here is that Black's minor pieces are restricted by the pawn centre, but the centre itself is not yet consolidated and is subject to counter-attack. Therefore (1) Black must use violent methods to hack away at the pawns: he cannot afford to delay; (2) The unnecessary exchange of even one pair of minor pieces is to be avoided by White because Black's cramp would be greatly relieved, yet the pawn centre would remain vulnerable. That is why 13 ♗×g4 would lead to even worse trouble and why he was obliged to play 15 ♔h2. And there is another variation which perhaps captures the spirit of this opening even better: (12 f4 ♘eg4 13 ♘f3) ♘×e4! 14 ♘×e4 ♗f5 15 ♗d3 c4 16 ♕×c4 ♖c8 17 ♕b4 ♗×e4 18 ♗×e4 a5 19 ♕a4 b5, regaining the piece with plenty of initiative.

Without these aggressive possibilities the . . . ♘bd7 line of the Benoni would simply be unplayable.

12 . . . ♘h5?

Though well aware of the deficiencies of this move, Nunn feels that with the white bishop committed to b2 Black's easier access to the squares g5 and f4 might tip the balance in his favour. This kind of thing is a matter of trial and error; of gradually improving the variations through home analysis. Here the note to Black's 15th move indicates that 12 . . . ♘h5 will not quite stand up; so we need to explore briefly a few alternatives. Notice how the startling move . . . g5 is essential in nearly all these lines: the knight's outpost must be maintained against White's threat of f4. Indeed, one of the problems created by provoking the exchange at h5 is that he lacks that resource thereafter.

(1) 12 . . . g5 13 ♗b2 g4 (getting the best of both worlds; this way he uses the g-pawn **and** gets in . . . ♘h5!) 14 a4 ♘h5, and now either 15 g3 ♖f8, intending . . . f5 with a double-edged position, or the simpler line 15 ♘c4

♘×c4 16 ♗×c4 ♘f4 17 ♘d1 ♗e5 18 ♗×e5 ♖×e5 19 ♘e3 ♕e7, which led to a quick draw in the game Gligorić–Tatai, Venice 1971. Here Black's nice active pieces easily compensate for any theoretical weakness in his pawn structure. Let me repeat that the advance . . . g5–g4, however odd it may seem, is absolutely correct positional play in the circumstances.

(2) 12 . . . a6 13 a4 (13 f4? ♘eg4 is still wrong, of course) g5 14 ♗b2 ♘g6 15 g3 ♗h3 16 ♖fe1 ♖b8 17 a5 ♘d7, with an unclear position, approximately equal (Gligorić–Sax, Niksić 1983). Incidentally, Black could also play 13 . . . ♘h5 here, reaching the position in the main game, but with . . . a6 and a4 thrown in. Then he would not face the threat of ♘b5 and would be a significant tempo ahead (see note to Black's 14th move).

(3) 12 . . . ♘fg4 (a recent, very sharp idea) 13 h3 ♘h6 14 f4 (otherwise comes . . . f5) ♘eg4 and White cannot capture with the pawn. After 15 ♘f3 ♕a5 16 e5 leads to unfathomable complications.

Enough opening theory! The rest of this game provides ample excitement.

13 ♗×h5 g×h5

14 ♗b2 ♗d7

Black has to play this rather useless bishop move because 14 . . . ♕h4 would be countered by 15 ♘b5 ♖d8 16 f4 ♘g4 17 ♘f3, and Nunn remarks that Black is crushed. 'Crushed', mind you, not just 'driven back'; as far as he is concerned, loss of initiative is tantamount to losing the game in this position.

15 ♖ae1 . . .

White would like to play 15 f4 ♘g4 16 ♘d1, exchanging Black's best minor piece, but 16 . . . ♗d4+! 17 ♗×d4 (17 ♔h1 ♘×h2!) c×d4 would provoke unwelcome complications. For example, 18 ♘c4 b5! 19 ♘×d6 ♕b6 wins for Black. The rook move covers e3 in preparation for 16 f4 ♘g4 17 ♘f3, then h3, forcing the knight to retreat.

15 . . . ♕h4 *(34)*

34
W

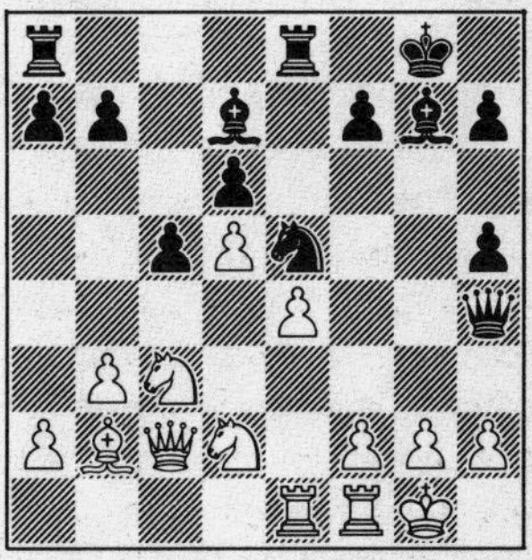

Nunn is still pursuing the basic theme of trying to prevent f4 (which now costs White the exchange) and is also ready to meet both 16 ♖e3 (third rank theme again) and 16 ♘d1 (heading for e3, but also preparing 17 f4 ♘g4 18 ♘f3, since Black could not play 18 . . . ♗d4+). His analysis is as follows: (1) 16 ♖e3 ♘g4 17 ♖h3 ♕g5; now the rook is vulnerable (. . . ♘×f2 is a threat) and 18 f4 fails on account of 18 . . . ♗d4+ 19 ♔h1 ♕g7 with several dangerous threats; (2) 16 ♘d1 ♕f4! and White has no satisfactory way to drive off the queen: (a) 17 g3? ♕×d2; (b) 17 ♔h1 h4 18 g3 ♕h6, and 19 f4 is still impossible because of 19 . . . h×g3; against other moves Black can just improve his position, by . . . h4, for example.

But there are two other possibilities for White. One is the game continuation, which after great complications is revealed as a mistake, and the other is the subtle move 16 ♔h1!, preparing 17 f4 (by cutting out . . . ♗d4+). This is the move which refutes 12 . . . ♘h5. The threat is 17 f4 ♘g4 18 ♘f3, expelling the queen, and 16 . . . ♘g4 17 ♘f3 ♕e7 18 h3 etc. is also unacceptable for Black, even though White's f-pawn is temporarily blocked. If 16 . . . ♕f4, of course, 17 ♘e2 again forces through f4.

Polugaevsky plays the move which 15 . . . ♕h4 was designed to prevent because he thinks, wrongly, that Black dare not win the exchange.

16 f4? . . .

The remainder of this game is a veritable witches' cauldron of tactics, impossible to explain in general terms. Therefore, most of what follows has to take the form of a set of (perhaps bewildering) variations. But if you find analysis difficult, they will repay close study. The notes try to indicate not only some ideas with which you may be unfamiliar, but also the way in which two first-rate tacticians would have been thinking during this phase. First of all, Polugaevsky's idea is based on the assumption that at move 20 he can withdraw his queen and trap the black one, either by ♖e2 or by ♘d1. But on re-examining the position Nunn now goes ahead with the win of the exchange (not that he has much choice!) because he has seen some flaws in White's analysis.

16 . . . ♘g4
17 ♘f3 ♗d4+
18 ♔h1 ♘f2+
19 ♖×f2 . . .

Too late to back out: 19 ♔g1 loses to 19 . . . ♘d3+ and 20 . . . ♘×e1.

19 . . . ♕×f2 *(35)*

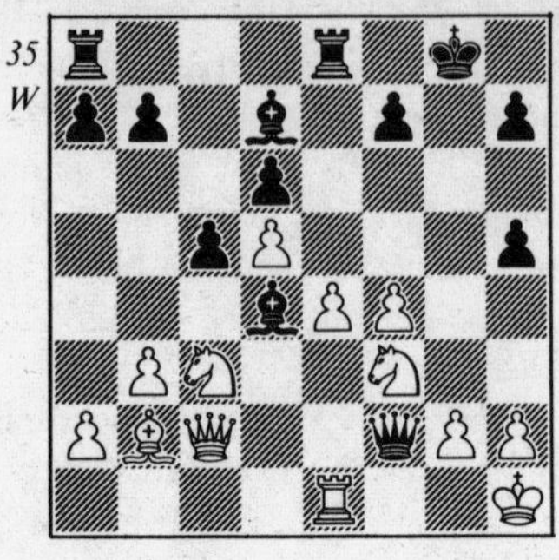

20 ♕c1 . . .

It must be either this or 20 ♕b1 – nothing else will worry Black – and White made the text move without much hesitation because 20 ♕b1 would at least permit 20 . . . ♗×c3 21 ♗×c3 ♗h3 22 ♖g1 ♗g4. Then, although he undoubtedly has fair compensation for the exchange (long black diagonal, pawn centre, weakened black pawns), he has no immediate threats (23 ♘g5 is safely met by . . . h6) and all danger to the queen is gone. In any case, Nunn had other plans. His intention was to answer 20 ♕b1 by 20 . . . ♗f5! It goes without saying that only the sharpest moves will do, and this one (threatening 21 . . . ♗×e4 22 ♖×e4 ♖×e4) exploits the overload on the white queen, the back-row mate possibility and the potential pin on the e-file. It is this feeling that White's game is tactically somewhat brittle which goads a player into finding such an extraordinary move. The position is actually extremely dangerous for White, so dangerous that Nunn could see no answer to 20 . . . ♗f5 during the game. Here is what he analysed: (a) 21 e×f5 ♖×e1+ 22 ♕×e1 ♕×b2; (b) 21 ♘d1 ♗×e4! 22 ♘×f2 (or 22 ♕×e4 ♖×e4 23 ♘×f2 ♖×e1+ 24 ♘×e1

♗×f2) ♗×b1 and White remains at least the exchange down; (c) ♖f1 ♗×e4! 22 ♖×f2 (or 22 ♘×e4 ♕×b2) ♗×b1, with the same effect; (d) 21 ♖e2 ♗×e4! 22 ♕c1! (22 ♘×d4 ♗×b1, or 22 ♖×e4 ♖×e4, or 22 ♖×f2 ♗×b1) ♗×f3! 23 ♖×f2 ♗×f2 and wins.

Surprisingly, though, there is a resource, spotted by the players after the game: White can hang on by 21 ♗a1! The f5 bishop is then *en prise* and Black cannot capture at e4, even if he exchanges first at c3, because after the final . . . ♕f1+ the knight can interpose at g1. In fact 21 ♗a1 is best answered by the original idea of 21 . . . ♗×c3 22 ♗×c3 ♗h3 etc., with transposition.

The subsequent course of the game appears to prove that 20 ♕c1 loses by force (the crucial difference being shown in the note to White's 23rd move), but one cannot reasonably criticise White's choice. To establish with certainty which is the better move would be beyond anyone's capacity over the board. Besides, 20 ♕c1 can only be refuted by Black's very accurate play in the sequel.

20 . . . ♗h3

The only defence against 21 ♖e2; 20 . . . ♗f5 is now useless, and after 20 . . . ♗×c3 21 ♕×c3 the mating threat is too powerful.

21 ♖g1 ♔f8!

This is the strongest move, played quickly by Black because the concrete threat of 22 . . . ♗×g2+ maintains his initiative and forces the reply. But White's compensation for his material is on no account to be underestimated. The beauty of . . . ♔f8 lies in the fact that there is a very plausible alternative in 21 . . . ♗g4, which also contains a concrete threat; yet Black's advantage would soon evaporate if he played that: 22 ♘×d4 (forced; 22 ♖f1 ♕e3 allows Black to consolidate at once) c×d4 (22 . . . ♕×d4 23 ♘b5) 23 ♖f1 (23 f5 is safely met by . . . f6, but not 23 . . . d×c3 24 ♕×c3, when the king cannot run), and then: (1) 23 . . . ♕e3 24 ♕×e3 d×e3 25 h3 ♗d7 26 ♖e1, with a most unattractive ending for Black in spite of his material superiority (wrecked pawn structure, exposed king and lack of useful files for his rooks); (2) 23 . . . ♕h4 24 ♘b5 ♖×e4 (or 24 . . . ♗e2 25 ♘×d6 ♗×f1 26 ♕×f1! ♖ed8 27 ♘f5 ♕f6 28 ♗×d4 ♕a6 29 ♕e1 and Black is in trouble) 25 ♘×d6 ♖e2 26 ♗×d4, and despite appearances this is not a good position for Black: his king is dangerously exposed and White can conjure up a lot of threats. Black for his part cannot do anything effective against the castled position and his other moves are relatively feeble: (a) 26 . . . ♖×a2 27 ♕c7 ♖f8 28 ♘e4 f6 29 ♕e7; (b) 26 . . . ♖d8 27 ♕c7; (c) 26 . . . ♗f3(!) 27 ♘f5! ♕h3! (27 . . . ♗×g2+ loses after 28 ♔g1 ♕h3 29 ♘h6+ ♔f8 30 ♕c5+ and 31 ♕b5+, picking up the stray rook) 28 ♘h6+ ♔f8 29 ♕c5+ ♔e8 30 ♕b5+ ♔f8, and the fun seems to peter out to a draw, since the liquidation 31 ♕×e2 would leave White with a bad ending.

22 ♘×d4 c×d4 *(36)*

23 f5 . . .

Another critical moment, where White has four reasonable options, apart from the text move. Three of them Polugaevsky would have rejected fairly promptly, though:

(1) 23 ♘d1 ♗×g2+ 24 ♖×g2 ♕e1+ 25

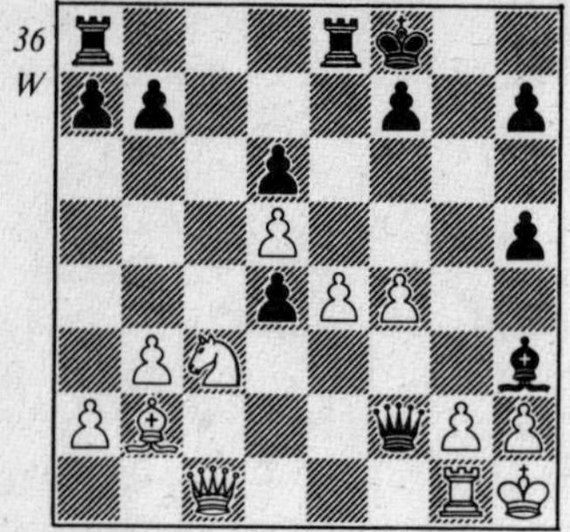

36
W

♖g1 ♕×e4+ 26 ♖g2 ♕e1+ 27 ♖g1 ♕e2!, with the decisive threat of 28 . . . ♕f3+ 29 ♖g2 ♖e1+. The defender is curiously helpless here.
(2) 23 ♘b5 ♖ac8 24 ♕b1 (24 ♗×d4 ♗×g2+ and mate) ♖c2 and wins. Notice that against 20 ♕b1 this variation would not have worked: with the queen guarding the e-pawn and . . . ♖ac8 not being a tempo gain, 23 ♘b5 would be a very good line for White. That is why Black would have had to content himself with the alternative method outlined earlier.
(3) 23 g×h3 ♕f3+ 24 ♖g2 d×c3 25 ♗×c3 ♖×e4, winning comfortably.

But the fourth option conceals a stunning tactical point, worthy of a study:
(4) 23 ♗a3. Now the knight cannot be taken (23 . . . d×c3 24 ♗×d6+ ♖e7 25 g×h3 etc.), and if Black covers his d-pawn by 23 . . . ♖ad8, there follows 24 ♘b5 ♖×e4 (with the seemingly devastating threat of 25 . . . ♗×g2) 25 ♘×d6!! ♗×g2+ 26 ♖×g2 ♖×e1+ 27 ♕×e1 ♕×e1+ 28 ♖g1, after which the queen can only escape the discovered check danger by 28 . . . ♕e2. Unfortunately, Black then gets mated by 29 ♘e4+ ♔e8 30 ♘f6! Not even the rook offer will save him: 29 . . . ♖d6 30 ♗×d6+ ♔e8 31 ♘f6+ ♔d8 32 ♖g8 mate. If 28 . . . ♕×g1+, of course, he will slowly lose the endgame. This amazing resource was spotted later by Jonathan Mestel: not surprisingly it escaped both players during the game. In fact, once this pitfall is noticed, the right answer is not hard to find: 23 . . . ♖ec8!, giving the king some air. Then 24 ♗×d6+ ♔e8 and White has nothing; for example, 25 ♕a3 ♖×c3 26 ♕a4+ ♔d8 and wins.

Obviously White is still alive and kicking! The text move is his final attempt to pin down the wandering king; but on the squares d7 and e8 the king will be safe, and this is the theme which dominates the last phase of the game.

23 . . . d×c3
24 ♕×c3 . . .

24 ♕h6+ is no good: 24 . . . ♔e7 25 ♗×c3 ♖g8 and it is White who gets mated (26 ♕f6+ ♔e8). But now he threatens 25 ♕g7+ ♔e7 26 ♗f6+ ♔d7 27 ♕×f7+ etc., and also covers f3, which in a moment will enable him to capture the bishop. Black solves the problem with an attacking move of his own, as you might guess.

24 . . . ♖×e4

Threatening 25 . . . ♗×g2+ and making space for his king. 25 ♕h8+ (or ♕g7+) now achieves nothing: 25 . . . ♔e7 26 ♕f6+ ♔e8 27 ♕h8+ ♔d7 and the king is safe.

25 g×h3 *(37)* **. . .**

Not 25 ♕×h3? ♖e1, when mate is unavoidable. Instead he plans a mate of his own – 26 ♖g8+ etc. – but . . .

25 . . . ♔e8!

is the move which seals his fate: the king simply walks away! The trouble is that White's forces are geared to an attack down the g-file and the long diagonal; were Black's position

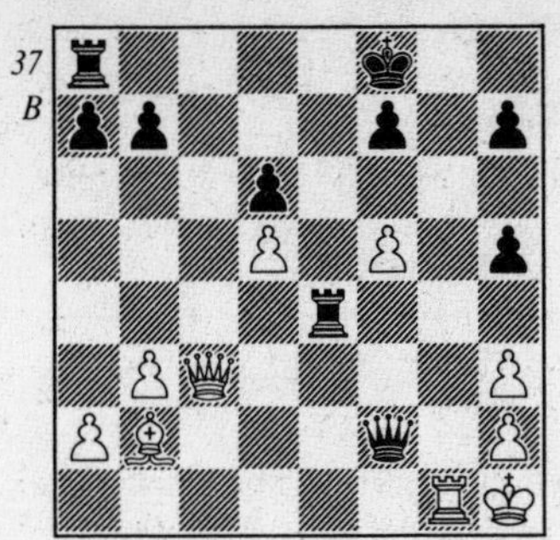

37
B

purely defensive, he might well spend a move or two rearranging them to meet the new situation. But Black is anything but passive: if now 26 ♕h8+ or ♖g8+, then . . . ♔d7 and White must go back again to cover f3 and e1. Meanwhile, Black is planning . . . ♔d7 and . . . ♖ae8 anyway.

26 ♕d3 . . .

Threatens a dangerous check at b5; so Black pins the rook to stop ♖g8+.

26 . . . ♖e1
27 ♖×e1 . . .

Equivalent to resigning, but 27 ♕b5+ ♔f8 28 ♗g7+ ♔g8! loses more material.

27 . . . ♕×e1+
28 ♔g2 ♖c8

Black will now go straight for a mating attack, his rook operating on the g-file. The point of . . . ♖c8 is to meet White's checks by playing the king via c7 to b8 without blocking in the rook. The rest is plain sailing.

29 f6 ♔d7
30 ♕×h7 ♕d2+
31 ♔g3 ♕×d5
32 ♔h4 ♖e8
0 – 1

Game 9

French Defence
Baden 1980

J. Nunn v. R. Vaganian

1	**e4**	**e6**
2	**d4**	**d5**
3	**♘d2**	**c5**
4	**♘gf3**	**a6**

A host of minor features add up to justify this move. The intention is partly to avoid White's ♗b5 lines, and in some variations to retreat the bishop to a7 after an exchange of pawns at c5. There are other points also, to which we refer later. But to understand the opening properly we should first examine the standard variation, which runs: 4 . . . ♘c6 5 e×d5 e×d5 6 ♗b5 ♗d6. Now here 7 d×c5 is more accurate than 7 0–0 (a point which has been overlooked in some opening books) because it keeps White's options open. After 7 . . . ♗×c5 8 ♘b3 ♗d6 9 0–0 ♘e7 he is by no means obliged to make the routine move 10 ♘bd4, but can more usefully play ♖e1 or ♗g5. On the other hand, the variation 7 0–0 c×d4 8 ♘b3 ♘e7 leaves him with nothing better than 9 ♘b×d4. Tactically the difference lies in the greater exposure of Black's pawn at d5. For instance, in the first case White might continue 10 ♖e1 a6 11 ♗e2 (anticipating Black's later pin . . . ♗g4) 0–0 12 ♗g5 (intending ♗h4–g3 with an exchange of Black's better bishop – a considerable gain) f6 13 ♗h4; and now 13 . . . ♘f5 is unplayable, but with the extra pawn at d4 it would suit Black admirably. In short, the black pawn at d4 is a nuisance and progress is difficult without removing it.

Black, of course, may also make the capture at move six, to try to reach the more favourable position, but he then runs into other problems because pieces tend to get exchanged too quickly for the player with the isolated pawn; for example: 6 . . . c×d4 7 ♕e2+ ♕e7 (this time . . . ♘e7 is not available; or if 7 . . . ♗e7 8 0–0 ♘f6 9 ♖e1 suits White) 8 ♘×d4 ♕×e2+ 9 ♔×e2 ♗d7 10 ♘2f3 ♘×d4+ 11 ♘×d4 ♗c5 12 ♖d1 ♘e7 13 ♗e3 ♗×d4 14 ♗×d7+ ♔×d7 15 ♖×d4 and White has a definite pull (Hübner-Korchnoi, match 1981).

That does not exhaust the theory of the variation, naturally, but this aspect of it happens to be relevant to the present game.

5	**e×d5**	**e×d5**
6	**♗e2**	**c×d4**

Rather than 6 . . . ♗d6 etc., as explained. Another possibility, which is beyond our scope here, is 6 . . . c4, meeting 7 b3 by 7 . . . b5 (8 a4? c3) – a further justification of 4 . . . a6.

7	**0–0**	**♗d6**
8	**♖e1**	**♘e7**
9	**♘b3**	**0–0**
10	**♘b×d4**	**. . .**

We can summarise the opening phase by saying that White has gained a tempo of sorts by moving his bishop only once (instead of ♗b5, . . . a6, ♗e2, as in the main line), but that he has used the extra move to play the not specially useful ♘b×d4.

10 . . . ♘bc6

11 ♗e3 . . .

Here is another reason why White would have preferred to avoid the early blockade of d4. With the knight at b3 he could play ♗g5, but as things stand Black has the awkward reply 11 . . . ♕b6.

11 . . . ♕c7

Revealing a further useful aspect of 4 . . .a6, in that ♘b5 is prevented.

12 h3 ♗d7

12 . . . ♘f5 is more accurate: Black offers an exchange but develops his bishop with gain of time. After 13 ♘×f5 ♗×f5 14 ♕×d5 (14 c3 ♖ad8 is also about equal) ♗×c2 15 ♖ac1 ♖ad8 16 ♕c4 ♗f5 17 ♕b3 ♗e6 he has equalised (Geller–Forintos, Moscow 1975).

13 ♕d2 *(38)* **. . .**

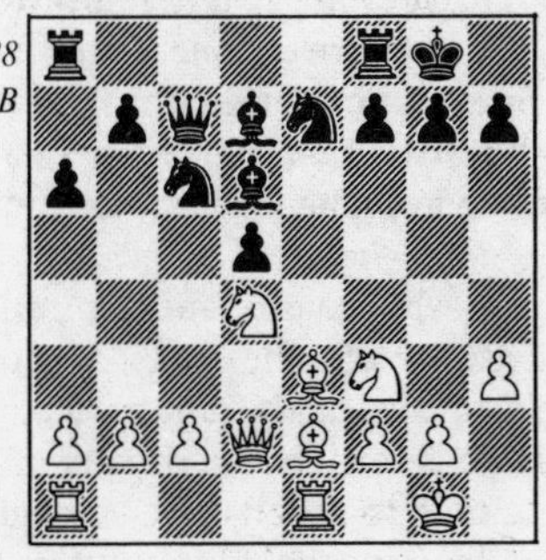

Broadly speaking, we can say that White's plan is to exchange **minor** pieces in the hope of exploiting Black's isolated pawn in the endgame. I stress minor pieces because in the nature of things queens and rooks are better equipped to attack weak pawns, and the more the board is cleared of obstructions the greater becomes their scope. White's ideal here would be something like: rooks at d1 and d4, queen at d2, no minor pieces left to harass the blockader at d4, and the remaining black pieces defending passively. From that position he might manoeuvre his pieces to create a new weakness in Black's game and thus a second target; perhaps in the Q-side, perhaps in the castled position.

At present exchanges are not easy to accomplish, since ♘×c6 b×c6 will improve Black's pawn structure and provide him with an open b-file. (Of course, when this same exchange is made in, for example, the QGD Tarrasch Defence, the resulting c-pawn is exposed on a half-open file; that is another matter entirely). But if White can combine the exchange with a quick c4 **in favourable circumstances**, Black will again be left with an isolated pawn. And here is where the practical difficulty of this opening arises for Black. He cannot really do anything direct; rather he must keep his pieces flexible, avoid too many exchanges and be ready to counter any of White's plans. If the opportunity arises he may play for a K-side attack.

Specifically, the success or failure of the c4 idea **will depend on the placing of the pieces**. Or, to put it another way, general thinking about the pawn structure cannot be divorced from piece play. That is what you may find hard to accept; one tends to think: 'Either c4 will give White some advantage or it won't.' The following notes should clarify this point.

13 . . . ♘g6(?)

This highlights the problem. Though an expert in the French Defence, Vaganian slips up at once. With an isolated d-pawn the position of the knight at e7 is unfortunate in that it cannot easily occupy the natural outpost at e4. Black therefore heads for the alternative square at c4, via e5, but his move is too casual because it permits c4 under favourable circumstances, as we shall see. . . . f6 is another common idea, intending . . . ♘e5–c4 without allowing White to exchange comfortably at e5; but here 13 . . . f6 14 ♘×c6 b×c6 15 c4 would open the position and reveal weaknesses at e6 and on the c4–g8 diagonal. On the whole, Black would do best to complete his development by the simple move 13 . . . ♖fe8.

14 ♘×c6! b×c6

14 . . . ♗×c6 is possible, but after 15 ♘d4 Black's pieces at c6 and g6 are misplaced (if 15 . . . ♘e5 16 ♘f5 is embarrassing) and White has moved in the right direction by exchanging a pair of pieces.

15 c4 . . .

Comparing this position with the one Black could have had after 13 . . . ♖fe8, you will see that 14 ♘×c6 b×c6 15 c4 would have permitted him a more active continuation in 15 . . . ♘f5 16 c×d5 ♘×e3 17 f×e3 c×d5 18 ♕×d5 ♗c5, or here 17 d×c6 ♗×c6 18 f×e3, and in both cases White's extra pawn is worthless. White's best reply is 16 c5 ♗e5 (16 . . . ♗g3 17 ♗g5! is also slightly better for White) 17 ♘×e5 ♕×e5 18 ♗f4 ♕d4 19 ♖ac1 ♕×d2 20 ♗×d2 ♘d4 21 ♗d1 with a small advantage, but Black stands better than in the actual game. As things stand, his d-pawn is under fire, his knight can do nothing useful and he is obliged to make a passive 16th move.

15 . . . a5

Threatening 16 . . . ♗b4. White now prefers to keep the d-pawn under attack, at the same time preparing b4. If 16 c5 ♗e7 17 a3, Black has 17 . . . a4, crippling the majority.

16 a3! ♗e6

There is little choice. 16 . . . d×c4? loses a piece (17 ♖ad1), while 16 . . . ♘f4 can be met by 17 c5 (17 ♗f1 is also very good) ♘×e2+ 18 ♖×e2 ♗e7 (18 . . . ♗e5 19 ♗d4 ♗f4 20 ♕c3 f6 21 g3) 19 ♗f4 ♕d8 20 ♖c1, leaving Black with a very poor bishop at d7. 16 . . . ♘e7 17 c5 would be even worse.

17 c5 . . .

17 ♘d4 may look tempting, but Black has 17 . . .a4; capturing on e6 would then only strengthen his pawn centre and open a file for his rook. But why play 17 c5, when all the time we have been claiming that the intention was to isolate Black's pawns?! Well, if things had developed differently over the last few moves, one could well imagine circumstances in which the isolating of the pawn would have been appropriate – but not now. Always the relative scope of the pieces is what counts, and here, after 17 c×d5 ♗×d5, the black bishops would be admirably centralised and ready to threaten the K-side. For White then to generate any pressure down the c-file would in practice be far too difficult. No, his thinking has to be a bit more flexible than that; and by 17 c5 he gains space in the centre and plans a blockade at d4, followed by the advance of his Q-side majority.

17 . . . ♗e7

17 . . . ♗f4, leaving himself with only the inferior white-square bishop,

would be a major concession; so he must remain constricted.

18 b4 ♖fb8

Apart from its obvious negative aspects (holes at e5 and e6) 18 . . . f5 would have no future as an attacking weapon because the pawn could get no further than f4. Simply 19 ♗d4, then ♗d3, ♕c3 and ♘e5 would refute it. Therefore, Black's only hope of play is along the a- and b-files.

White can now continue with the natural move 19 ♘d4, meeting 19 . . . ♕b7 by 20 ♖ab1, then ♖ec1 and ♕c2, gradually preparing b5 and the creation of a very strong passed pawn. Nunn avoided this because he reckoned only on the immediate 20 b5 c×b5 21 ♘×b5 ♖c8, when the c-pawn can be comfortably blockaded (. . . ♘e5–c6). Not that his chosen move is bad; it is merely more ambitious and more complex.

19 ♗d4 . . .

The main purpose of this is to secure the b-pawn by ♗c3 and follow up with ♘d4. For the moment it also threatens to overrun the centre and cramp Black severely by 20 ♗d3 and later ♘e5; hence the reply.

19 . . . ♗f5

Psychologically this is a critical moment, for with the Q-side pawn structure clearly defined and White happily manoeuvring around the d4 square, there would be a tendency with many players to do no analysis at all; simply to drop the pieces on to the obvious squares and expect the game to win itself. There would be talk of White playing 'smoothly', or of his game 'flowing', and a corresponding disdain for Black's awkward-looking pieces. But just play a couple of casual moves without analysing and see where 'smooth' play gets you: 20 ♗c3 ♗e4 21 ♘d4 ♘f4! 22 ♗f1 (22 f3 ♘×h3+) ♗g5 and the despised black pieces have come to life alarmingly: 23 ♕d1 a×b4 24 a×b4 ♖×a1 25 ♕×a1 ♘d3, for instance, with at least equality. So beware of smoothness; it is something which you can appreciate **afterwards**; during the game it can be a deadly delusion.

Instead of this Nunn blends accurate tactical play with his basic plan by means of a nice multi-purpose move:

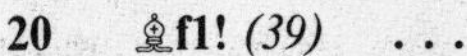

20 ♗f1! *(39)* **. . .**

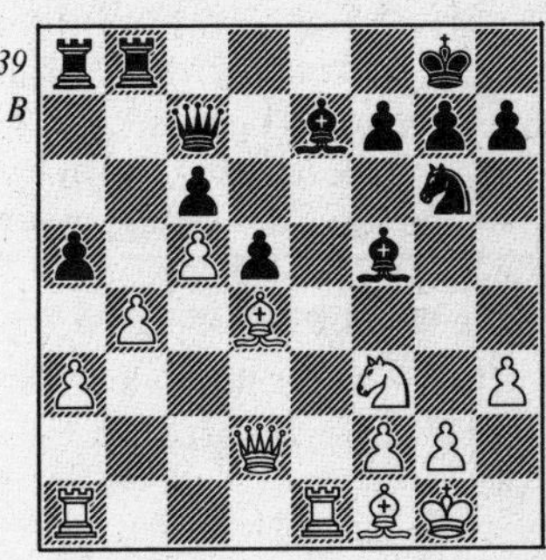

Anticipates . . . ♘f4 and clears the way for ♘e5, if required. Also a reply to 20 . . . ♗e4 is being prepared. Now Black does not have much margin of error; he has to appreciate that his position will become intolerably passive if the white knight is allowed to reach d4 without a fight. This is another difficult point: it is a question of recognising initiative; of realising that although the two sets of pieces may at first sight appear to have about the same level of activity, in reality one set is doing something **relevant**. For instance, the knight at d4 will attack c6 permanently; the black knight may reach c4, but will have little or no effect there. White's 27th move drives this point home very forcefully.

20 . . . f6?

A very weak move which not only does nothing to obstruct White's plan but also blocks the K-bishop and seriously weakens e6. ♘e5 is prevented, but Black seems to overlook the regrouping plan of ♗c3 and ♘d4. The best idea was still 20 . . . ♗e4, driving the knight away at a moment when d4 is inaccessible; then White's advantage is kept within reasonable bounds: 21 ♘g5! ♗f5 22 ♗c3 a×b4 23 a×b4 h6 24 ♘f3 ♗d7, and if 25 ♘d4 ♗f6. Notice that if Black tries to win a pawn by 21 . . . ♗×g5 22 ♕×g5 a×b4 23 a×b4 ♖×a1 24 ♗×a1 ♖×b4?, he loses at once by 25 f3 f6 (mate in two if the bishop moves) 26 ♕d2. He could also try 21 . . . ♗×g5 22 ♕×g5 f6 23 ♕d2 ♘e5, but here the two bishops guarantee White a plus.

21 ♗c3 ♗e4(?)

21 . . . ♗f8 22 ♘d4 ♗d7 is a more resilient defence, though 23 ♘e6 ♗×e6 24 ♖×e6 would be unpleasant. The rook cannot be trapped (24 . . . ♘e5 25 ♖e1 ♕f7 26 ♗×e5; or 24 . . . a×b4 25 a×b4 ♖×a1 26 ♗×a1 ♘e5 27 ♕f4); so Black would have passive pieces and no compensation for the bishop-pair. After the text move White can demonstrate a forced win.

22 ♘d4 a×b4

23 a×b4 . . .

Now 24 f3 is threatened; so the knight must move. If Black exchanges first we have: 23 . . . ♖×a1 24 ♗×a1! ♘e5 (24 . . . ♘f8 is much the same) 25 f3 ♗g6 26 f4 ♘c4 27 ♗×c4 d×c4 28 ♖×e7, winning a pawn for nothing. If 23 . . . ♘f8 24 f3 leads to the same thing.

23 . . . ♘e5

24 ♖×a8 ♖×a8

White exchanges rooks because he has seen a way to win which is even more conclusive than 24 f3 etc., and which requires the black rook to be undefended at a8.

25 f3 ♗g6

26 f4 ♘c4 *(40)*

40
W

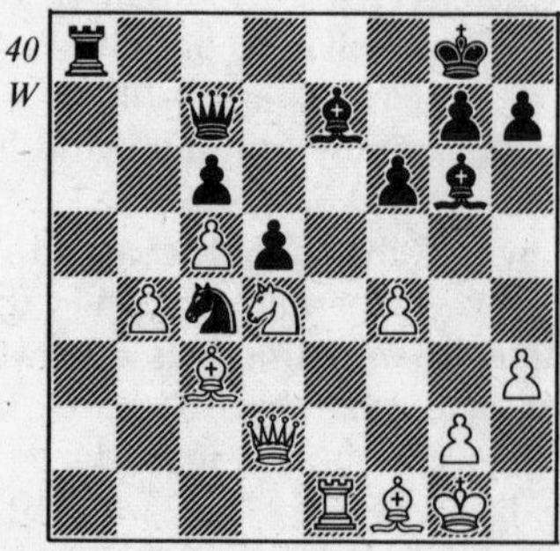

If 26 . . . ♘f7 27 f5 ♗h5 28 g4 ♕g3+ 29 ♔h1 wins the bishop; or 28 ♘e6 ♕ moves 29 ♘f4, if you prefer. After 26 . . . ♘c4 Black's pieces seem to be reasonably placed, but . . .

27 ♕e2! . . .

. . . and the game is over. White threatens 28 ♕e6+ and 29 ♕×c6 as well as the bishop, and will answer 27 . . . ♖e8 by 28 ♕e6+ ♗f7 (28 . . . ♔h8 29 f5, or 28 . . . ♔f8 29 ♕×c6 and 29 . . . ♕×f4 cannot be played) 29 ♕×c6 ♕×f4 30 ♗×c4 d×c4 31 ♕d7 ♔f8 32 ♘f5, winning a piece. If 27 . . . ♕×f4, White could win material by 28 ♕×e7 ♖e8 29 ♕×e8+ etc., but would probably prefer to transpose into the line above by 28 ♕e6+ ♗f7 (28 . . . ♔h8 29 ♕×e7!) 29 ♕×c6 ♖e8 (if 29 . . . ♖a7 30 ♕c8+ ♗f8 31 ♘c6 and 32 ♘e7+) 30 ♗×c4 etc. Black settles for his only other option, but the second hammer-blow threatens four more things!

27 . . . ♗e4

28 ♕g4! ...

Now he faces 29 ♖×e4, ♗×c4, ♘e6 and ♕e6+ and heavy material loss is inevitable.

28 ... ♗f8

If 28 . . . ♗g6 29 ♘e6, followed by f5; if 28 . . . f5 29 ♘×f5 uncovers the bishop with a mate threat. White can now win two pawns by 29 ♗×c4 f5 30 ♘×f5 ♗×f5 31 ♗×d5+ c×d5 32 ♕×f5, but he chooses the alternative.

29 ♖×e4 1 – 0

(29 . . . d×e4 30 ♗×c4+ ♔h8 31 ♕e6 ♗e7 32 ♕×e4 etc.)

Game 10

Sicilian Defence
Baden 1980

J. Nunn v. A. J. Miles

1	**e4**	**c5**
2	**♘f3**	**d6**
3	**d4**	**c×d4**
4	**♘×d4**	**♘f6**
5	**♘c3**	**g6**
6	**g3**	**. . .**

This method of meeting the Dragon is soundly based on the idea of controlling d5. With the bishop on g7 the d-pawn will become very weak if Black counters the control by playing . . . e6. The drawback is that it is very slow.

6	**. . .**	**♘c6**
7	**♘de2**	**. . .**

Avoiding an exchange; a difficult move to understand, perhaps, but in most openings Black is bound to be cramped for a while, and the exchange of even one pair of pieces can provide considerable relief. This is especially relevant here, where White is playing a slow variation and must rely on subtler methods than would be appropriate in the usual, more violent anti-Sicilian lines. On the whole he feels that this factor outweighs the time loss.

7	**. . .**	**♗g7**

7 . . . ♗d7 8 ♗g2 ♕c8 9 h3 is the main alternative, whereby Black plays to prevent White castling. On the other hand, the queen on c8 gets in Black's way, and if it is later moved to c7, White castles and gains a tempo.

8	**♗g2**	**♖b8**

A new idea. Black develops Q-side counterplay as quickly as possible. Perhaps influenced by the result of this game, the idea seems to have been abandoned after this one appearance; but Black's loss was not due to the opening.

9	**a4**	**a6**
10	**0–0**	**b5**
11	**a×b5**	**a×b5**
12	**♘d5** *(41)*	**. . .**

41
B

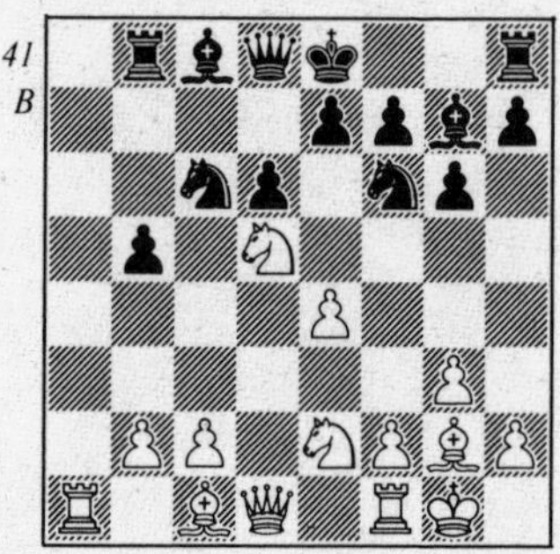

This knight is still in position fifteen moves later, with the battle raging all around him! Meanwhile, several questions arise: (1) Why play ♘d5 at once? (2) What if Black takes it? (3) What if he plays 12 . . . e6?

In answer to (1) the whole theme of the variation is to occupy d5, and other, more formal developing moves would not be appropriate at this point. For example, the right square for the Q-bishop is not yet clear (12 ♗e3 ♘g4, or 12 ♗g5 h6), though an exchange against Black's strong K-bishop is likely to be the best solution. Another move which might strike you is 12 f4, but that would block the bishop and make it an inferior piece; in any case there is no guarantee that White will want to continue with e5 or f5. Balancing all these thoughts leads naturally to 12 ♘d5.

Number (2) is fairly straightforward: if 12 . . . ♘×d5 13 e×d5 ♘e5 14 ♘d4, the weak square c6 in conjunction with the a-file is bound to lead Black into trouble, e.g. 14 . . . ♕b6 15 ♘c6 ♘×c6 16 d×c6 0–0 17 ♗e3 etc., or 14 . . . ♗d7 15 ♘c6 ♗×c6 16 d×c6 ♕c7 17 ♖a6 ♖b6 18 ♖a8+ ♖b8 19 ♖×b8+ ♕×b8 20 ♕d5 with advantage.

As for (3), 12 . . . e6 13 ♘×f6+ ♗×f6 is very good for Black unless White can do something immediate to exploit his delay in castling, and this gives us an excellent insight into Nunn's thinking. He knows that he simply must keep the initiative or get into trouble. Therefore he considered only 14 ♗f4 and 14 ♗h6; nothing else is worth a second look, and if the b-pawn has to be ditched, so be it. Most players, while appreciating that ♗h6 is an interesting move and that the b-pawn might be sacrificed, would not sense the urgency of the situation. 14 c3 would probably be preferred, because it seems safe; yet after 14 . . . 0–0 Black's somewhat more aggressive position would definitely give him the edge, since 15 ♗h6 ♖e8 16 ♕d2 may be met by 16 . . . ♘a5 threatening . . . ♘b3 or . . . ♘c4.

Once this is understood the following variations fall into place. Notice how almost every move is a direct threat; this is part of the secret – White knows he must keep it going!:

(a) 14 ♗f4 ♘e5 (14 . . . ♗×b2 15 ♗×d6 ♗×a1 16 ♕×a1 wins for White) 15 ♗h6 ♘g4, which is unclear.

(b) 14 ♗h6! ♗×b2 15 e5! (to trap the bishop) ♘×e5 16 ♖a2 ♘g4 (16 . . . ♘c4 17 ♖×b2 ♘×b2 18 ♕d4) 17 ♘d4 ♘×h6 (17 . . . ♗×d4 18 ♕×d4 e5 19 ♗c6+ and now 19 . . . ♔e7 20 ♖a7+ is very good for White, so 19 . . . ♗d7 20 ♕×d6 ♗×c6 21 ♕×c6+ ♕d7 22 ♕e4 is better, though even here White has a very dangerous attack) 18 ♘c6 ♕c7 19 ♘×b8 ♗g7 20 ♘c6, followed by ♖a7, when White is probably slightly better.

All these variations were visualised when playing 12 ♘d5.

12	**. . .**	**0–0**
13	**♗g5**	**. . .**

Virtually a tempo gain; Black cannot permit the splitting of his pawns by a capture on f6, because the d-pawn would become fatally weak.

13	**. . .**	**♘d7**
14	**♕c1**	**♘c5**
15	**b4(?)** *(42)*	**. . .**

42
B

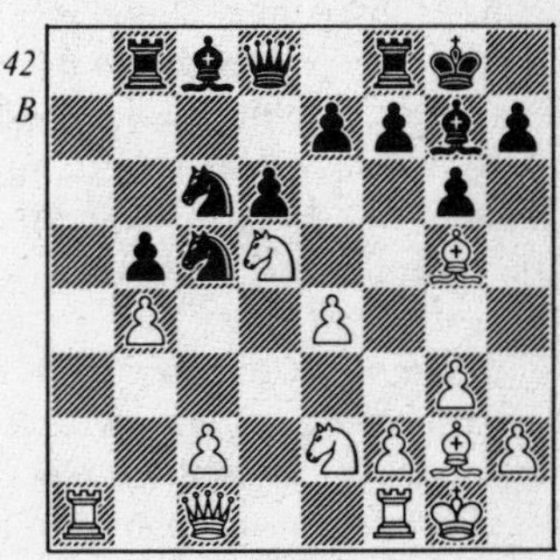

Strictly speaking, a slower treatment is best here and 15 ♖d1 is the natural move. This was rejected during the game on account of 15 . . . ♗g4, but then 16 f3 ♗d7 17 ♗h6 b4 18 ♗×g7

♔×g7 19 b3, followed by ♕b2+, should give White an edge.

The move chosen is a bold attempt to maintain the initiative at the cost of the exchange. Black would like to develop his Q-side play by . . . b4 and even . . . b3, and 15 b4 stops this advance and fixes the b-pawn as a potential target.

The line intended after 15 . . . ♗×a1 was 16 ♕×a1 ♘e6 17 ♗h6 (not 17 ♗×e7 ♘×e7 18 ♘f6+ ♔h8 19 ♘d7+ f6 20 ♘×b8, because 20 . . . ♕b6 wins a piece) ♖e8 18 f4 (other moves are also met by 18 . . . f6) f6 19 f5 ♘c7 20 ♕a2 (20 f×g6 h×g6 21 ♖×f6? e×f6 22 ♘×f6+ ♔f7 23 ♘×e8 ♘×e8 wins for Black), with a dangerous attack, for example 20 . . . ♔h8? 21 ♘×c7 ♕×c7 22 f×g6 h×g6 23 ♕f7 ♖g8 24 ♖f4 (threatening 25 ♗g7+ as well as 25 ♖h4) g5 25 ♗×g5! f×g5 26 ♕h5+ and mates.

Now let us pause for a moment! First of all, learning to visualise sequences of moves like that only comes with hard practice. If you find it very difficult, the sooner you begin practising, the better! There is no other way. More generally, if you feel nervous about sacrificing in these situations, where there is no certainty of a mate or of swiftly regaining the material, remember that the exchange is often not a great deal to give up. If a Grandmaster has worked through a number of variations to test his idea, and can see that his pieces are aggressively placed and will continue to generate threats, such a sacrifice may be almost routine. The present position happens to be a hard one to assess and Nunn has decided to take the risk. In the event neither player realised that 20 . . . e6! is a much better move, for example:

(1) 21 ♘×c7 ♕×c7 22 f×g6 h×g6 23 ♖×f6 ♔h7, followed by . . . ♘e5 and the excellent knight stops the attack.
(2) 21 e5 (ingenious, but it doesn't work) ♘×d5 (21 . . . e×d5? 22 ♗×d5+ ♘×d5 23 ♕×d5+ ♔h8 24 ♕f7 ♖g8 25 e×f6 wins) 22 ♗×d5 ♘×b4 23 f×e6 (23 e×f6 ♕×f6! wins, but not 23 . . . ♘×a2 24 f7+ ♔×f7 25 f×e6+ ♔g8 26 e7+, or 24 . . . ♔h8 25 f6!, both lines winning for White) ♘×d5! (23 . . . ♕b6+ 24 ♖f2 ♘×a2 25 e7+ ♔h8 26 e×f6 wins for White) 24 e×f6 ♗×e6 25 f7+ ♗×f7 26 ♖×f7 ♔×f7 27 ♕×d5+ ♖e6 28 ♘f4 ♕f6 and White's attack cannot proceed further.

Incredible variations, most of which would have been worked out after the game; only the outlines of (2) could have been glimpsed over the board.

15	**. . .**	**♘e6(?)**
16	**♗h6**	**♘ed4**

Again Black should have taken the rook, when 17 ♕×a1 transposes. This time, though, White could play 17 ♗×f8 ♗h8 18 ♗h6 ♖a8 (18 . . . ♘ed4 19 ♘×d4 ♘×d4 20 ♕g5 is awkward) 19 c3, followed by f4, with roughly level chances. The text move wins a pawn, but in very dangerous circumstances.

17	**♘×d4**	**♘×d4**
18	**♔h1**	**♗×h6**
19	**♕×h6**	**♘×c2**

White was obliged to sacrifice the pawn, but that would hardly have bothered him: he now has plenty of compensation in the form of aggressive pieces. Perhaps that is obvious to you, but from now on we are concerned with making the most of a powerful position; of not losing our grip on the game. Loss of control is something many people would fear, even though they might judge the original sacrifice correctly.

First of all Black is by no means dead yet. There is scarcely anything in his position which could be called a serious structural weakness. Therefore White cannot take his time. He must be precise and not allow the game to simplify until he has achieved something concrete - winning his pawn back and keeping positional superiority, for example, or maybe weakening Black seriously in some other way. Above all, the knight is his key attacking piece and he must play to prevent Black from exchanging his bishop for it. The choice of moves is obvious: 20 ♖a7 or 20 ♖ac1; but 20 ♖a7? ♗b7 21 ♕d2 ♗×d5 22 e×d5 ♕b6! 23 ♖×e7 ♘a3, followed by . . . ♘c4–e5, would enable Black to defend comfortably, and White would face the danger of being left with a poor bishop.

This is altogether a very good variation, typical of returning material to wrest the initiative. Compare also the note to White's 12th move, where the capture at d5 was bad. The difference, of course, is that White cannot make use of c6 this time.

20 ♖ac1 ♘d4

21 ♖c7 . . .

It must be a direct threat, otherwise Black plays 21 . . . e6 or 21 . . . ♗b7; and if 21 ♖fd1, ♘e6 prevents ♖c7. Then, after for example 22 e5 ♗b7! 23 ♕h4 ♗×d5 24 ♖×d5 ♘c7, Black is no worse and may even have an advantage.

21 . . . ♗d7

Forced; if 21 . . . ♖e8 or 21 . . . ♖b7 22 ♖×e7! wins. Quite apart from the comments on general thinking, a number of tactical ideas are appearing in this game which are instructive in themselves. If 21 . . . e6, White has 22 ♘e7+ and 23 ♘×g6+.

22 f4 *(43)* **. . .**

43
B

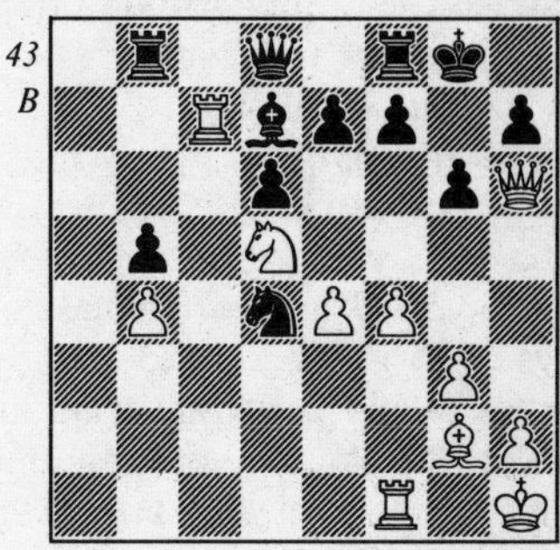

A difficult moment; although White seems to have a variety of good attacking lines, none of them is really clear-cut. Again he will consider only aggressive moves, preferably direct threats. He will first identify 22 ♗h3, 22 f4 and 22 ♖d1 as the likely contenders, and his analysis will be an attempt to choose between them.

Later examination indicates that 22 f4 allows Black equality more or less by force; so one of the alternatives should really have been preferred. Here are the variations:

(1) 22 ♗h3 and now:
(1a) 22 . . . ♗×h3? 23 ♖×e7! and wins (but not 23 ♘×e7+? ♕×e7 24 ♖×e7 ♗×f1, which is very good for Black).
(1b) 22 . . . e6? 23 ♖×d7 and wins.
(1c) 22 . . . ♘e6 23 ♖a7 (Black is badly tied up now) ♖e8 (23 . . . ♖a8 24 ♖×a8 ♕×a8 25 ♘×e7+ ♔h8 26 ♗g2 is positionally very good for White; or if 23 . . . f5 24 e×f5 g×f5 25 ♖c1 exerts unpleasant pressure) 24 f4 ♗c6 25 f5 (not 25 ♖×e7 ♗×d5) ♗×d5 26 e×d5 ♘c7 (or 26 . . . ♘f8 27 ♖×e7! and wins) 27 f×g6 h×g6 28

♖×c7 ♕×c7 29 ♗e6! f×e6 30 ♕×g6+ ♔h8 31 ♖f7 ♕c1+ 32 ♔g2 ♕d2+ 33 ♔h3 and wins.

(1d) 22 . . . f5! and now neither 23 ♖d1 e6! nor 23 e×f5 ♘×f5 offers anything clear to White.

(2) 22 ♖d1 ♘c6! (22 . . . ♘e6 23 ♖a7, followed by f4, gives White a dangerous attack as in 1c above) 23 ♗h3 (23 ♖c1 ♘e5 is unclear) f5! (23 . . . ♗×h3 24 ♖×e7! and 23 . . . ♘e5 24 f4 ♗×h3 25 f×e5 ♗d7 26 e×d6 e×d6 27 ♖×d7 are wins for White) 24 e×f5 g×f5, and although White has a promising attack, there doesn't seem to be anything definite. However, his pressure must be worth more than a pawn.

Notice in particular the return of material (23 . . . ♖a8 etc.) which fails here because White keeps a hold on the centre, and the counter-attacking move 23 . . . e6! in conjunction with . . . f5. This move saves Black, yet it is a point which may escape you when analysing. Black needs to ask: 'Can I hit back?', not simply 'Where shall I move my attacked knight?'

A Grandmaster is quite capable of working out the above variations over the board, but in the end he has to judge between the final position of (2) and the one he gets in the game. This is extremely difficult and the conclusion is that 22 ♖d1 would have been slightly better (see note to Black's 23rd move).

22 . . . f5

Absolutely necessary; against 22 . . . ♘e6 White is preparing another thunderbolt – 23 f5! ♘xc7 24 f6 ♘e6 25 f×e7 and wins!

23 e5 . . .

Once again 23 ♖d1 e6! would ruin everything. He must be ready with ♘f6+.

23 . . . ♖f7?

Too passive; 23 . . . ♖c8 was correct, with the following continuation being virtually forced: 24 ♖×c8 (24 ♖a7 ♘c6, or 24 ♖b7 ♘c6) ♗×c8 25 ♖d1 ♘e6 26 ♕h4 ♖f7 27 e×d6 e×d6 28 ♕×d8+ ♘×d8 29 ♘b6 ♖c7 30 ♘×c8 ♖×c8 31 ♗f1 ♘f7 32 ♗×b5 ♖b8 33 ♗c4 ♖×b4 34 ♗×f7+ ♔×f7 35 ♖×d6 with a draw. Perhaps White could try delaying the recapture of the pawn by 29 ♔g1, but it is hard to believe that this would bring any advantage.

24 ♖d1 ♘e6
25 ♖a7 ♘f8

White has no tangible threats for the moment; so Black should probably have tried 25 . . . ♖c8. Neither 26 ♖×d7 nor 26 ♘b6 leads to anything apart from a few exchanges.

26 ♕h4! . . .

Black is now in serious difficulties. He is almost paralysed by the pressure from every side, even though White has no immediate threat. His next move eliminates the possibilities of ♘×e7+, ♗d5 and ♖×d7, which crop up in several variations.

26 . . . ♔g7

If 26 . . . ♖c8 27 ♖×d7 ♕×d7 28 ♘b6 ♕c7 29 ♘×c8 ♕×c8 30 e×d6 e×d6 31 ♗d5 ♘e6 32 ♖e1 wins. If 26 . . . d×e5 27 f×e5 ♕e8 28 ♖×d7! etc.

27 ♘c7 . . .

The game is now approaching its crisis. White must identify his opponent's weak spot (the centre pawns now, not the K-side) and liquidate into a favourable ending by playing e×d6 at a suitable moment. In other words, he must win back his sacrificed pawn and be certain of winning at least the b-pawn in the endgame. Black can hardly avoid this simplification; for example 27 . . .

♘e6 28 e×d6 e×d6 29 ♕×d8 and 30 ♖×d6 is worse than the game; if 27 . . . d×e5 28 f×e5 ♕c8 29 ♕d4 ♗e6 30 ♘a6 and White wins. He therefore decides to force his opponent into an immediate liquidation, otherwise White could improve his position, by 28 ♔g1 for instance.

27	**. . .**	**♖c8**
28	**e×d6**	**e×d6**
29	**♕×d8**	**♖×d8**
30	**♖×d6**	**♖c8** *(44)*

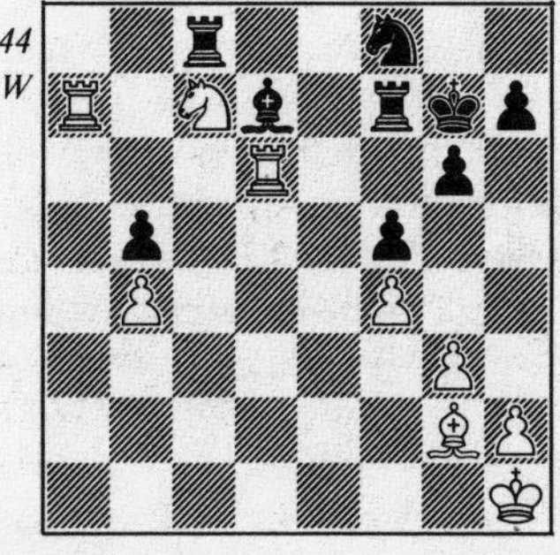

In this last phase the difference between aggressive and defensive pieces is made very clear by the variations. Black is now fighting a losing battle and can easily forfeit more than just his b-pawn. However, he sets a good trap here; 30 . . . ♖b8 is no good because of 31 ♗d5 ♖e7 (or . . . ♖f6) 32 ♘e6+ and he loses at least the exchange. But if now 31 ♗d5 ♖e7 32 ♘e6+ ♔h6 (32 . . . ♘×e6? 33 ♖d×d7 ♖×d7 34 ♖×d7+ ♔f6 35 ♖d6 ♖e8 is a case of paralysis; if here 35 . . . ♖c1+ 36 ♔g2 ♖e1 37 ♔f2 ♔e7 38 ♖b6 wins) 33 ♘×f8, Black draws by 33 . . . ♖c1+ 34 ♔g2 ♖c2+ 35 ♔f3 (35 ♔h3? even loses) ♖c3+ etc.

31	**♔g1**	**. . .**

The black pieces are terribly restricted; so White takes his time and refuses to win material prematurely. For the time being, having dismissed the aggressive 31 ♗d5, his analysis will simply aim to control the position and ensure that Black cannot free himself without unacceptable material losses.

31	**. . .**	**♔h6**

Trying to get his king away from the knight check at e6. The other freeing attempts are 31 . . . ♖f6, met by 32 ♘×b5 ♖c1+ 33 ♗f1, and 31 . . . ♖e7 32 ♗f1, which will transpose into the game after 32 . . . ♔h6. Black has nothing better than this king move, since 32 . . . ♔f7 loses to 33 ♘d5 ♖e1 34 ♖d×d7+ ♘×d7 35 ♖×d7+ ♔f8 36 ♔f2 ♖a1 37 ♗×b5.

32	**♗f1**	**♖e7**

32 . . . ♗e8 33 ♘×b5 ♖×a7 34 ♘×a7 would have lasted longer, but White should win, since Black's pieces are still very passively placed. Instead Black hopes in vain that White will miss the winning combination.

33	**♘d5!**	**. . .**

Suddenly there is a more attractive and convincing win than continuing to persecute the b-pawn. White simply resumes his attack.

33	**. . .**	**♖e1**
34	**♘b6**	**♖c6**

If 34 . . . ♖cc1 35 ♘×d7 ♖×f1+ 36 ♔g2 ♖g1+ 37 ♔h3 and White's attack hits h7 one tempo before Black's reaches h2!

35	**♘×d7**	**♖×d6**
36	**♘×f8**	**♔h5**
37	**♖×h7+**	**♔g4**
38	**♔f2**	**♖×f1+**
39	**♔×f1**	**♔f3**
40	**♖d7**	**♖c6**
41	**♖d3+**	**♔e4**
42	**♔e2**	**1 – 0**

Game 11

Sicilian Defence
Bristol Weekend Open 1981
J. Nunn v. G. Anthony

1	**e4**	**c5**
2	**♘f3**	**♘c6**
3	**d4**	**c×d4**
4	**♘×d4**	**e5**
5	**♘b5**	**♘f6**

After 4 . . . e5 Black usually intends to play the Löwenthal Variation, 5 . . . a6 6 ♘d6+ ♗×d6 7 ♕×d6 ♕f6, one of the very oldest Sicilian lines. 5 . . . ♘f6 aims to transpose into the Pelikan Variation, a more modern (and well-analysed) version of the old system. Nunn, therefore, knowing his opponent to be a Pelikan specialist, decides to avoid the book move 6 ♘1c3 and take the game straight out of theory; a somewhat risky procedure which Grandmasters are more inclined to adopt in weekend tournaments with fast time limits than in serious international play.

6	**♘5c3**	. . .

The moves which test the Pelikan are always those which exert immediate pressure on the weak spots at d5 and d6; quiet play generally permits Black easy equality by means of an early . . . d5. Apart from that there are, in the main lines, certain positional aspects which make the opening hard to understand: in some cases White's control of d5 is significant, in others it is not; sometimes Black gets weak, doubled f-pawns, sometimes they are not weak and he can undermine White's centre by . . . f5, or use the g-file; and so on. We cannot go into detail here, but we will have a quick look at an interesting alternative to the normal 6 ♘1c3, namely 6 ♗g5 ♗c5 (not to be recommended against 6 ♘1c3, because both 7 ♘d6+ and 7 ♗e3, aiming at the weakness on d6, favour White).

White can then play 7 ♗×f6 ♕×f6 8 ♕d2 0–0 9 ♘c7 ♖b8 10 ♘d5 ♕g6 11 ♘bc3, when his grip on d5 appears to give him a clear advantage (ECO's assessment). But things are not so simple; he has wasted a good deal of time with his knight manoeuvres and with sharp play Black can exploit that: 11 . . . b5! 12 ♗×b5 (12 f3 weakens the black squares) ♘d4 13 ♗d3 ♖×b2 (13 . . . ♕×g2 14 0–0–0 favours White) and if 14 ♘a4, still not 14 . . . ♕×g2? 15 0–0–0, but the surprising combination 14 . . . ♖×a2! 15 ♖×a2 ♕×g2, with advantage.

White's alternative is a pawn sacrifice: 7 ♘d6+. If Black declines, we have 7 . . . ♔e7 (7 . . . ♔f8? 8 ♗c4) 8 ♘f5+ ♔f8 9 ♘c3 d6 10 ♘e3 h6 11 ♗×f6 ♕×f6 12 ♘cd5, with considerable advantage because Black now has no counterplay and he is the one who will have to waste time, playing . . . g6 and . . . ♔g7. So 7 . . . ♗×d6 8 ♕×d6 ♘×e4 9 ♗×d8 ♘×d6 10 ♗c7, and then, for example, 10 . . . ♔e7 11 ♘c3 ♘e8 12 ♘d5+ ♔f8 13 0–0–0 ♘×c7 14 ♘×c7 ♖b8 15 ♗c4 with lasting pressure for the pawn, though not necessarily an overall advantage, since Black's game is quite solid.

In theory at least Black should not have much trouble equalising against Nunn's move. Compared with the normal variations he is immediately freed from any concern over d6 and c7.

6 . . . h6

Prevents 7 ♗g5, but 6 . . . ♗c5 would have served the purpose (7 ♗g5? ♕b6) and excluded the white bishop from its natural square at e3. Another reasonable system of development would be 6 . . . ♗e7 7 ♗c4 d6, followed by . . . ♗e6.

7 ♗e3 ♗b4

The plan of . . . ♗e7, . . . d6 and . . . ♗e6 would still offer comfortable equality because White has a problem organising his knights; for example, ♘d5 and ♘1c3 cannot be played without losing the e-pawn. Instead Black initiates a very different kind of game by developing his bishop outside the pawn chain. Quite an acceptable idea, but he must take care. Exchanging off the potentially bad bishop might seem to make sense, but it could expose a serious weakness at d6 **while he is still undeveloped.** A similar situation can arise in the French Defence, where Black may get into trouble on the white squares if he exchanges his bad bishop prematurely.

8 a3 ♕a5!

The best move because 8 . . . ♗a5 would give rise to the black-square weakness: 9 ♗c4 ♗b6 (not much choice: if 9 0–0 10 ♗c5 and ♗d6, or if 9 . . . ♘×e4 10 ♕d5 ♘g5 11 ♗×g5 ♕×g5 12 ♕×f7+ ♔d8 13 0–0 to White's advantage; incidentally, without a3 and . . . ♗a5 Black could quite happily meet ♕d5 by . . . ♘d6 here!) 10 ♗×b6 ♕×b6 11 ♘d2 0–0 (11 . . . ♕×b2? 12 ♘b5) 12 ♗b3, followed by ♘c4. A potential weakness such as d6 always has to be seen in the context of the piece grouping; that is why we stressed earlier that Black should retain his bishop **until his development was well-advanced**. If, in the variation just examined, he were able to get in the moves . . . d6, . . . ♗e6 and . . . ♖fd8, there would be no problem: d6 would be securely defended and he would have adequate counterplay along the c-file.

9 a×b4 . . .

Nunn is feeling adventurous. Having left the books at move 6, he continues the theme of setting his opponent unfamiliar problems and now wrenches the game out of anything resembling a book position! Alternatives lead to approximate equality: 9 ♗d3 d5 10 e×d5 ♗×c3+ 11 ♘×c3 ♘×d5 12 ♗d2 ♘×c3 13 ♗×c3 ♕c7; or 9 ♗d2 ♗c5! (because the bishop is of no further use at b4, and because 10 ♘d5? and 10 ♗c4? are both met by 10 . . . ♗×f2+; 10 ♘b5 ♕b6 achieves nothing) 10 ♗d3 ♕c7 (or 10 . . . ♕b6 11 0–0 ♗d4, but not 11 . . . ♕×b2? 12 ♖a2 ♕b6 13 ♘a4).

9 . . . ♕×a1

10 ♕d6 *(45)* **. . .**

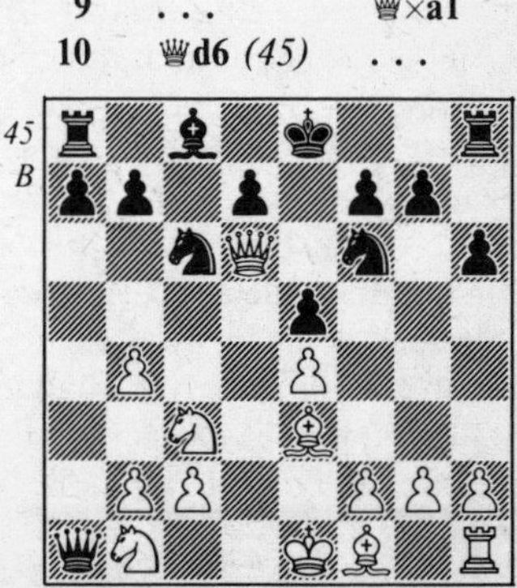

In making the sacrifice Nunn has taken into account that the black king is trapped in the middle, his queen cannot easily come back into play and the mobilisation of his other forces can only proceed slowly. He has also analysed Black's two aggressive replies 10 . . . ♘×e4 and 10 . . . ♕×b2 and concluded that there is a good practical chance of success. And although analysis indicates that a perfect defence should lead either to perpetual check or an approximately equal endgame, his judgement proves correct, because the difficulties of beating off such an attack over the board are quite formidable – certainly beyond Black in this game.

In fact both . . . ♘×e4 and . . . ♕×b2 should lead to a draw with best play; but you don't meet this sort of position every day, so let us first probe one or two variations, to try and get the feel of the tactics; at the same time we can eliminate a third option for Black. If he tries 10 . . . ♘g4? 11 ♗c1! imprisons the queen and threatens, among other things, to win the e-pawn by a combination of b5 and ♗e2; if he persists, we have 11 . . . ♘d4 12 h3 ♘×c2+ 13 ♔d1 ♘×f2+ 14 ♔×c2 ♘×h1 15 ♘d5 and mate.

The next point is that against slow play White has a basic attacking plan of ♗b5 (in many cases better than b5 because it stops . . . b6), ♗×c6 and ♗c5. In some lines early development of the K-bishop might also enable him to castle and keep a very comfortable, fully mobilised position, still with plenty of attack in return for the exchange. For example, 10 . . . b6 11 ♗b5 ♗b7 12 0–0 ♕×b2 13 ♗×c6 ♗×c6 (13 . . . d×c6 14 ♕c7) 14 b5 ♗b7 15 ♕c7 ♗c8 16 ♕×e5+ ♔f8 17 ♕d6+ ♔g8 18 ♗d4 with a substantial advantage. In short, Black's only respectable moves at this point are the ones which attempt an immediate disruption of White's position.

Now after 10 . . . ♕×b2 11 b5 will not quite stand up. Most variations are good for White, such as 11 . . . ♘×e4 12 ♘×e4 ♕×b1+ 13 ♔d2; then (a) 13 . . . ♕b4+ 14 ♕×b4 ♘×b4 15 ♗c5 ♘d5 16 ♘d6+ ♔e7 17 ♘×c8+ ♔e6, which gives White a very good ending because his pieces are active and the black rooks cannot easily come into play; or (b) 13 . . . ♘b4? 14 ♗d3! ♕×h1 15 ♗c5, which yields a winning attack (15 . . . ♔d8 16 ♕e7+ ♔c7 17 ♕×e5+ and mates, or 15 . . . ♘d5 16 ♕×d5 and still Black cannot organise any defence); or (c) 13 . . . ♘e7, which gives rise to the delightful variation 14 ♗c5 ♘g6 15 ♗d3! ♕×h1 16 ♘×f6+ g×f6 17 ♗×g6 ♔d8 18 ♕×f6+, with the familiar mating pattern appearing again. 11 . . . ♘b4? also fails after 12 ♗c5 ♘×c2+ (12 . . . ♕c1+ 13 ♔e2 ♕×c2+ 14 ♘d2) 13 ♔d1 ♔d8 14 ♕e7+ etc., but Black unfortunately has 11 . . . ♘d4!, cutting out the main danger. Then 12 ♕×e5+ ♘e6 13 ♕d6 b6! again stops ♗c5 and threatens to mobilise by . . . ♗b7 and . . . ♖c8. That would mark the end of White's attack, and indeed he seems to have nothing better than 14 e5 ♘e4 15 ♘×e4 ♕×b1+ 16 ♔d2 ♗b7, with insufficient compensation for the exchange (17 ♘f6+ g×f6 18 e×f6 0–0–0!).

So it has to be 11 ♗b5! Then both 11 . . . ♕×b4? and 11 . . . ♘×b4? again fail dismally after 12 ♗c5. And this time 11 . . . ♘d4 will not suffice either, on account of 12 ♕×e5+ ♘e6 13 ♕d6; then 13 . . . ♘×e4 14 ♘×e4 ♕×b1+ 15 ♔d2 ♕×h1 16 ♘c5 ♕×g2 17 ♘×d7 and wins, or 13 . . . b6 14 0–0, and 14 . . . ♗b7 is refuted by 15 e5.

It follows that Black must play 11 . . . ♘×e4, which give us: 12 ♘×e4 ♕×b1+ 13 ♔d2 ♕×b4+ (not 13 . . . ♕×h1 14 ♗c5 ♔d8 15 ♗×c6 b×c6 16 ♕e7+ ♔c7 17 ♕×e5+ ♔b7 18 ♘d6+ ♔b8 19 ♘c4+ and mate in three; if here 17 . . . d6 18 ♗×d6+ ♔b7 19 ♘c5+ ♔b6 20 ♗c7+ leads to mate) 14 ♕×b4 ♘×b4 15 ♗c5, and the same peculiar, unbalanced ending crops up again. Although Black has an extra pawn this time, it would seem that White's aggressive minor pieces assure him at least equal chances. For example: 15 . . . ♘a6 16 ♗×a6 b×a6 17 ♘d6+ ♔e7 18 ♘×c8+ ♔e6 19 ♘d6, and White controls all the useful squares down the b-file and can support his knight by c4, ♗a3 and c5, if need be; also the a-pawns are very weak. If 15 . . . ♘c6 16 ♘d6+ ♔e7 17 ♘×c8+ ♔f6 18 ♘d6 b6 19 ♗a3 a6 20 ♗d3 (not 20 ♗c4 b5) and . . . b5 can be met by ♗c5. Again the rooks will have great difficulty coming into play.

In the event Black decides to take the e-pawn at once, probably as sound a move as any, even though in effect it advances White's development by exchanging f6 for b1.

10 . . . ♘×e4
11 ♘×e4 ♕×b1+
12 ♔d2 ♕×b2
13 b5 . . .

Or 13 ♗b5 ♕×b4+, reaching the same ending; if 13 . . . ♘×b4 14 ♗a4 b6 15 ♘g3! is very good (15 . . . g6 16 ♘e4, or 15 . . . ♔d8 16 ♘f5 ♖e8 17 ♕×b6+!).

13 . . . ♘b4

13 . . . ♘e7 leads to serious trouble, thus: 14 ♗c5 ♘f5 15 ♕d5, and Black, very short of moves anyway, is faced with the threats of g4 and ♗c4; if here 14 . . . ♘g6 15 ♗c4 b6 16 ♗a3 ♕d4+ 17 ♕×d4 e×d4 18 ♘d6+ is devastating (White actually forces mate after 18 . . . ♔d8). Of course, the old idea of . . . ♘d4 and back to e6 is no longer possible; so the choice lies between 13 . . . ♕b4+ and 13 . . . ♘b4. 13 . . . ♕b4+ transposes into the inferior form of the ending previously discussed (line (a)), with Black having only two extra pawns, but 13 . . . ♘b4 does not transpose into line (b) because the queen is now at b2 instead of b1. With the queen not exposed to the rook at h1, it follows that 14 ♗d3 is now useless. The text move is therefore clearly Black's best.

14 ♗c5! . . .

Definitely the best chance. 14 ♕c5 (covering c2 and threatening ♘d6+) is the sort of preparatory move which you can sometimes afford in the middle of an attack, but not here. Black lets fly with a nice vigorous 14 . . . d5! and takes over control of the centre at once: 15 ♘d6+ ♔d7 16 ♘×f7 b6! 17 ♕d6+ (17 ♕c3 ♕×c3+ 18 ♔×c3 ♖e8 19 ♔×b4 ♔e6 and Black wins the endgame) ♔e8 18 ♘×e5 ♕×c2+ 19 ♔e1 ♕b1+ 20 ♔d2 ♗f5, followed by . . . ♖c8 and Black has an excellent position with serious threats against the king. White's queen and knight look menacing, but his attacking force lacks manoeuvrability and the one check he needs to deliver mate is not forthcoming.

14 . . . ♕×c2+
15 ♔e3 ♕b3+ *(46)*
16 ♔e2? . . .

This is the game's crisis. White has

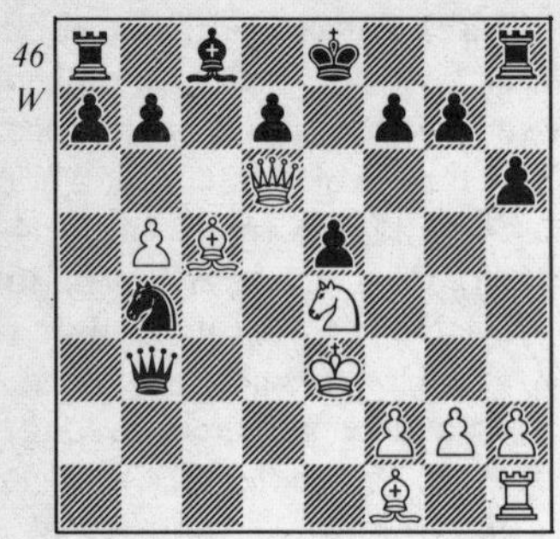

no more than a draw and he should therefore allow perpetual check by 16 ♔d2 ♕c2+ etc. Black cannot do better either; if he tries 16 . . . ♘d5 he loses to 17 ♕×e5+ ♔d8 18 ♘d6, then ♗c4, however he covers the mate threat at f7; 18 . . . ♕a2+ 19 ♔c1 only makes things worse. Nunn's move stops the perpetual (16 . . . ♕c2+ 17 ♘d2), but his winning attempt is misguided because he is obstructing his K-bishop and thus presenting Black with a vital tempo.

16 . . . ♘d5! is now the right move. It threatens 17 . . . b6; so White has to keep going: 17 ♕×e5+ ♔d8 18 ♘d6 and with an extra tempo Black can make the earlier variation work: 18 . . . ♖f8! 19 ♔d2 (nothing better) f6 20 ♕d4 b6 21 ♗c4 b×c5 22 ♕×d5 ♕b2+ and the queens will be exchanged, leaving White with a lost ending.

16 . . . ♕c4+?

Although 16 ♔e2 was wrong, it had the merit of setting Black another problem, in that he was forced to find 16 . . . ♘d5! Not perceiving the strength of that move, he is still looking for perpetual check, on the assumption that White dare not advance any further. However . . .

17 ♔f3 ♕b3+

18 ♔g4 *(47)* **. . .**

47
B

The king proposes to join in the attack along with his other forces! Actually Nunn is something of a specialist in wandering kings, as several of his recent games confirm, but this one cuts quite a figure by any standards. Black had thought this last move to be impossible in view of 18 . . . f5+ 19 ♔×f5 ♕e6+ 20 ♕×e6+ d×e6+ 21 ♔×e5 ♘d5. Then there is indeed no reason why he should not complete his development in peace and win the endgame. But he had overlooked 21 ♔g6!, threatening to win the rook as well as the knight! For a king to win the game by trapping a rook on its original square at move 22 must be unique, I should think. Nor can Black exploit the king's advanced position: 21 . . . ♘d5 (letting the knight go by 21 . . . ♖f8 would certainly lose) 22 ♔×g7 b6 (22 . . . ♗d7 23 ♔×h8 ♔f7+ 24 ♔h7 is safe) 23 ♗a3 ♗b7 24 ♔×h8 ♔f7+ 25 ♔h7 ♘e7 (25 . . . ♘f6+ 26 ♘×f6 ♔×f6 27 ♗d3 e4 28 ♗b1 is OK – White follows with ♖e1 or f3 or ♗b2+ and f4) 26 ♘d6+ ♔f6 27 ♗d3 (or 27 ♘×b7 ♘g6 28 ♗e7+!) ♖g8 28 ♘×b7 ♖g7+ 29 ♔×h6 and he escapes.

So what is Black to do? In the end he settles for 18 . . . f5+ and 19 . . .

♕f7+, which the conclusion of the game shows to be inadequate. 18 . . . ♕e6+ 19 ♕×e6+ d×e6 20 ♘d6+ ♔d7 21 ♗×b4 produces the same bad ending we have seen before; so there remain only 18 . . . h5+ and 18 . . . ♘d5. In fact, after 18 . . . h5+ 19 ♔h4, Black has to play 19 . . . ♘d5 anyway (19 . . . g5+ 20 ♘×g5 is useless) and for tactical reasons which will become clear in a moment it is much better for him to keep the king at g4.

After 18 . . . h5+ 19 ♔h4 ♘d5 20 ♕×e5+ ♔d8 21 ♘d6 we have: (a) 21 . . . ♖f8 22 ♗c4 and wins; (b) 21 . . . ♕a4+ 22 ♗c4 and wins; (c) 21 . . . g5+ 22 ♕×g5+ f6 23 ♕g7 ♕a4+ (if 23 . . . ♖e8 simply 24 ♘×e8) 24 ♗c4 ♖e8 25 ♘f7+ ♔c7 26 ♕g3+ and wins; (d) 21 . . . ♘e7 (21 . . . ♘ any other 22 ♗c4 wins) 22 ♗d3! and White wins, if necessary by bringing his rook into play, though the threat of 23 ♘×b7+ is hard enough to cope with: (i) 22 . . . f6 23 ♘×b7+ ♗×b7 24 ♗×e7+ ♔c8 25 ♖c1+ and wins; (ii) 22 . . . ♘g6+ 23 ♗×g6 f×g6 24 ♕×g7 ♕a4+ 25 ♗d4 and wins; (iii) 22 . . . ♕a4+ 23 f4 or 22 . . . g5+ 23 ♕×g5, which are both useless.

But if Black begins with 18 . . . ♘d5 things are rather different. This position offers such a feast of unusual tactical play that we shall go into more detail than would normally be appropriate for one move. First of all the danger to the white king becomes apparent: if 19 ♕×e5+ ♔d8 20 ♘d6, as before, Black suddenly catches him by 20 . . . ♘f6+ 21 ♔f4 (21 ♔f5 ♕e6+ wins) g5+ 22 ♔f5 ♕c2+ 23 ♔×f6 ♕g6 mate!

So it has to be a change of theme; White has to pause for breath and bring out his last two pieces: 19 ♗e2 b6 20 ♖d1 (20 ♗a3 is too slow: 20 . . . ♗b7 21 ♖d1 ♔d8! and the attack grinds to a halt after 22 ♖×d5 ♕×d5 23 ♕e7+ ♔c7 24 ♗d6+ ♔c8) b×c5 21 ♖×d5 f6. Up to about here the players could have analysed during the game (when thinking about the 18th move, that is) and then relied on judgement; beyond this point we are decidedly in the realms of home analysis. Black is forced to weaken his white squares with this last move because he cannot tolerate the threatened 22 ♖×e5+ ♔d8 23 ♕e7+ ♔c7 24 ♖×c5+ ♔b7 25 ♗f3 etc. If he runs (21 . . . ♔d8), then 22 ♘×c5 threatens ♘b7+ as well as the queen; if then 22 . . . f5+ 23 ♔h5 avoids a queen check and wins. If 21 . . . f5+ 22 ♔×f5 ♖f8+ 23 ♔g6 ♖f7 24 ♖×e5+ ♔d8 25 ♖×c5 and wins by the two threats of 26 ♕c7+ and 26 ♗c4 (if 25 . . . ♖e7 26 ♕c7+ ♔e8 27 ♕×c8+).

After 21 . . . f6 White continues 22 ♔f5 and apart from the new possibility of a bishop check the king is threatening his demolition act again! If 22 . . . h5 (22 . . . ♖f8? 23 ♗h5+) 23 ♔g6 ♖f8 24 ♔×g7 ♖f7+ 25 ♔g8 ♖e7 26 ♗×h5+ ♔d8 27 ♔f8 etc. Black may also try 23 . . . ♖b8 here, but 24 ♔×g7 ♖b6 25 ♕×c5 still wins. Another defence is 22 . . . ♕c2, which is a very tough nut to crack from the point of view of demonstrating a forced win. There are many false trails, lines where Black escapes by a whisker. However, it seems that 23 ♗h5+ ♔d8 24 ♗f7! is good enough (not 24 ♖×c5 ♕a2, threatening to exchange queens, but from f7 the bishop is ready to descent on d5 or e6, as appropriate). Black then has a choice of eight possible queen moves or 24 . . . h5 (which is a serious possibility, believe it or not!).

We then have:

(a) 24 . . . ♕c1 (or . . . ♕a2, . . . ♕b3, or . . . ♕b2) 25 ♔g6 and wins;

(b) 24 . . . ♕b1 (or 24 . . . ♕a4) 25 ♖×c5 with the winning threat of 26 ♗d5;

(c) 24 . . . ♕c4 25 ♗e6 and then: (i) 25 . . . ♕×b5 26 ♔g6; (ii) 25 . . . ♔e8 26 ♗×d7+ ♗×d7 27 ♕×d7+ ♔f8 28 ♕d6+! ♔g8 (28 . . . ♔f7 29 ♕e6+) 29 ♕e6+ ♔h7 30 ♘×f6+ and wins; (iii) 25 . . . g6+ 26 ♔×f6 ♕×e4 27 ♕e7+ ♔c7 28 ♖×c5+ and wins.

24 . . . ♕e2 and 24 . . . h5 are definitely the two toughest defences. For example, 24 . . . ♕e2 25 ♖×c5 h5! Then 26 ♕c7+ leads nowhere and both 26 ♘×f6? ♕×f2+ and 26 f3 ♕×g2 are bad; so 26 h3 would be forced, but then 26 . . . h4! and White, faced with the threat of 27 . . . ♖h5+ 28 ♔g6 ♕×e4+, has no way of improving his position: 27 ♕d5 ♖b8, for instance, and he is tied up through having to defend f2, e4 and h5.

Looking at 24 . . . h5 for a moment, 25 ♗e6 ♕e2 26 h3 h4! would be another dead end for White; in fact Black is winning this one because he has access to h5: (a) 27 ♔g6 ♕h5+, leading to mate; (b) 27 ♗×d7 ♕h5+ 28 ♘g5 (28 ♔e6 ♖e8+!) ♕×g5+ 29 ♔e4 ♕f4+ 30 ♔d3 e4+; (c) 27 ♘×c5 ♖h5+ 28 ♔g6 ♖g5+ and mate in five moves; (d) 27 f3 ♕×g2 with even stronger threats; (e) 27 ♕×d7+, which is unsound because the king slips away to h7.

Now all this is frankly a bit hard to swallow, considering the difference in activity between the two sets of pieces. Since Black can only use his queen and his h-pawn, one feels there must be a way to win, and if you look long enough you find 25 ♖d2!, a complete answer to both 24 . . . ♕e2 and 24 . . . h5. The analysis is as follows: 24 . . . ♕e2 25 ♖d2 ♕×b5 (if 25 . . . ♕f1 or . . . ♕e1 26 ♘×c5 ♕b1+ 27 ♖d3, threatening two mates) 26 ♘×c5 and then: (a) 26 . . . ♕b1+ 27 ♖d3 ♖e8 28 ♗×e8 ♔×e8 29 ♔g6 ♕c1 30 ♘e6! and wins; if here 29 . . . ♕b6 30 ♕d5, or 29 . . . ♕b5 30 ♘e6!, or 29 . . . ♕b4 30 ♕d5 ♕g4+ 31 ♔h7 ♖b8 32 ♔g8 ♕h5 33 ♘×d7 and wins; (b) 26 . . . ♖e8 27 ♔g6! (if 27 ♗×e8 ♔×e8 28 ♔g6 Black slips out with 28 . . . ♕c6) and then (i) 27 . . . ♕b1+ 28 ♔×g7 and wins; (ii) 27 . . . ♖b8 28 ♗×e8 ♔×e8 29 ♔×g7 and wins; (iii) 27 . . . ♕b8 28 ♘e6+ ♖×e6 29 ♕f8+ ♔c7 30 ♗×e6 and wins; (iv) 27 . . . ♖e7 28 ♘e6+ ♖×e6 29 ♗×e6 and Black has no adequate defence to the main threat of ♖c2, followed by ♕f8+; (v) 27 . . . ♕b6 28 ♕d5 ♖e7 29 ♘e6+ ♖×e6 30 ♗×e6 and Black cannot stop the chief threat of ♗×d7 without losing his rook (if 30 . . . ♕b7 31 ♕×b7 ♗×b7 32 ♖×d7+ ♔c8 33 ♖×g7+ etc. liquidates right down to a winning pawn ending).

After that the analysis of 24 . . . h5 25 ♖d2 seems a lot simpler: (a) 25 . . . ♕c1 26 ♘×c5 ♕b1+ 27 ♖d3 and wins; (b) 25 . . . ♕a4 26 ♗d5 ♕×b5 27 ♗×a8 and the piece is worth far more than four feeble pawns; (c) 25 . . . ♕b1 26 ♗d5 ♕g1 27 ♘×c5 (rather than the awkward 27 ♗×a8 ♕×g2) and wins.

For all his inspired wriggling Black is really up against enormous odds in these variations; with only his queen developed he is powerless to stop the attack if it is correctly played. But he does seem to have one saving move; after 22 . . . ♖b8! the services of one or two extra pieces make all the difference. First of all it puts a stop to the king's activities: 23 ♔g6 ♖b6 24 ♕×c5 ♗b7! (not 24 . . . ♔d8 25 ♘d6, nor 24 . . . f5+ 25 ♘d6+) 25 ♗c4 (or 25 ♘d6+ ♖×d6 26 ♖×d6 ♕f7+ etc.) ♕c2 and White is struggling badly.

Secondly, White get nowhere by taking the rook: 23 ♕×b8 ♕×d5; then 24 ♕×c8+ ♔f7 leads to trouble because the pieces are highly vulnerable: 25 ♕×h8 ♕e6 mate, or 25 ♘g5+ h×g5 26 ♕×h8 g6+ 27 ♔g4 ♕×g2 mate, or 25 ♗h5+ g6+ 26 ♗×g6+ ♔g7 27 ♕a6 ♕e6+, winning material. Therefore he would have to continue 24 ♘d6+ ♔e7 25 ♘×c8+ ♖×c8 26 ♕×c8; but this is the kind of endgame where three connected pawns are superior to the minor piece: unless the bishop can assist the queen in a direct attack he is likely to be something of a lost soul – that is in addition to the now awkward placing of the white king. Black can take an easy draw here by 26 . . . g6+ 27 ♔×g6 ♕e4+, or he can try for more with the surprising continuation 26 . . . ♔f7 27 ♗h5+ (otherwise he cannot fend off the threats of 27 . . . g6+, leading to mate, and 27 . . . ♕e6+ 28 ♔e4 d5+) g6+ 28 ♗×g6+ ♔g7 and the bishop must be abandoned at once, to meet the threat of 29 . . . ♕e6+. Since the g-pawn is being troublesome in this variation, White might attempt 23 ♘×f6+ g×f6 24 ♕×b8; but instead of taking the rook Black simply castles (none too soon, you may think!) and after 24 . . . 0–0 25 ♖×c5 ♕e6+ he has a winning position.

So far White has not done very well after 22 . . . ♖b8, but he has two more possibilites. He can either take perpetual check by 23 ♘×f6+ g×f6 24 ♗h5+ ♔d8 25 ♕×f6+ ♔c7 26 ♕d6+ (not 26 ♖×c5+? ♔b7 27 ♗f3+ e4! 28 ♗×e4+ d5+, and certainly not 26 ♕e5+?? d6+) ♔d8 etc. (26 . . . ♔b7 27 ♗f3 being too dangerous), or he can play 23 ♗h5+. As far as we can tell this represents the best winning attempt. The continuation would be 23 . . . ♔d8 24 ♘×c5 ♕c2+ 25 ♔g4 ♖e8! (the only defence; further checks don't help, since there is no perpetual, and 25 . . . g6 26 ♕×f6+ ♔c7 27 ♕×e5+ loses at once) 26 ♗×e8 (nothing better; 26 ♘e6+ leads nowhere and 26 ♘×d7? ♖b6 would be disastrous) ♔×e8 27 ♕×b8 (27 ♘×d7? ♕g6+ picks up the knight in two moves) ♕c4+ 28 ♔h3 (28 ♔f5? ♔f7 leads to mate, 28 ♔h5 ♔f7 is also too dangerous, and 28 ♔g3 ♕f4+ 29 ♔h3 ♕f5+ is perpetual: 30 g4? ♕f3+ 31 ♔h4 g5+ 32 ♔h5 ♔f7!) ♕×d5 29 ♕×c8+ ♔e7; and here White's complete lack of co-ordination and centralisation, together with the black queen's checking power, argue against his making much progress. If, for example, 30 ♕c7 e4! threatens a perpetual check which cannot be prevented by 31 g3 (or if 31 g4 h5). The best he can do is 30 f3, preparing a possible ♘e4 and cutting out the check at d3, so that ♘b7 with a direct attack may be contemplated. But then Black makes full use of his pawn majority: 30 . . . f5 31 ♘b7! (The b-pawn is safe because 31 . . . ♕×b5? 32 ♕d8+ ♔e6 33 ♕g8+ ♔f6 34 ♘d6, followed by ♕f7+ would yield a winning attack. The other point of the move is to exchange queens, White's last hope of winning. If 31 ♕c7 g5 32 ♕×a7 ♕d4! and again the black queen is much too strong: 33 g3 ♕d1 and White has to allow perpetual by 34 ♔g2 etc.; 33 ♕×d7+ will not work here because White's king is too far away) g5! 32 ♕c5+ ♕×c5 34 ♘×c5 34 ♘×c5 d5.

Beginning way back with 18 . . . ♘d5, then, this ending seems to be the result of best play on both sides! It is hard to assess because Black has all the positional trumps: strong pawns, control of the centre, weak b-pawn, white king misplaced. Probably it amounts to a slight overall advantage to White.

18 . . . f5+
19 ♔×f5 ♕f7+
20 ♔×e5 . . .

There are bound to be a few pitfalls with the king out in the open, 20 ♔g4? h5+, for instance, and Black wins. But on e5 the king is safe enough and White's position is a picture of centralisation.

20 . . . ♘c2

Having covered the mate at e7 with gain of time, Black can now save his knight; on c2 it will deny the king a safe retreat to d4 and prevent the white rook from occupying e1. Of course, 20 . . . ♕h5+ 21 ♔d4 ♕d1+ 22 ♔c4, or here 21 . . . ♘c2+ 22 ♔c3, would defeat the object of his last move.

21 ♗c4 . . .

Forcing Black to waste more time maintaining control of e7.

21 . . . ♕h5+
22 ♔f4 ♕h4+

If 22 . . . g5+ 23 ♔f5 g4+ 24 ♔f4 wins immediately.

23 ♔f3 b6 *(48)*

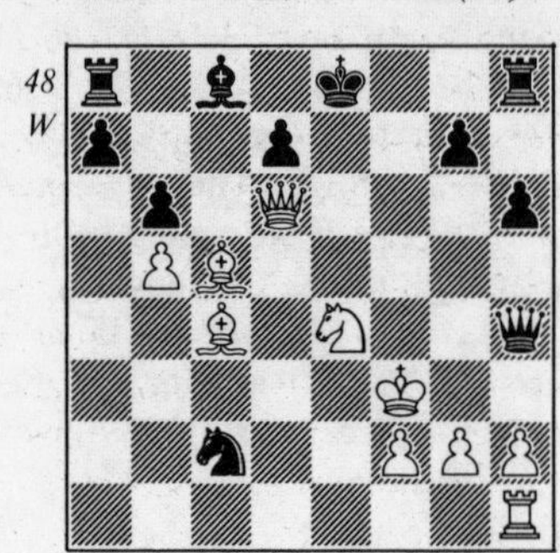

If 23 . . . ♕h5+ 24 ♔g3 ♔d8 25 ♕e7+ ♔c7 26 b6+ a×b6 27 ♕d6+ ♔d8 28 ♕×b6+ ♔e8 29 ♘d6+ and mate in two more moves; or if 23 . . . ♔d8 24 b6!, and the threat of ♕c7+ and ♘d6+ is equally catastrophic. Therefore Black creates threats of his own (. . . ♗b7 as well as . . . b×c5) and even now White can go badly astray. Nunn's original intention was 24 ♕e5+ ♔d8 25 g3, but this has two refutations(!): 25 . . . ♖e8! 26 ♕×e8+ ♔×e8 27 g×h4 b×c5 28 ♘×c5, and 25 . . . ♕g4+! 26 ♔×g4 d6+, both of which are unclear.

On further inspection he finds the winning combination.

24 ♕g6+ ♔d8
25 g3 ♕h3
26 ♗e7+! ♔×e7
27 ♕×g7+ ♔d8
28 ♕×h8+ ♔c7
29 ♕e5+ ♔d8
30 ♘d6 1 – 0

Game 12

King's Indian Defence
Johannesburg 1981

V. Korchnoi v. J. Nunn

1	**c4**	**♘f6**
2	**♘c3**	**g6**
3	**e4**	**d6**
4	**d4**	**♗g7**
5	**♗e2**	**0–0**
6	**♘f3**	**♘bd7**
7	**0–0**	**. . .**

White has the option of a sharper variation here, namely 7 e5 d×e5 8 d×e5 ♘g4 9 e6 f×e6; but after, for example, 10 0–0 ♘de5 11 ♗g5 ♘×f3+ 12 ♗×f3 ♘e5 13 ♗e2 ♘c6, followed by . . . ♘d4, he has no more than equality.

7	**. . .**	**e5**
8	**♕c2**	**a5(?)**

For a fuller appreciation of the opening you may like to compare the notes on Ftačnik–Nunn (Game 20). At the time of the present game Nunn had only just taken up the King's Indian and was not sufficiently familiar with this unusual variation; in the later game against Ftačnik he played the more accurate line 8 . . . c6 9 ♖d1 e×d4 10 ♘×d4 ♕e7. The move . . . a5 could amount to a tempo loss, since Black may well be able to manage without it; besides that the weakening of b5 and b6 may later prove a handicap.

9	**♖d1**	**. . .**

Threatening the e-pawn; Black must therefore either play 9 . . . ♕e7 or exchange pawns. But after 9 . . . ♕e7 White can gain some advantage, for once, by 10 d×e5. Usually that exchange is not to be recommended against the King's Indian because the weakness at d4 is laid bare, while Black's equivalent square d5 can still be covered by . . . c6. Here, though, White has one or two tactical points in his favour, thanks to the placing of his queen and rook. He can throw in a quick ♘d5 and Black's weakness at c7 is revealed, thus: 10 d×e5 ♘×e5 (or 10 . . . d×e5 11 ♘d5 ♘×d5 12 c×d5 and the c-pawn is weaker still – 12 . . . ♘f6 13 ♗e3, for instance, with ♖ac1 to follow; 11 . . . ♕d8 12 ♗e3 here would be terribly passive) 11 ♘×e5 d×e5 (11 . . . ♕×e5 merely exposes the queen to a later f4 or ♗d4 without giving her any significant activity) 12 ♘d5 (12 ♗g5 c6 13 ♘a4 ♗e6 14 ♗e3 ♘d7 would be less effective) ♘×d5 13 c×d5 f5 14 ♗e3 b6 15 f3 and the c-pawn is an embarrassment.

9	**. . .**	**e×d4**
10	**♘×d4**	**♖e8?** *(49)*

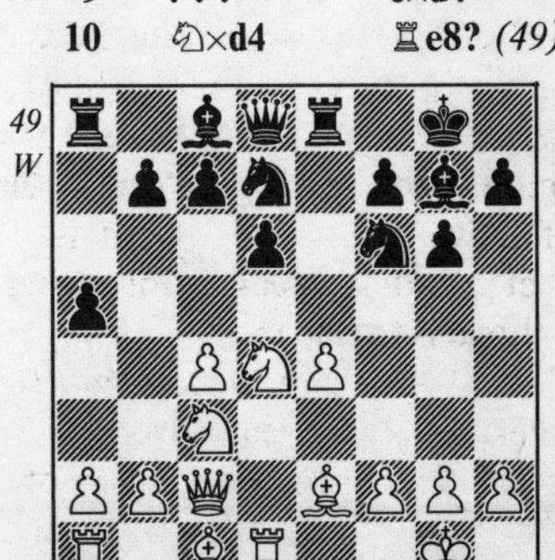
49
W

This is a serious mistake, as Korchnoi's reply demonstrates. The point is that Black must somehow shake the grip of the pawns at c4 and e4; failing that, White's control of the centre will become more and more stifling as he completes his development and consolidates the position. And Black can only tackle these pawns either by exchanging them off or by working round them, so to speak, by means of black-square counterplay. In some King's Indian lines this second plan would be put into effect by such moves as . . . c6, . . . ♕b6, . . . ♘c5 (or . . . ♘e5), . . . ♕b4 etc. Here e7 happens to be a more appropriate square for the queen (because White will play ♗e3), but either way 10 . . . c6 must come first; if then 11 ♗e3 ♕e7 (but not 11 . . . ♘c5? 12 ♘×c6, nor 11 . . . ♘e5 12 h3, threatening c5 or f4) and we would have a position similar to Game 20.

11 ♘db5! . . .

This is what Nunn overlooked. He cannot shake off the knight, and, with . . . c6 now unplayable, his queen is badly restricted. With that hope gone he concentrates on liberating his position in the only other way: by making the break . . . f5. The drawback to that plan is that he may be obliged to recapture at f5 with a pawn, weakening his formation without obtaining sufficient piece play in return.

11 . . . ♘c5

12 ♗g5 . . .

For all Black's positional difficulties he is not without tactical resources, especially on the K-side, which White has left a little exposed by massing most of his forces on the other flank. If White plays the obvious move 12 f3, here are two examples of what could happen: (a) . . . ♘h5 13 g4? ♗e5 14 g×h5 ♗×h2+ with at least a draw (15 ♔h1 ♕h4 16 ♗f1 ♗g3+ 17 ♔g1 ♖e5 18 ♕g2 ♖×h5); (b) 12 . . . ♘h5 13 ♗e3 ♗e5, and if 14 ♗×c5 ♕h4 with a dangerous attack if White does not return the piece at once, e.g. 15 ♗e3 ♗×h2+ 16 ♔f1 ♘g3+, or 15 ♗f2 ♕×h2+ 16 ♔f1 ♘f4 and the g-pawn goes (17 g3 ♕h1+ 18 ♗g1 ♕g2+). Nevertheless, 12 f3 is still the best move; our analysis is short-circuited by the fact that White can answer 12 . . . ♘h5 by 13 ♗e3 ♗e5 14 g3!, stopping the attack and threatening both 15 f4 and 15 ♗×c5. Black would thus be driven back with loss of time.

12 ♗g5 sets a cunning trap – easily overlooked – but in the end it amounts to a tempo loss because White has to retire his bishop to e3 and still play f3.

12 . . . ♗d7

The trap lies in the variation 12 . . . h6? 13 ♗×f6 ♗×f6 14 ♘d5 ♘e6 15 ♘d×c7! ♘×c7 16 ♖×d6 ♕e7 (if 16 . . . ♗d7 still 17 ♘×c7) 17 ♘×c7 and White wins material; but now 13 . . . h6 would force White to exchange unprofitably at f6 or lose his e-pawn: hence the following move.

13 f3 ♘e6

The other way of breaking the pin would be less satisfactory: 13 . . . h6 14 ♗e3 ♘h5 15 f4, for instance, and 15 . . . f5 can be answered by 16 e5. In any case . . . f5 is going to make quite enough holes in Black's K-side without increasing the damage by more pawn moves. Having the c-pawn and the square f4 covered by the knight may also prove useful. The one drawback to . . . ♘e6 is that the bishop's path to f5 is obstructed.

14 ♗e3 . . .

Permitting the black knight to settle on f4 would be unwise; certainly progress would be difficult thereafter: 14 ♗h4 g5 15 ♗f2 ♘f4 and the outpost is secure, at least for the time being. If 15 ♗g3, still 15 . . . ♘f4 and White would lose more than he gained by exchanging; his black squares would be weak, his bishop bad, and Black could easily defend the front f-pawn and subsequently make use of the g-file.

14 . . . ♘h5

15 ♗f1 . . .

Anticipating a later . . . ♘f4. Now although it looks hazardous, Black has to take the plunge with his . . . f5; the longer he delays, the more White will build up and strengthen his position along the lines of ♕f2, ♖d2 and ♖ad1, then eventually a pawn break of his own – c5 maybe, or f4–f5. Nor can Black achieve anything by piece play alone: 15 . . . ♘hf4 and 15 . . . ♗e5 are both answered by 16 g3, and 15 . . . ♘ef4 by 16 g4. And 15 . . . ♖f8 is useless because recapturing with the rook at f5 would cost a piece.

15 . . . f5

16 e×f5 g×f5

17 ♗f2 . . .

The tactical justification for 15 . . . f5 is simple enough: if 17 ♕×f5? ♘ef4 and wins. And positionally there is a bright side to the pawn recapture in that the opposing pieces are denied the use of e4. But Black has had to delve a little deeper than that to keep the game under control, for after this last move he must be ready to make a sacrifice. The following note explains this point.

17 . . . ♖f8

First of all this is forced because the f-pawn is now genuinely *en prise*, and neither 17 . . . f4 18 ♗d3 nor 17 . . . ♕g5 18 c5 can be seriously considered. In the first case Black would be reduced to a terribly passive move like 18 . . . ♘f8 or be overrun by 18 . . . ♘f6 19 ♗h4 h6 20 ♗g6; and in the second case the only reasonable try 18 . . . ♗×b5 19 ♘×b5 d×c5 would be met by 20 ♗c4!

Secondly, White could now play 18 c5, more or less compelling Black to surrender the queen, but he would be ill-advised to do so: 18 . . . ♘×c5 (not 18 . . . d×c5? 19 ♗c4 ♕c8 20 ♘d5 and wins, nor 18 . . . ♗×b5 19 ♘×b5 d5 20 c6 b6 21 ♗c4) 19 ♗×c5 d×c5 20 ♗c4+ ♔h8 21 ♗e6 ♗×e6 (much better than 21 . . . ♘f6 22 ♕×f5 ♗×e6 23 ♕×e6 ♕c8 24 ♕e5 c6 25 ♘d6 etc.) 22 ♖×d8 ♖a×d8, and in return for a small material investment Black has conspicuously increased his control of the centre and has excellent play for all his pieces. In fact Grandmasters would almost regard such a sacrifice as routine, though in this case, of course, Nunn has had to anticipate it when contemplating 15 . . . f5. One likely continuation of this variation leads to a lightning attack which White can only just beat off: 23 ♘×c7 ♗d4+ 24 ♔h1 ♘g3+ 25 h×g3 ♖f6 26 ♕c1 f4 27 ♕×f4 ♖×f4 28 g×f4 ♗c4 and Black's aggressive bishops at least compensate for the pawn. Quieter play also favours Black; for example 23 ♖e1 ♗c4, with a similar attack looming, or 23 ♘e2 c6 24 ♘bc3 b5 etc.

In a way that is typical King's Indian play. Black's pieces seem to be lying in wait, ready to burst into life at the first opportunity. White for his part does much better not to look for any quick gain of material; his plan is rather to eliminate any counterplay and gradually exchange Black's best minor pieces – the pawn weaknesses will tend to show up more prominently in a major piece ending.

18 g3 . . .

Keeping the knights out and preparing ♗g2 and f4 when appropriate. Now any further aggression by 18 . . . f4 would react against Black after 19 g4 ♘f6 20 h4, with ♗d3 to follow. Here the pawns would restrict his knights severely, yet would not be in any way vulnerable themselves. Since the knight is no longer doing much work at h5, Nunn now recentralises it, at the same time setting a trap of his own . . .

18 . . . ♘f6

19 ♕×f5? *(50)* **. . .**

50
B

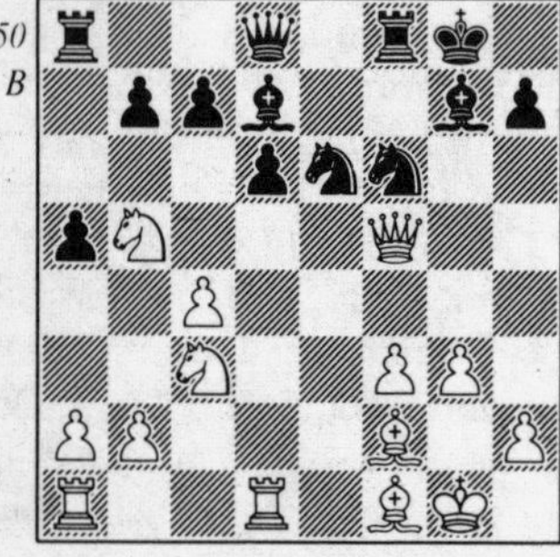

. . . into which White falls. Obviously one has to be wary about putting the queen on such an exposed square, but it is very much in Korchnoi's style to grab material if, as here, he can see no concrete reason for not doing so. In fact he has mistakenly assumed that Black is sacrificing the pawn for general reasons, i.e. to obtain better piece play. Much sounder would be 19 ♘d4, which maintains a clear advantage without any risk. After the exchange of knights he could occupy the ideal blockade square by ♘e2–f4, then play ♗d4 and ♗d3, bringing tremendous pressure to bear against Black's fragile K-side. Nor could Black oppose this plan to seize f4: 19 . . . ♘×d4 20 ♗×d4 ♘h5 would play into White's hands by allowing his best minor piece to disappear, while 20 . . . ♗h6 and then . . . ♗×♘at f4 would leave him desperately weak on the long black diagonal and the g-file.

19 . . . ♘g4!

A most surprising combination! For all Korchnoi's vast experience it seems that this move never crossed his mind. If the white queen now takes the knight, she suddenly runs alarmingly short of squares; if she doesn't take, Black gets an extremely dangerous initiative, thus: (a) 20 ♕c2 ♖×f3,then . . . ♕f6 and . . . ♖f8; (b) 20 ♕d3 ♘e5; (c) 20 ♕e4 ♘g5; (d) 20 ♕d5 ♘×f2 21 ♔×f2 c6 22 ♕×d6 ♖f7 23 ♗h3 (or 23 ♘a3 ♕b6+ and . . . ♕×b2) ♕f6 24 ♗×e6 ♕×f3+ 25 ♔g1 ♕e3+ 26 ♔h1 ♗×e6 27 ♘d4 ♗g4 and wins; (e) 20 ♕h5 ♘g5! and if now 21 f×g4 ♗e8 traps the queen in circumstances much more favourable than the game continuation because the f-file is open: 22 ♕×g5 ♕×g5 23 ♘×c7 ♖×f2! 24 ♘×a8 (24 ♔×f2 ♕c5+) ♖×b2 and wins; if, on the other hand, 21 f4, then 21 . . . ♘f3+ 22 ♔g2 ♘fe5! (not 22 . . . ♘f×h2? 23 ♗d3) threatens both 23 . . . ♖f5 and 23 . . . ♘×f2 with . . . ♗g4 and yields a strong attack. Notice that (20 ♕h5) ♖×f3 is not so good because the rook temporarily blocks the knight's forking square; for example 21 ♕×g4 ♘g5 22 ♕h5 (or ♕h4 at once, but he wishes to inconvenience Black as much as possible) ♗e8 23 ♕g4 h5 24 ♕h4 ♖×c3 25 ♗g2 and the position is unclear.

Much the best chance is to take the knight and then surrender the queen. 19 ♕×f5 has thrown away White's advantage, but no more than that; he still has approximate equality.

20	**♕×g4!**	**♘g5**
21	**♕h5**	**♗e8**
22	**♕×g5**	**. . .**

Strictly speaking not the most accurate, though the reason is very hard to foresee at this stage. It happens that . . . ♗h5+ will be a useful move for Black as his attack develops; therefore 22 ♕g4 is better, when Black either has to repeat moves by 22 . . . ♗d7 etc. (there is no way White can avoid the repetition) or block the square by 22 . . . h5, in order to win the queen. If he chooses the latter, he will be obliged to adopt a quieter continuation at move 23 instead of the sacrificial attack.

22	**. . .**	**♕×g5**
23	**♘×c7** *(51)*	**. . .**

51
B

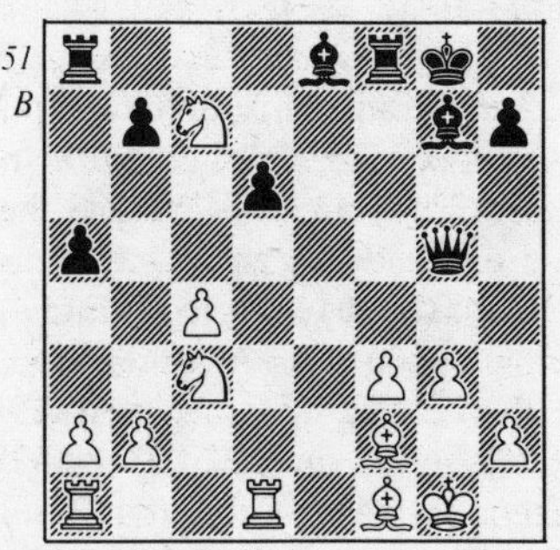

The guaranteed win of another exchange (by ♘×a8 or ♘e6) might justify White in claiming a slight material advantage. But that does not tell the full story. When the forces are unbalanced, as here, both sides are eager to create the kind of position which will suit their set of pieces best. That applies especially in the case of queen vs. odds and ends. The queen likes an open game with the material scattered far and wide, in which her mobility and forking power may be exercised to the full. The odds and ends prefer every thing to be anchored down, securely protected from the queen's roving eye. Once their position is consolidated they can begin to take the initiative, combining against some weak pawn, for instance; and in the process they may well find that they are gaining many tempi harassing the queen.

Of course, control of the centre is as crucial a factor as ever; therefore White's plan, after taking the exchange, will be to consolidate by ♗g2 and f4 and to occupy d5 as soon as possible. This is the key square. In the following analysis of Black's two most likely moves watch how White is fighting to get a firm grip on it, especially with his knights, and how Black is forever trying to oppose that and at the same time to stir things up for his queen:

(1) 23 . . . ♗c6(?) (obvious, but rather feeble) 24 ♘×a8 ♖×a8 25 ♗g2 ♖f8 26 ♘d5! ♗×b2 27 ♖ab1 ♗g7 28 f4 ♕d8 (must cover e7) 29 c5! and White has a wonderful set of pieces; if 29 . . . ♔h8, for example, he might continue 30 ♘b6 ♖f6 31 ♗d4 ♖g6 32 ♗×g7+ ♔×g7 33 ♘c4 d5 34 ♘e5.

(2) 23 . . . ♕f5 24 ♘×a8 (24 f4, declining the win of the exchange, is one ambitious possibility; White is hoping here that his hold on the centre will offset the material deficit. And indeed after 24 . . . ♖ac8 25 ♘7d5 that might well be so; but Black

has 24 . . . ♗×c3! 25 b×c3 ♗c6 26 ♘d5 (26 ♘×a8? ♕e4) ♗×d5, and with both knights eliminated, the c-pawns weak and the queen free to roam around White cannot have sufficient compensation) ♕×f3 25 ♖d2 ♗c6 (if 25 . . . ♗×c3, hoping to follow with . . . ♗c6, White has 26 ♗g2! before recapturing; 26 . . . ♕×g2+ 27 ♔×g2 ♗×d2 28 ♘b6 would not then be enough for a pawn) 26 ♘d5 ♗×d5! (everything is done to neutralise d5: 26 . . . ♖×a8 27 ♗g2 ♕f7 28 ♖f1 would be dangerous for Black) 27 c×d5 ♖×a8 28 ♗g2 ♕f7 29 ♖e1, followed by ♖e6, and although Black now has a slight material advantage, White's pieces are working well and there are no suitable targets for the queen. Most likely the result would be a fortress draw.

Some analysis along these lines has convinced Nunn that he cannot win by normal means; that somehow the position needs to be 'thinned out' for his queen to make any progress. And that leads him to the interesting idea which follows.

23 . . . ♖×f3!

Certainly the best practical chance of winning. The material cost is high, but White's king will be exposed, he will be vulnerable on the black squares (after the further . . . ♖×f2) and the queen will get the sort of position in which she excels above all – attacking in co-operation with one or two smaller pieces.

24 ♘×a8 . . .

Another try is 24 ♘e4, but that only encourages the queen: 24 . . . ♕e7 25 ♘×a8 ♕×e4 (threatening 26 . . . ♖×f2 27 ♔×f2 ♗d4+) 26 ♖e1 (if 26 ♗g2 ♗c6 contains a drop of poison: 27 ♘c7? ♖×g3! and wins; or if 27 ♖e1 ♕f5 with advantage) ♕g6 27 ♘c7 (again, if 27 ♗g2 ♗c6 and taking the rook would be too dangerous; or if 28 ♘c7 ♖×f2 29 ♔×f2 ♕f7+) ♗c6 28 ♘d5 ♗×d5 29 c×d5 ♕f5, and this time there is no chance of a fortress draw: Black's rook is much more lively and he stands to win at least a pawn immediately.

24 . . . ♖×f2

25 ♔×f2 ♕c5+ *(52)*

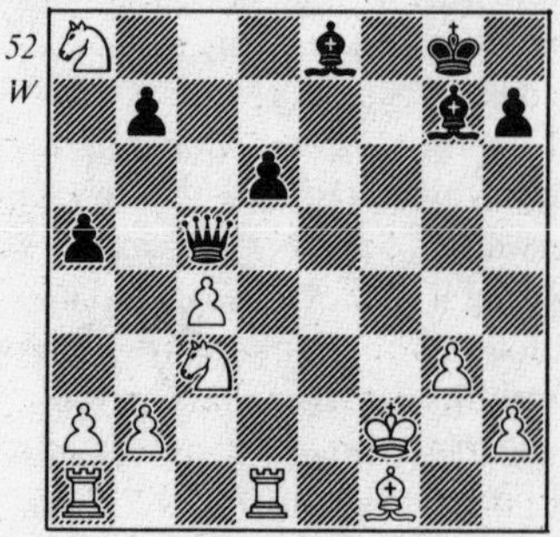

52
W

And here White faces a real crisis, for the wrong choice of square will cost him the game. First of all, 26 ♔e1 and 26 ♔e2 can be refuted without much trouble: (a) 26 ♔e1? ♗×c3+ 27 b×c3 ♕e3+ 28 ♗e2 ♗h5 29 ♖d2 ♗×e2 30 ♖×e2 ♕g1+ and wins; or (b) 26 ♔e2? ♗×c3 27 b×c3 ♗h5+ 28 ♔d3 (no choice; if 28 ♔d2 ♕f2+ 29 ♔d3 ♗g6 mate, or if here 29 ♔c1 ♗×d1 etc.) ♕f5+ (making use of a recurring pattern is a valuable aid to analysing quickly; he already knows that d2 is off limits to the king) 29 ♔e3 (29 ♔d4 ♕f2+ is one move shorter) ♕f3+ 30 ♔d4 ♕f2+ 31 ♔e4 (31 ♔d5 ♗×d1 32 ♖×d1 ♕f3+) ♗g6+ 32 ♔d5 ♕c5+ 33 ♔e6 ♗f5+ 34 ♔e7 (or 34 ♔f6 ♕e5+ 35 ♔g5 ♗g6+ and mate in two) ♕e5+ 35 ♔d8 d5! and mate in two more moves, either by . . . ♕b8+ or by . . . ♕d6+.

All this Nunn worked out when playing 23 . . . ♖×f3, but now things get a little more complicated. Of the other two squares, neither player took 26 ♔f3 very seriously, yet oddly enough it is the one which holds the draw. At g2, on the other hand, the king gets trapped on the diagonals because he dare not venture out to h3. The reason why f3 is correct is that the king can retreat either towards the Q-side or to g2 and h1, depending on where the black bishop decides to check (h5 or c6). At least that is the pattern which emerges when you examine the position afterwards. To avoid any misunderstanding it must be stressed that you cannot possibly solve the problem according to such general principles during play; only concrete analysis will provide the answer.

Now in reply to 26 ♔f3 Black would have to choose between 26 . . . ♗h5+ and 26 . . . ♕f5+ (if 26 . . . ♗c6+ 27 ♘d5, and 26 . . . ♗×c3 would not do because the king slips safely away after 27 b×c3 ♗c6+ 28 ♔e2):

26 . . . ♗h5+ (this alone may have deterred Korchnoi from making the correct move; he has to realise not only that 27 ♔g2 will not suffice, but also that 27 g4, allowing . . . ♕f5+, is good for White!) If now 27 ♔g2 ♕e3! threatens 28 . . . ♗f3+ 29 ♔h3 ♕h6 mate, and we have: (a) 28 ♔h3 ♗f3 and wins; (b) 28 h3 ♗f3+ and wins; (c) 28 h4 ♗f3+ 29 ♔h2 ♕f2+ 30 ♔h3 ♕g1 31 ♖d2 h5 and wins; (d) 28 ♗e2 (the only hope) ♗×e2 29 ♘×e2 ♕×e2+ 30 ♔h3 ♗×b2 (Black would like to trap the knight, but his queen cannot get to d8 with tempo gain, i.e. by checking) 31 ♖ab1 ♗e5, and Black can claim some advantage: the knight is temporarily out of play, the white king is exposed (a major handicap when playing against the queen) and if White loses his a-pawn the black passed pawn will be a real menace.

But 27 g4! is much better. After 27 . . . ♕f5+ 28 ♔g2 Black's Q-bishop is pointing in the wrong direction and 28 . . . ♕×g4+ 29 ♔h1 ♕f4, with the idea of . . . ♗e5, is well met by 30 ♘d5; or if here 29 . . . ♗e5 30 ♗e2! (but not 30 ♘d5? ♕h4 31 ♖d2 ♗f3+ 32 ♔g1 ♗d4+) ♕f4 31 ♖g1+ ♔h8 32 ♖g2, halting the attack.

Black does better with 28 . . . ♗×g4, but after 29 ♖d3 ♗d4 30 ♖×d4 ♕f3+ 31 ♔g1 ♕e3+ 32 ♔h1 ♗f3+ 33 ♗g2 ♗×g2+ 34 ♔×g2 ♕×d4 35 ♖g1, although his queen is still active, he is really the one who is fighting to draw.

If we now analyse the stronger move 26 . . . ♕f5+, we can soon eliminate two possible replies: (a) 27 ♔g2? ♗c6+ 28 ♘d5 ♕e4+ 29 ♔g1 (29 ♔f2 ♗d4+ is much the same) ♗d4+ 30 ♖×d4 ♕×d4+ 31 ♔h1 ♗×d5+ 32 c×d5 ♕×b2 33 ♖d1 ♕×a2, with winning chances because the white pieces are badly out of position and will have great difficulty co-ordinating their efforts to stop the a-pawn. Apart from anything else there is a grave danger of forks (34 ♘b6 ♕b3, for example); (b) 27 ♔e3? ♗h6+ 28 ♔e2 ♗h5+ 29 ♔e1 ♗×d1 30 ♘×d1 (if 30 ♖×d1 ♗e3 wins) ♕g5! 31 ♗e2 ♕d8 and Black should win, having a slight material advantage and good play on the black squares – 32 ♘c3 ♕×a8 33 ♘d5 ♕a7, for instance.

However, this last variation is something of a fluke; it only works because Black has gained a tempo by . . . ♗h6+. Much better is 27 ♔e2, and then, although the king cannot readily escape the cross-fire in the centre, he has plenty of pieces with which to cover up, and can even sacrifice a bit back, if need be. In this line it is suddenly Black who is searching for a way to equalise!

The two obvious checks are ineffective: (a) 27 . . . ♕c2+ 28 ♖d2 ♗h5+ 29 ♔e1 ♗×c3 30 b×c3 ♕×c3 (there is a trap here: 30 . . . ♕e4+ and if 31 ♔f2? ♕f3+ 32 ♔g1 ♕×c3 33 ♖ad1 ♕e3+ 34 ♔h1 ♗×d1 35 ♖×d1 ♕f3+ and wins; unfortunately 31 ♖e2! ♗×e2 32 ♗×e2 gives White the advantage, since the queen can neither trap the knight nor give perpetual check) 31 ♖d1 (or 31 ♖b1, but after 31 . . . ♕e3+ White will sacrifice the exchange anyway) ♗×d1 (31 . . . ♕e3+ is similar to the last note) 32 ♔×d1 with advantage; (b) 27 . . . ♗h5+ 28 ♔e1 ♗×c3+ (if 28 . . . ♕f3 29 ♖d3) 29 b×c3 ♕e5+ (Black will soon run out of checks; his only hope is to pick up the knight as well as the exchange) 30 ♔d2 ♕g5+ 31 ♔c2 ♗×d1+ 32 ♖×d1 ♕d8 33 c5 ♕×a8 34 c×d6 and White should win.

It begins to look bad for Black. Even if he tries to prepare . . . ♗h5+ by 27 . . . ♗h6, the answer is 28 ♖d3 ♗h5+ 29 ♔e1 ♕e5+ 30 ♗e2, and he makes no progress; he has also lost the option of the useful move . . . ♗×c3. Yet there is a way out. The best move, believe it or not, is the obscure but remarkably effective 27 . . . a4! pinpointing two of White's weak spots. The double threat is to trap the advanced knight by . . . ♕a5 and to undermine its colleague by . . . a3. We then have: (a) 28 ♖ac1 (or 28 a3) ♗h5+ 29 ♔e1 ♗×c3+ 30 b×c3 ♗×d1 31 ♖×d1 ♕a5, with a likely draw; (b) 28 ♖d3 a3 29 b×a3 (not 29 ♘c7? a×b2 30 ♖ any ♗×c3) ♗h5+ 30 ♔e1 (30 ♔d2 ♕f2+) ♕a5 31 ♔d2 ♕×a8, and the powerful bishop at g7 provides plenty of attacking chances to compensate for the pawn deficit; (c) 28 ♔d2 a3 29 b×a3 ♕a5 30 ♖ac1 ♕×a8, as in (b); (d) 28 ♘b6 a3 29 ♘bd5 ♕c2+ 30 ♖d2 ♗h5+ 31 ♔e1 a×b2! and wins; (e) 28 ♘c7 ♗h5+ 29 ♔e1 ♗×d1 30 ♖×d1 (30 ♘×d1 ♕a5+) a3 31 ♘7d5 ♕c2 (better than 31 . . . ♕e5+ 32 ♗e2 a×b2 33 ♖b1 ♕g5 34 ♔c1) 32 ♗d3 (not 32 ♖d2? ♕c1+ 33 ♖d1 a×b2) ♕×h2, and the most likely outcome is a draw; for example 33 b×a3 ♗h6 34 ♘e4 ♕h1+ 35 ♔e2 ♕h5+ with perpetual check.

We now return to the game (Diagram 52). Korchnoi has run short of time and makes a fatal mistake.

26 ♔g2? ♗×c3

White must have overlooked that the recapture costs him a rook as well as the exchange: 27 b×c3 ♗c6+ 28 ♖d5 ♗×d5+ 29 c×d5 ♕×c3 and 30 . . . ♕c2+. He still has a nominal material advantage, but his forces are hopelessly scattered and Black's attack persists. First of all the threat of 27 . . . ♗c6+ must be attended to. If 27 ♔h1 ♗c6+ 28 ♗g2 ♗×g2+ 29 ♔×g2 ♗e5 and there is no defence against 30 . . . ♕c6+ and . . . b6, winning the knight (if 30 ♖d5 ♕×c4 31 ♖ad1 – 31 ♖×a5? ♕b4 wins a rook – b5 32 ♘b6 ♕c6 33 ♘d7! ♗g7! 34 ♘b8 ♕b7 still traps it). White therefore takes his only other chance.

27 ♘c7 . . .

So that 27 . . . ♕×c7 can be met by 28 b×c3, or 27 . . . ♗c6+ by 28 ♘d5; but Black solves the problem by going to the other side of the blockading square d5. His threat of mate in two provides the necessary tempo to trap the rook at a1.

27 . . . ♗g6

28 ♘d5 . . .

If 28 ♗d3, there is a delightful variation: 28 . . . ♗×b2 29 ♖ab1 ♗×d3 30 ♖×d3 (30 ♖×b2 ♗e4+ and 31 . . . ♕×c7) ♕×c4 31 ♖dd1 (the rook at b1 must be defended against . . . ♕e4+ or . . . ♕c2+, and of course it must continue to threaten the bishop) ♕×a2, threatening 32 . . . ♗c1+, thus gaining another tempo, and the a-pawn wins comfortably. The rest is easy.

28 . . . ♗e4+

29 ♔h3 ♗×b2

30 ♖ab1 ♕f2!

Black's Q-bishop happens to be the more useful attacking piece at present; therefore, by threatening both 31 . . . ♗f5+ and 31 . . . ♗×b1 32 ♖×b1 ♕f5+, he forces White to surrender his rook for the other bishop. If 31 ♘f4 ♗f5+ 32 ♔h4 ♗f6+ wins.

31 ♖×b2 ♕×b2

32 ♘f4 ♗f5+

33 g4 ♕f2

0 – 1

Game 13

Sicilian Defence
Wijk aan Zee 1982

J. Nunn v. M. Tal

1	**e4**	**c5**
2	**♘f3**	**e6**
3	**d4**	**c×d4**
4	**♘×d4**	**♘c6**
5	**♘c3**	**a6**
6	**g3**	**. . .**

The fianchetto has the advantages of controlling d5, protecting the e-pawn so that the Q-knight may move, and in some circumstances threatening Black's rook. These points will become clear in a moment when we examine some variations.

6	**. . .**	**♕c7**
7	**♗g2**	**♘f6**
8	**0–0** *(53)*	

53
B

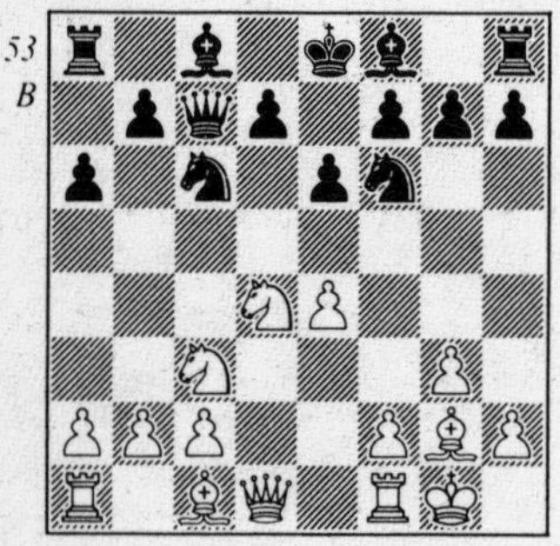

8	**. . .**	**h6**

Hereabouts the opening play is becoming subtle. In adopting the Paulsen System Black is willing to let his normal development lag slightly in the interests of quick counterplay on the Q-side. At the same time he retains the option of transposing into the more straightforward Scheveningen variation by . . . d6, . . . ♗e7 and . . . ♗d7. But at this early stage he may have no wish to transpose in that way, and in any case it could get dangerous: 8 ♗e7 9 ♖e1 d6 10 ♘×c6 b×c6 11 e5 d×e5 12 ♖×e5, for example, making full use of the long diagonal; or again 8 . . . d6 9 ♖e1 ♗d7 10 ♘×c6, and if 10 . . . ♗×c6 11 ♘d5!

So for the moment Black is looking for a different line of development, and the obvious way is 8 . . . ♘×d4 9 ♕×d4 ♗c5. Then comes 10 ♗f4! because White would welcome the endgame after 10 . . . ♗×d4 11 ♗×c7 ♗×c3 12 b×c3 d5 (or 12 . . . 0–0 13 e5) 13 e×d5 ♘×d5 14 ♗e5 f6 15 c4: here the power of the bishops will count for far more than the theoretical weakness of the c-pawns. Black would therefore play instead 10 . . . d6 (10 . . . ♕b6 11 ♕d2 ♕×b2 12 ♘a4 ♕a3 13 ♘×c5 ♕×c5 14 ♗d6 is not worth a second glance), but after 11 ♕d3 ♘d7 (to have . . . ♘e5 ready in reply to ♖ad1) 12 ♘a4 e5 13 ♗d2 b5 14 ♘×c5 ♘×c5 15 ♕a3 White still keeps a slight advantage.

Looking for improvements we find 8 . . . ♗e7 9 ♖e1 ♘×d4 10 ♕×d4 ♗c5, a more refined version of the line given above, the point being that 11 ♗f4 allows 11 . . . ♕b6 12 ♕d2 e5! 13 ♗×e5 ♗×f2+, equalising (or if 13

♘d5 ♘×d5 14 e×d5 d6). So White would prefer something like 11 ♕d1 (stops . . . ♘g4) d6 12 ♗e3 e5 13 ♕d2 ♗e6 14 ♖ad1, again with a slight pull.

This variation was played occasionally in the seventies, but never achieved any great popularity. And very recently another objection to it has arisen: after 9 . . . ♘×d4 White can even play 10 e5, leading to seemingly favourable complications. That had not been thought of when the present game was played, but Tal avoids the line anyway, which brings us back to the text move. In playing 8 . . . h6 he hopes for 9 ♖e1; then 9 . . . ♘×d4 10 ♕×d4 ♗c5 gains a tempo on the main line because his bishop has only moved once and because . . . h6 is a move which Black always needs to play sooner or later, principally to avert ♗g5. Now 9 ♘×c6 d×c6 10 ♗e3 e5 11 ♘a4 ♘d7 12 ♗h3 would guarantee a slight advantage, but Nunn prefers another move, avoiding the exchange altogether.

9 ♘b3 ♗e7

Wisely settling for development and a transposition into Scheveningen channels. To pursue the Q-side play would attract one of those lightning attacks to which Black is always susceptible in the modern Sicilian variations: 9 . . . b5? 10 a4 b4 11 ♘d5! e×d5 12 e×d5 ♘a7 (otherwise the coming d6 will hit him even harder; nor can he return the piece to cover up: 12 . . . ♗e7 13 d×c6 d×c6 14 ♘d4 ♗d7 15 ♖e1 leaves him hopelessly exposed) 13 d6 ♕b8 14 ♖e1+ ♔d8 15 ♗e3 (threatens 16 ♗×a8 and if 16 . . . ♕×a8 17 ♗b6 mate; if 15 . . . ♗b7 16 ♗b6+ ♔c8 17 ♗c7!) ♘c6 16 a5 ♗b7 (d-pawn cannot be captured) 17 ♗b6+ ♔c8 18 ♗c7 ♕a7. Black is now paralysed and there are many ways to win: 19 ♕e2 ♘d8 20 ♕c4 ♘c6 21 ♘d4, for instance.

10 a4 . . .

Still . . . b5 is not a threat, but White is keeping all his options open here: he plays the move which he knows will soon be necessary without committing himself in any other way. And a4 is necessary because his aim at this stage is to forestall the aggressive development of the black bishop at b7. Even 10 . . . b6 would now be met by the same attack – 11 ♘d5! etc., which explains Tal's next move.

10 . . . d6

11 f4 . . .

There are now two ways to stop . . . b6: 11 a5 and the text move. Nunn's choice makes it too risky on account of 12 e5, and at the same time he is attracted by the idea of a general pawn advance against Black's K-side, which has been slightly weakened by . . . h6. Specifically, 11 . . . b6 would be met by 12 e5 d×e5 (12 . . . ♘d7 13 e×d6 ♗×d6 14 f5 e5 15 ♘d5 is worse) 13 f×e5 ♘d7 14 ♕g4 g6 15 ♕f4, when Black is in trouble because he cannot capture the e-pawn.

The other way is 11 a5, which has also been tried in a master game, the intention being to attack the Q-side (11 . . . 0–0 12 ♗e3 etc.) and to expose . . . h6 as a time loss rather than a weakness. This may be slightly better than 11 f4, which leads to approximate equality with best play. After 11 a5 it would again be much too risky to play 11 . . . b6 because of 12 a×b6 ♕×b6 13 ♗e3, with the threat of e5 hanging over Black – 13 . . . ♕c7 14 ♘b5, for example.

11 . . . 0–0

11 . . . ♗d7 is also perfectly playable. White would then delay his pawn advance until the black king was committed, 12 ♗e3 0–0 13 g4 being the likely continuation.

12 g4 *(54)* . . .

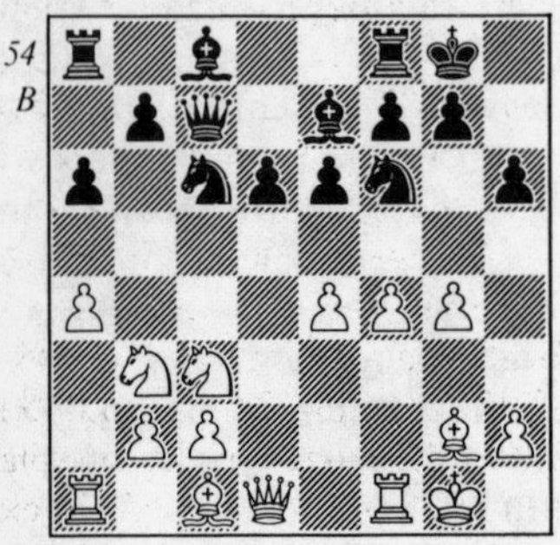

54
B

With this move the most instructive positional part of the game begins. Obviously control of the centre is important on all occasions, but here its effect is particularly striking. The advance 12 g4 must be seen as a **positional manoeuvre**, not the start of a mating attack. It may eventually result in an attack, but White cannot possibly generate any real threats against the king while his knights are far away and while only his queen can participate quickly. For the moment the intention is to gain space and drive the black knight from f6, thus augmenting White's control of the centre.

But we need a little more justification than that for 12 g4. Suppose Black tries to break open the centre – the standard response to the threat of a flank attack? In fact a closer look reveals that White is effectively restraining both . . . e5 and . . . d5 here (and even . . . b5, which might affect the centre by driving the knight from c3). We shall have more to say about this matter in a moment; but there is one final point: if the loss of tempo in playing 6 g3 and then 12 g4 seems hard to accept, remember that the fianchetto development (compared to the commoner ♗e2) has already gained time for White in the sense that . . . d5 has always been prevented. Therefore White does not now have to waste another move to achieve that aim.

So all these things justify 12 g4; but no more than that can be claimed. Black's game is still quite sound and it is only his ensuing mistake which leads him into such trouble.

12 . . . ♗d7?

Tal observes that 13 g5 would be a first-rate positional blunder, ruining everything for White, because 13 . . . h×g5 14 f×g5 ♘h7, followed by . . . ♘e5, would give Black a rock-solid position on the K-side (control of the centre square e5!); but he doesn't notice that g5 can be prepared by h4. He should at all cost have prevented any further expansion by playing 12 . . . ♘d7!, after which White would have nothing better than to continue with straightforward development: 13 ♗e3 b6 14 ♕e2 ♗b7, for example, with a double-edged middle-game and approximately equal chances.

13 h4! . . .

It seems that at least one of the watching Grandmasters was inclined to laugh at this! But Nunn knows exactly what he is doing: the further pawn advance is not only logical, but even strategically decisive, because from now on Black will be unable to obtain any decent play for his pieces. After g5, which cannot be averted, . . . h×g5 can now be met by h×g5, **without yielding the point e5**. In fact it would be most unwise for Black to exchange pawns: with the opening of the h-file his king really would be in trouble (♕h5, then ♖f3–h3, or ♔f2 and ♖h1). In a moment, then, Black will have a choice of knight retreats: to e8 where it will interfere with his rooks and leave his K-side exposed (13 . . . ♖fd8 14 g5 ♘e8 would expose it even more), or to h7, defending the K-side, but leaving the knight permanently marooned. Tal decides that . . . ♘h7 is the lesser evil.

13 . . . b5

Perhaps you are still worried because White's row of pawns looks unwieldy? How is he going to control events when the real fighting begins? What if Black sacrifices a pawn to break up the centre? That has happened frequently enough in such positions; in the resulting open game the white king could be seriously harassed down the diagonals.

Well, Nunn makes the interesting comment that he hardly calculated a single variation more than a couple of moves deep during the entire game. And here surely lies the secret. He does not need to analyse in great detail. In a moment Black will indeed make the pawn sacrifice . . . d5; and White, **with his pieces established in the centre**, will then maintain tactical control by working out a series of short variations. If he starts out with a firm grip on the centre, he never need permit the black pieces any dangerous activity. At move 13 he will have concentrated on Black's pawn breaks to make sure no mischief is possible, namely (a) 13 . . . e5? 14 f5 (or even g5 at once) followed by g5 and ♘d5, and Black is hopelessly weak and cramped; (b) 13 . . . d5 14 e×d5 ♘×d5 15 ♘×d5 e×d5 16 g5, winning a pawn safely. The actual choice, 13 . . . b5, is not a sacrifice (14 a×b5 a×b5 15 ♖×a8 ♖×a8 16 ♘×b5? ♕b6+ and 17 . . . e5 would be disastrous); so White just pushes the knight back and develops.

14 g5 ♘h7

15 ♗e3 . . .

And here is our proof that White cannot think in terms of an immediate attack: if he is tempted into 15 g×h6 g×h6 16 ♕h5, his lack of preparation will suddenly turn against him: 16 . . . ♔h8 17 ♕×h6 ♖g8 (threatening 18 . . . ♖g6 19 ♕h5 ♖ag8 with dangerous counterplay) and if 18 f5 b4 19 ♘e2 e×f5 20 e×f5 ♘e5, with . . . ♗c6 to come, and Black's threats are becoming very unpleasant. Definitely not the sort of position to have against Tal!

15 . . . b4

15 . . . b×a4 16 ♖×a4 ♖fb8 is an attempt to get some play, but after 17 ♖c4 ♕d8 the opening of another line favours White, if anything: the rook is quite handily placed at c4.

16 ♘e2 *(55)* **. . .**

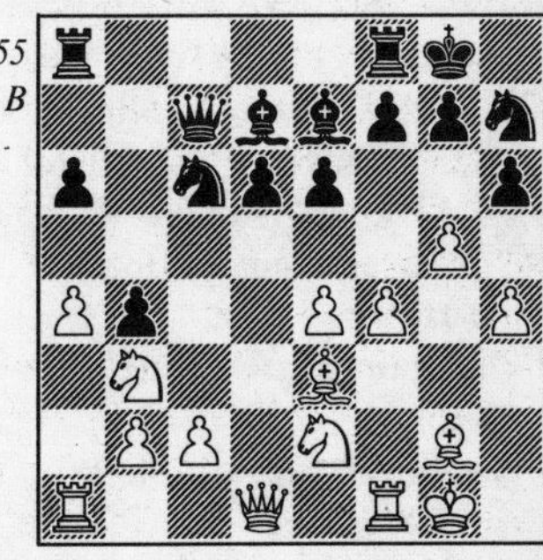

16 . . . d5

Black decides that desperate measures are necessary and sacrifices a pawn. If this appears premature, bear in mind that White is planning

♘g3 and ♕g4, when he really will have an irresistible attack. Meanwhile, Black lacks counterplay. Why? Because, barring . . . d5 and . . . e5, he has no pawn breaks which would open up play for his pieces. And the only other possibility, play down the c-file, achieves nothing since he has no good square for his knight: if 16 . . . ♘a5 17 ♘×a5 ♕×a5, not only is his queen misplaced, but White's weakest minor piece has been exchanged; or if 16 . . . ♖ac8 17 ♘g3 ♘b8 18 ♖f2 and Black is making no progress.

But what about 16 . . . e5? In many such positions it would hardly be worth considering because White could simply reply f5, and his dominance of the weak square at d5 would leave Black without a shred of counterplay. Here, though, 17 f5 would be an unclear pawn sacrifice; so Black will have a chance of some play by occupying e5 with his knight. Even so, White keeps the advantage, partly because he can expose the black king, partly because his own occupation of d5 will be very powerful: 16 . . . e5 17 g×h6 and then: (a) 17 . . . e×f4 18 h×g7, followed by ♘×f4 and the knight is heading for d5 or h5; (b) 17 . . . g×h6 18 f×e5 ♘×e5 19 ♗×h6, with a similar effect, apart from the extra pawn; (c) 17 . . . ♗×h4 (best) 18 h×g7 ♔×g7 19 ♕d2! ♖g8 20 ♖ad1 ♗e7 21 f×e5! ♘×e5 22 ♘f4, with advantage because all White's pieces are ideally poised for attack (♘d5, ♘d4-f5, ♗h6 or ♗d4 in some cases, open f-file etc.). What is instructive about these variations is that, **with the black king exposed**, White gains far more than he loses by exchanging at e5. He concedes Black a square, but opens up many more possibilities for his own pieces. I stress this point because of the earlier remarks about f5 being the thematic move in this kind of situation: and I suspect that the majority of players would prefer 21 f5 in line (c), for example. But the white knights would have some unflattering remarks to make about that move! Black would reply 21 . . . ♔h8 and operate on the g-file in relative security.

17 e×d5 . . .

Blocking the centre usually enhances the power of a flank attack, but not here. 17 e5? would be answered by 17 . . . h5! and . . . g6, bringing White to a dead stop. In any case there is no reason not to accept the pawn.

17 . . . e×d5

18 ♕×d5 . . .

Here is the position anticipated in the note to Black's 13th move, with White controlling the board by a massive concentration of pieces in the centre. This will shortly make an even greater impression when he completes his mobilisation by ♘ed4 and ♖ae1. **And that is why Black's pawn sacrifice fails**: his pieces simply cannot get through to exploit the theoretical weaknesses in White's K-side. Two more points favour White: (1) The g2 bishop shields the king and exerts considerable power down the long diagonal; (2) Black is playing a piece down in the main battle area (that knight at h7!). This factor alone is enough to seal his fate.

18 . . . ♖ac8

Not the square Black really wants for his rook, but after 18 . . . ♖ad8 (the only way he can hope to frighten the queen) 19 a5 threatens 20 ♗b6 and 19

. . . ♗g4 loses the knight at c6. If 18 . . . ♖fd8, White has 19 g6.

19 a5 . . .

Still a good move: the black rooks are kept out of d8 and at the same time White is thinking about his endgame prospects. If . . . a5 were permitted, Black's pawn structure would be more solid; now the a- and b-pawns are both fixed and subject to attack and any ending would therefore be easier to win. For example, Black could now try 19 . . . ♗e6, but after 20 ♕×c6 ♕×c6 21 ♗×c6 ♖×c6 22 ♘ed4 there is no reason why White should not win with correct play.

19 . . . ♘b8

20 ♘ed4 . . .

More centralising, this time restricting the movement of Black's Q-bishop. The game is now won without too much difficulty, but Nunn's technique is of some interest. In what follows he does not insist on trying to force exchanges, which might cause him to misplace some of his pieces. Nor does he insist on a K-side attack at any cost. He combines the two ideas in a flexible way by threatening action on the K-side: then it is Black who has to come scrambling for exchanges in order to avoid a worse fate.

20 . . . ♗g4

21 ♖ae1 ♖fd8

22 ♕e4 . . .

Those pawns could soon be on the move again. White threatens 23 f5, burying the bishop at h5, with worse to follow. Black avoids the danger by himself threatening 23 . . . ♗×g5.

22 . . . ♖e8

23 ♗f2 *(56)* **. . .**

Pins the bishop and forces a retreat by the renewed threat of f5.

56
B

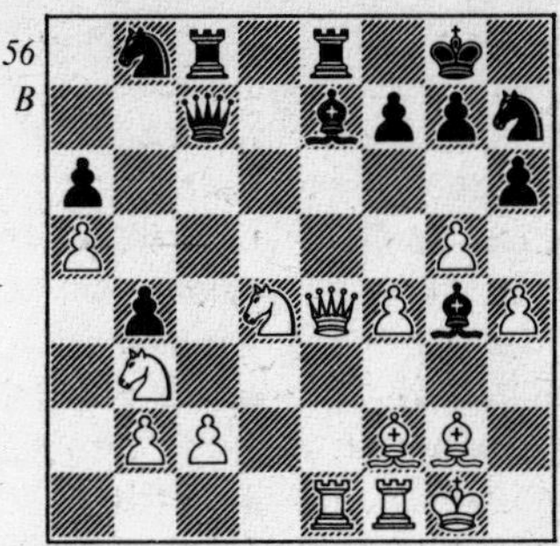

23 . . . ♗d7

The only other move worth considering is 23 . . . h×g5 (23 . . . g6 24 f5 is very bad; so is 23 . . . h5 24 f5, with further advances of f6 or g6 in the air). Then 24 h×g5 ♗d7 25 g6 ♘f6 (25 . . . f×g6 26 ♕×g6 is no better, with ♗d5+ threatened, among other things) 26 g×f7+ ♔×f7 27 ♕d3 and White is planning f5 or ♘f5 according to circumstances. If Black now grabs the (extremely hot) f-pawn, all the latent power in White's position is suddenly released: 27 . . . ♕×f4 28 ♗g3 ♕g4 (or 28 . . . ♕h6 29 ♗b7 ♖cd8 30 ♗c7) 29 ♖e4 ♕g6 (or 29 . . . ♕g5 30 ♖e5 ♕g4 31 ♖f4, or if here 30 . . . ♕h6 31 ♗d5+ ♔f8 32 ♖f2-h2 etc.) 30 ♖×e7+ ♖×e7 31 ♗d5+ and wins. If Black declines the bait, he simply remains a pawn down with an exposed king.

24 ♕d5 . . .

White can quite safely use his pawns as a battering-ram. He now threatens 25 g6, meeting 24 . . . ♘f8 by 25 h5, then g6 anyway. If 24 . . . ♔f8 25 ♗e4. Black's only defence is to exchange queens, but with a pawn to the bad and the h7 knight still out of play the situation is hopeless.

24 . . . ♕d6

25 ♘f5! . . .

White is still in no great hurry to

exchange queens: he permits his opponent the option of 25 . . . ♗×f5 26 ♕×f5 instead of the game continuation. Either way his bishop-pair will dominate the board. But he is also returning the extra pawn temporarily: possibly as instructive a piece of Grandmaster thinking as anything which has gone previously. The point is not that the variations are difficult to calculate, but that Nunn is thinking boldly; dynamically. Time and again we see how his thinking is the **reverse** of that of a weaker player. It is not, 'If I play ♘f5 I shall lose a pawn; I will only do that as a last resort'; but rather, 'I can simplify the position by ♘f5 and continue to generate powerful threats; it would be a miracle if Black could get away with . . . ♖×c2.'

And so he is able to finish off the game quickly and convincingly.

25	. . .	♕×**d5**
26	♘×**e7+**	♖×**e7**
27	♗×**d5**	♖×**e1**
28	♖×**e1**	♖×**c2**
29	♖**e7**	. . .

Suddenly it is obvious. White threatens 30 g6, 30 ♗a7 and worst of all 30 ♖×f7. Since Black cannot defend the f-pawn, he at least forces White to take it with the bishop.

29	. . .	♗**c6**
30	♗×**f7+**	♔**f8**

Or 30 . . . ♔h8 31 g×h6!

31	♖**c7**	. . .

The two threats of ♗c5+ and ♗g6 gain more material.

31	. . .	**h×g5**
32	♗**c5+**	**1 – 0**

Game 14

Sicilian Defence
Wijk aan Zee 1982

J. Nunn v. J. van der Wiel

1	e4	c5
2	♘f3	♘c6
3	d4	c×d4
4	♘×d4	♘f6
5	♘c3	d6
6	♗c4	e6
7	♗e3	♗e7
8	♕e2	. . .

Velimirović's system, in which White prepares a quick 0–0–0 followed by a K-side pawn storm; from e2 the queen keeps an eye on Black's outpost square at c4 and continues to support g4 for the pawn thrust at move 11. The whole variation is very fast-moving and in complete contrast, for example, to Nunn-Gheorghiu (Game 19), where White had to build up his attack very slowly and carefully. Incidentally, van der Wiel was in the tricky psychological position of wanting a half-point from this game to make his first Grandmaster norm. Even though he lost, he was probably wise to choose a sharp variation in keeping with his own style. If you play for a draw, there is a very fine line between trying to play solidly and in practice playing too passively and losing. Nunn for his part is pressing hard for a win, to have a chance of first prize, and is quite happy with the choice of opening.

8	. . .	a6

Or Black may castle; for example 8 . . . 0–0 9 0–0–0 a6 10 ♗b3 ♕c7 11 ♖hg1 ♘d7 12 g4 ♘c5 13 g5 ♗d7 14 ♖g3, intending ♕h5 and ♖h3, with equally sharp play.

9	0–0–0	♕c7
10	♗b3	♘a5
11	g4	b5

This is intended as an attack on White's e-pawn (by . . . b4), with the added option of a Q-side fianchetto. It is not a preparation for . . . ♘c4 because after . . .

12	g5	. . .

. . . 12 . . . ♘d7? would be refuted by 13 ♗×e6 etc. Therefore Black is forced to exchange.

12	. . .	♘×b3+
13	a×b3	. . .

Not 13 ♘×b3. the doubling of the pawns is insignificant and White does better to keep his knight on the aggressive square d4.

13	. . .	♘d7
14	h4 *(57)*	. . .

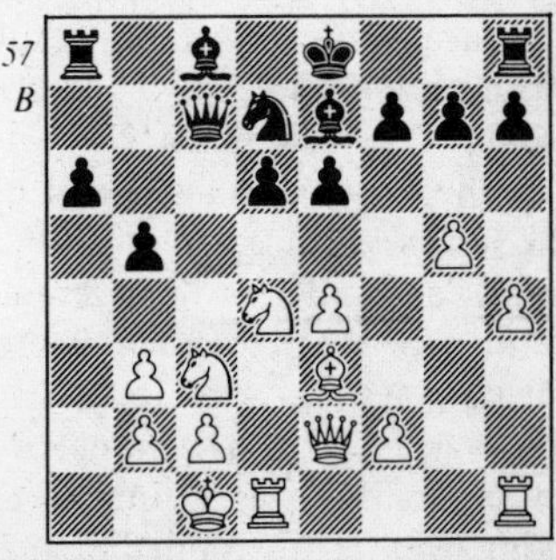

This variation has been adopted

many times in Grandmaster practice (we are still in the books at move 20 of the main game) and currently 14 h4 is considered the strongest move, being a kind of happy medium between the violent piece sacrifice 14 ♘f5 (leading to about equality, it seems) and slower moves such as 14 ♔b1 and 14 b4.

In such a well-analysed opening the obvious practical question is: how much of all this theory does a Grandmaster remember and how much does he work out over the board? Since much of it is concrete analysis, it is actually possible to remember a great deal; and if you play a system regularly the process of memorising tends to happen automatically, without much conscious effort. But in this regard Nunn makes the point that learning typical ideas is much more valuable than remembering lots of specific variations. His 21st move is a good example, of which more later. Meanwhile, here are some general remarks concerning what follows:

(1) Control of the centre is approximately balanced. Black's pawn position, though defensive, is restraining White's pieces quite effectively; on the other hand, any disturbance of his pawns may result in serious weaknesses.
(2) The basic idea of 14 h4 is to undermine the e-pawn by h5 and g6. As the pawns advance castling K-side becomes less and less of a serious possibility for Black to contemplate, and if he plays . . . ♗b7 for Q-side castling he will have problems defending e6. If the bishop stays at c8 his king will be marooned in the centre.
(3) If Black does not make a capture after h5 and g6 White may continue h6, opening lines for his pieces or obtaining a passed pawn. Alternatively he may play g×f7+ ♔×f7, and, if the bishop has gone to b7, sacrifice a knight at e6 to draw the black king into the open.
(4) Black can often win a pawn, either at e4 or a4, but as a rule the capture is likely to be fraught with danger.

Bearing these points in mind, we can now analyse 14 . . . b4, the main alternative to the game continuation: 14 . . . b4 15 ♘a4 ♘c5 16 h5, and now the win of the a-pawn, leaving the queen offside, is simply not worth the trouble. For example 16 . . . ♘×a4 17 b×a4 ♕a5 18 g6 ♕×a4 19 ♔b1 ♗d7 (or 19 . . . f×g6 20 h×g6 h6 21 e5! d5 22 ♕g4 ♕d7, which is very passive) 20 g×f7+ ♔×f7 21 ♕f3+ ♗f6 (21 . . . ♔e8 22 e5 d5 23 ♕g4) 22 h6 ♖hg8 23 h×g7 ♕a5 24 ♖h6 ♕e5 25 ♖h5 1–0 (Hartston–Mestel, British Championship 1973).

It looks more reasonable to take the e-pawn, but still White develops a dangerous initiative: 16 . . . ♘×e4 17 g6 and now any capture leads to trouble; if 17 . . . f×g6 18 h×g6 h6 19 ♕f3, while 17 . . . h×g6 18 h×g6, yielding White the h-file, is bad on general grounds in all these variations. But ignoring the g-pawn permits White the strong idea of h6, no matter what Black plays in between. For instance 17 . . . ♘f6 18 h6! (generally it is much better for the attacker to complicate the position like this than to give the defender only one thing at a time to think about, as after 18 g×f7+ ♔×f7 19 h6 g6) f×g6 (if 18 . . . h×g6 19 h×g7 ♖g8

20 ♖h8 ♗b7 21 ♗g5 0-0-0 22 ♗×f6 ♗×f6 23 ♘×e6 wins neatly, or if 18 . . . g×h6 19 g×f7+ ♔×f7 20 ♖×h6, favouring White strongly because the g- and h-files have opened up) 19 h×g7 ♖g8 20 ♗g5 and Black is threatened in every corner – if 20 . . . e5 White has 21 ♗×f6 ♗×f6 22 ♕f3 ♗g5+ 23 ♔b1 ♗b7 24 ♕f8+! Another try is 17 . . . f5, but still it is 18 h6! h×g6 (or 18 . . . ♗f6 19 h×g7 ♕×g7 20 f3 ♘c5 – 20 . . . ♘g3 21 ♕c4 – 21 ♘×f5, which is very strong) 19 h×g7 ♖g8 20 ♖h8, and then: (a) 20 . . . ♘f6 21 ♘b6! ♖b8 (21 . . . ♕×b6 22 ♘×f5 ♕d8 23 ♘h6 ♔d7 24 ♕f3 ♖b8 25 ♘f7 ♕e8 26 ♘×d6 ♗×d6 27 ♗c5 ♘d5 28 ♗×d6 and wins) 22 ♘×f5! e×f5 (22 . . . g×f5 23 ♖×g8+ ♘×g8 24 ♕h5+ ♔d8 25 ♕h8) 23 ♖×g8+ ♘×g8 24 ♘d5 ♕b7 (Zaitsev–Utemov, USSR 1983 up to here) 25 ♕c4!, threatening chiefly 26 ♘c7+, with a very strong attack; or (b) 20 . . . ♔f7 21 ♖×g8 ♔×g8 22 f3 ♘f6 (22 . . . ♘g5 23 ♕g2, or 22 . . . ♘c5 23 ♕h2) 23 ♕h2! ♘h5 (23 . . . ♔×g7 24 ♕h6+ ♔f7 25 ♖g1, or 23 . . . e5 24 ♖g1 e×d4 25 ♖×g6 ♗b7 26 ♗×d4) 24 ♖g1, with dangerous threats.

But Black has two other possibilities yet. With f5 still covered by the bishop, and with a white knight unable to occupy d5 directly, he can just about contemplate . . . e5. Even so, he is likely to suffer on his white squares before long, as another of Nunn's games confirms: 16 . . . e5 17 ♘f5 ♗×f5 18 e×f5 ♘×a4 (or 18 . . . ♘×b3+ 19 ♔b1 ♘c5 20 ♘×c5 d×c5 21 ♕c4, with a classic white-square bind which will be intensified by ♖d5 and ♖hd1 – more than enough for a pawn) 19 b×a4 ♕c6 20 ♔b1 (a subtle point: not 20 b3 because the a-pawn is unimportant; White wishes to answer 20 . . . d5 by 21 ♗c1, and if 21 . . . f6 22 h6) ♕×a4 21 ♖h4 ♖b8 22 ♖d5 ♕d7 23 ♕d3, again with a crushing bind, this time to be reinforced by such moves as b3, ♖c4, ♖a5, g6 etc. (Nunn–Murshed, Commonwealth Championship 1985). An interesting example of a complete change of theme, given the normal sharp character of this opening.

Currently the best move is reckoned to be 16 . . . ♗d7, by which Black develops a piece, keeps e6 covered and preserves his threats against e4 and a4. White's best response is not clear, but the immediate 17 g6 seems most in the spirit of the variation: 17 . . . ♘×b3+ 18 ♘×b3 ♗×a4 19 h6! f×g6 20 h×g7 ♖g8 21 ♘d4, for instance, with initiative in return for the pawn. The narrow line between success and failure, between a devastating attack and one which never gets off the ground, is evidenced by two games in which White played the slower move 17 ♔b1. Planinc–Belyavsky (Hastings 1974–5) continued 17 . . . ♗×a4 18 b×a4 ♘×a4? (leaving e6 vulnerable) 19 g6 ♗f6 20 g×f7+ (not 20 h6 first this time, on account of 20 . . . h×g6) ♔×f7 21 h6 g6 22 ♕f3 ♖hf8 23 e5! d×e5 24 ♘×e6! (24 . . . ♔×e6 25 ♕g4+ ♔e7 26 ♕×b4+) and the attack won easily. But in Quinteros–Popović (Novi Sad 1982) there came the much better move 18 . . . ♕b7!, in the knowledge that White would not wish to shut out his queen from the squares g4 and h5 by playing 19 f3. He therefore sacrificed the pawn, but after 19 g6 ♗f6 20 g×f7+ ♔×f7 21 e5 d×e5 (21 . . . ♗×e5 22 ♘f3 would be less good) 22 ♘b3 ♘×a4 23 ♕g4 ♖ac8

24 h6 ♕c6 was simply two pawns down for nothing.

Returning now to the main game, 14 . . . ♗b7 is just playable, but Black has to be extremely careful because he is leaving e6 unsupported again.

14 . . . ♗b7

15 f3 . . .

The choice between this and the sharper move 15 h5 is really a matter of taste. Nunn prefers the text move because he considers that **with e6 weakened** White can gain the advantage by slower methods, without needing to sacrifice the centre pawn. In other words, shutting the queen out of g4 and h5 (see the last note) doesn't matter if White can keep his attack moving by the natural plan of h5 and g6; with the black bishop at d7 something sharper is called for.

One example of 15 h5 will suffice: 15 h5 b4 16 ♘a4 (16 ♘a2 has also been tried) ♗×e4 17 f3, and now 17 . . . ♗d5, covering e6, would be the crucial test; 17 . . . ♗b7 is decidedly inferior: 18 g6 h×g6 19 h×g6 ♖×h1 20 ♖×h1 ♘c5 (or 20 . . . ♗f6 21 ♘×e6 f×e6 22 ♗b6 and wins) 21 ♘×c5 d×c5 22 g×f7+ ♔×f7 23 ♘×e6 ♕c6 24 ♘×g7! ♔×g7 25 ♗d4+ 1 – 0 (Podgaets–Butnoris, USSR 1975).

15 . . . b4

Black may decide to castle Q-side hereabouts, or he may leave his king in the centre for a while. The difference is not especially significant; what matters is that he must play . . . b4 first, otherwise (after 15 . . . 0–0–0, say) White could play b4 himself, keeping the knight out of its best square, or even sacrifice a knight for two pawns at b5.

16 ♘a4 . . .

Now Black cannot permit h5 and g6 without a fight; so his choice lies between (a) the risky text move 16 . . . ♘c5, which aims to win a pawn at a4; (b) 16 . . . d5, opening the game for his bishops, but much too dangerous with his king stuck in the centre; and (c) 16 . . . g6 (the best chance), restraining White's advance and intending . . . 0–0–0 at a suitable moment.

First of all, 16 . . . d5 can be dealt with in quite a clear-cut manner: 17 e×d5 ♗×d5 18 ♘f5 ♗×b3 19 ♖×d7! ♕×d7 20 ♘b6 ♕c6 21 ♘×g7+ ♔f8 22 ♘×a8 ♗c4 (or 22 . . . ♔×g7 23 ♗d4+ f6 24 ♘b6 ♖d8 25 g×f6+ ♗×f6 26 ♖g1+ ♔f7 27 ♗×f6 ♔×f6 28 ♕g2+ and wins) 23 ♕d2 ♕×f3 24 ♖d1 ♕×a8 25 ♕d4 ♖g8 26 ♕×c4 ♖×g7 27 ♗c5, and White's attack is worth far more than a pawn.

Secondly, 16 . . . g6 does not quite equalise because the b-pawn shows up as a weakness; for example 17 ♕d2 ♕a5 18 h5 0–0–0 19 ♔b1 d5 (or 19 . . . ♘c5 20 h×g6 h×g6 21 ♖×h8 ♖×h8 22 ♘×c5 d×c5 23 ♘×e6 and wins) 20 e5! (a surprising sacrifice; this time opening the centre does not benefit White much, but it is worth a pawn to keep the b7 bishop blockaded) ♘×e5 21 ♕h2 ♗d6 (if 21 . . . ♘d7, just 22 h×g6 h×g6 23 ♕×h8 etc.) 22 ♗f4 ♕c7 23 ♘c5! ♗×c5 24 ♗×e5 ♗d6 25 f4, and again White has plenty of compensation (black-square control) for a pawn.

Finally there is the text move, which appears to be not quite adequate.

16 . . . ♘c5

17 ♔b1! . . .

This is a subtle move which requires some explanation. White is actually anticipating the variation 17 . . . ♘×a4 18 b×a4 ♖c8 19 ♗c1! He would then proceed by b3 and ♗b2 and Black would be saddled with a lifeless Q-side position: no pawn breaks to open up more lines and no way to make effective use of the c-file; White would then prepare h5 and g6 at his leisure. But after 17 h5 the g-pawn would be unprotected and this manoeuvre would be harder to carry out.

In view of this Black persists with his plan to win the a-pawn, but since no improvements are apparent for him between now and White's very strong 21st move, he would most likely have done better with 17 . . . g6. That would lead, after 18 ♕d2, to positions similar to the last note.

17	**. . .**	**♕a5**
18	**h5**	**♘×a4**
19	**b×a4**	**♕×a4**

If 19 . . . ♗×g5 20 ♘b3 ♕d8 21 e5 ♗×e3 22 ♕×e3 d5 23 ♖hg1 (23 . . . 0–0? 24 ♕h6), or if here 20 . . . ♕e5 21 ♗d4 ♕f4 22 ♘a5 ♗c8 23 ♗×g7, with a clear advantage in each case.

20 g6 *(58)* **. . .**

58
B

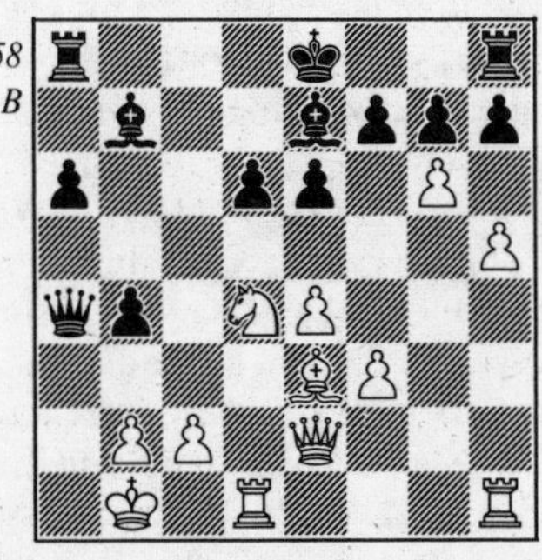

Black is now in real trouble. If 20 . . . h×g6 21 h×g6 and he cannot exchange rooks without allowing the nasty check on the following move, 21 . . . ♖×h1 22 ♖×h1 ♖c8 23 ♖h8+ ♗f8 24 ♕h2, for example. Or if 21 . . . ♖g8 22 g×f7+ ♔×f7 23 ♕g2! with an easy attack against the numerous weaknesses, especially e6 and g6; if, for instance, 23 . . . g6? 24 ♖h7+, or if 23 . . . ♗f6 24 ♖dg1 ♖ac8 (24 . . . g6? 25 ♖h7+ again, or 24 . . . ♗×d4 25 ♕g6+ ♔e7 26 ♗×d4 e5 27 ♗e3 with tremendous pressure) 25 ♕g6+ ♔e7 26 ♗g5 etc.

If 20 . . . h6 21 g×f7+ ♔×f7 22 ♕g2 is even worse for Black; so he must not touch his pawns. That really leaves only 20 . . . ♗f6 and the game continuation 20 . . . ♖c8 for serious consideration. And this is yet another position which has been reached in previous games! In Čabrilo–Sindik (Kecskemét 1979) 20 . . . ♗f6 came unstuck as follows: 21 g×f7+ ♔×f7 22 h6 (usefully loosening up f6 before the intended knight sacrifice) g6 23 ♘×e6! Now 23 . . . ♔×e6 loses quite simply to 24 ♕c4+ ♔e7 (or 24 . . . d5 25 ♖×d5 ♖ac8 26 ♖c5+ ♔e7 27 e5) 25 ♖×d6! ♔×d6 26 ♖d1+. Black therefore tried to hit back by 23 . . . b3 24 c×b3 ♗×e4+ 25 f×e4 ♕×e4+ 26 ♔a2; but he is fighting a lost cause because the white rooks have already developed too much power along the open files, and his king is the worse exposed. There is also the weak spot at f6 to worry about. If 26 . . . ♔×e6 27 ♕d2 ♗e5 28 ♗d4, threatening both 29 ♖he1 and 29 ♗×e5 etc., is overwhelming; he therefore played 26 . . . ♕×e6 27 ♖hf1 ♖he8 (or 27 . . . ♔e7 28 ♖×f6 anyway), and lost after 28 ♖×f6+! ♔×f6 29 ♕f3+ ♕f5 30 ♗d4+ ♔f7 31 ♕b7+.

Now after Black's next move Nunn could not remember any more theory, but his familiarity with the ideas and themes inherent in the position nevertheless enabled him to work out the best move – an innovation as it turned out, and one moreover which should have won by force.

20 . . . ♖c8

21 h6! . . .

An earlier game (Platonov–Polugaevsky, Kharkov 1967) had continued 21 ♕g2, which is much less potent. In defending c4 Black's 20th move has largely cut out the possibility of the knight sacrifice, and if he can get in . . . ♗f6 as well he will be covered against the threat of h6 (meeting it by . . . h×g6). It follows that White has to act at once if he wants to keep the initiative. After 21 ♕g2 ♗f6! 22 ♗g5 ♗e5 (provoking a weakness at e4 before taking the knight; 22 . . . ♗×g5 23 ♕×g5 would leave him exposed, the knight being the more dangerous piece here) 23 f4 ♗×d4 24 g×f7+ ♔×f7 25 ♖×d4 ♕b5 the players agreed to a draw in a still very murky position.

But 21 h6 gives Black no such chance. White's plan is to create threats on both sides of the board by making a strong passed pawn at g7 and then harassing the king, who will inevitably be driven across to d7 or c7.

21 . . . h×g6

This is forced; if 21 . . . g×h6 22 g×f7+ ♔×f7 23 ♖×h6 ♗f6 24 ♕h2 White has a crushing attack, with threats of 25 ♖×f6+ and 25 ♘×e6 as well as the more obvious ones at h7 and d6.

22 h×g7 ♖g8

23 ♖h8 ♔d7

White can tackle this position in two ways: he can intensify the pressure on the h-file and hope to paralyse Black by forcing him to defend the g8 rook (Plan A), or he can attack the Q-side at once, while the black rooks are busy watching the g-pawn (Plan B). In fact the two ideas are very closely linked, but only analysis will reveal which one should take precedence at any given moment. Here it happens that the immediate Q-side strike is superior; therefore . . .

24 ♘b3! . . .

The other way would be 24 ♕h2, threatening ♕h7. Then 24 . . . ♖×g7 would be refuted simply by 25 ♖×c8 ♗×c8 26 ♕h8 ♗f6 27 ♗h6, and 24 . . . ♗f6? 25 ♘×e6 would be catastrophic. And since 24 . . . ♔c7 (allowing . . . ♕e8) 25 ♗g5! ♕d7 (25 . . . ♗×g5 26 ♘×e6+) 26 ♗×e7 ♕×e7 27 e5 d5 28 ♕h7 ♕d8 29 ♖h1 practically cripples him, the outlook appears grim for Black (even though the win would take some time in this last line). But 24 . . . ♕a5!, intending . . . ♕d8, is a hidden resource. In that way he can cover the back rank without permitting the exchange of his better bishop – 25 ♕h7 ♕d8 26 ♖h1 ♗f6, for instance – and there seems to be nothing conclusive for White.

Now after 24 ♘b3 Black's rooks are temporarily out of action; so the fork threat can only be met by a king or a queen move or by 24 . . . d5. And against 24 . . . d5 or 24 . . . ♕b5 White switches back to his other plan, while still eyeing the Q-side, thus: 24 . . . d5 25 ♕h2, and nothing can stop ♕h7 (25 . . . ♖×g7 26 ♖×c8 etc.); or 24 . . . ♕b5 25 ♕h2! and then (a) 25 . . . ♖×g7 26 ♖×c8 ♗×c8 27 ♕h8 ♗f6 (27 . . . ♕e2 28 ♖d3 ♗f6 29 ♗d4 e5 30 ♗c5 is worse) 28 ♗d4! (not 28 ♗h6? ♕h5) ♕g5 (or 28 . . . e5 29 ♗c5, or 28 . . . ♗e5 29 ♘c5+, or 28 . . . ♗×d4 29 ♘×d4 ♕e5 30 f4 ♕f6 31 e5) 29 ♗×f6 ♕×f6 30 f4! ♔c7 (30 . . .

e5 31 f×e5 ♕×e5 32 ♖d5 and 33 e5) 31 ♖×d6 ♕×f4 32 ♕d8+ and wins; (b) 25 . . . ♔c7 26 ♗c5 e5 27 ♗×b4!, and since neither capture (at b4 or g7) is permissible, White keeps a winning positional advantage without any material sacrifice. Finally, 24 . . . ♕c6 is refuted by 25 ♘a5 ♕c7 26 ♘c4!

24 . . . ♔c7

Black settles for the king move and for the moment the attack is going to be directed more against the king himself; though a very striking feature of the game is how the activity on the Q-side is intimately involved with the passed g-pawn. You actually get the distinct impression that the whole board is wired up!

25 ♕c4+ ♗c6 *(59)*

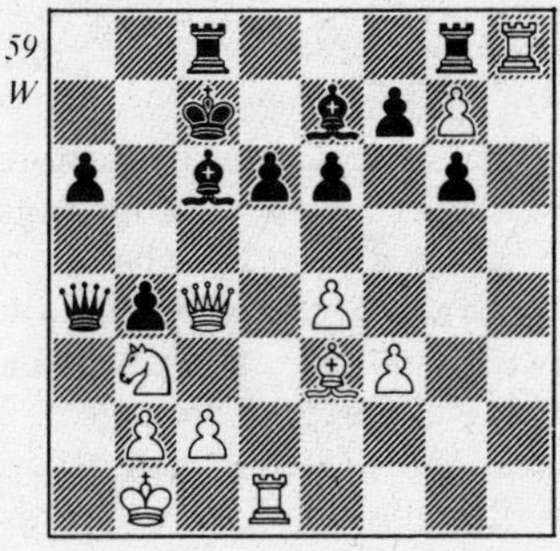

There is no choice; if 25 . . . ♔b8 26 ♕×c8+, or if 25 . . . ♕c6 26 ♖×g8 ♖×g8 27 ♕×b4 ♖×g7 28 ♘a5, picking up the rook by ♕c3+. If Black refuses the pawn, say 27 . . . ♔b8, then 28 ♕d4 and the combination of ♕a7+, ♘a5 and ♖d3 is altogether too much.

26 ♕d4(?) . . .

Not a serious mistake, but 26 ♘d4! is the quickest way to decide the game. Probably the naturalness of ♕d4, looking towards a7 and g7, together with the fact that the knight has just come from d4, contributed to the error. The strength of ♘d4 lies in Black's inability to use his rooks for the defence of the bishop; thus the threat of 27 b3 can only be fended off by a fatal loosening of his central position, namely 26 . . . d5 27 e×d5 e×d5 28 ♗f4+ ♔b7 (or 28 . . . ♔d7 29 ♘×c6, or 28 . . . ♗d6 29 ♗×d6+ ♔×d6 30 ♘×c6 ♕×c6 31 ♕f4+ and wins) 29 ♕e2 ♗f6 (if 29 . . . ♗c5 30 ♕h2 turns up again) 30 ♖×g8 ♖×g8 31 ♗e5 and Black is helpless: 31 . . . ♗×g7 yields the delightful variation 32 ♗×g7 ♖×g7 33 b3 ♕a5 34 ♘×c6 ♔×c6 35 ♕e8+ ♔b7 36 ♕h8, or if 31 . . . ♗d8 32 ♕h2 (-h7), or 31 . . . ♗h4 32 ♕h2 g5 33 f4 and wins, or 31 . . . ♗×e5 32 ♕×e5 and White's game is overwhelming. Finally there is the amusing line 26 . . . b3 27 ♕×a4 ♗×a4 28 c×b3, when Black again loses because of the inevitable rook exchange!

26 . . . ♕b5

27 ♕a7+? . . .

This, of course, was planned on the previous move. Nunn has been led astray by thinking that the queen check wins by force, but he has overlooked Black's 28th move. The right way is 27 ♖dh1! (back to plan A), threatening 28 ♖×g8 ♖×g8 29 ♖h8 ♕b8 30 ♕b6+, and White can demonstrate a forced win as follows: (a) 27 . . . ♕b8 28 ♖×g8 ♖×g8 29 ♖h8 ♕e8 (must defend against ♕b6+) 30 ♕a7+, followed by ♘a5; (b) 27 . . . ♗b7 28 ♖×g8 ♖×g8 29 ♖h8 ♕e8 30 ♕b6+, again followed by ♘a5; (c) 27 . . . e5 28 ♕a7+ ♕b7 29 ♕×b7+ ♗×b7 30 ♖×g8 ♖×g8 31 ♖h8 ♖×g7 32 ♗h6 ♗f6 33 ♗×g7 ♗×g7 34 ♖h7 and wins; (d) 27 . . . f6 (looks like a defence, threatening the g-pawn and vacating f7 for the rook, but e6 is exposed) 28

♖1h7 (threatens 29 ♗h6, then ♖×g8 and ♖h8) e5 (or 28 . . . ♕b8 29 ♕c4, and ♘d4 to follow) 29 ♕a7+ ♕b7 30 ♕×b7+ ♔×b7 (to keep . . . ♗e8 and . . . ♗f7 available) 31 ♘a5+ ♔c7 32 ♘×c6 ♔×c6 33 ♗h6 and wins.

27 . . . ♗b7

If 27 . . . ♕b7? 28 ♗b6+ ♔c7 29 ♘c5+.

28 ♘d4 ♕a4! *(60)*

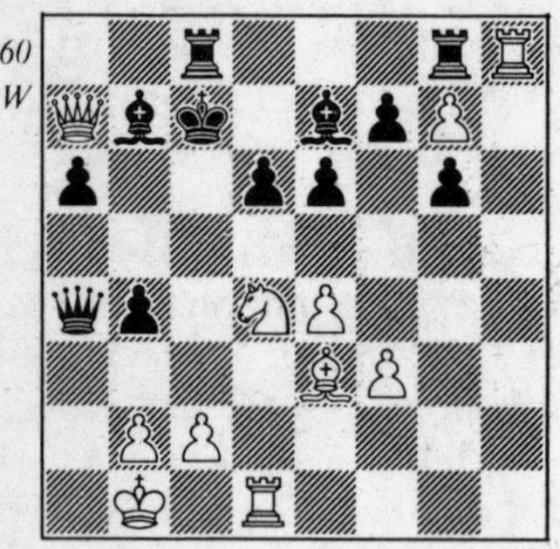

60
W

After this Black just about survives; but nothing else will do: (a) 28 . . . ♕e5 29 ♘c6! ♔×c6 30 ♕b6+ ♔d7 31 ♕×b7+ and wins; (b) 28 . . . ♕d7 29 ♘f5! (threatens ♗b6+; so Black must take) e×f5 30 ♗b6+ ♔c6 31 ♗a5 with a decisive attack; (c) 28 . . . ♕a5 29 c4! (threatens 30 ♘b3 ♕a4 31 ♗b6+) b×c3 (or 29 . . . ♕a4 30 ♖c1, followed by ♘b5+) 30 ♖c1, and Black cannot meet the check on the c-file; (d) 28 . . . ♕e8 29 ♖×g8 ♕×g8 30 ♘b3 ♖a8 31 ♕b6+ ♔c8 32 ♖d4 (or ♘a5) and wins; (e) 28 . . . ♕c4 29 b3 ♕c3 30 ♘e2 ♕c6 31 ♖d4 d5 32 e×d5 e×d5 33 ♘f4 and wins.

Now the course of the game indicates that White is probably still winning at this point, but there is nothing immediate. He would like to play 29 ♖dh1, intending 30 ♖×g8 ♖×g8 31 ♖h8 ♕e8 (31 . . . ♖×g7 32 ♕b8+) 32 ♘b3, with a winning threat of ♗b6+, but Black has 29 . . . ♗f6! Then the desirable 30 ♘×e6+ f×e6 31 ♕b6+ ♔b8 32 ♕×d6+ ♔a8 33 ♖×g8 will not do because Black has a mate at c2 and b2; and if he exchanges rooks first, c8 is left open for the king, thus: 30 ♖×g8 ♖×g8 31 ♘×e6+ f×e6 32 ♕b6+ ♔c8, and now 33 ♕×d6 is no longer check and Black escapes by 33 . . . ♕d7 or . . . ♕e8.

All of which is very frustrating! But we know that Black is only hanging on by his fingernails; so perhaps a little more pressure or an extra line-opening somewhere will do the trick and push him over the edge. And sure enough that thought encourages Nunn to find the following very fine move, which largely makes up for his previous error.

29 e5! . . .

First of all this prevents . . . ♗f6, so that if Black tries to keep the position blocked by 29 . . . d5, 30 ♖dh1 wins: 30 . . . ♖×g7 31 ♖×c8+ as before, or 30 . . . ♕e8 31 ♘b3 with ♗b6+ to follow. 29 . . . ♕a5 meets a similar fate: 30 ♘b3 ♕b5 31 ♖dh1 and again Black cannot defend both wings. Secondly, 29 . . . d×e5 opens the d-file fatally: 30 ♘b3 ♕b5 31 ♗b6+ ♕×b6 32 ♖d7+ ♔c6 (32 . . . ♔×d7 33 ♕×b6 ♗d5 34 ♕a7+ and wins) 33 ♘a5+ ♕×a5 34 ♕×b7+ ♔c5 35 ♖×g8 ♖×g8 36 ♖c7+, mating or winning the queen.

Therefore, however Black reacts, he cannot prevent a breakthrough at d6. And if he takes at g7 he falls victim to another blistering combination: 29 . . . ♖×g7 30 ♘×e6+ f×e6 31 e×d6+ ♗×d6 32 ♕b6+ ♔b8 33 ♕×d6+ ♖c7 (33 . . . ♔a8 34 ♕c5! ♔b8 35 ♗f4+) 34 ♖×c8+ ♗×c8 35 ♗a7+ and wins. There remains only the text move, and here the main line of the attack is revealed. Nunn's tactical control is the point to bear in mind here. Having worked out that 29 . . . ♖×h8 is forced, he has visualised as far as move 40, by which time he has an extremely favourable ending of queens and opposite bishops. And don't forget the defender! In a game like this his part is all too easy to overlook; van der Wiel actually deserves a lot of credit for walking through this minefield and surviving as far as the endgame!

29 . . . ♖×h8!
30 e×d6+ ♗×d6

Now the simple sequence 31 ♘×e6+ f×e6 32 ♕b6+ ♔b8 33 ♕×d6+ ♔a8 34 g×h8/♕ fails for the same reason as before – Black has 34 . . . ♕×c2+ and perpetual check. Therefore White must take on h8 first, leaving c8 for the king, and Black escapes immediate ruin.

31 g×h8/♕ ♖×h8
32 ♘×e6+ f×e6
33 ♕b6+ ♔c8
34 ♕×d6 . . .

Opposite bishops are bound to favour White as long as he can keep his attack going, because his queen and bishop combine so well on the black squares. But were the queens to disappear, even if he regained two pawns for the one sacrificed, his weak f-pawn and the small number of pawns remaining would argue against his making much progress. Now in the face of White's threats of ♗a7, ♗f4 and ♗b6 the next move is compulsory.

34 . . . ♕c6 *(61)*

If 34 . . . ♗d5 35 ♗f4 wins because the rook is in danger as well as the king: 35 . . . ♔b7 36 ♕c7+ ♔a8 37 ♗e3 ♗b7 38 ♖d8+.

35 ♕e5! . . .

Another excellent move, all the more so because it was foreseen at the outset. 35 ♕d4 ♖e8 36 ♗f4, threatening 37 ♕e5, looks good, but Black has a complete defence in 36 . . . ♕d5. With the text move White is not only permitting the exchange of rooks, but refusing the b-pawn; and that, I'm sure, is where many players would have gone astray. One has to appreciate two unobvious things: that White still has a very powerful attack with only his queen and bishop, and that the attack will simply not work with the queen on the inferior square b4 – a classic case of the power of centralisation. After 35 ♕×b4 (threatening ♖d3) there is 35 . . . ♖d8 36 ♖×d8+ ♔×d8, and then, for example, 37 ♗g5+ ♔c7 38 ♕a5+ ♔b8 39 ♕d8+ ♗c8 and White is achieving very little. The point is that with only a relatively small force remaining some precision is required, and the queen must be in the right spot to begin with. It is not good enough to claim that White will always be able to take over the black squares and regain the attack whenever he wishes.

35 . . . ♖d8

Still forced, otherwise ♗f4 wins (35 . . . ♖h5 36 ♗g5 ♖h8 37 ♗f4). Now the exchange must be made, or Black will occupy the centre (. . . ♕d5) and it will be impossible to generate threats against his king.

36 ♖×d8+ ♔×d8

37 ♗g5+ . . .

And here is the first taste of what is to come. If 37 . . . ♔c8 38 ♕h8+ wins, or if 37 . . . ♔e8 38 ♕h8+ ♔f7 39 ♕h7+ ♔f8 40 ♕e7+ ♔g8 41 ♗f6 and wins; therefore the king is driven into the centre. A useful point of technique to note is the queen's occupation of a white square at move 39, complementing the black-square bishop, and a big improvement on the obvious 39 ♕f6+.

37 . . . ♔d7

38 ♕g7+ ♔d6

39 ♕f8+ ♔d5

39 . . . ♔e5 40 ♗f4+ ♔d5 41 ♕×b4 would be better still for White; from f4 the bishop confines the king and prevents . . . e5 (because of ♕e4+).

40 ♕×b4 . . .

Why should the attack be so strong, even allowing that the king is uncomfortably exposed? Chiefly because the pawns can be used on white squares to co-operate with the bishop in weaving a mating net, precisely the same principle as when the queen used a white square in the earlier note. The f-pawn is already conveniently in place, and b3 + c4 is also available when required. Already White threatens 41 c4+ ♔d4 (41 . . . ♔e5 42 ♕c3+ ♔d6 43 ♕d4+) 42 ♕c3+ ♔c5 43 b4+ ♔b6 44 ♕d4+ and mate, and it is impossible for Black to beat off the threats and still co-ordinate his pieces properly. His queen also has to look after the bishop, who remains a spectator for the rest of the game, and if she occupies a black square she is in mortal danger of a skewer. A further practical difficulty is that White's threats are not obvious two-move mates, but are based on much longer variations, and it is very easy to get caught in a trap. The truth is that the more you analyse this position and appreciate White's resources, the more hopeless it seems to be for Black.

40 . . . e5!

Very short of time, Black nevertheless finds the best defence, giving his king access to another white square. He might easily have blundered into 40 . . . ♔e5?, for there are mates lurking in this position where you would hardly expect them: 40 . . . ♔e5? 41 ♗f4+ ♔f5 (or . . . ♔f6) 42 ♕f8 mate!

If he can't move his king, the threat of 41 c4+ has to be met either by the text move or by 40 . . . ♕d7; and 40 . . . ♕d7 41 ♗f4! (confining the king and threatening 42 c4+ ♔c6 43 ♕a4+) leads to a forced win as follows:

(a) 41 . . . ♔c6 42 ♕c4+ ♔b6 43 ♗e3+ ♔a5 44 ♕c5+ ♕b5 45 ♗d2+ and mate.

(b) 41 . . . ♗c8 42 ♕e4+ ♔c5 43 ♗e3+ ♔b5 (43 . . . ♔d6 44 ♕b4+ ♔e5 45 ♕f4+ ♔d5 46 ♕d4+ ♔c6 47 ♕b6+ ♔d5 48 ♕c5 mate) 44 b3! ♔a5 45 ♕e5+ ♕d5 46 ♕c7+ ♔b4 47 ♗d2+ ♕×d2 48 ♕c4+ and mate.

(c) 41 . . . ♗c6 42 c4+ ♔d4 43 b3, and there is no defence to the threats of 44 c5+ and ♕c4 mate, or 44 ♕d2+ and ♗e3+.

(d) 41 . . . ♕c6 42 c4+! ♔d4 43 ♕c3+ ♔c5 44 b4+ ♔b6 45 ♕d4+.

(e) 41 . . . ♕c8/f7/g7/h7 42 ♕d6+

♔c4 43 b3+ and wins.

(f) 41 . . . e5 42 ♕e4+ ♔c5 43 ♕×e5+ ♕d5 (If 43 . . . ♔b4 44 b3!, leaving no adequate reply to the threat of ♔b2 and c3 mate – 44 . . . ♕d5 45 ♕e1+ ♔c5 46 ♕a5+ and wins; if 43 . . . ♔c6, still 44 b3! is best, preparing ♕e4+ and/or c4. No matter how Black plays in this line, he either loses the g-pawn with check or gets into a mating net) 44 ♕c7+ ♕c6 (44 . . . ♔b5 45 c4+) 45 ♕a5+ ♕b5 (45 . . . ♔d4 ♕e5+) 46 ♕c3+ ♕c4 (46 . . . ♔d5 47 ♕e5+) 47 ♕e3+ ♔c6 (47 . . . ♔b5 48 b3 ♕f1+ 49 ♔b2, then c4+; 47 . . . ♔b4 48 b3; 47 . . . ♕d4 48 ♕e7+) 48 ♕e8+ ♔c5 49 ♗e3+, winning either the bishop or the g-pawn with check.

41 ♕e4+ . . .

The sealed move, and some adjournment analysis has now convinced Nunn that he has every chance of winning. To start with he picks up a pawn with check. Black decides to surrender the g-pawn rather than the e-pawn, in order to restrict the scope of the opposing bishop as much as possible.

41 . . . ♔d6

If 41 . . . ♔c5 42 ♕×e5+ ♕d5 43 ♕c7+ ♕c6 (43 . . . ♔b5 44 c4+, or 43 . . . ♗c6 44 ♗e3+ ♔b4 45 b3 ♕×f3 46 ♕b6+ ♗b5 47 ♕d4+ and wins, or here 45 . . . ♔c3 46 ♕g7+ ♔b4 47 ♔b2) 44 ♕e7+ ♔b5 (or 44 . . . ♔d5 45 b3) 45 ♗e3!, followed by b3 and c4+. White's plan is simple enough to understand in principle, but getting the tactics right is far from easy. Here, for instance, 45 b3 might allow Black to escape with 45 . . . ♕×f3 46 c4+ ♔c6. Hence the more accurate 45 ♗e3.

42 ♕×g6+ ♔d5(?)

If 42 . . . ♔c7 43 ♕g7+ ♔d6 44 ♕e7+ ♔d5 45 ♗f6, winning the e-pawn. But surprisingly there is a distinction to be made between the text move and 42 . . . ♔c5, which puts up more resistance. The difference is that after . . . ♔c5 White has to begin his attack by ♗e3+; he therefore loses the option of playing ♕e7+ and ♗f6, and Black's defence is consequently eased. Even so White should still win, though nothing is quite forced. Best play seems to be as follows: 42 . . . ♔c5 43 ♗e3+ ♔d5 (43 . . . ♔b4 44 ♕d3, or 43 . . . ♔b5 44 ♕d3+ ♕c4 45 ♕d6! ♕f1+ 46 ♔a2 ♕c4+ 47 b3 ♕×c2+ 48 ♔a3 and wins) 44 ♕f7+ ♔d6 45 c4! ♕d7 (45 . . . ♕c7? 46 c5+ ♔c6 47 ♕e6+ ♔b5 48 c6!) 46 ♕f8+ ♔e6 (46 . . . ♔c7 47 ♕c5+ ♔d8 48 ♗g5+ and takes on e5 with check) 47 ♕h6+ ♔f7 (47 . . . ♔e7 helps White because the bishop can check) 48 ♕h7+ ♔e8 (48 . . . ♔e6 49 ♕g6+ etc. is similar) 49 ♕g8+ ♔e7, and here, oddly enough, there is no forced win. White therefore plays 50 ♔c1!, cutting out . . . ♕d1+ and keeping open his options of ♗c5+ or ♗g5+ and in practice an adequate defence will be impossible. If the black queen strays too far she will be inviting disaster, and the capture of the f-pawn will cost Black his bishop.

43 ♕f7+ ♔d4 *(62)*

If 43 . . . ♔c5 44 ♕e7+, and then: (a) 44 . . . ♔c4 45 ♕×e5, threatening 46 b3+; (b) 44 . . . ♔b6 45 ♗e3+ and 46 ♕×e5+; (c) 44 . . . ♔d5 45 ♗f6; (d) 44 . . . ♔d4 45 ♕d8+! and another unexpected mating pattern emerges by 45 . . . ♕d5 46 ♕b6+ ♔c4 47 b3+ ♔c3 48 ♕e3+ ♔b4 49 ♗e7+ ♔a5 50 ♗d8+! ♔b4 51 ♕e1+ ♔c5 52 ♕a5+

♔d6 (52 . . . ♔c6 53 ♕b6+ and mates) 53 ♕c7+ ♔e6 54 ♕e7+ ♔f5 55 ♕f6 mate! If here 45 . . . ♔c5 46 ♗e3+ ♔b5 (or 46 . . . ♔b4 47 ♕d2+ first) 47 b3, with a decisive attack (47 . . . a5 48 ♕d3+).

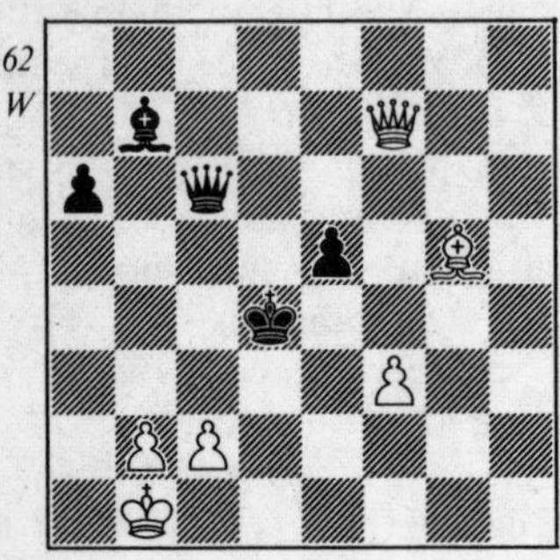

62
W

44 ♕b3! . . .

Threatens 45 ♗e3 mate, to which Black has only one defence. As an aid to systematic thinking in this type of position, you may find it useful to ask: (1) Can the king run? (2) Can the black queen deal with the threat? If the answers are both no, the chances are that you have a pretty powerful threat; then you can look around to see if there is any defence at all. Here 44 . . . ♔c5 is refuted by 45 ♗e7+ and 44 . . . ♕×f3 by 45 ♕b4+; the only hope is to make more air for the king.

44 . . . e4
45 ♗e3+ . . .

The disadvantage of 44 . . . e4 is that White can now obtain a passed f-pawn, which, together with the continuing attack, is bound to be decisive. Nunn spent a few minutes looking at other promising lines, beginning with ♗f6+ or ♕e3+, but without success. The sheer number of alternative checks at every move makes it hard over the board to be sure of anything, especially when the king has more squares available; therefore the sensible, practical way is to keep it simple.

45 . . . ♔e5
46 f4+ ♔f6

This helps White a little; he could have put up more fight by going behind the f-pawn and threatening the bishop. In the end, though, it makes no essential difference; for example 46 . . . ♔f5 47 ♕f7+ ♔g4 48 ♕g7+ (48 f5 ♔f3) ♔f3 (not 48 . . . ♔h3 49 ♗f2!) 49 ♕g1 ♕d5 50 ♕f2+ ♔g4 51 ♕g2+ ♔h5 (or ♔f5) 52 ♕h3+ ♔g6 53 ♕g4+ ♔f6 54 b3, with a position much like the game.

47 ♕g8 ♕d5
48 ♗d4+ . . .

White's plan is straightforward enough: secure the king by b3, anchor the bishop at e5 and advance the f-pawn, without, of course, permitting an exchange of queens or allowing the e-pawn to surge forward.

48 . . . ♔e7
49 ♕g7+ ♔d6
50 b3 ♔c6
51 ♗e5 . . .

The advance of the passed pawn will be combined with new threats against the king, the current one being 52 ♕c7+ and 53 c4+. Nor does Black have the resources to make his own passed pawn dangerous; if 51 . . . ♔b6 52 f5 e3 53 ♗d4+ ♔c6 54 ♕g6+ ♕d6 55 ♕e8+ and wins.

51 . . . ♕d7
52 ♕h6+ ♔d5
53 ♕b6! ♕c6
54 ♕d8+ ♔e6
55 ♕f6+ ♔d7

If 55 . . . ♔d5 56 c4+ ♔c5 57 ♕e7+ ♔b6 58 ♗d4+ wins.

56 ♕g7+ ♔e6

Or 56 . . . ♔c8 57 f5 e3 58 f6 e2 59 ♕g4+.

57	**♕g4+**	**♔f7**
58	**f5**	**♕h6**
59	**f6**	**1 - 0**

One possible finish would be 59 . . . ♗c6 (stopping ♕d7+) 60 ♕c8 ♕h1+ 61 ♔b2 e3 62 ♕c7+ ♔g6 63 ♕g7+ ♔f5 64 f7.

Game 15

Modern Benoni Defence
Marbella (Zonal) 1982

G. Ligterink v. J. Nunn

1	**d4**	**♘f6**
2	**c4**	**c5**
3	**d5**	**e6**
4	**♘c3**	**e×d5**
5	**c×d5**	**d6**
6	**♘f3**	**g6**
7	**g3**	**. . .**

In Game 8 Polugaevsky played 7 e4 and 8 ♗e2 here. A fianchetto might seem to make Black's thematic pawn advance . . . b5 easier, but it also affords White certain tactical chances based on the sudden opening of the long diagonal.

7	**. . .**	**♗g7**
8	**♗g2**	**0–0**
9	**0–0** *(63)*	**. . .**

63
B

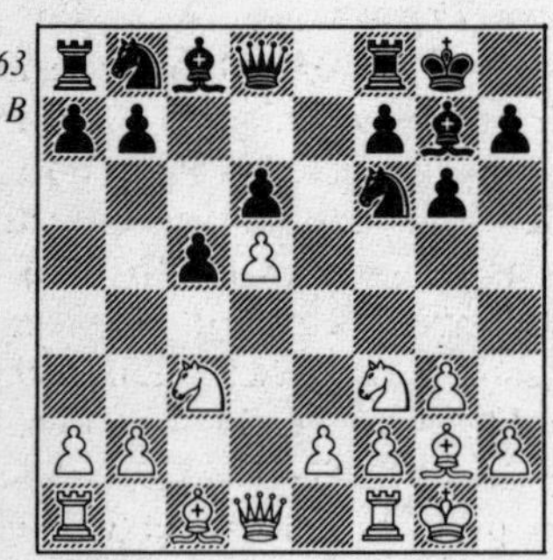

9	**. . .**	**♘bd7**

9 . . . ♘a6 is also possible, and straightaway there is a variation which demonstrates the dangers: 10 ♘d2 ♘c7 11 ♘c4, and if 11 . . . b5? 12 ♘×d6 ♕×d6 13 ♗f4, recovering the knight with advantage. Nunn prefers the systems based on . . . ♘bd7, but in any case the long diagonal theme crops up again before long.

Now there are two aspects of this opening which we need to think about. The first concerns some new ideas which have arisen for White, and whether they are likely to give him a better chance of initiative than the older, standard plan of ♘d2–c4 (+ a4) followed by a central pawn push. The second concerns Black's move-order in reaction to these ideas, specifically in what order he should play . . . a6, . . . ♖e8 and . . . ♘bd7, or indeed whether he should play these moves at all. We are not pretending that there are clear-cut answers to these questions. What follows is a review of the kind of shape the game may take, rather than an attempt to come to any definite conclusions.

Suppose we start with 9 . . . a6 10 a4 ♘bd7. Then, apart from ♘d2–c4 etc., White can try the immediate advance 11 e4, planning a knight move followed by f4, or he can hit the d-pawn by 11 ♗f4. These are basically the two new ideas. Black for his part has to think in terms of occupying e5 with a knight, but with f4 imminent and having both knights to juggle with, he will not find it easy to secure a foothold in the centre. It goes almost without saying that any exchange of pieces would be a welcome relief.

Reducing these thoughts to some concrete analysis give us 11 e4 ♖e8 12 ♖e1; and now 12 . . . ♘e5 13 ♘×e5 ♖×e5 14 f4 is obviously unsatisfactory, while 13 . . . d×e5 14 a5 also has many positional disadvantages – K-bishop blocked, passed d-pawn, hole at b6 and weak c-pawn. Another idea which has been tried is 12 . . . c4, intending . . . ♘c5–d3 and planning to meet 13 ♕e2 by 13 . . . ♘c5 14 ♕×c4 b5 15 ♕f1 b4 etc. That is fine for Black, but 13 ♗f4 ♘c5 14 e5 is a much better reply. The quick break in the centre without the preliminary f4 is another characteristic of this variation; White gets a secure passed pawn and plenty of scope for all his minor pieces. In fact Black usually plays 12 . . . ♘g4, and then 13 ♘h4! ♘f8 (or 13 . . . ♘ge5 14 f4 ♘c4 15 ♘f3 ♖b8 16 ♕c2 ♕a5 17 ♖a2!, which is even worse; White's last move prevents . . . b5 and prepares ♗f1, driving the black pieces into a huddle – Ligterink–Short, Plovdiv 1983) 14 h3 ♘e5 15 f4 ♘c4 16 ♗f1 ♘a5 17 ♘f3 gives White the upper hand; for example 17 . . . c4 18 ♗e3 ♗×c3 19 b×c3 ♖×e4 20 ♘d2, regaining the pawn with good black-square play in prospect (Ligterink–Franco, Arnhem/Amsterdam 1983).

The whole idea of having the knight kicked round the board from f6 to a5 is most unconvincing. Black does better to forget . . . ♖e8 and concentrate on Q-side play, thus: 11 e4 ♖b8 12 ♖e1 (if 12 a5 b5 13 a×b6 ♕×b6, the b-pawn is at least as weak as the a-pawn; instead White permits the advance and seeks to immobilise the enemy pawns) b5 13 a×b5 a×b5 14 ♗f1 (Black is ready to neutralise the central push here: 14 ♗f4 ♘e8 15 e5 d×e5 16 ♘×e5 ♘×e5 17 ♗×e5 ♗×e5 18 ♖×e5 ♘d6 is equal) b4 15 ♘b5 ♘e8. Now here the awkward appearance of the black pieces is something of an illusion. The white knight looks aggressive at b5, but is actually rather inflexible; at the same time the thrust e5 has lost a lot of its punch compared with previous variations and Black may be able to counter-attack by . . . f5. Two examples, briefly, are (1) 16 ♗f4 ♖b6 17 ♕c2 ♗b7 (Ree–Sax, Arnhem/Amsterdam 1983 up to here) 18 ♖a7 ♕b8 19 ♖ea1; and (2) 16 ♕c2 ♘e5 17 ♘×e5 ♗×e5 18 ♗h6 ♗g7 19 ♗×g7 ♔×g7 20 e5 ♗f5 21 ♕c1 d×e5 22 ♕×c5 ♖c8 (Sosonko–Danner, Salonika 1984), with approximate equality in each case.

Returning to move 11 (after 9 . . . a6 10 a4 ♘bd7), White can introduce the other new idea by 11 ♗f4. On the whole, though, it is not regarded as very promising because it blocks the f-pawn. For instance: 11 . . . ♕e7 12 ♕d2 (or 12 e4 ♘g4 and we are dealing with positions similar to the game, which are discussed in a later note; if 12 h3, Black can still obtain active play by 12 . . . ♖b8 13 ♖b1 ♖e8 14 ♖e1 ♘h5 15 ♗g5 ♕f8 16 e4 b5 – Hansen–Cebalo, Banja Luka 1981) ♘g4 13 ♖ab1 ♘de5 14 b4 b6 15 b×c5 b×c5 16 h3 ♘×f3+ 17 e×f3 ♘e5 and the position is roughly level (Korchnoi–Hulak, Wijk aan Zee 1983).

Since e4 is beginning to look more dangerous than ♗f4, Black could well try a different move-order, 9 . . . a6 10 a4 ♖e8, in which he tries to cut out this possibility and at the same time prepare some immediate action (and a welcome exchange of pieces) in the centre. He also hopes to avoid wasting a move by having to defend his d-pawn (as after 10 . . . ♘bd7 11 ♗f4). The problem is that after 11 ♗f4 ♘e4 12 ♘×e4 ♖×e4 13 ♘d2 ♖b4 (must keep active – 13 . . . ♖e8 14 ♘c4 is no good at all) White has 14 ♖a2! ♗×b2 15 ♘e4 (or even ♘c4) with advantage. If Black declines the b-pawn, he cannot easily continue his neglected development.

After 11 ♗f4, then, Black probably does best to play 11 . . . ♕e7, which leads to positions already dealt with. But there is one further subtlety here, which introduces the final move-order question: can Black do without . . . a6? After 9 . . . ♘bd7 (the main game) he certainly cannot delay it for long because the danger of ♗f4 and ♘b5 is too great, but 9 . . . ♖e8 is a possibility, again cutting out White's e4 and preparing . . . ♘e4 if circumstances are favourable. If then 10 ♗f4, Black could play 10 . . . a6 11 a4 ♕e7, transposing into the line suggested above, or he could try an extremely complicated variation beginning with 10 . . . ♘e4 (10 . . . ♘h5 11 ♗g5 ♕b6 is yet another plan) 11 ♘×e4 ♖×e4 12 ♘d2 ♖b4, since 13 ♖a2 is not available this time! One example of that is 13 a3 (or 13 ♘e4 ♗f5, meeting 14 ♘×d6 by . . . ♖×f4) ♖×f4 14 g×f4 ♗×b2 15 ♖a2 (Black provoked a3 to make the rook go to this now useless square) ♗g7 16 e4 ♘a6 17 ♖e1 b5 18 e5 ♗f5, with a very unclear position (Alburt–Peters, USA Championship 1981). If instead 10 ♖e1, Black will wish to weaken White's Q-side first with 10 . . . a6 11 a4 and then again play 11 . . . ♘e4 12 ♘×e4 ♖×e4 13 ♗g5 (before ♘d2, of course, but now Black's d-pawn is under less pressure) ♕c7 14 ♘d2 ♖b4 15 ♘e4 ♘d7, with a satisfactory game. Naturally this line could also have arisen via 9 . . . a6 10 a4 ♖e8 11 ♖e1 etc.

10 e4 . . .

Plenty of transpositions are possible around here. 10 ♖e1 a6 11 a4 would turn into a variation already examined, while 10 ♗f4 ♕e7 11 ♖e1 a6 12 e4 simply becomes the main game. But in this line (or with the move-order adopted in the game) you will notice that Black's choice of 9 . . . ♘bd7 has given his opponent an additional option. After 9 . . . a6 10 a4 is unavoidable, but if Black delays . . . a6 the threat of a quick central breakthrough by e5 appears again; and since that is far stronger than Black's thrust . . . b5, White can manage without a4. The drawback to all this is the old objection to ♗f4, namely that it obstructs the f-pawn, and the continuation of the game suggests that 10 e4 a6 11 a4 would be a slightly better chance of initiative than the line adopted.

10 . . . a6

11 ♗f4 ♕e7

Not 11 . . . ♕c7, because of 12 e5 d×e5 13 d6 ♕b6 14 ♘×e5 ♕×b2 15 ♘a4 ♕d4 16 ♕×d4 c×d4 17 ♘c4! with a very strong position. But now 12 e5 would be premature: 12 . . . ♘×e5 13 ♘×e5 d×e5 14 d6 ♕e6, and although White does not lose a pawn overall he gets an inferior endgame by 15 ♗g5 (15 ♖e1 ♘e8) ♖d8 16 ♗×f6 ♗×f6 17 ♘e4 ♗g7 18 ♘×c5 ♕×d6; he therefore prepares the pawn thrust.

12 ♖e1 ♘g4

Forced, to avoid 13 e5, and this is the parting of the ways for White. He can still continue quietly with 13 a4, or he can set the game ablaze with the fierce continuation in the text. Here are two examples of 13 a4, which have their own points of interest: (a) 13 a4 ♖b8 14 ♗f1 ♘ge5 15 ♘d2 (avoiding an exchange) ♖e8 (a convenient regrouping, leaving f8 for the queen) 16 ♗e3 f5! (because Black would gain more than he would lose by the pawn exchange – the pawn would not be a burden to defend and he would control e4; meanwhile 17 . . . ♘g4 is threatened) 17 h3 ♕f8 18 f4 ♘f7, and the game is equal because Black has had plenty of time to organise his position against the pawn advance (Inkiov–Ermenkov, Bulgarian Championship, 1977); (b) 13 a4 ♖b8 14 ♘d2 ♘de5 15 ♘f1 (or 15 h3 g5!) ♘c4 16 ♕e2 b5 17 a×b5 a×b5 18 h3 ♘ge5 with equality (Smyslov–Portisch, Hungary 1978).

Ligterink is looking for something altogether sharper than that.

13 ♗g5 ♕e8

Nunn deliberately allows the following combination because he has seen a remarkable counter-sacrifice at move 16. In any case he is playing the whole game uncompromisingly since he needs a win to have a chance of qualifying for the Interzonal tournament. Of the two possible alternatives, 13 . . . ♗f6 is definitely too passive: 14 ♗×f6 ♕×f6 15 h3 ♘e5 16 ♘×e5 ♘×e5 17 f4 ♘c4 18 e5! d×e5 19 b3 ♘b6 (19 . . . e×f4 20 ♘e4) 20 f×e5 with a tremendous position; nor is 14 . . . ♘ (either) ×f6 any better: 15 e5 ♘×e5 16 ♘×e5 d×e5 17 d6 ♕e6 (or 17 . . . ♕e8 18 ♘d5) 18 f4 etc. But 13 . . . f6 14 ♗c1 b5 is perfectly satisfactory. During the game Nunn (and perhaps Ligterink too) felt that in this line the bishop would remain imprisoned for too long, with . . . f5 being difficult to organise. That is a needless worry, though: the bishop is far from being buried alive, and he can generate plenty of Q-side play after, for instance, 15 a4 b4 16 ♘b1 a5 17 ♘bd2 ♗a6, or 15 h3 ♘e5 16 ♘×e5 d×e5! This last move may seem a surprising choice, but 17 d6 would expose the pawn too much; therefore Black can follow up with . . . ♕d6 and the blockade cannot be lifted, at any rate for a long time; meanwhile he will have much more scope, especially for his queen and bishop, than after 16 . . . f×e5. It would also be difficult to devise a plan after . . . f×e5 because the f-file could not easily be put to use. But after . . . d×e5 and . . . ♕d6 Black has, for example, . . . ♘b6, . . . ♗d7, . . . ♖ec8, . . . ♖ab8 and the advance of the Q-side pawns.

14 e5 . . .

This is a clever idea, which deserved a better fate, for if Black deviates at all from the game continuation he gets into trouble. First, he must keep taking with his knights at e5; if 14 . . . d×e5 15 d6 threatens both ♗e7 and ♘d5 (15 . . . f6 16 ♘d5! ♕d8 17 ♘c7), or if 14 . . . ♘d×e5 15 ♘×e5 d×e5 16 d6 f6 17 ♘d5 ♕d8 18 ♘c7 ♖b8 19 ♕d5+ ♔h8 20 ♗d2, with a very strong position.

14 . . . ♘d×e5

15 ♘×e5 ♘×e5

16 f4 *(64)* **. . .**

And here Black is forced to sacrifice his queen; not that he has any objection – he is guaranteed at least a draw.

16 . . . ♘g4!

The only other moves Black could

64
B

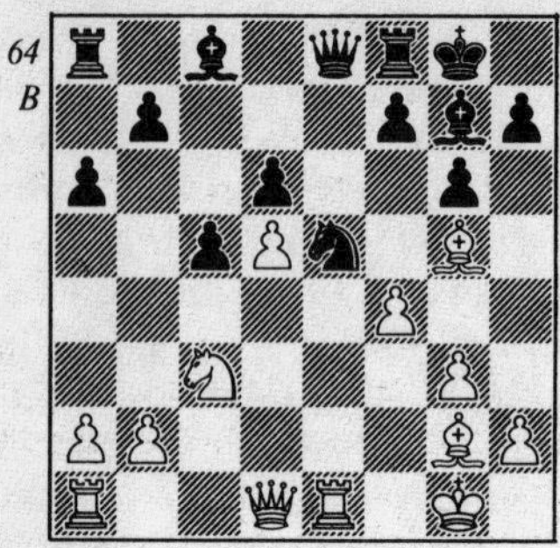

consider are 16 . . . h6 and 16 . . . ♗g4 (followed by . . . h6). 16 . . . f6 is decidedly inferior because of 17 f×e5 f×g5 18 e6, with a massive pawn wedge that could never be undermined.

If 16 . . . h6 17 ♗h4 (not 17 f×e5 h×g5 18 e6 this time, on account of 18 . . . ♗e5!, when White has to exchange his e-pawn) g5 18 f×e5 (18 f×g5 h×g5 19 ♗×g5 f5 is not so clear; Black's well-placed knight and control of e4 give him some return for his exposed king) g×h4 19 e6!, and now Black cannot cover up by 19 . . . ♗e5 because his king is too open – 20 ♕g4+ ♔h8 21 ♕×h4, for instance, would be very strong; meanwhile 20 e7 is threatened and the e-pawn remains a terrible thorn in his side, impossible to dislodge.

The analysis of 16 . . . ♗g4 contains a few tactical curiosities. White might be tempted into 17 ♖×e5, which wins two pieces for a rook, but then comes 17 . . . ♕c8! 18 ♖e2 c4 19 ♕d2 ♗×e2 20 ♘×e2 ♕c5+ 21 ♔h1 f5 and suddenly the white bishops are quite badly restricted and Black has all the play with his mobile Q-side majority. The best move is 17 ♕c1! because he wishes to cover g5 (17 ♕d2 permits complications by 17 . . . ♘c4 18 ♕d3 ♗d4+ 19 ♔h1 ♘e3), and after 17 . . . h6 18 f×e5 h×g5 19 ♕×g5 ♗f5 20 g4 ♗c8 (or 20 . . . ♗d7 or 20 . . . ♗d3) 21 e6 (21 . . . ♗e5? 22 e7) Black's Q-side is again seriously blockaded.

17 ♖×e8 ♖×e8

You may like to compare this queen sacrifice with the one in Game 5 (Augustin–Nunn). On that occasion the queen was ineffective because the whole pawn structure was against her. To open up the position and gain manoeuvring space for her was not possible within a reasonable time. Here it is not so much the weakness of the queen which is striking – before too long she manages to obtain some active play – but rather the enormous power of the black pieces, especially their control of the centre. They seem to sweep into White's position almost as they please, first on one side of the board, then on the other. The white minor pieces, on the other hand, are very poorly placed, particularly the g5 bishop, and none of them can get any kind of foothold in the centre.

Now at this point there is a terrifying collection of forks, discovered checks and even mates based on the threat of 18 . . . ♗d4+, and it is the realisation that White's choice of replies is very restricted which has led Nunn to give serious consideration to what is, after all, a substantial sacrifice. In fact White has only three possibilities here: (a) the immediate return of the queen by 18 ♘e4; (b) 18 ♕f1 (best); and (c) 18 ♘e2. He cannot move his king, rook, either bishop or any pawn without allowing a quick win by . . . ♗d4+, and he cannot move the queen to any other square (say 18 ♕b3) because Black has 18 . . . ♗d4+ 19 ♔h1 (19 ♔f1 ♘×h2 mate) ♘f2+ 20 ♔g1 ♘d1+ 21 ♔f1 (21 ♔h1 ♖e1+) ♘e3+ 22 ♔g1 ♘c2+ 23 ♔f1 ♘×a1 24 ♕d1 ♗f5 etc. As a general rule, if Black regains even a minor piece, let alone a rook, he has at least material equality and should maintain enough positional advantage to win.

18 ♘e4 is not quite satisfactory because of 18 . . . ♗d4+ 19 ♕×d4 (19 ♔h1 ♖×e4 20 ♕×g4 ♗×g4 21 ♗×e4 and Black emerges a good pawn up) c×d4 20 ♘×d6 ♖e2! (the white pieces have suddenly woken up and Black has to return the exchange without further ado; but still he has enough to win. 20 . . . ♖f8 21 ♗e7 would be too passive, while 20 . . . ♖e3 21 ♘c4 ♗f5 – he cannot permit ♘b6 combined with d6 – 22 ♘×e3 ♘×e3 23 ♗f6 ♘×g2 would lead to a draw) 21 ♘×c8 ♖×g2+ (21 . . . ♖×c8? 22 ♗f3) 22 ♔×g2 ♖×c8 23 f5 (must release the bishop) f6 24 ♗f4 g5 25 h3 ♖c2+ 26 ♔g1 ♘h2 27 ♗d6 (27 d6 ♔f7) ♘f3+ 28 ♔f1 ♔f7, and White has a thoroughly miserable position.

The two other moves, ♕f1 and ♘e2, both lead to a draw with correct play, but 18 ♕f1 is much simpler because Black would have nothing better than an immediate repetition by 18 . . . ♗d4+ 19 ♔h1 ♘f2+ etc. He could try for more, but it would be very risky. But even if White had thought of ♕f1, he would understandably have been reluctant to accept a draw so soon after beginning his combination. That was really his best option, though; after the text move his position is harder to handle than Black's and he is more likely to make a mistake.

18 ♘e2(?) ♘e3

19 ♕d2 . . .

This is forced; 19 ♕e1? ♘×g2 20 ♔×g2 ♗g4 would lose a piece, while 19 ♕d3 would just encourage 19 . . . ♗f5.

19 . . . ♘c4

20 ♕c2 . . .

Again there is no choice; against other moves Black plays . . . ♘×b2 with tempo gain. In a way Black's plan is quite simple. He will win the b-pawn and then advance his 3:1 Q-side majority supported by all his pieces. He will also double rooks on the e-file. And in spite of his large material disadvantage the pressure generated in this way will suffice to win the game unless White can obtain some genuinely active play for his queen.

20 . . . b5! *(65)*

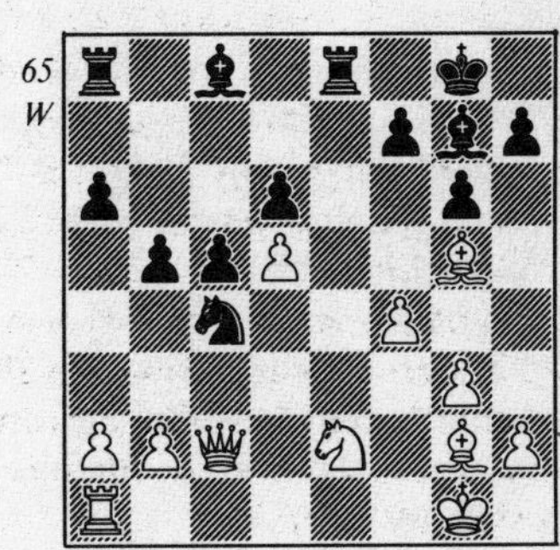

65
W

Obviously Black will operate with direct threats and tempo gains whenever possible, but he will not automatically grab material at the first opportunity, if in so doing he allows the white pieces some scope. Here a combination of . . . ♘×b2 and . . . ♗f5 is what he wants, but 20 . . . ♘×b2 21 ♗e4! is inferior – 21 . . . f5, to drive away the bishop, would block his own piece. Therefore Nunn prepares . . . ♗f5 in another, more flexible way. He retains the option of either capture at b2 or of . . . ♘e3. But what is rather startling is that he actually has the time to play 20 . . . b5 in the circumstances. The explanation is that 21 . . . ♗f5 has now become such a serious threat (22 ♕d1 ♘×b2, or even 22 . . . ♗×b2 23 ♗f3 ♘e3) that White has to direct all his attention to stopping it.

Now there are not many ways to prevent . . . ♗f5. If 21 ♗f3 (guarding the knight) ♗f5 22 ♕d1 ♗×b2 wins at least the exchange, and . . . ♖e3 plus . . . ♖ae8 can also follow. There is not much hope in that. If 21 ♗e4 ♗g4 threatens 22 . . . ♗×e2 and 23 . . . f5, and if 22 ♗d3 ♘×b2 is catastrophic. It would have to be 22 ♖e1, but then comes 22 . . . f5 23 ♗g2 (23 ♗d3 ♘×b2 threatens . . . c4) ♗d4+ 24 ♘×d4 (24 ♔h1 ♗f2) ♖×e1+ 25 ♔f2 ♖d1 26 ♘f3 ♗×f3 27 ♔×f3 ♖d2, followed by . . . ♖e8, and the king is fatally exposed. Finally, 21 ♘c3 ♗f5 22 ♗e4 (or 22 ♕c1 or ♕b3 ♗d4+ 23 ♔h1 ♘×b2 24 ♕×b2 b4 25 ♖c1 b×c3 26 ♕b6 c2 and wins) b4 23 ♗×f5 b×c3 24 b×c3 ♘e3 25 ♕d2 ♘×f5, though better than some variations, is distinctly favourable to Black because his pieces are still much the more aggressive. If here 24 ♗d3 c×b2 25 ♖f1 (♖b1 and ♖d1 are no better) ♘e3 26 ♕d2 ♘×f1 27 ♔×f1 h6 28 ♗h4 ♗d4, followed by doubling rooks, and Black will win with his passed pawns.

After long thought White finds what is unquestionably his best chance; he gives his queen and knight some scope and simultaneously prevents . . . ♗f5.

21 g4! ♗×g4

22 ♘g3 h6

Usefully driving the bishop to h4. White's counter-attack is going to be based on the pawn advance f5, which will now cost him a piece after . . . g5. White will also be very reluctant to move his knight again; so the bishop cannot easily return into play via the h4–e1 diagonal.

23 ♗h4 ♗×b2

24 ♖c1 ♗d4+!

The bishop is Black's most useful piece, both in attack and defence (holding the K-side together and preventing ♘e4–f6+, for instance), and it would be unwise to surrender it for a passive rook, even though Black could then claim a slight material advantage. On the other hand, he would happily exchange his knight for the rook, making way at the same time for his Q-side pawns. That is why the rook had to go to c1. And now there is another dynamic aspect of the position which needs some explanation. White's very good 21st move has changed the picture somewhat. Since he now has counter-chances on the K-side, the slow advance of the pawn majority will no longer suffice for Black. The time factor has become crucial and he must act swiftly before White's attack develops. Nunn therefore adopts a rather surprising plan: he exchanges White's passive K-bishop for his own active knight, but in so doing he gains time to complete his development and maintain the initiative. 24 . . . ♖e3 was a tempting alternative, intending . . . ♖ae8 and . . . ♗×c1, but 25 h3 ♗d7 26 ♘f1 is a good reply, since White can always return the material – 26 . . . ♖c3 27 ♕×c3.

25 ♔h1 ♘e3!

26 ♕d2 ♘×g2

An example of the slower method would be 26 . . . ♘f5 27 ♘×f5 ♗×f5 28 ♗f2 ♗g7; but the pawns cannot advance easily here – . . . c4 is met by ♗d4, or if . . . b4 Black will need to use his a-pawn as well, to make progress. Even more seriously the thinning out of the position is helping the queen more and more. White would probably try to exchange a pair of rooks and penetrate via a5.

27 ♕×g2 . . .

If 27 ♔×g2 ♗e3 and . . . ♗×f4 would kill any hopes for White on the K-side, and his minor pieces would be badly misplaced.

27 . . . ♖e3

Doubling rooks with gain of time and highlighting another favourable aspect of his 26th move; White is going to miss his K-bishop, even though it was a passive piece.

28 ♖f1 . . .

Black has also had to take into account the possibility of a liquidation, but after 28 ♘f1 ♗f3 29 ♘×e3 ♗×g2+ 30 ♘×g2 c4 the ending favours him because White's pawns are rather weak and he cannot transfer his pieces smoothly to the Q-side. For example, if 31 ♘e1 ♗e3 wins a pawn; or if 31 ♗e1 ♖e8 32 ♗b4 ♔g7 (or perhaps 32 . . . ♖e2) 33 ♗×d6 ♖d8 34 ♗b4 ♖×d5, followed by . . . ♔f6–f5.

28 . . . ♖ae8 *(66)*

This is the crisis of the game. Black has completed the plan outlined in the note to his 24th move and his pieces are beautifully placed. He has total control of the centre and the queen has not managed to penetrate anywhere. On the other hand, White is now ready to begin his counterplay. Obviously a K-side attack is the only option open to him; his pieces are too awkwardly placed to consider anything else. And he must begin at once because Black is preparing to push his c-pawn. Analysis indicates a draw with best play, as follows:

29 h3 ♗c8 30 f5 g5 31 ♘h5, threatening to sacrifice at g5 and also to play 32 ♗f2. In reply it seems that Black cannot do better than the obvious move 31 . . . ♖e2. There is one other try, 31 . . . ♗b7, which sets a beautiful trap, but is sadly unsound. If (31 . . . ♗b7) White is tempted into 32 ♗×g5, he loses to 32 . . . ♖×h3+! 33 ♕×h3 ♗×d5+ and then: (a) 34 ♖f3 h×g5 and amazingly he must part with a whole rook, having no defence against . . . ♖e3 (if 35 ♔h2 ♖e2+ 36 ♔g3 ♗×f3 wins, or if 35 ♕g3 or ♕g4 f6! and nothing is changed); or (b) 34 ♔h2 ♖e2+ 35 ♔g3 h×g5 36 ♔g4 (no other way to prevent . . . ♖e3+) ♖g2+ 37 ♘g3 ♗e5, and the inevitable outcome is a winning endgame for Black with four pawns against the exchange. The problem, of course, is that 31 . . . ♗b7 does not prevent the other threat – White plays 32 ♗f2, either gaining time for 33 h4 (after 32 . . . ♖e2) or exchanging the bishops; and we know that the disappearance

of his K-bishop would weaken Black's attack substantially.

So 31 . . . ♖e2 32 ♕g4 (the only useful square) and here the position is balanced on a knife-edge. What appeared to be a rather clumsy attacking set-up for White, compared with Black's more orthodox piece placing, actually has a lot of power behind it. He is basing his assault on the sacrifice ♗×g5, together with the rickety-looking but quite effective move ♘f4 (making way for ♕h5, among other things). If Black defends with 32 . . . f6 33 ♘f4 ♖2e4 34 ♕h5 g×f4 35 ♕g6+ is disastrous for him; and 34 . . . g×h4 35 ♕g6+ ♔f8 36 ♘e6+ is no better. Therefore he must rely on threats of his own, and only one will do. 32 . . . ♗b7 is natural, but fails against 33 ♘f4 ♖2e4 34 ♗×g5 h×g5 35 ♕×g5+ ♔f8 (35 . . . ♔h7 or . . . ♔h8 36 f6) 36 ♘e6+ and the attack breaks through to win. Again 32 . . . ♖8e4 is inadequate: 33 ♘f4 and White threatens ♕×e2, ♘×e2 and ♗×g5.

The right way is 32 . . . ♖2e4! and now it is White who has to be careful. Is it 33 ♘f4 or 33 ♖f4 ? If 33 ♖f4 ♖×f4 34 ♘×f4 ♖e5! and then (a) 35 ♗×g5 ♗×f5 36 ♕g3 (36 ♕h5 is the same) ♗e4+ 37 ♔h2 ♖×g5 and wins; (b) 35 ♘h5 ♗×f5 36 ♕g3 (or White may insert 36 ♘f6+ ♔g7 37 ♘h5+ ♔f8 – it makes no difference) ♗e4+ 37 ♔h2 ♖×d5 (threatens . . . ♗e5) 38 ♕g4 (or 38 ♕e1 g×h4 39 ♕×e4 ♖×h5 40 ♕a8+ ♔g7 41 ♕×a6 b4 and Black wins the endgame) ♗e5+ 39 ♔g1 (or 39 ♗g3 ♖d2+ 40 ♔g1 f5) f5 40 ♕e2 g×h4 and wins; (c) 35 ♕h5 ♗×f5 36 ♕×h6 g×f4 37 ♕×f4 (there is no better move; if 37 ♗f6 ♖e1+ and mate, or if 37 ♕×d6 ♖e2 ♕d8+ ♔h7 and wins; nor is 37 ♕g5+ ♗g6 any improvement) ♗g6. Black now threatens above all 38 . . . ♖e2 and . . . ♗e4+, and after capturing the d-pawn should win with his material advantage. In every case Black either liquidates into a winning ending with rook, bishop and several pawns against the queen, or gets a mating attack.

But if White keeps his rook, the back rank is safe and he can just manage to draw, thus: 33 ♘f4! ♖8e5 34 ♗×g5 ♗×f5 35 ♕h4 h×g5 36 ♕×g5+ ♗g6 37 ♕d8+ (but not 37 ♕g3 ♖f5, with . . . ♗e5 to follow, nor 37 ♕g2 ♖×f4! 38 ♖×f4 ♖e1+ 39 ♖f1 ♖×f1+ 40 ♕×f1 c4, when Black should win by advancing his pawns, because the queen will have no weaknesses to attack, nor any checks) ♖e8 38 ♕×d6 ♖e1 (38 . . . ♗e5 39 ♕d7) 39 ♖×e1 ♖×e1+ 40 ♔g2 ♗e4+ 41 ♔h2 ♖h1+ 42 ♔g3 ♖g1+, and neither side dare try for more (if 43 ♔h4? ♗f3 wins).

After all these delicately-balanced variations the final moves of the game are something of an anti-climax. White unfortunately neglects to drive the bishop away before playing f5 (probably hoping to trap it) and as a result loses at once.

29	**f5?**	**g5**
30	**f6**	**. . .**

White's intention was 30 ♗×g5 h×g5 31 h3, regaining the piece, but he had overlooked 31 . . . ♗e5! In that event 32 h×g4 ♖×g3 is the same hopeless ending as occurs in the game, while 32 ♘e4 ♖×h3+ 33 ♔g1 ♗d4+ 34 ♖f2 (or 34 ♘f2 ♖ee3!) ♗×f2+ 35 ♔×f2 ♖f3+ etc. is even worse. 30 h3 g×h4, of course, amounts to much the same thing.

30	**. . .**	**♔h8!**

Not 30 . . . g×h4 31 ♘f5, but now White has to lose material – if 31 ♘f5 ♗h3, for example.

31	**♗×g5**	**h×g5**
32	**♘f5**	**♗×f5**
33	**♖×f5**	**♖e1+**
34	**♖f1**	**♗×f6**
35	**♕h3+**	**♔g7**
36	**♖×e1**	**♖×e1+**
37	**♔g2**	**c4**

0 – 1

Black's king is perfectly safe from checks and the c-pawn cannot be stopped. For example: (a) 38 ♔f2 ♖b1 39 ♕a3 c3; (b) 38 ♔f2 ♖b1 39 ♕d7 c3 40 ♕c6 c2; (c) 38 ♕d7 c3 39 ♕c6 ♖e2+ 40 ♔g3 ♖×a2 41 ♕×d6 c2 42 ♕c6 ♖a3+ and . . . ♖c3.

Game 16

Two Knights Defence
London (Phillips & Drew) 1982
J. Nunn v. L. Christiansen

1	**e4**	**e5**
2	**♗c4**	**♘f6**
3	**d3**	**♘c6**
4	**♘f3**	**h6**

Broadly speaking, Black can choose a system of development based on the obvious . . . ♗c5, or he may opt for the more restrained . . . ♗e7. After the latter move the position resembles a Closed Ruy Lopez in which he may continue manoeuvring along the lines of . . . d6, . . . 0–0, . . . ♖e8, . . . ♗f8 and perhaps . . . g6 and . . . ♗g7. Christiansen intends to adopt that variation, but wishes to save time by fianchettoing immediately. The point of his surprising fourth move is twofold: (i) that 4 . . . g6 would be disastrous on account of 5 ♘g5 (5 . . . d5 6 e×d5 ♘×d5 7 ♘×f7; or 6 . . . ♘a5, as per the normal Two Knights line, 7 ♕e2 and he cannot justify the pawn sacrifice); and (ii) that the loss of tempo and hence neglect of development involved in 4 . . . h6 can only be exploited by opening up the centre; and White can only achieve that by d4, which would in itself amount to a loss of time after his third move.

5	**0–0**	**d6**
6	**c3**	**g6**
7	**d4** *(67)*	**. . .**

Although the d-pawn moves twice, c3 and d4 is most likely the best chance of maintaining the initiative. Now Black must be careful to keep the position stabilised; otherwise his backward development and the weaknesses created at f6 and h6 will be exposed. For example: (a) 7 . . . ♗g7 8 d×e5 d×e5 9 ♕×d8+ ♘×d8 10 ♘×e5 ♘×e4 11 ♖e1; or (b) 7 . . . ♘×e4 8 ♗d5 ♘f6 9 ♗×c6+ b×c6 10 d×e5 ♘d5 11 e×d6 e×d6 12 ♖e1+ ♗e7 (12 . . . ♗e6 13 ♘d4) 13 c4, and he has a weak d-pawn, is unpleasantly pinned on the e-file and cannot castle; or (c) 7 . . . e×d4 8 c×d4 ♘×e4 9 ♖e1 d5 10 ♗×d5 ♕×d5 11 ♘c3; if here 8 . . . d5 9 e×d5 ♘×d5 10 ♖e1+ ♗e7 11 ♗×d5 ♕×d5 12 ♘c3, followed by d5 and ♕e2.

Clearly Black needs to retain a pawn at e5.

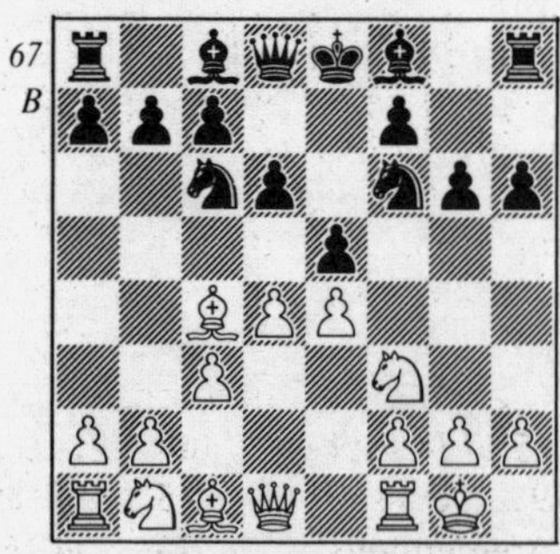
67
B

7	**. . .**	**♕e7**
8	**♘bd2**	**♗g7**
9	**♖e1**	**. . .**

The same kind of position arises in Nunn–Olafsson (Game 18), and the placing of the queen on e7 has comparable objections here: she is bound to feel uncomfortable opposite the white rook. But in this case at least Black already has f5 under control; so the queen cannot be disturbed by the appearance there of a white knight. Having accepted a restricted position in the centre, Black's most natural plan will be to liberate himself and at the same time counter-attack by working for the move . . . f5; but the timing will be critical since he is bound to suffer from weaknesses after White has exchanged pawns at e5 and f5. This is, of course, a very different situation from the typical King's Indian formation where White has blocked the centre by d5, a move which he has no intention of making here. In that case the centre would not open up completely and Black could confidently aim for . . . f5 at the earliest opportunity.

9	**. . .**	**0–0**
10	**h3**	**. . .**

A necessary precaution since 10 ♘f1 would be met by 10 . . . ♗g4. This position has been reached on a number of occasions, with Black experimenting in various ways to try to obtain some play. For instance: (1) 10 . . . ♔h7 11 ♘f1 ♘d8 (a puzzling move, whose intention is actually to forgo . . . f5 altogether and make use of the outpost at f4 – . . . ♘e6–f4 – for some piece play against the K-side) 12 ♘g3 ♘g8 13 ♗d3 ♕f6 14 d5! (but just at the right moment White cuts across the plan; blocking the centre is quite in order now because Black has wasted time and will experience great difficulty in achieving . . . f5 – the move to which he must revert) ♕e7 15 ♕c2 (Psakhis–Nei, Tallinn 1983) and Black's game is unacceptably passive – if 15 . . . ♕d7 16 c4 and still 16 . . . f5 is unplayable: 17 e×f5 g×f5 18 ♘×f5 ♖×f5 19 ♘h4 ♘e7 20 g4. (2) 10 . . . ♕d8(!) 11 ♗b3 ♖e8 (quite a good scheme, though it has only been tried once; the queen is removed from the e-file without further ado and still White's e-pawn is under some pressure. 12 a3 a5 13 ♗c2 ♗d7 14 ♘f1 a4 15 ♘g3 b5, with a comfortable game (Gavrikov–Eingorn, USSR 1981). (3) 10 . . . ♘h7 (the normal move, preparing . . . f5; at the same time his position is relieved by an exchange of knights and he threatens the d-pawn) 11 ♘f1 ♘g5 12 ♘1h2 ♘×f3+ 13 ♘×f3 ♔h7 14 a4 f5 15 d×e5 d×e5 16 a5 f×e4 (or 16 . . . a6 17 ♕b3, making Black's development difficult) 17 ♘d2 e3 18 ♖×e3 ♗f5 19 a6 b6 (Ghinda–Belyavsky, Lvov 1981). White should now blockade by 20 ♘e4, and although Black's pieces are quite lively, the weakness at e4 may tell against him in the long run. Ghinda neglected the crucial square e4 and got into trouble; after 20 ♗d5? ♕d7 21 ♗f3 ♖ad8 22 ♕a4 e4! 23 ♘×e4 ♘e5 Black's piece activity had reached alarming proportions (if 24 ♕×d7 ♘×f3+ 25 ♖×f3 ♖×d7 26 ♘g3 ♖d1+ 27 ♔h2 ♗e5, for instance) and Belyavsky went on to win.

In an earlier round of the present tournament Spassky had tried a refined version of this normal scheme against Nunn, developing his Q-side pieces first, and Christiansen now adopts the same approach.

10	**. . .**	**♗d7**
11	**♘f1**	**♖ae8**
12	**♘g3**	**♔h8** *(68)*

If Black can organise . . . ♘h7 and . . . f5 his attack will begin to look

68
W

menacing, but the drawback to his plan is that **he is committed to it**. If White can find some slight weakness in it; if he can interfere somehow, then Black will be in difficulties because a change of plan will require much regrouping. In the first game Nunn reacted feebly by 13 ♗d2 ♘h7 14 d×e5 ♘×e5 15 ♘×e5 d×e5 16 ♕b3 b6, with no more than equality. The second time round, characteristically, he is ready with a big improvement.

13 a4! . . .

The drop of poison in this move is that it looks so innocent! It is just the kind of semi-waiting move which you expect White to play in such a situation. He wants to wait a little while longer for Black to commit himself definitely by . . . ♘h7 and . . . f5, and he also wishes to make some progress by nibbling away at the Q-side, trying to weaken Black by a5–a6, or gain some space, or perhaps follow with a5 and ♕b3. But the tactical point, which escapes Christiansen entirely, is that White is preparing a central pawn exchange followed by b3 and ♗a3. Had he spotted that, Black would probably have continued 13 . . . ♖d8. Then the immediate pawn exchange would merely expose White's queen prematurely to the black rook, while 14 ♕e2 would permit 14 . . . ♘a5 15 ♗d3 ♘b3. Therefore 14 a5! would be the best multi-purpose move, preparing a6, or ♕b3, or d×e5 with ♕e2, all according to circumstances. The game might develop in various ways, but White would certainly maintain his initiative.

13 . . . ♘h7?
14 d×e5 ♘×e5

If 14 . . . d×e5 15 b3, Black would have to jettison a pawn to avoid worse: 15 . . . ♘a5 16 ♗a3 c5 17 ♗×c5 ♕×c5 18 ♕×d7 ♘×c4 19 b×c4 ♕×c4 20 ♕×b7 etc., with no compensation.

15 ♘×e5 d×e5

If 15 . . . ♕×e5, 16 ♕b3 ♗c6 17 ♗×f7? ♕f6 is unplayable, but 16 ♗e3 genuinely threatens the a-pawn (meeting a subsequent . . . b6 by a5) and if 16 . . . a6 17 ♕b3 does win a pawn.

16 b3 . . .

Faced with ♗a3, Black now resigns himself to making the enormous positional concession . . . c5, leaving a hole at d5 which torments him for the rest of the game. But his prospects were dismal anyway: if 16 . . . ♖g8 17 ♗a3 either wins a pawn (17 . . . c5 18 ♗×c5) or forces the queen to abandon f7 or d7; if 16 . . . ♗e6 17 ♗a3 c5 18 ♗×e6 forces 18 . . . f×e6. And to avoid any confusion by comparison with Game 6 (Britton–Nunn), this is not a position where the f-file would compensate Black for his weakened pawns. The reason is twofold: (1) His minor pieces are very inferior and could not assist with any K-side attacking operations, by establishing a knight outpost at f4, for example; therefore White would simply play f3 and Black's chances of using the f-file would be practically zero. (2) White's own pieces are active and before long he will organise some exchanges along the d-file. Sooner or later Black's pawn weaknesses will show up in the endgame.

16 ... ♖d8

17 ♗a3 c5

If you are wondering why we are making such a fuss about d5, the endgame may provide the clearest illustration of what a dreadful positional liability it represents. Meanwhile, the game continuation is also very much to the point; White uses the square at once to bring the black pawns under fire.

18 ♕d5 ...

Quiet lines are also favourable, 18 ♕e2 ♖fe8 19 b4 c×b4 20 ♗×b4 ♕f6 21 ♖ed1, for instance, or here 18 ... ♗c6 19 b4! ♗×a4 (19 ... b6 20 b×c5 b×c5 21 ♕e3 and wins) 20 b5 a6 21 b×a6 b×a6 22 ♗×a6, threatening ♕c4. The text move is even better.

18 ... b6

19 ♕b7 ...

The queen is in no personal danger here and White's decision to go plundering deep in enemy territory is quite acceptable in this instance; all the same, a certain amount of analysis was necessary to estimate the strength of Black's counterplay, which is bound to hit his castled position in the queen's absence.

19 ... ♕f6 *(69)*

If 19 ... ♖b8 20 ♕×a7 is safe enough, or if 19 ... ♖a8, simply 20 ♗d5 and 21 ♕×a8.

20 ♖ad1 ...

In fact the power of Black's attack is far from easy to assess and Nunn

69
W

decides to play safe for the next few moves, guaranteeing himself a more modest advantage than he might have had. The best move is to capture at once: 20 ♕×a7, and here we have a clear picture of how his analysis ran during the game: 20 ... ♗×h3 (although this sacrifice is an obvious possibility, one feels at first that it must be unsound because the white bishop can quickly return to e2 or f1; but it is f2 that is hard to defend in the absence of the queen) 21 g×h3? ♘g5 and then: (a) 22 ♔g2 ♕f3+ 23 ♔f1 ♘×h3 24 ♖e2 (24 ♖a2 ♘f4 and ... ♖d1+) ♘f4, with numerous threats, chiefly mate in three by 25 ... ♕g2+ etc.; (b) 22 ♗f1 ♘f3+ 23 ♔g2 (or 23 ♔h1 ♘×e1 24 ♖×e1 ♕×f2 and Black wins) ♘h4+, with perpetual check since White dare not abandon f2; (c) 22 ♖e2 ♘×h3+ 23 ♔f1 h5!, with dangerous threats – 24 a5 h4 25 ♕×b6 ♕f3, for instance; if here 25 ♘h1, then still 25 ... ♕f3, of course.

Thus Nunn's calculations; but he overlooked that he need not take the bishop. After 21 a5! Black's Q-side collapses so quickly that he has no time to generate any real threats. His only hope is to eliminate the g-pawn by the sacrifice ... ♗×g2, but that brings the white king one move sooner to g2 and makes the defence easy. If 21 . . . b×a5 22 ♗×c5 threatens to take the bishop (as well as the rook) because f2 is now covered; if 21 . . . ♘g5 22 ♕×b6 ♕f4 (22 . . . ♘f3+ 23 g×f3 ♕×f3 24 ♗f1) 23 ♕×c5 ♗×g2 (otherwise ♕e3) 24 ♔×g2 ♕f3+ 25 ♔h2 and Black has nothing. Nor can he sacrifice any earlier: if 21 . . . ♗×g2 22 ♔×g2 ♘g5 23 ♖e3 ♖d2 24 ♖f1 and the attack is over.

20 . . . ♗×h3!

21 ♖×d8 . . .

Again 21 g×h3 is bad because of 21 . . . ♘g5 22 ♗f1 ♘f3+ 23 ♔g2 ♘h4+ and perpetual check; 22 ♖×d8 ♖×d8 23 ♖e2 ♖d1+ would be even worse: 24 ♔h2 ♘f3+ 25 ♔g2 ♘h4+ 26 ♔h2 ♕f3, or 24 ♔g2 ♕f3+ 25 ♔h2 ♖h1+ and mate.

21 . . . ♖×d8

22 ♕×f7 ♗g4

Not, of course, 22 . . . ♕×f7 because his g-pawn would go. Now, should White grab the a-pawn or exchange queens? It may be a matter of personal style. I think there are many Grandmasters who, seeing how favourable the endgame is, would swap without further ado. Nunn also settles for the ending, but points out that 23 ♕×a7 should really be preferred because Black's counterplay can be contained fairly comfortably. Two general points will make the following analysis easier to comprehend and explain why White can get away with the pawn grab: (1) The white queen is not completely cut off; she can create threats against the back rank which deter Black from throwing his whole force into the attack. (2) The demolition of Black's Q-side by a5 is imminent. That will bring the white queen and bishops quickly back into circulation. Therefore the move ♘h1, on which White is relying heavily in these variations, should be regarded as only temporarily passive.

After 23 ♕×a7 the best try is 23 . . . ♖d2, giving the rook as much scope as possible; if 23 . . . ♘g5, there is 24 a5 ♖d2 25 ♕a8+ ♗f8 26 ♘h1 ♗f3 27 ♗f1 and Black has nothing, or if 23 . . . ♖f8, again 24 ♘h1 ♘g5 25 a5 and neither 25 . . . ♘f3+ nor 25 . . . ♘h3+ is any good (generally speaking, Black has to try and sacrifice his bishop here, not his knight).

So 23 . . . ♖d2 24 ♘h1! (24 ♖f1 ♖a2 25 ♗c1 h5 26 ♕f7 is also good) ♖a2 (if 24 . . . ♘g5? 25 ♗c1, but from a2 the rook can prevent a5) 25 ♗c1 ♖a1 (otherwise b4 may come) 26 ♕a8+ ♘f8 27 ♖f1, and there is no compensation whatever for the lost pawn because White still has plenty of initiative. He can consolidate by ♗e3 and f3, he can play ♕d5, and so on.

23 ♕×f6 ♘×f6

Since no improvements are apparent for Black in the remainder of the game, this position must be regarded as lost for him, even though White still has quite a lot of work to do. He is handicapped by his very bad bishop, his isolated pawn and above all the ruinously weak square d5 which White can seize and occupy. The same pawn formation can arise out of many differenct openings (King's Indian, for example, with colours reversed) and the fact that the corresponding square d4 is still controlled by a pawn is of crucial importance because it prevents Black from occupying a similar outpost.

These disadvantages need not be fatal in themselves; Black might well overcome his problems if only he had some counterplay. His crushing burden is that he has none. His control of the d-file is spurious because his rook has no entry points; he has no pawn breaks by which he might open another file or create some play – to organise . . . a6 and . . . b5 would be virtually impossible even if White did nothing in the meantime; and his minor pieces have no chance of occupying any good outposts. By contrast **White's position can unfold**, i.e. he can make progress by taking possession of d5 and then organising a break on the left flank by a5. Summing it up, what might at first appear to be tiny advantages for White are actually enormous; in fact by Grandmaster standards the whole game is very one-sided.

24 ♘f1 . . .

In a moment White will centralise his king and free the other pieces from the duty of defending d2 and d3. Meanwhile, the knight covers d2 and takes a step towards d5. At the same time 24 . . . ♖d1 is forestalled because 25 ♖×d1 ♗×d1 26 f3 ♗c2 27 ♔f2 would leave the bishop in trouble. It is possible, though, that 24 f3 ♗c8 25 ♗c1 would have been a marginally more accurate move-order, leaving the knight a little longer at g3 to discourage any counterplay by . . . g5 (see the next note). Not that the counterplay seems to help Black much, given the right response.

24 . . . ♗c8

25 ♗c1 . . .

Not 25 b4; Black is helpless as things stand, and White has no wish to alter the pawn formation in any substantial way, other than to play a5 when he is good and ready.

25 . . . ♗b7

Black's choice lies between passive defence (which he prefers here) and an attempt at counterplay, which risks the creation of further weaknesses. The active plan would be . . . ♔h7, . . . g5, . . . ♔g6, . . . g4, . . . h5 and . . . ♗h6, gaining space and exchanging his bad bishop. That is why a slight preference was expressed earlier for keeping the knight on g3 a little longer, meeting . . . g5 by ♘f5.

But in reality the K-side play doesn't seem to improve Black's chances significantly. Here are one or two likely variations: (1) 25 . . . ♔h7 26 f3 g5 27 g4! ♔g6 28 ♘g3; then White can occupy f5 whenever he wishes and an exchange will only deprive Black of his better bishop and expose his e-pawn. If 28 . . . h5 29 g×h5+ ♘×h5 30 ♘×h5 ♔×h5 31 ♔f2 (threatens ♗f7+) ♗f6 32 ♗d5 and Black has only given himself a weak g-pawn. White's plan here would be ♗e3, ♖a1 and a5; or if Black plays . . . a5, then ♖b1 and b4. (2) 25 . . . g5 26 f3 g4 (a different move-order, to cut out White's g4) 27 ♘g3 ♔h7 28 ♔f2 ♔g6 29 ♖h1 h5 30 f4 e×f4 31 ♗×f4 ♗b7 32 ♔e3, and White has a useful target in the weak h-pawn and a dangerous passed pawn of his own.

Black decides to wait.

26 f3 ♗f8

27 ♘e3 ♔g7

28 ♔f2 ♗e7 *(70)*

29 ♖h1! . . .

This is where many players would have slipped up. Remember that White's advantages are permanent;

70
W

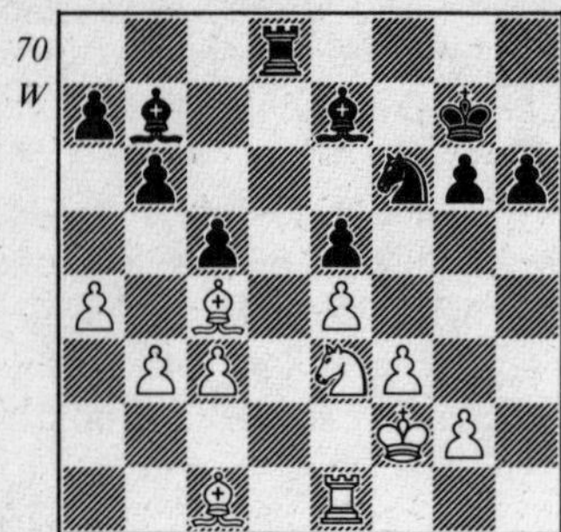

therefore he should take his time and stamp out any hint of counterplay. On the previous move 28 . . . ♘h5 was unplayable because of 29 ♘g4, but if White innocently continues with the next part of his plan by 29 ♔e2, there comes 29 . . . ♘h5, aiming at f4 and g3 with . . . ♗g5 or . . . ♗h4 also in the air, and 30 ♘g4 ♘f4+ 31 ♔f2 ♗f6 32 g3 ♘d3+ (or perhaps 32 . . . ♘h3+ 33 ♔g2 ♘g5) 33 ♗×d3 ♖×d3 34 ♗×h6+ ♔f7 gives Black just the kind of active chance he is looking for.

The point of the subtle text move is to force . . . h5 (since the pressure against h6 cannot be tolerated for long) and thus eliminate any counterplay. If Black now tries 29 . . . ♘h7, aiming for . . . ♗g5, the answer is definitely less subtle: 30 ♖×h6 ♔×h6 31 ♘f5+ ♔h5 32 g4 mate! Meanwhile 29 . . . ♘h5 is still refuted by 30 ♘g4.

29 . . . h5

30 ♔e2 ♗c8

During this phase White is keeping control by analysing two- or three-move variations – nothing elaborate, just keeping alert to any little tricks. For example, 30 . . . ♗×e4 31 f×e4 ♘×e4 is refuted by 32 ♔e1! ♘×c3 33 ♗b2 and Black gets only two pawns for the piece.

31 ♗d2 . . .

The Q-bishop is not pulling his weight; so the next part of the plan is to transfer him to g3, in order to tie Black down to the defence of the e-pawn. Meanwhile, Black cannot undertake anything constructive. One frustrating aspect of the situation is that he cannot benefit by exchanging off one or two minor pieces. In the resulting simplified position the helplessness of his remaining black bishop (the one piece which White would not exchange) would be even more glaringly apparent. In fact the exchange of white-square bishops, to leave d5 wide open for his other pieces, is one of White's primary objectives in the next few moves. For the moment, though, he is in no hurry to occupy d5: a knight exchange would give Black access to f6 and make the defence of the e-pawn easier.

31 . . . ♗b7

31 . . . a5 would create a new target at b6, which White could attack by ♘c4 or ♘d5. At a later stage, after the exchange of bishops, the king would also have a clear path into Black's position via c4 and b5.

32 ♗e1 ♘e8

If 32 . . . ♗d6 33 ♗g3 and ♖d1 would be very hard to meet.

33 ♗g3 ♗f6

34 a5! . . .

The breakthrough comes on the extreme flank, where the defender's resistance is bound to be lowest. And it is most important to appreciate that the chain a7, b6, c5 must be classed as a weakness **because of White's control of d5** and hence superior pieces. The immediate 34 ♗d5 is avoided because of 34 . . . ♗a6+.

34 ... ♘d6
35 a×b6 a×b6
36 ♖a1 *(71)* **...**

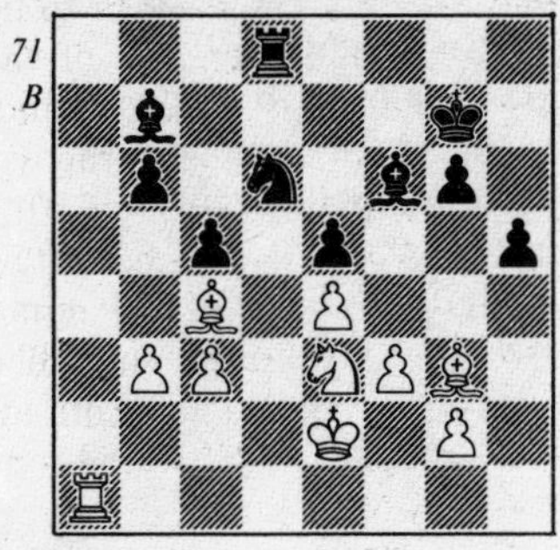

36 ... ♗c6

Black again decides to wait. If 36 . . . ♘×c4 37 ♘×c4 b5, both 38 ♘×e5 ♗×e5 39 ♗×e5+ ♔f7 40 ♖a7 and 38 ♖a7 b×c4 39 ♖×b7+ ♔g8 40 b×c4 ♖a8 41 ♖c7 would be quite sufficient to win. And if 36 . . . ♖a8, the variations are even more clear-cut: 37 ♖×a8 ♗×a8 38 ♗d5 ♗×d5 39 ♘×d5 and then: (a) 39 . . . ♘c8 40 ♔d3 ♔f7 (40 . . . b5 41 ♗f2) 41 ♘×f6 ♔×f6 42 ♔c4 ♔e6 43 ♔b5 ♔d6 44 c4 Zugzwang, because Black will soon have to permit ♔c6 and ♔c7; (b) 39 . . . b5 40 ♗f2 c4 (or 40 . . . ♘b7 41 ♘c7 b4 42 ♘e6+ ♔f7 43 ♘×c5 ♘×c5 44 ♗×c5 b×c3 45 ♔d3; or here 41 . . . c4 42 b4 ♘d6 43 ♗c5) 41 b×c4 b×c4 (41 . . . ♘×c4 42 ♘c7 ♘d6 43 ♗c5) 42 ♗c5 ♘b5 (42 . . . ♘b7 43 ♗b4, then ♘e3 or ♘b6) 43 ♔d2 ♗g5+ 44 ♔c2 and wins the c-pawn by ♘b6.

37 ♗d5 ♗e8

Black naturally avoids the exchange, but has to concede more space in so doing.

38 ♖a7+ ♔h6

If 38 . . . ♖d7, there is 39 ♖a6!; then either 39 . . . ♘c8 40 ♗e6, picking up the b-pawn, or 39 . . . b5 40 ♗c6 ♖d8 (or . . . ♖e7) 41 ♗×e8 ♘×e8 42 ♘d5 and the e-pawn goes. But after 38 . . . ♔h6 Black is still holding on by his fingernails. In order to increase the pressure just a little more White persists with his basic plan: to eliminate the opposing Q-bishop and leave Black with a stone-dead position. Against passive play the plan will be executed by ♔d3–c2, ♖c7 and ♗c6. If Black then allows an exchange, ♖c6 and ♘d5 will win a pawn; if he plays . . . ♗f7, ♘d5 will force him to capture the knight; the bishop will retake and again ♖c6 must result in the win of a pawn.

39 ♔d3 ...

The king manoeuvre must come first, to avoid . . . ♘b5.

39 ... g5 *(72)*

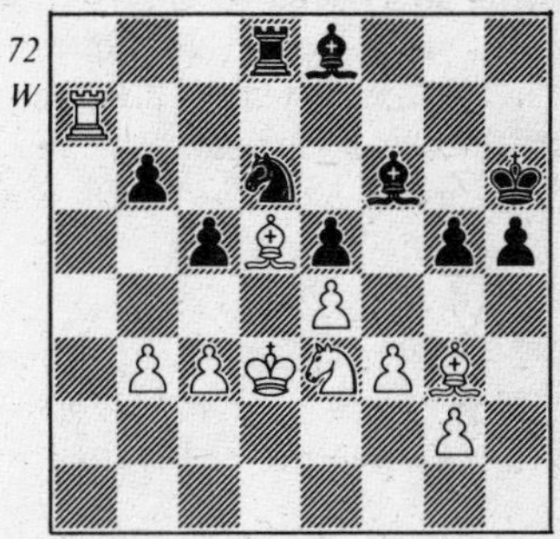

Come what may, he must interfere with White's plan; hence this rather desperate attempt at counterplay. Although f5 is seriously weakened, it certainly represents his only chance; in fact it provokes an error at once!

40 ♔c2? ...

The problem of preventing counterplay largely explains the mystery of why Grandmasters use up so much time during a game. The broad outlines of a position they perceive readily enough; it is the precision work which takes its toll on the clock. And both here and at move 29 we can see how fatally easy it is to let a strong opponent (i.e. one who is searching for some piece play at all cost) throw a spanner in the works, if constant vigilance is not exercised. In the last move before the time-control White very naturally continues with his main plan, avoiding a pin on the d-file. But this 'safe' move actually provokes unnecessary complications. Black's K-side activities are based on . . . ♗g6 and . . . g4, and if the e-pawn is solidly protected, f×g4 is a perfectly good reply. But if Black is permitted to exchange at f3 a passed h-pawn will appear and the f-pawn itself may become a target.

So 40 ♖c7! is correct, leaving Black woefully short of moves; in fact he has no choice but to continue his attack: that apart, he is in Zugzwang. If 40 . . . ♗g6 41 ♖c6, or 40 . . . ♘b5 41 ♖b7, or 40 . . . ♖d7 41 ♖c6, or 40 . . . ♗g7 41 ♖e7 ♗f6 42 ♖e6; of course, if 40 . . . ♗b5+ 41 ♔c2 is quite in order.

Therefore 40 . . . g4 is the only try and White then has: 41 f×g4 ♗g6 42 ♘f5+ ♗×f5 (42 . . . ♘×f5 43 g×f5 ♗×f5 44 ♔c4 and 45 ♖c6) 43 g×f5 ♘×f5 44 ♖c6 ♔g7 (44 . . . ♘×g3 45 ♖×f6+ is hopeless, and 44 . . . ♖d6 loses to 45 e×f5 ♖×d5+ 46 ♔e4) 45 ♗f2 ♘e7 (45 . . . ♖d6 46 ♔c4 ♖×c6 47 ♗×c6, followed by ♔d5 or ♔b5) 46 ♖×f6 ♖×d5+ (46 . . . ♘×d5 47 e×d5) 47 e×d5 ♔×f6 48 ♗h4+ ♔f7 49 d6 (or 49 ♗×e7) and wins.

40	**. . .**	**♗g6**
41	**♖c7**	**g4**
42	**♖c6**	**b5**

Part of Black's plan is to drive the knight away by . . . ♗g5 and perhaps follow with . . . ♖f8, but 42 . . . ♗g5 fails against 43 ♗×e5. He therefore provokes 43 ♖×c5, hoping to continue 43 . . . ♗g5 44 ♗f2(?) g×f3 45 g×f3 ♖f8 with quite good play. In fact, 44 ♘f1, keeping the bishop trained on e5, would be acceptable here, but Nunn much prefers not to have a passive knight. Instead he removes his king from the awkward c2–g6 diagonal and then continues with a more aggressive plan, more in the spirit of the position.

43	**♔b2**	**c4?**

After this Black's game disintegrates completely; he has overlooked the threat behind White's last move. His only hope was to exchange pawns first; then, after 43 . . . g×f3 44 g×f3 c4, White still has enough to win, but only with accurate play. For instance, 45 f4, as in the game, fails against 45 . . . e×f4 46 ♗×f4+ ♗g5 47 ♗×d6 ♗×e3 and the outcome is unclear. Apart from anything else the pawns are disappearing at an alarming rate.

White would play instead 45 b×c4 b×c4 46 ♗×c4! (again, 46 ♘×c4 ♘×c4+ 47 ♗×c4 ♖d2+ encourages counterplay) and there is no reason why his extra pawn should not eventually win the game. In fact Black has to be very careful here: 46 . . . ♗e8? 47 ♖×d6, 46 . . . ♘×c4+ 47 ♘×c4 and 46 . . . h4 47 ♘g4+ all lose at once. It follows that White can safely consolidate on the next move by 47 ♗d5.

44	**f4!**	**. . .**

White now gets a strong attack because the same continuation 44 . . . e×f4 45 ♗×f4+ ♗g5 46 ♖×d6 ♖×d6 47 ♘×g4+ h×g4 48 ♗×d6 is an easy win. The desperado capture at move 47 explains why Black should have started with 43 . . . g×f3. Failing this, Black makes a desperate piece sacrifice, trying to eliminate as many pawns as possible, but the remainder is plain sailing.

44	**. . .**	**b4**
45	**f×e5**	**b×c3+**
46	**♔×c3**	**c×b3**

Or he could rescue the piece by 46 . . . ♘b5+ 47 ♔c4 ♘a3+ 48 ♔d3 ♗g5; but then comes 49 ♘f5+ ♔h7 50 ♖c7+ ♔h8 51 e6 ♖×d5+ (or 51 . . . ♗×f5 52 ♗e5+ ♔g8 53 ♖g7+ ♔f8 54 e7+ ♗×e7 55 ♖g8 mate) 52 e×d5 ♗×f5+ 53 ♔e2 ♘b5 54 ♗e5+ ♔g8 55 ♖g7+ and wins.

47	**♗f4+**	**♔h7**
48	**e×f6**	**♘×e4+**
49	**♔×b3**	**♖d7**
50	**♔c4**	**g3**
51	**♗×e4**	**♗×e4**
52	**♖e6**	**♗g6**
53	**♖e7+**	**1 - 0**

Game 17

Modern Benoni Defence
London (Phillips & Drew) 1982
L. Portisch v. J. Nunn

1	**d4**	**Nf6**
2	**c4**	**c5**
3	**d5**	**e6**
4	**Nc3**	**e×d5**
5	**c×d5**	**d6**
6	**e4**	**g6**
7	**Nf3**	**Bg7**
8	**Be2**	**0–0**
9	**0–0**	**Re8**
10	**Nd2**	**. . .**

So far the moves are the same as in Game 8, and, as we explained there, the modern method of treating the Benoni begins with 10 . . . Nbd7. In view of Portisch's impressive record of wins against . . . Nbd7 Nunn prefers to switch back to the older system, popular in the Sixties.

10 . . . Na6 *(73)*

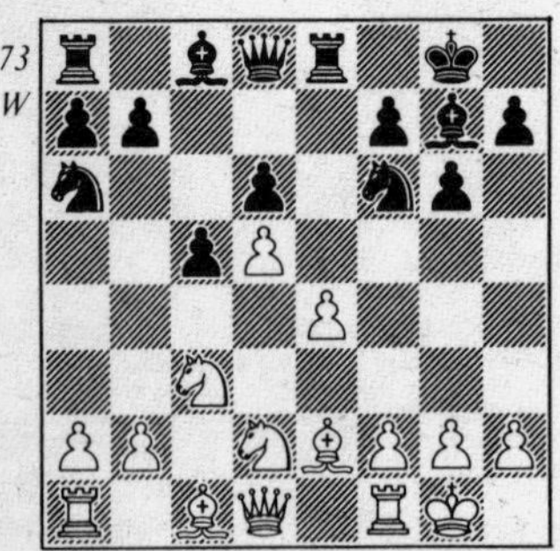

The intention, of course, is . . . Nc7, . . . a6, possibly . . . Rb8 and ultimately . . . b5; should White play B×a6 the two bishops and open b-file will more than offset the pawn weakness. But this plan is rather slow, and White has time to oppose it by the far from obvious manoeuvre Rb1 and b4 (after . . . b5, that is). If he can then induce Black to close the Q-side by . . . c4, he will have a relatively free hand in the centre and can get on with his own aggressive plan of f4 and e5.

Let us now look at some theory to see how these ideas work out. The main line continues 11 f3 Nc7 12 a4 b6 (not . . . a6 yet; he must be ready with . . . Ba6 in order to capture the knight on c4; otherwise Bf4 will follow and he will be reduced to playing the unacceptably passive move . . . Bf8. After the exchange on c4 Black need not worry about the white-square weakness, provided he can keep his pawns rolling. That is what counts in this variation: whether Black can maintain some initiative on the Q-side, or whether he will be stopped dead in his tracks by b4) 13 Nc4 Ba6 14 Bg5 (no point in Bf4 now) and then: (a) 14 . . . Qd7 15 Rb1 B×c4 16 B×c4 a6 17 b4 (17 Qd3 Reb8 is pointless) b5 (17 . . . c×b4 18 R×b4 leaves the b-pawn weak; nor can Black take any advantage of the loose knight at c3 or the long diagonal generally) 18 a×b5 a×b5 (18 . . . N×b5 would be desirable, either exchanging a passive piece or occupying d4, but White wins a pawn by 19 B×b5 a×b5 20 b×c5) 19 Bd3 c4 (otherwise Black can't do much anyway) 20 ♗c2, and White has reached the kind of position he wants, with his bishop conveniently posted at c2 to support f4 and e5. Evans–Kane (US Championship 1973) continued 20 . . . ♖a3 21 ♘e2 ♖a2 22 ♔h1 ♘a8 23 ♗c1! (the bishop is more effective at b2 now) ♘b6 24 ♘c3 ♖a6 25 ♗b2 ♕b7 26 f4 and White won fairly quickly. The rook's careering up and down the a-file hardly contributed to Black's cause here, but in any case it is difficult for him to find suitable counterplay; (b) 14 . . . h6 (hoping to show that squares other than g5 are inferior) 15 ♗e3 (space forbids any examination of other moves; 15 ♗h4 and ♗d2 are also possible, but White would like later to play ♕d2, covering c3 with tempo gain as a preparation for b4) ♗×c4 16 ♗×c4 a6 17 ♕d2 ♔h7 18 ♖ab1 ♕d7 19 b4 b5 20 ♗e2 (One of the advantages of . . . h6: this bishop has to occupy a slightly worse square because 20 ♗d3 allows 20 . . . ♘f×d5! 21 e×d5 ♖×e3 etc. White is also avoiding a×b5 here in favour of a later a5, thus denying Black use of the a-file, but whether that benefits him is arguable, since a5 costs a tempo) c4 (20 . . . c×b4 21 ♖×b4 b×a4 22 ♘×a4 leaves b6 exposed and the a-pawn fatally weak) 21 a5. This position has also occurred several times in Grandmaster practice. Black has gained a tempo over line (a) because ♗d1–c2 still has to be played before White can advance in the centre (♗d1–c2 is two moves, but Black lost one with . . . ♔h7). The question is to what extent Black can profit from that. Here are three examples: (i) 21 . . . ♕e7 22 ♗d4 ♕f8 23 ♗d1 ♘d7 24 ♗×g7 ♕×g7 25 ♗c2 ♖e7 26 ♖be1 ♘e8 27 f4 (Reshevsky–Garcia, Buenos Aires 1970) and Black's game is too passive; (ii) 21 . . . ♘g8! (the best move, preparing . . . f5 at once before the bishop reaches c2; note that this was impossible in line (a)) 22 ♗d4 ♗×d4+ 23 ♕×d4 f5 24 ♗d1 ♕g7 25 ♕d2 f×e4 26 ♘×e4 ♖e5 27 ♘c3 ♖ae8 (Ree–Evans, Amsterdam 1971) with approximate equality; (iii) 21 . . . ♘g8 22 ♗d1 f5 23 ♗c2 f×e4 24 f×e4 ♗e5 25 ♖f3 ♕g7 26 ♘e2 ♘f6 (Ogaard–Nunn, Gjøvik 1983) again with equality. On the whole Black is struggling a bit in these lines, but if he can exchange enough pieces he may eventually hope for some endgame advantage.

If we now return to the main game we shall observe the same type of position emerging, but with one extra move on each side.

11 ♔h1 ♖b8

The king move is always useful, given the potential danger on the g1–a7 diagonal, while . . . ♖b8 helps to prepare . . . b5. Notice that if 11 . . . ♘c7 12 a4 b6 13 f3, Black could hardly do better than transpose into the game by 13 . . . ♖b8: 13 . . . a6? would permit 14 ♘c4 without the necessary . . . ♗a6 being available.

12 f3 ♘c7

13 a4 b6

Black decides to stick to the main line. 13 . . . a6 is actually possible here (with . . . ♖b8 having been played), since 14 ♘c4 could be met by 14 . . . b5. After that 15 a×b5 a×b5 16 ♘a5, with subsequent occupation of c6, would normally be dangerous, but in this case 16 . . . ♗d7 17 ♗f4 b4 18 ♘a4 ♘b5 produces more of a double-edged position, rather than one unfavourable to Black, since his knight may be able to settle on d4. A positional point worth noting is that the seemingly strong 14 a5 is ineffective because it does not genuinely hamper . . . b5. For example 14 a5 ♗d7 15 ♘c4 ♗b5 16 ♗g5 ♗×c4 17 ♗×c4 h6 18 ♗e3 b5 19 a×b6 ♖×b6 and the game is level because the b-pawn is as weak as the a-pawn.

14 ♘c4 ♗a6

15 ♗g5 . . .

Reaching the same position as in the earlier analysis, but with ♔h1 and . . . ♖b8 included. And although these two moves amount to a fair exchange in terms of the overall situation and the tempi used up, they do leave Black slightly ahead in his preparations for . . . b5, while White's plan of ♖b1 and b4 has been delayed. On his next move, therefore, Portisch adopts a different method, i.e. b3 instead of b4. More about that in a moment.

15 . . . ♕d7

The best move. 15 . . . ♗×c4? 16 ♗×c4 a6 is a serious mistake because of 17 ♕d3!, which drives Black into a passive position and prevents . . . b5 altogether; for example 17 . . . ♕c8 18 ♗f4 ♗f8 19 ♖ab1 ♘d7 (or 19 . . . ♕b7 20 b4 b5 21 a×b5 a×b5 22 ♘×b5 ♘×b5 23 b×c5 and wins) 20 b4, and White stands very well (Browne–Torre, Manila 1976). Also inferior is 15 . . . h6 16 ♗e3 ♗×c4 17 ♗×c4 a6 18 ♕d3 ♕c8 19 ♗f4 ♖d8 20 ♖ab1 ♗f8 21 b4 (Polugaevsky–Bouaziz, Riga 1979), when Black is in the same miserable state as in Browne–Torre. 15 . . . ♕d7 is much better because Black prepares . . . a6 and . . . b5 **before** exchanging at c4, thus denying White the ♕d3 manoeuvre. And of course he avoids 15 . . . h6 16 ♗e3 ♕d7 because by a subsequent ♕d2 White would gain a useful tempo in defending c3; at the same time . . . h6 no longer has the compensating advantage which it held before.

Now if White sticks to the ♖b1/b4 plan, we get: 16 ♖b1 ♗×c4 17 ♗×c4 a6 18 b4 b5 19 ♗d3 (an important point: if 19 a×b5 Black can now play 19 . . . ♘×b5! without losing a pawn, and the exchange of his passive knight against either White's bishop or knight equalises comfortably; if 20 ♘×b5 a×b5 21 ♗d3 c4, the blockader of the passed pawn would also have disappeared) c4 20 ♗c2 b×a4! (same idea, the exchange of the knight) 21 ♗×a4 ♘b5, with at least equality (Kane–Enklaar, Skopje 1972). Another line is 16 ♕d2 ♗×c4 17 ♗×c4 a6 18 ♗d3 b5 19 a×b5 a×b5 (Enklaar–Szabó, Amsterdam 1972) 20 ♖a7, again with a roughly equal game. This is why Portisch now prefers the alternative plan.

16 b3 . . .

The intention is to exploit Black's delay in playing . . . ♗×c4 by preparing to retake with the pawn. His centre will then be fortified and his grip on b5 will paralyse the opposing pawn majority. And for Black that spells the same kind of danger as we have come across in other King's Indian/Benoni games in this collection (compare the notes at an equivalent point in Games 8, 12 and 20). **He must strike back at once**; any hesitation in activating his pieces is likely to lead him into the hopelessly passive type of position which we have already observed. With the Q-side neutralised, his counterplay must come via . . . f5; and even the tempo gain resulting from his next move is important.

16 . . . ♘h5

17 ♖c1 . . .

With best play on both sides 17 ♖c1 and 17 ♕d2 seem to be of equal merit; in fact they are most likely to transpose. 17 ♕d2 is slightly more complex because it offers a pawn, one, however, which Black would be unwise to accept: 17 . . . ♗×c3 18 ♕×c3 ♘×d5 19 ♕d2 (not 19 e×d5? ♖×e2 20 ♗h6 ♕e7 21 ♖fe1 ♗×c4 22 b×c4 ♕h4! and it is Black who has the attack) ♘c7 (no better square) 20 ♖ad1 ♘e6 (20 . . . ♖e6 would result in something equally unpleasant, such as 21 ♗h6 ♖be8 22 ♕b2 f6 23 f4 ♖×e4 24 ♗×h5 ♗×c4 25 b×c4 g×h5 26 ♕×f6) 21 ♗e3 ♗×c4 22 ♗×c4 ♖ed8 23 f4, and he faces an extremely dangerous attack.

Assuming that he declines the pawn, Black really needs to begin with 17 . . . ♗×c4, otherwise the white knight will be too much of a nuisance as the complications develop. So 17 . . . ♗×c4 18 b×c4 f6 (first driving the bishop to what is likely to be an inferior square, whether h4 or e3) and then: (a) 19 ♗h4 f5! (Threatening 20 . . . f4 and . . . ♗e5 with a grip on the whole centre and K-side. White must stop that at any price, but 20 e×f5? ♗×c3 costs a piece; hence his following vigorous move) 20 g4 f×g4 21 f×g4 ♗e5 (intending to meet 22 g×h5 by 22 . . . ♕h3 23 ♗f3 ♕×h4 24 ♖g1 ♕f6 with advantage; Black seems to be sailing close to the wind here, but that is typical of the Benoni) 22 ♖f3 ♘g7 23 ♖af1 ♖f8 with an unclear position. Black's bishop is very good, but his knights are poorly placed. On the other hand, if all the rooks disappear, as seems likely, White probably cannot achieve much while the knights get themselves organised; (b) 19 ♗e3 f5. Now the quiet 20 ♖ac1 is best (and if 20 . . . ♕e7 21 ♗g5), transposing into what could have happened in the main game, had White played correctly at move 19. In this case White maintains a small advantage. There is a complication here in that he can try 20 e×f5 and parry the seemingly strong 20 . . . ♕e7 by 21 ♗g1 ♗×c3 22 ♕×c3 ♕×e2 23 ♖fe1, trapping the queen (if here 21 . . . ♕h4 22 ♗f2, or if 21 . . . g×f5 22 ♗d3 with obvious advantage). The trouble is that Black has simply 20 . . . ♕×f5, threatening . . . ♕e5, and an answer is not easy to come by: if 21 g4? ♕e5, or 21 ♗f2? ♗×c3, or 21 f4? ♖×e3! 22 ♕×e3 ♖e8 and 23 . . . ♗×c3. Best seems to be 21 ♖ae1 ♖×e3 (21 . . . ♕e5 22 ♘d1) 22 ♕×e3 ♘g3+ (if 22 . . . ♗d4 first, trying for mate, then 23 g4) 23 h×g3 ♕h5+ 24 ♔g1 ♗d4 25 ♕×d4 c×d4 26 ♘e4 ♕e5 27 ♗d3, and White can probably claim equality (by continuing with f4 and ♘g5, while it is difficult to see how Black can achieve anything effective), but no more.

17 . . . f6

18 ♗e3 . . .

Not 18 ♗h4 because Black could play . . . ♘f4. 18 ♗d2 blocks the queen, and if White plays it with the intention of answering 18 . . . f5 by 19 e×f5, then, after 19 . . . g×f5 20 f4 ♘f6, the square e4 is weak and the d-pawn is as much a liability as the f-pawn.

18 . . . f5 *(74)*

19 g4(?) . . .

It is often difficult to judge whether

74
W

g4 is appropriate. Sometimes it can be extremely strong and lead to positions where the black knights are denied the use of any good squares for a long time to come. But here Portisch is being a bit too optimistic; his gain of time and space does not in the long run compensate for the weakness of his backward pawn and the blockade point e5. The soundest move is 19 ♕d2.

Another pawn sacrifice is possible here, interesting to compare with the earlier one (17 ♕d2 ♗×c3 etc.) just because of its unsoundness. After the tempting 19 f4 there comes 19 . . . ♗×c4 20 b×c4 ♘f6 21 e5 (forced to sacrifice now) d×e5 22 d6 (22 f×e5 ♖×e5 23 ♗f4 ♖ee8 24 ♘b5 ♘×b5 25 ♗×b8 ♘d4 doesn't work) ♘a6 23 f×e5 ♖×e5 24 ♗f4 ♖ee8, and you might expect the passed pawn and bishop-pair to give White some advantage, as in countless other examples of this typical Benoni idea. But this judgement fails to take into account that the black pieces are also quite lively and that he possesses good outposts for his knights at e4, d4 and b4. Add to that the control of the sensitive spot d5 which a knight will exert from b4, and it should become clear that White does not have sufficient return for his pawn.

19 . . . ♗×c4
20 b×c4 . . .

20 ♗×c4 f×g4 21 f×g4 ♘f6 would cost a pawn, as would 20 g×h5 ♗×e2 21 ♕×e2 ♗×c3 22 ♖×c3 f×e4.

20 . . . f×g4
21 f×g4 ♘f6

The game now enters a tough manoeuvring period in which Black attempts to exploit his long-term positional advantages by occupying e5 with a knight and by finding useful squares for his other minor pieces, while White opposes him by more dynamic means, trying to build up a compensating initiative based on his command of the f-file and greater control of space. The problem is whether he can achieve this before Black's grip tightens.

22 ♗f3 ♕e7

Freeing d7 for the knight; not 22 . . . ♕d8 23 ♗f4 etc.

23 ♗g5 . . .

On the surface an obvious move, forestalling Black's manoeuvre . . . ♘d7–e5, but there may be an instructive point concealed here. Notice how Portisch uses every weapon he can find to interfere with Black's plan. Weaker players are sometimes inclined to underestimate the use of tactics in this way. They feel: 'Well, ♗g5 is a waste of time; it pins the knight, but Black can solve that problem easily enough. Why bother?' But the problem may not be so easy to solve; the move you have in mind may be more of a nuisance than is immediately apparent. The present position is a good example. The knight cannot be unpinned by . . . ♕f7/♕f8 because of ♗g2; so Black has to choose between 23 . . . h6 (plus

. . . g5) and 23 . . . ♕e5. And on reflection Nunn is not satisfied with his decision to advance the pawns because a hole is created at f5. Straightaway, then, ♗g5 has provoked an inaccurate response. The best move is 23 . . . ♕e5, which, though apparently illogical, seems to guarantee a small advantage; but that does not alter the fact that ♗g5 has posed Black an awkward question over the board. 23 . . . ♕e5 produces something like 24 ♕d2 ♘d7 25 ♘e2 (there is no way to exploit the queen's shortage of squares) ♗f6 26 ♗f4 ♕e7 27 g5 ♗g7 28 ♗g3 ♘e5 29 ♗g2 ♖f8. The knight has finally made it and Black stands a little better.

23	**. . .**	**h6**
24	**♗h4**	**g5**
25	**♗e1**	**. . .**

White avoids blocking g3 in anticipation of playing ♘e2–g3–f5.

25	**. . .**	**♖f8**

By threatening . . . ♘×g4 Black holds up ♘e2 for one more move.

26	**♗g2**	**♘d7**
27	**♖×f8+(?)**	**♖×f8(?)**

Both moves are inexact, though in White's case the difference between ♖×f8+ and his main alternative ♖f5 is not very clear-cut. If Black exchanges rooks after 27 ♖f5, the e-pawn recaptures and the weakness has disappeared. The dark side of the move is that White would much prefer his knight to occupy this vital square. Black can almost ignore the intruding rook and work around it, so to speak, something he certainly could not do if the knight were installed there. For example, 27 ♖f5 ♘e5 (incidentally preventing ♘e2; Black is now using tactics to interfere with his opponent's strategic aims) 28 ♕e2 (now hoping for ♘d1–e3, ♖ moves away and ♘f5) ♖be8!, and if 29 ♘d1 ♖×f5 and the g-pawn must retake (30 e×f5? ♘×g4). Black is keeping an edge here then, but for all that the rook does have some influence at f5 and it seems that with this move White would have reduced his disadvantage to a minimum.

Black for his part should have recaptured with his knight, because he needs to find good squares for **all** his minor pieces as quickly as possible. After 27 . . . ♘×f8 this knight can head for f4 (at the same time usefully anticipating White's possible h4); then . . . ♗e5, . . . ♖f8 and . . . ♘e8–f6 can follow and he stands very well. After 27 . . . ♖×f8 there is temporary congestion because both the bishop and the knight want e5.

28	**♘e2** *(75)*	**. . .**

75
B

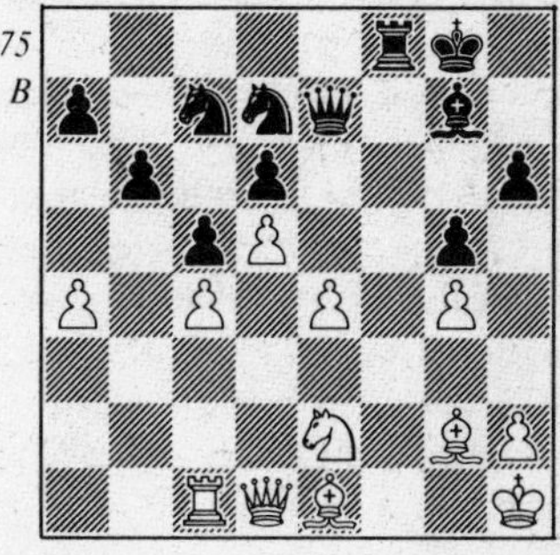

28	**. . .**	**♗e5!**

Yet again one of the players is obliged to frustrate his opponent's strategic designs. Black must now be willing to part with his fine bishop in order to prevent ♘g3–f5; and indeed, after 29 ♘g3 ♗×g3 30 ♗×g3 ♘e5, followed by . . . ♘e8–f6, he would have the upper hand because the blocked position would favour knights rather than bishops. White therefore postpones ♘g3 (in fact he never plays it), forcing the bishop to stand guard at e5; in that way he makes it harder for the d7 knight to find a desirable square.

29 ♕d3 ♘e8

30 ♗d2 ♕g7

Black continues to manoeuvre. If he is left in peace, the plan is . . . ♖f7, . . . ♘f8–g6 and . . . ♘f6. The queen is ideally posted at g7, looking down the long diagonal and cutting out any possible counterplay by h4.

31 ♖f1 ♖×f1+

Avoiding ♖f5 the second time around!

32 ♗×f1 ♕f7

And the same applies to the queen; if 32 . . . ♘f8 White has 33 ♕f3–f5. Best play now would be 33 ♗g2 ♕f2 34 ♕f3 ♕×f3 35 ♗×f3, and then either (a) 35 . . . ♔g7 36 ♔g2, followed by ♘g3 and . . . ♗×g3, which is like the game continuation except that White has not lost a pawn, or (b) 35 . . . ♘ef6 36 h3 (36 h4 is another playable line) ♗b2 (threatens . . . ♘e5) 37 ♘g3 ♘e5 38 ♗e2, and, with his weakness at f5 balancing White's at e5, Black can scarcely claim much advantage. If he starts with 33 . . . ♘f8, then 34 h4 or ♕f3 amounts to the same thing. Instead Portisch, a little pressed for time, makes a serious error.

33 ♔g2? . . .

He covers the weak spots on the f-file and plans to answer 33 . . . ♗×h2 by 34 ♕h3, but overlooks that his e-pawn has inadequate protection.

33 . . . ♘ef6

34 h3 . . .

Better to abandon the e-pawn, which is obstructing his pieces, than the g-pawn.

34 . . . ♕g6

35 ♘c3 . . .

If 35 ♔f3 ♗d4 36 ♕c2 (or 36 ♔g2 with transposition) ♘e5+ 37 ♔g2 ♕×e4+ 38 ♕×e4 ♘×e4 39 ♘×d4 c×d4 (or . . . ♘×d2) and White has a worse ending than actually occurs.

35 . . . ♗×c3

Black cannot benefit from delaying the capture, hoping to make it in more favourable circumstances; if 35 . . . ♗d4, for example, intending . . . ♘e5, 36 ♕f3 threatens ♕f5 and Black must take at once or lose his chance.

36 ♗×c3 ♕×e4+

37 ♕×e4 ♘×e4 *(76)*

76
W

The knights are at least the equal of the bishops because the position remains largely blocked and because they have convenient protected squares near the centre from which they can operate (e5, d4, f4). These are the criteria by which you judge whether a knight can stand up to a bishop in the endgame. The problem is that sooner or later Black will have to open the game by pawn exchanges, if he wants to exploit his extra material; and then the bishops will show their teeth. Analysis indicates that he can win against a perfect defence, but he has to take great care.

First a few general remarks: (1) If Black could exchange a knight for the dark-square bishop he would win easily by invading the centre with his king via e5 and d4; (2) If the other bishop were exchanged for a knight the situation would be quite different: Black could not invade the centre and his own pawns would be highly vulnerable to attack. In that event the correct result would be a draw; (3) If no piece exchanges occur for a while, and if Black cannot make progress by infiltrating with his knights, he will eventually have to initiate some kind of Q-side action. An obvious plan is . . . a6 and . . . b5, but this advance must at the very least be thoroughly prepared, or the position will open prematurely and White will create a dangerous passed pawn by c×b5, . . . a×b5, a5. If the circumstances are wrong, the whole scheme may have to be abandoned; (4) Certain pawn endings resulting from a double exchange are drawn, even though Black is a pawn up.

Now 38 ♗e1, as played by Portisch, is certainly the best and most obvious move. But to illustrate one of the drawn pawn endings and to show how the knights might invade White's position, here is the analysis of 38 ♗b2: (a) 38 . . . ♘d2 39 ♗c3 ♘×f1? 40 ♔×f1 ♘e5 41 ♗×e5! d×e5 42 ♔e2 ♔f7 43 ♔e3, and, as long as he is careful with his tempo moves, White's protected passed pawn will save him – 43 . . . ♔e7 (43 . . . ♔f6 44 ♔d3 leads nowhere; White now waits for . . . a6 and . . . ♔d6 before playing ♔e4) 44 ♔d3 ♔d6 45 ♔e3 a6 46 ♔e4 (White to move would now lose) a5 47 ♔e3, and if 47 . . . b5 48 c×b5 ♔×d5 49 ♔d2 draws (White can hold the two pawns and play b6 if their king attempts to support them); (b) 38 . . . ♘e5! 39 ♗c1 (otherwise . . . ♘d2) ♘c3 40 ♗b2 (or 40 a5 b×a5 41 ♗d2 ♘a4 42 ♗×a5 ♘b2 and wins) ♘×a4 41 ♗a1 ♔f7 42 ♔f2 b5! 43 c×b5 ♘b6 44 ♗g2 ♘d3+ and . . . ♘f4, and Black stays two pawns up.

To demonstrate Nos. (2) and (3) above, we can return to the game.

38	**♗e1**	**♘e5**
39	**♗e2**	**♔f7**
40	**♗f3**	**♘f6!**

This is where Black must retreat, and not exchange the wrong bishop. If 40 . . . ♘×f3? 41 ♔×f3 ♘f6 42 ♗c3, and there is simply no suitable winning plan: (a) 42 . . . ♘d7 43 ♔e4 ♘f8 (heading for f4; even without White's king move we know that . . . ♘e5 only leads to a draw) 44 ♗a1 ♘g6 45 ♗b2 ♘f4 46 h4, and Black is getting nowhere; (b) 42 . . . ♘e8 (trying for . . . a6 and . . . b5, but this is too dangerous because White's king and bishop become very active and he gets a passed pawn; nor can Black use his own king) 43 ♔e4 ♔g6 44 ♗b2 ♘c7 45 ♗a1 a6 46 ♗c3 b5 47 c×b5 a×b5 48 ♗a5 ♘e8 49 a×b5 ♘f6+ 50 ♔d3 ♘×d5 51 b6, and Black is in trouble.

Clearly one knight cannot hope to win this ending against the dark-square bishop under the present circumstances. The right plan is to keep both knights and ultimately turn his attention to Q-side play. Whether that will involve . . . a6 and . . . b5 or some other manoeuvre remains to be seen; meanwhile, he has one more task to carry out on the other wing, in order to guarantee himself as much positional advantage as possible.

41	**♗e2**	**♘g6!**

Very good play. By menacing the h-pawn he forces White to withdraw the bishop to f1, to avoid some worse fate, and that paves the way for the main idea, . . . h5. If this pawn is taken, the square f5 opens for the black king (solving another problem, the narrow entry through the centre), and if not, another weakness will be created at g4.

42 ♗f1 . . .

This is nevertheless the best defence. Other moves allow an invasion by the knights or the king, thus: (a) 42 ♗f3 ♘f4+ 43 ♔g3 ♘d7 44 ♗d1 ♘e5 45 ♗b3 ♘e2+ 46 ♔g2 ♘d4 47 ♗a2 ♘c2, and wins by . . . ♘e3+ or . . . ♘a3; (b) 42 ♗d1 ♘f4+ 43 ♔h2 (if 43 ♔g3 ♘d3 wins) ♘d7 44 ♗c3 ♘e5 45 ♗b3 ♘e2 46 ♗b2 ♘d4 47 ♗a2 ♘df3+ and . . . ♘d2; (c) 42 ♔f3 ♘h4+ 43 ♔f2 (if 43 ♔g3 ♘e4+ 44 ♔h2 ♔f6 and the king walks in, or if 43 ♗×h4 g×h4 44 ♔f4 ♘h7 45 ♔f5 ♘g5 46 ♗f1 ♘f3 and a check at d4 drives the king back) ♘e4+ 44 ♔e3 ♘g2+ 45 ♔×e4 ♘×e1, and wins because the knight escapes and the white king cannot penetrate; (d) 42 ♗d2 ♘e4 43 ♗c1 (or ♗e3) ♘c3; (e) 42 ♗g3 ♘e4 43 ♗h2 ♘e5 and 44 . . . ♘d2.

42 . . . h5

42 . . . ♘f4+ 43 ♔f3 is pointless (43 . . . ♘d7 44 ♔e4 or 44 h4). Now if White defends the pawn he loses rapidly: 43 ♔g3 h×g4 (not 43 . . . h4+ because analysis shows that g4 will be a weaker target than h3 here) 44 h×g4 ♘e5 45 ♗e2 ♘e4+ 46 ♔g2 ♔f6 47 ♗f3 (otherwise there is nothing to be done about the threat of . . . ♘g6 and . . . ♔e5–d4, but we have now returned to the game position after 40 ♗f3, minus the h-pawns and with Black's king one decisive square ahead) ♘×f3! 48 ♔×f3 ♔e5 49 ♔e3 a5, and White is in a thoroughly nasty Zugzwang, despite retaining his 'better' bishop! He therefore exchanges pawns, and Black spends the next few moves establishing his king at f5.

43	**g×h5**	**♘×h5**
44	**♔f3**	**♘e5+**
45	**♔e4**	**♔g6**
46	**♗e2**	**. . .**

If 46 h4 ♘f6+ 47 ♔e3 ♔f5 48 h×g5 ♘fg4+ 49 ♔d2 ♘f3+ and wins.

46	**. . .**	**♘f6+**
47	**♔e3**	**♔f5**
48	**♗c3**	**. . .**

48 ♗d3+ ♘×d3 49 ♔×d3 ♘e4 would produce that Zugzwang again – 50 h4 g4 51 h5 g3 etc. In any case, once his king has penetrated the opposing position Black can afford to make the hitherto forbidden exchange of knight for white-square bishop. One point which has to be borne in mind in this endgame is that the elimination of the h- and g-pawns will not save White. That is unusual; the defender normally breathes a sigh of relief if he can reduce the pawns to one side. But two knights against two bishops is something of a special case. In a confined space the knights are just too good; and as the sequel shows, it is well-nigh impossible to stop them gradually working their way in, if White is brought to a purely defensive rôle. If the K-side pawns disappear and White exchanges either bishop for a knight, he is still unlikely to survive, because of the agility of the remaining knight, the dominating position of the black king and the weakness of the c-pawn.

Now here Black would like to make the exchange of K-side pawns immediately, i.e. 48 . . . g4, hoping for 49 h×g4 ♘f×g4+ 50 ♔d2 (or 50

♗×g4 ♘×g4+ and wins by . . . ♘e5) ♔e4, with a decisive penetration, as in the game. Unfortunately he is thwarted by a simple tactical point: 48 . . . g4 49 ♗×e5 d×e5 50 h×g4+. He therefore has to recognise that he has made the maximum improvement to his chances on the K-side and turn his attention to the other flank. His next move is designed to make . . . b5 available as an option, rather than to play it at once. In fact it would be better described as a last resort. Nunn was most reluctant to permit the opening of the position which it would involve, and the following analysis (note to White's 49th move) justifies his mistrust of it. As things turn out he is not obliged to find the very best plan because White makes a further mistake.

48 . . . a6 *(77)*

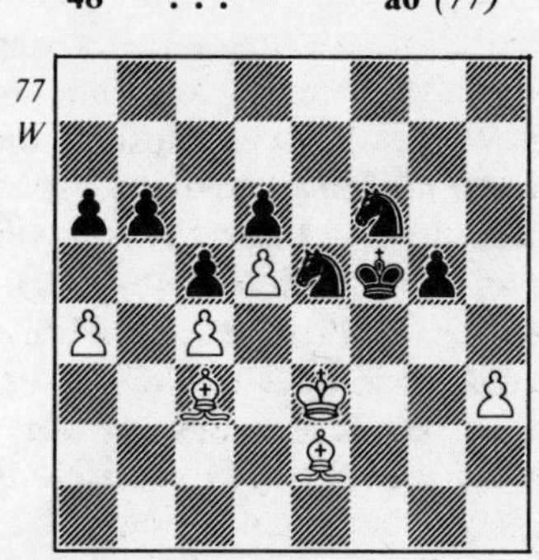

There is one more possibility here: since White can apparently do little in the meantime it may occur to Black to manoeuvre his f6 knight round to a5. That would certainly be decisive if he could achieve it, but tactically it is impossible because the bishops are not as helpless as all that! After 48 . . . ♘g8 they may set an ambush for the king, thus: 49 ♔f2! (to avoid check on c4 in a moment) ♘h6 (if 49 . . . ♔e4 50 ♗d2 is awkward) 50 ♗d1! ♘×c4 (50 . . . ♔e4 51 ♗c2+) 51 ♗c2+ ♔f4 52 ♗d3 ♘a5 53 ♗d2+ ♔e5 54 h4 and the passed pawn will be extremely dangerous in view of the offside knight at a5. It follows that Black would have to retreat his king to f6 after 50 . . . ♘hf7 51 ♗c2+, but then the white king would settle on e4 and progress would be extremely difficult. Although the . . . ♘g8 idea does not work here, it has an important part to play in subsequent variations.

49 ♗e1? . . .

A tactical error which allows Black to win fairly comfortably because ♗×e5 is no longer available in reply to . . . g4. Looking for the most resilient defence, we find, firstly, that any move by the K-bishop permits either . . . ♘×c4+ or, again, . . . g4 (or if 49 ♗d3+ ♘×d3 50 ♔×d3 ♘e4 51 ♗e1 ♔f4 and wins). Secondly, the counter-attack 49 a5 can be dismissed as follows: 49 a5 b×a5 50 ♗×a5 g4 51 h×g4+ (if 51 h4 g3 and both 52 ♗c7 and 52 ♗e1 lose to 52 . . . ♘fg4+ 53 ♗×g4 ♔×g4; if 52 ♗c3 g2 wins) ♘f×g4+ 52 ♗×g4+ (if 52 ♔d2 ♔e4 53 ♗c7 ♔d4 wins at once, or if here 53 ♗c3 ♘h2, followed by . . . ♘hf3+, which is similar to the main line) ♘×g4+ 53 ♔d3 ♘e5+ 54 ♔c3 ♔e4 55 ♗c7 ♘f7 56 ♗b8 ♔e3 57 ♔b3 (otherwise comes . . . ♘g5–e4+ etc.) ♔d4 58 ♗c7 ♔d3 and White is in Zugzwang: 59 ♗b8 a5, or 59 ♗a5 ♘e5. It may seem awkward to have to defend the d-pawn with the knight, but in the end there is no way in which Black's invasion can be repelled.

That leaves only 49 ♗b2, continuing to cover e5, and here we can see why Nunn was so keen to avoid the

. . . b5 break if at all possible. After 49 . . . b5 50 c×b5! (activating the K-bishop) ♘×d5+ 51 ♔f2 (out of range of knight forks) a5 (if 51 . . . a×b5 52 ♗×b5 and the supported a-pawn is very dangerous) 52 ♗c1! (prevents . . . ♔e4) ♘b6 53 ♗d2 ♘bc4 (53 . . . ♘×a4 54 ♗×a5, followed by b6, would be worse – 54 . . . ♘d7? 55 ♗g4+) 54 ♗×c4 ♘×c4 55 ♔e2 d5 56 ♔d3 Black runs into another drawn pawn ending if he exchanges (again because of White's protected passed pawn), and if he keeps the pieces on he also faces insoluble problems, despite his united passed pawns, because of his weaknesses at a5 and g5. The analysis of the pawn ending would be as follows: 56 . . . ♘×d2 57 ♔×d2 ♔e5 58 ♔d3 d4 59 ♔c4 ♔d6 60 ♔d3 ♔d5 61 ♔d2 c4 62 ♔c2 d3+ (62 . . . c3 63 ♔d3 ♔c5 64 ♔c2 ♔c4 65 b6 would be worse, if anything, since he dare not play his king to b3) 63 ♔c3 ♔c5 64 ♔d2 ♔d4 65 b6 c3+, and we have one of those positions where two moves lose and one draws: (a) 66 ♔e1? ♔e3 67 ♔d1 d2; (b) 66 ♔c1? ♔e3 67 b7 d2+ 68 ♔c2 ♔e2 69 b8/♕ d1/♕+ 70 ♔×c3 ♕c1+ 71 ♔d4 ♕f4+; but (c) 66 ♔d1! ♔e3 67 b7 c2+ 68 ♔c1 ♔e2 69 b8/♕ d2+ 70 ♔×c2 d1/♕+ 71 ♔b2 with a draw.

Evidently Black has to be more patient. The best way seems to be the knight manoeuvre which he wanted to try before (. . . ♘g8–h6–f7 etc., across to a5), but with a better chance this time owing to the slightly inferior position of the Q-bishop. After 49 . . . ♘g8 the ambush idea of the previous note will not work, and letting the king in is disastrous: 50 ♔f2 ♔e4 51 ♗c1 (or 51 ♗c3 ♘h6, and if 52 ♗d2 ♘hf7 is available) ♘d3+ 52 ♗×d3+ (the bishop was on d2 before and White did not have to take) ♔×d3 53 ♗×g5 ♔×c4 54 h4 b5 55 a×b5 a×b5 56 h5 b4 57 h6 ♘×h6 58 ♗×h6 ♔d3 59 ♔e1 b3 60 ♗g7 ♔c2 and Black wins.

So White has to play another waiting move: 50 ♗c3 ♘h6 51 ♗b2 (or 51 a5 b×a5 52 ♗×a5 g4, winning as before, or 51 ♔f2 ♔e4, and if 52 ♗d2 ♘hf7) ♘hf7 52 ♗c3 ♘d8 53 a5 (he has to take some action now; if 53 ♗b2 ♘b7 54 ♗c3 ♘a5 55 ♗×a5 b×a5 56 ♗f1 g4 57 h×g4+ ♘×g4+ 58 ♔d3 ♔f4 59 ♗e2 ♘e5+ 60 ♔c3 ♔e3 and wins by a knight check at e4; if 57 h4 g3 58 ♗e2 ♘d7 59 ♔f3 ♘b6 60 ♔×g3 ♘×a4 and wins, or if here 58 h5 ♔g5 59 ♗e2 ♘d7) b×a5 54 ♗×a5 ♘b7, and now White has the choice between passive defence (55 ♗c3) and sharper play (55 ♗c7), which gives us: (a) 55 ♗c3 a5 56 ♔d2 (the king has to stop the a-pawn; if 56 ♗b2 a4 and . . . ♘a5) ♔e4 57 ♗f1 a4 58 ♗e2 ♘f3+ 59 ♔c2 ♔e3 60 ♗f1 (60 ♗d1 ♘e5, or 60 ♗×f3 ♔×f3 61 ♗f6 g4 62 h×g4 ♔×g4 63 ♔b2 ♔f5 64 ♗e7 ♔e4 and wins) ♔f2 61 ♗d3 ♘e1+ 62 ♔d2 ♘×d3 63 ♔×d3 a3 64 ♔c2 ♔g3 65 ♗f6 ♔×h3 66 ♗×g5 ♔g4 67 ♗e7 ♔f4 68 ♔b3 ♔e5 69 ♔×a3 ♘a5 and wins; or (b) 55 ♗c7 (ties up the knight, but also the bishop) a5 56 ♔d2 ♔e4 57 ♔c3 (otherwise . . . ♔d4) a4 58 ♗d1 a3 59 ♗b3 (if 59 ♗a4, heading for c6, then . . .. ♘×c4) ♔e3 60 ♗b6 ♘d3 61 ♗c7 a2! (the point of this pawn sacrifice is to gain a tempo by making the bishop take three moves instead of two to attack the b7 knight; if 61 . . . ♘f4 62 ♗a4 etc., with the king stopping the a-pawn) 62 ♗×a2 ♘f4 63 ♗b1 ♘×h3 64 ♗f5 ♘f2 65 ♗c8 g4 66 ♗×b7 g3 and wins. This analysis is difficult and complicated, but the impression remains that against a perfect defence Black has just enough to win.

49	**. . .**	**g4!**
50	**h×g4+**	**. . .**

50 h4 is no better: 50 . . . ♘h5 51 ♗f1 (aiming to meet . . . g3 by ♗h3+; if 51 ♗c3 ♘f4, threatening the h- and c-pawns, and if 52 ♗×e5 ♔×e5 53 ♗×g4 ♘g2+, or if 52 ♗f1 g3 etc.) ♘f3 52 ♗d3+ ♔e5 53 ♗c3+ (or 53 ♗f2 ♘d4 and . . . g3) ♘d4 54 ♗g6 ♘f4 55 h5 g3 56 ♗b2 ♘×g6 57 h×g6 ♔f6 and wins.

50	**. . .**	**♘f×g4+**
51	**♔d2**	**♔e4**
52	**♔c3**	**♔e3**
53	**♗d1**	**♘f3** *(78)*
54	**♗g3**	**. . .**

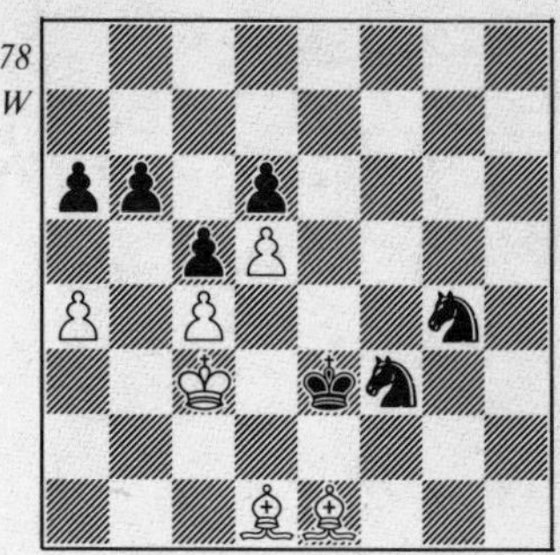

Earlier variations should have made it clear that even the exchange of the worse bishop does not save White. If 54 ♗×f3 ♔×f3 55 ♗h4 ♔e2 56 ♗d8 (or 56 ♗e7 ♘f2) ♘f2 57 ♗×b6 ♘e4+ 58 ♔c2 ♔e3 59 ♗a5 ♔d4 60 ♔b3 ♔d3, and wins by . . . ♘d2+.

54	**. . .**	**♘f2**
55	**♗c2**	**. . .**

If 55 ♗×f2+ ♔×f2 56 ♗×f3 ♔×f3 57 ♔d3 a5 and wins.

55	**. . .**	**♘g5**
56	**♔b2**	**♘ge4**
57	**♗h4**	**♔d4**
58	**♗b3**	**♘d3+**
59	**♔a3**	**♘e5**
	0 – 1	

Game 18

Bishop's Opening
Teesside 1982 (England–Iceland match)
J. Nunn v. F. Olafsson

1	e4	e5
2	♗c4	♘f6
3	d3	♘c6

One reason for White's innocent-looking opening is that with 2 ♗c4 the Petroff Defence is avoided. Around 1982 the Petroff was proving an efficient equalising weapon in Grandmaster play, though more recently Karpov and others have found some new ideas for White. Nunn scored a number of successes with 2 ♗c4 at that time, beating Korchnoi and Hort in addition to Olafsson, but since then has largely abandoned it and returned to the Ruy Lopez. Notice that 3 . . . d5 is too dangerous, unless Black wishes to play a rather questionable gambit, because the e-pawn gets into trouble: 4 e×d5 ♘×d5 5 ♘f3 ♘c6 6 0–0 and the subsequent ♖e1 will be embarrassing.

4	♘f3	♗c5

After 4 ♘c3 White would still retain the option of f4; therefore Black would be well advised to play 4 . . . ♗b4, meeting 5 f4 by . . . d5, rather than 4 . . . ♗c5 5 f4 d6 6 ♘f3 etc., which would result in a difficult form of the King's Gambit.

5	0–0	d6
6	c3	. . .

6 ♘c3 would produce the Giuoco Pianissimo, much favoured by schoolboys! In spite of its simple appearance this opening has its finer points, like any other, but is unlikely to appeal to Grandmasters. In any event it would be inappropriate here because of White's early castling. After 6 . . . ♗g4 his K-side would come under pressure through his inability to retreat the bishop to e2 and the threat of . . . ♘d4. Nor could he easily achieve the central break c3 and d4. In other words, he would have no useful play. Had he not castled, he could answer . . . ♗g4 by h3 and g4, marooning the black bishop at g6, and then castle Q-side.

6	. . .	♕e7?

After 6 c3 the outline of White's plan is revealed: he will continue ♖e1, ♘bd2–f1–g3 as in the Ruy Lopez, and eventually d4, which should prove all the more effective with his development completed. In face of this the placing of the black queen at e7 has many negative features: the queen is likely to be hit sooner or later by ♘f5, the move . . . d5 (or any action in the centre) can hardly be contemplated in view of the reply e×d5 followed by d4, and generally it is undesirable to have the queen opposed by a white rook. Oddly enough, 4 . . . ♕e7 (after 4 c3) is quite a well-known book line of the Giuoco Piano; yet there the move is open to precisely the same objections as 6 . . . ♕e7 here.

So what should Black do? 6 . . . ♗g4 would now be met by 7 ♘bd2, then ♖e1 and ♘f1, as in the game. Thereafter White's natural continuation of ♘g3 and h3 would automatically break the pin: a manoeuvre worth remembering. If Black plays for . . . d5, say 6 . . . ♗g4 7 ♘bd2 0–0 8 h3 ♗h5 9 ♖e1 d5, then White may continue 10 e×d5 ♘×d5 11 ♘e4 ♗b6 12 ♘g3, either winning the e-pawn or gaining the two bishops. In another game (against Nunn) Korchnoi played what must really be the soundest and most flexible line: 6 . . . 0–0 7 ♘bd2 a6 8 ♗b3 ♗a7. The bishop will have to retreat to a7 after White's d4; so here Black plays it at once and delays the decision on the placing of his other pieces until he sees more of White's plan of development.

7 ♘bd2 . . .

In the past Nunn has had some success by combining White's other manoeuvres with a Q-side pawn advance. But experience against the strongest opponents has convinced him that the pawn push is a strike into thin air unless it is connected with action in the centre. One example will suffice: 1 e4 e5 2 ♘f3 ♘c6 3 ♗c4 ♗c5 4 c3 ♘f6 5 d3 d6 6 b4 ♗b6 7 a4 a6 8 0–0 0–0 9 ♘bd2 ♘e7 10 ♗b3 ♘g6 11 ♘c4 ♗a7 12 h3 h6 13 ♖e1 ♗d7 (Nunn–Byrne, Baden 1980). If White had played d4 at an earlier stage, pressing on e5, there would have been a strong threat of b5 to push away the knight. As it is, he has no more than equality.

In the present game, although 7 b4 etc. is quite playable, he prefers to concentrate on exploiting the bad queen move in a more direct way.

7 . . . a6

Black would like to exchange knight for bishop at c4, but 7 . . . ♘a5? would be a mistake: 8 ♗b5+ c6 9 ♗a4 b5 10 ♗c2 ♗b6 11 b4 ♘b7 12 a4 and his position will be seriously weakened because 12 . . . a6 is unplayable.

8 ♗b3 . . .

White now avoids the threat of 8 . . . ♘a5.

8 . . . 0–0

9 ♖e1 ♗e6 *(79)*

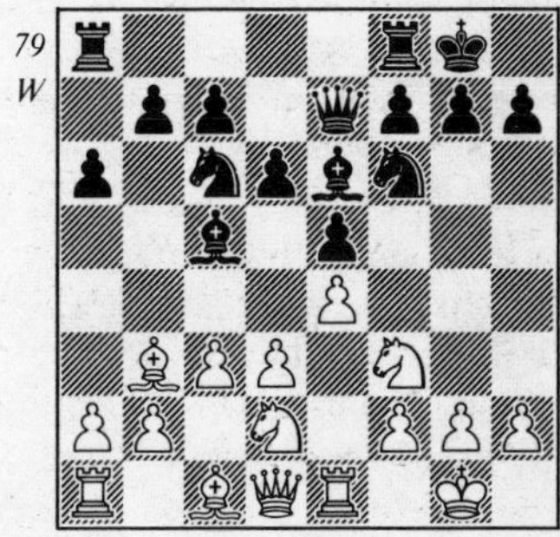

9 . . . ♘g4 10 ♖e2 has no point, since Black is unable to continue immediately with . . . f5. After 11 h3 the knight would be driven back with loss of time.

10 ♘f1 . . .

On reflection Nunn is inclined to prefer 10 ♗c2, avoiding what might be a relieving exchange for Black and shortly causing his opponent to lose more time fending off the threat of d4–d5. During play he was worried that 10 ♗c2 ♘g4 11 ♖e2 f5 might expose the weakness at f2, but analysis indicates that the attack is unsound: 12 e×f5 ♗×f5 13 d4 ♗×c2 14 ♕×c2 ♗b6 15 h3 ♘f6 16 d×e5 ♘×e5 17 ♘×e5 d×e5 18 ♘c4, and Black has to surrender his aggressive bishop, remaining with a much inferior position, or abandon his e-pawn at once.

But there is another line here which reveals that Black's activities along the f-file are certainly not to be despised: if 12 d4(?) e×d4 13 e×f5, Black has 13 . . . ♘×f2! 14 ♖×f2 (14 ♖×e6 ♘×d1 15 ♖×e7 ♘×e7 16 ♗×d1 d×c3+ loses material) d×c3 15 b×c3 ♗×f5, finishing up with rook + two pawns vs. bishop and knight and good open files for his rooks. In view of this Nunn's decision to steer clear of the whole thing is understandable. It also has its practical value in saving clock time: from now on . . . ♘g4 can always be met simply by d4.

10 . . . ♗a7

Although it simplifes a little, 10 . . . ♗×b3 does not quite equalise: 11 ♕×b3! (because of the useful threat at b7; creating an open file by the pawn capture is often preferred in such cases) ♖ab8 (if 11 . . . ♕d7 12 ♗g5 ♘g4 13 ♖e2, followed by h3, also preserves an edge; if 11 . . . ♗b6 12 ♗e3 etc.) 12 ♗e3 ♗×e3 13 ♘×e3; and then, for example, 13 . . . ♕e6 14 ♘d5, threatening ♘×c7 and ♘g5, or 13 . . . ♘d8 (for . . . c6) 14 d4 e×d4 (14 . . . c6? 15 ♘f5) 15 ♘d5 ♘×d5 16 e×d5, then 17 ♘×d4 and the black knight is immobilised.

11 ♗c2 . . .

Offered the choice again White now prefers to retain the pieces. But already this opening has certain puzzling aspects. Why should White consistently maintain his initiative, both in the variations we have looked at and in those to come? Why should Black's position be so awkward? The question really boils down to a more basic one: why is the Ruy Lopez (which this opening has now virtually become) so difficult for Black to combat? Look at the present position. Black's pieces are sensibly developed; he has as much space as White; his pawns are strong. Yet he has problems. The answer seems to be that in this type of Ruy Lopez position Black can easily get caught in a situation **where his game cannot unfold**. Here, for instance, White has his plans of ♘g3–f5 and later d4, but it is less easy for Black to find something profitable to do without weakening himself or making some serious concession. His pieces may look reasonably placed, but they cannot readily achieve anything constructive or relevant. I should make it clear that this does not have to happen to Black in a Lopez; it is far from being a bad opening for him. But in practice one error (here 6 . . . ♕e7) can leave him in misery. And so, if a player seems to have a respectable game (in a Ruy Lopez or any other opening, for that matter), yet still loses, his misfortune may often be traced back to this lack of life in his position.

Now here Black's only hope of play lies in organising . . . f5; but it must be very carefully prepared. The knight would interfere with the rooks at e8; therefore he plans . . . ♘g8, . . . g6 and eventually . . . f5. If he plays 11 . . . h6, to stop 12 ♗g5, then . . . g6 and . . . f5 would become more difficult to arrange.

11 . . . ♔h8

12 ♘g3 . . .

12 ♗g5 would have been a more troublesome move to meet. Among other things it makes plain the drawback of having the K-bishop at a7 instead of e7 or g7. The advantage

of a7 lies in its aggressive aspect, but that is only useful **if Black can take the initiative**. After 12 ♗g5 the only way to break the pin is by 12 . . . h6 13 ♗h4 g5 14 ♗g3, but there is no good follow-up: 14 . . . ♘h5? 15 ♘xe5 ♘xg3 16 ♘xc6 etc., or 14 . . . ♗g4 15 ♘e3, exposing the weakness at f5. If Black had time to consolidate his K-side by . . . ♖g8 and . . . h5 he would be quite well placed to start an attack; but the whole point is that he cannot. White hits back smartly in the centre and all his opponent's hopes are dashed: 14 . . . ♖g8 15 d4 g4 16 ♘h4 exd4 17 ♕d2 ♕f8 18 ♗f4 h5 19 ♘g3 with a very dangerous attack for the sacrificed pawn. White could also win a pawn here by 16 dxe5 gxf3 17 exf6 etc.

The heart of the matter, then, is that Black's pawn advance fails here **because he cannot gain the initiative**: it is White who seizes it by 15 d4 and goes on to demonstrate the serious weakness created by the advance. And in practice the only way you can be sure which way things will turn out is by doing the necessary analysis. The same principle would apply if Black allowed his pawns to be broken up by (12 ♗g5) ♕d7 13 ♗xf6 gxf6. If he could develop some attack along the g-file the idea would be acceptable, but after 14 ♘g3 he has no prospects of an attack and White's domination of f5 is too much to stand. For example: (a) 14 . . . f5 15 exf5 ♗xf5 16 ♘xf5 ♕xf5 17 d4 with a strong attack on h7 and/or e5: 17 . . . ♕f6 18 ♕d3, or 17 . . . ♕h5 18 dxe5 dxe5 19 ♘xe5; (b) 14 . . . ♘e7 15 d4, preventing . . . f5 and shutting out the K-bishop; (c) 14 . . . ♖g8 15 ♘h4 ♘e7 (15 . . . ♗g4 16 ♕d2–h6) 16 ♘h5; (d) 14 . . . ♗g4 15 h3 ♗xh3? (unsound) 16 gxh3 ♕xh3 17 d4 ♖g8 18 ♖e2 and the attack is easily beaten off.

12 . . . ♕d7

13 d4? . . .

This move has always been part of White's plan, but the timing is difficult and in playing it here he loses the advantage temporarily. It would be much more effective to prepare the advance by 13 h3, not only preventing . . . ♗g4, but also threatening to trap the bishop, as well as to fork, by a subsequent d4–d5. As at move 10, Nunn was afraid of a sacrifice: 13 . . . ♗xh3 14 gxh3 ♕xh3 (hitting the knight); and indeed there is a nasty variation after 15 d4?, namely 15 . . . exd4 16 cxd4 ♘g4, threatening both 17 . . . ♘xd4 and 17 . . . ♘ce5! But White can safely rely on 15 ♗e3 ♗xe3 16 ♖xe3 ♘g4 17 ♖e2, followed by ♕f1. If Black insists on throwing everything at his opponent, we get 17 . . . f5 18 exf5 e4 19 dxe4 ♘ce5 20 ♘xe5 ♕h2+ 21 ♔f1 dxe5 22 ♖d2!, then ♕f3 and the attack is exhausted.

13 . . . ♗g4

Another interesting and difficult positional point arises here. After 13 . . . exd4 14 cxd4 ♗g4 15 ♗e3 ♗xf3 16 gxf3 White would quite happily accept the doubled pawn because he gains so many advantages in return: two bishops, strong and mobile centre, g-file and open diagonal c2–h7. But after 13 . . . ♗g4 the line 14 ♗e3 ♗xf3 15 gxf3 is by no means the same thing. Here Black has not surrendered the centre by . . . exd4; therefore White has no open c2–h7 diagonal and no chance to make the thrust e5; nor can he resolve the central tension in any satisfactory way. In the second case Black could continue, for example, 15 . . . ♕h3, followed by . . . ♖ad8 or . . . ♖ae8, completing his development harmoniously. Later he might play . . . d5 to activate his knights, which would then comfortably match the white bishops. On the other hand, 16 . . . ♕h3 in the first line could be met by 17 ♔h1, then ♖g1, ♘f5, ♖g3 etc., or f4 and e5, and Black would be unable to find any decent play for his pieces, . . . d5 now being countered by e5.

It follows that White now has nothing better than to block the centre.

14 d5 **♘e7**
15 h3 *(80)* **. . .**

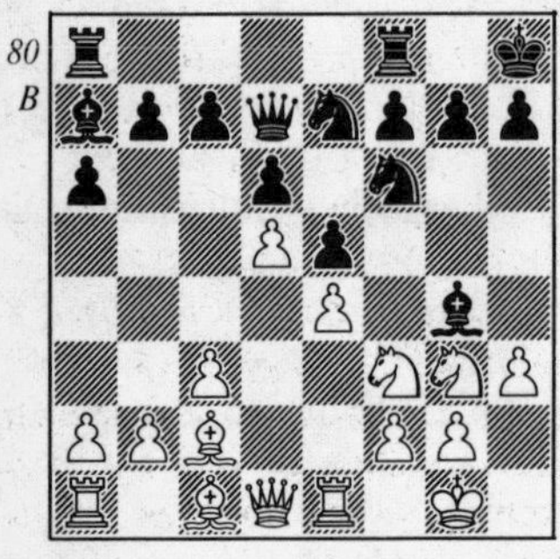

15 . . . ♗×f3

Black has a draw by sacrificing his bishop because he can use an extra piece in the attack this time (the knight at e7).

The analysis runs as follows: 15 . . . ♗×h3 16 g×h3 ♕×h3 17 ♗e3 (if 17 ♘h1 ♘g4 and White cannot adequately cope with the two threats of . . . ♘×f2 and . . . ♘g6–h4) ♗×e3 18 ♖×e3 ♘g4 19 ♖d3 (19 ♕f1 ♕×f1+ 20 ♘×f1 ♘×e3 21 ♘×e3 promises no advantage: although Black has no open lines for his rooks, White also lacks good squares for his knights) ♘g6 20 ♕f1 ♕h6, and White is in no position to avert the threat of . . . ♘f4, then . . . ♘h3+ and perpetual check. The only try is the ingenious 21 ♘f5 ♕h5 22 ♘3h4, hoping for 22 . . . ♘×h4? 23 ♕h3 g5 24 ♗d1; but Black has 22 . . . ♘f4! 23 f3 (23 ♖ moves g6) ♘×d3 24 ♗×d3 ♘h6, and the exchange of a pair of knights leaves him, if anything, with the better of it in view of White's feeble bishop.

That, of course, is quite a lot to see over the board. The text move also leads to approximate equality with correct play.

16 ♕×f3 **♘fg8**

Still working for . . . g6 and . . . f5, but the timing is a delicate business because he must take care not to open the position prematurely: the usual problem when you are facing two bishops. Nor could his own bishop help much from a7, should the king become exposed after these pawn advances. The bright side of this bishop is its aggressive potential. White cannot entertain the idea of exchanging it (♗e3), since he would remain with only the inferior specimen at c2. Therefore, he must aim for c4, b4 and ♗b2 (or ♗d2–c3), hoping that the pressure against e5 will eventually make c5 possible, with tactical chances down the long diagonal. At the same time he must ensure that Black is obliged, after . . . g6 and . . . f5, to recapture on f5 with a pawn: if the file were to open there would be serious trouble at f2. With best play the game appears at this point to be roughly balanced, though in practice it will be easier for Black to go wrong.

17 ♗d2 . . .

17 c4 would not save time because the back rank has to be cleared first. After 17 . . . g6 18 b4 Black has 18 . . . a5, and if 19 a3? a×b4 20 a×b4 ♗×f2+.

17 . . . g6

18 c4 f5?

And this error is serious enough to lose the game. In the end everything reverts to the two fundamental principles: control of the centre and optimum use of the pieces, i.e. making sure that your pieces are operating in a relevant way **now**. Not on the last move, but **now**, because the situation can change in the twinkling of an eye. Up to now the a7 bishop has had quite an influence on the game, and, had Black played 18 . . . ♗d4!, it could have continued to do so, because it would be interfering forcefully with White's Q-side plans. If 19 ♖ab1 (19 ♗e3 c5 20 d×c6 ♘×c6 suits Black admirably; in any case White should not offer this exchange) Black could choose between: (a) 19 . . . a5 20 ♘e2 ♗c5, when the knight must return to g3 because . . . f5 (recapturing with pieces) would now be timely; or (b) 19 . . . c5 20 ♘e2 f5 21 ♘×d4 c×d4, when he has a central pawn mass and play along the f-file to compensate for the loss of his bishops. In each case the position is about equal.

19 e×f5 ♘×f5

19 . . . g×f5 would be worse, as both black knights would be paralysed.

20 ♘×f5 g×f5

If 20 . . . ♘e7, trying to take with a piece, 21 ♗h6 ♖f7 22 ♗g7+ wins material.

21 ♗c3 *(81)* **. . .**

81
B

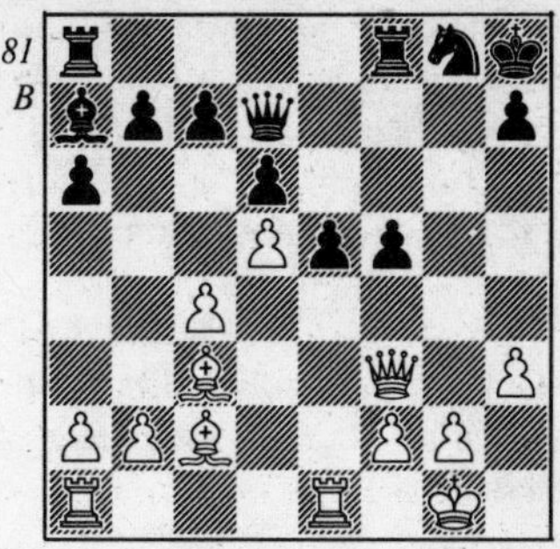

Now see the difference: White's pieces have control of the centre and are doing the things that matter. Black's bishop is denied d4 and will presently be buried alive by b4 and c5. The sturdy-looking pawn centre is actually highly vulnerable **because White's pieces are better**, and the decision will be brought about by smashing it with a rook sacrifice.

21 . . . ♖ae8

22 b4 ♘e7

23 h4! . . .

A nice touch, anticipating the defence of e5 by . . . ♘g6, after which c5 could be met by . . . d×c5. The pawn itself will also become a powerful factor in the main assault. White is willing to risk the slight weakening of g4 in view of the positive aspects of this move.

23 . . . ♖g8

Black's only hope of any play is to occupy the g-file at once. If he does nothing, White can win in several ways: h5 and ♕g3, for instance, then a sacrifice at e5; or c5, then a queen move and f4.

24 h5 ♖g7

The rooks must first be doubled at g7 and g8. As a foretaste of what is looming on the long diagonal we might offer the variation: 24 . . . ♖g4? 25 c5 ♖eg8 26 ♖×e5! ♖×g2+ 27 ♔h1 d×e5 28 ♗×e5+ ♖2g7 29 h6 and wins.

25 c5 . . .

25 h6 ♖g6 would be premature. Now if black refuses to double rooks, to avoid shutting in his king, the only other move worth analysing is 25 . . . f4: against slow play such as 25 . . . ♔g8 or 25 . . . ♖f8 White has 26 ♖ad1, then ♗b3 followed by either the sacrifice ♖×e5 or a queen move preparing f4.

In fact 25 . . . f4, threatening 26 . . . ♕g4, is probably the defence which would hold out the longest. It is a passive one though; normally a strong player will prefer an active defence such as Olafsson chooses because there is more chance of inducing an error that way.

After 25 . . . f4 26 h6 we have: (a) 26 . . . ♖g4? 27 c6! b×c6 28 d×c6 ♕c8 (28 . . . ♕e6 29 ♗b3 ♕f5 30 ♖×e5 d×e5 31 ♕×g4 etc.) 29 ♖×e5 d×e5 30 ♗×e5+ ♔g8 31 ♖e1! (quietly bringing in the last piece because Black is irrecoverably exposed and scattered; this is better than the extremely tempting line 31 ♗b3+ ♔f8 32 ♕×f4+ ! because Black has 32 . . . ♕f5) ♔f8 32 ♗g7+ ♖×g7 33 h×g7+ ♔×g7 34 ♕c3+ ♔f7 (or 34 . . . ♔h6 35 ♖×e7 ♖×e7 36 ♕f6+ ♔h5 37 ♗d1+) 35 ♗b3+ ♔g6 36 ♖e6+ and wins. All other defensive attempts lead to a similar type of catastrophe, 31 . . . ♖g6 32 ♗b3+ ♔f8 33 ♗g7+, for instance. (b) 26 . . . ♖f7 27 ♖ad1 ♘g6 28 ♕h5 ♖f6 (28 . . . ♘f8 29 ♗a4), and although a clear win is not apparent, Black has a miserable, passive position and a very bad bishop. White's best plan would seem to be ♗e4; then c6 if an opportunity arises, but otherwise ♖d3 and g3, working to open more lines on the K-side.

25 . . . ♖eg8

26 g3 *(82)* **. . .**

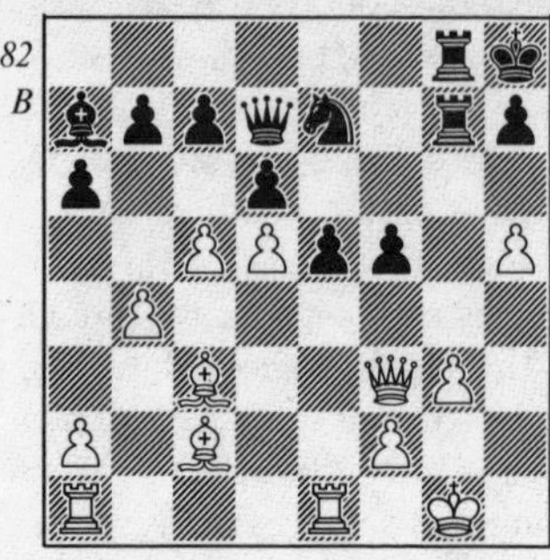

82
B

Not yet 26 ♖×e5? d×e5 27 ♗×e5 h6. Nor can White permit exchanges at g2, because the black queen would rapidly infiltrate via g4 or b5 and take advantage of the exposed king and bishops.

We are now at a critical moment where Black can force events by 26 . . . f4, obliging White to sacrifice at once. In the analysis which follows the main point of interest is the crushing power which the bishops develop, once the central barricades are broken down; notice especially the way White makes use of the newly opened c2–h7 diagonal and the h-file. If Black manages to cope with all these perils, the d-pawn will be the straw to break the camel's back:

26 . . . f4 27 ♖×e5 (27 h6? ♖×g3+) d×e5 28 ♗×e5, threatening 29 h6, and the only hope is to try 28 . . . ♕h3 (28 . . . h6 29 ♕d3, or 28 . . . ♘f5 29 ♕×f4 ♖f8 30 h6). Then comes 29 ♖e1!, once again the quiet move because it is much better for the moment to hold on to the d- and h-pawns, restricting the black knight, than to be tempted into 29 ♕f4. The result of that would be 29 . . . ♕×h5 30 ♖e1 (or 30 ♔g2 ♘g6) ♘×d5 31 ♕d4 c6 32 ♔g2 ♗b8! and Black can defend

himself. After 29 ♖e1 f×g3 30 f×g3 Black is facing 31 ♗f6, among other things, and is very short of constructive moves: if 30 . . . h6 31 ♕d3 again, or if 30 . . . ♖e8 31 ♗×g7+ ♔×g7 32 ♖f1 is disastrous. But he can try one more shot: the odd-looking 30 . . . b6! Now White will be in trouble if the a7-g1 diagonal opens (31 ♗f6 b×c5, for example); so 31 ♕d3! ♕×h5 32 ♔g2, securing the king and threatening ♖h1, and he can now demonstrate a forced win as follows:

(1) 32 . . . ♕g6 33 ♖h1! ♖e8 (33 . . . ♕×d3 34 ♗×d3 wins, while otherwise ♕×g6 decides) 34 ♗×g7+ ♔×g7 35 ♕d4+ ♕f6 36 ♖×h7+ and wins.
(2) 32 . . . ♘g6 33 ♗×g7+ ♔×g7 (33 . . . ♖×g7 34 ♖e8+ and 35 ♕d4+) 34 ♕d4+ ♔f7 35 ♗×g6+ ♖×g6 (35 . . . ♔×g6 36 ♖e6+; 35 . . . h×g6 36 ♕f4+ ♕f5 37 ♕×c7+ and mate; or 35 . . . ♕×g6 36 ♕f4+ ♕f6 37 ♕×c7+) 36 ♕e4! and Black cannot defend himself: 36 . . . ♔g7 37 ♕e7+ ♔h8 38 ♕e8+ ♔g7 39 ♖e7+ ♔h6 40 ♕f8+; or 36 . . . ♖g5 37 ♖f1+ ♔g7 38 ♕e7+ ♔h6 39 ♕f8+; or 36 . . . ♕g5 37 ♕e8+ ♔g7 38 ♖e7+ ♔h6 39 ♕f8+ ♔h5 (39 . . . ♖g7 40 ♖e6+ ♔h5 41 ♕e8+) 40 ♖×h7+ ♖h6 41 ♕f3+ and wins.
(3) 32 . . . ♖e8 (meets the threat: 33 ♖h1? ♕×e5 34 ♖×h7+ ♔g8, but now the d-pawn joins in) 33 d6 ♘c6 (exchanging pawns makes no difference; if 33 . . . ♘g8 34 ♗×g7+ ♔×g7 35 ♖×e8 ♕×e8 36 d7 ♕d8 37 ♕×h7+ ♔f8 38 ♗b3 wins) 34 ♗×g7+ ♔×g7 35 ♖×e8 ♕×e8 36 ♕×h7+ ♔f6 (36 . . . ♔f8 37 ♕h8+ ♔f7 38 ♗g6+) 37 ♕h6+ ♔e5 38 ♕e3+, winning the queen.

Instead Black decides simply to create a flight square for his king.

26 . . . h6

27 ♖ad1 . . .

The sacrifice is still not correct, with the black pawn remaining at f5, but White now prepares it by supporting the further thrust d6. The rook may then recapture and bring the fragile h-pawn under fire, or White may retake with his pawn, dislodging the knight and leaving the f-pawn in trouble. From now on White can guarantee a minimum of three pawns and an enduring attack for his sacrificed piece.

27 . . . ♕e8

Against any non-committal move (not that Black has many) White will sacrifice; or if 27 . . . ♔h7 28 ♖×e5 d×e5 29 d6 and the knight cannot move. After 27 . . . f4 28 ♖×e5 d×e5 29 ♗×e5 f×g3 30 f×g3 the enormous energy of the bishops reveals itself in a new set of tactical points: 31 ♕d3 is threatened again and the best Black can do is 30 . . . ♖e8 (if 30 . . . ♖d8, or anywhere except e8, 31 ♕f6 ♘g8 32 ♕g6! finishes the game; if 31 . . . ♘c8 here, then 32 ♗f5), remaining two pawns down in a lost endgame after 31 ♕d3 ♘f5 32 ♕×f5 ♕×f5 33 ♗×g7+ ♔×g7 34 ♗×f5. In the circumstances he seems lucky to manage even that.

28 ♖×e5! d×e5
29 ♗×e5 b6

This is too slow, but even the best move 29 . . . ♖f8 loses after 30 d6 c×d6 (30 . . . ♘c6 31 ♗×g7+ ♔×g7 32 d×c7 gives White three pawns and an attack in return for the a7 bishop!) 31 ♖×d6 ♘g8 (31 . . . ♔h7 32 ♕f4, or 31 . . . ♔g8 32 ♗b3+ ♔h7 33 ♗×g7 ♔×g7 34 ♕×b7 ♗b8 35 ♖e6 ♖f7 36 ♖e3 wins) 32 ♗×g7+ ♔×g7 33 ♕×b7+ ♖f7 34 ♕×a6, with four pawns and an attack for the piece.

30 d6 ♘c6 *(83)*

83
W

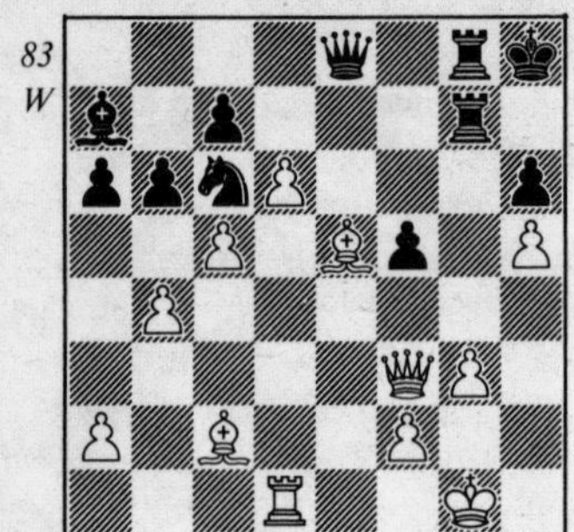

31 ♗f6 . . .

The black bishop is still trying to get back into the game; if 31 ♗b2? b×c5 32 ♕×f5 ♘d4 unpins the rook!

31 . . . ♕e6

31 . . . ♘×b4 32 d7 and 31 . . . ♖f8 32 ♕×f5 ♖×f6 33 ♕×f6 are hopeless; so Black plays for a final trap.

32 ♗×g7+ ♖×g7

33 ♕×c6 b×c5

34 ♕a8+ . . .

White has to go into this with his eyes open, because his queen will be temporarily out of action at a7 and the perpetual check can only be averted in one way.

34 . . . ♖g8

After 34 . . . ♔h7 the easiest win is by 35 ♕f3 ♖f7 (35 . . . ♔h8 36 ♗×f5) 36 d7.

35 ♕×a7 ♖×g3+

36 ♔h2 . . .

Surprisingly 36 f×g3? ♕e3+ is perpetual, or if 36 ♔f1? ♕c4+.

36 . . . ♕e5

37 ♕×c5! 1 – 0

Game 19

Sicilian Defence
Biel 1983

J. Nunn v. F. Gheorghiu

1	**e4**	**c5**
2	**♘f3**	**e6**
3	**d4**	**c×d4**
4	**♘×d4**	**a6**
5	**♗d3**	. . .

Black's move order permits his opponent a choice between simple development (5 ♘c3) and a Maroczy Bind system in which he plays the space-gaining move c4. Gheorghiu is prepared for either type of game, but happens to be a specialist in the 'hedgehog' formation, i.e.. . . b6, . . . e6 and . . . d6, accepting a restricted position, but one in which it is far from easy for White to judge when and where to attack.

Gheorghiu is also the kind of player who tends to repeat the same openings, not changing his repertoire for years. Obviously you become an expert by adopting that approach, but the drawback is that your opponents can prepare for the game more easily. In this instance Nunn has taken the opportunity to examine thoroughly a game Tringov–Gheorghiu (Lucerne Olympiad 1982) and has spotted an improvement for White at move 17. More of that later; suffice to say here that in order to reach move 17 without arousing Black's suspicions, he is deliberately playing his opening moves rather slowly!

5	. . .	**♘f6**
6	**0–0**	**d6**
7	**c4**	. . .

Black's plan can be summed up by saying that he wishes to be ready for anything White may throw at him. After completing his development he will have a cramped but flexible game, able to react swiftly to any loose play or premature attacks. The trouble is that there is very little margin of error. Here is one example of Black's problems (Commons–Peev, Plovdiv 1976): 7 . . . ♗e7 8 ♘c3 0–0 9 ♔h1 ♘bd7 10 f4 ♕c7 11 ♕e2 b6 12 ♗d2 (not 12 ♗e3, blocking the queen's support for e5) ♗b7 13 ♖ac1 g6 14 b4 ♖ac8 15 a3 ♕b8 16 ♘f3 ♖fe8 17 ♖ce1 ♗f8 18 ♘g5 h6 19 ♘×f7! ♔×f7 20 e5, with f5 to follow, and White's attack won.

It's hard to detect Black's errors in that game, but generally speaking the plan of f4, ♕e2, ♘f3 and a quick e5 is dangerous for him if he has played an early . . . ♘bd7 and if his other knight cannot therefore retreat from f6 to d7. (If the Q-knight makes room by occupying c5, White plays ♗c2 and b4.) In Gheorghiu's more subtle treatment of the problem the development of the knight is delayed until White has shown his hand: if he seems to be preparing e5, the knight goes to c6 instead.

7	. . .	**b6**
8	**♘c3**	**♗b7**
9	**f4**	**♗e7** *(84)*

84
W

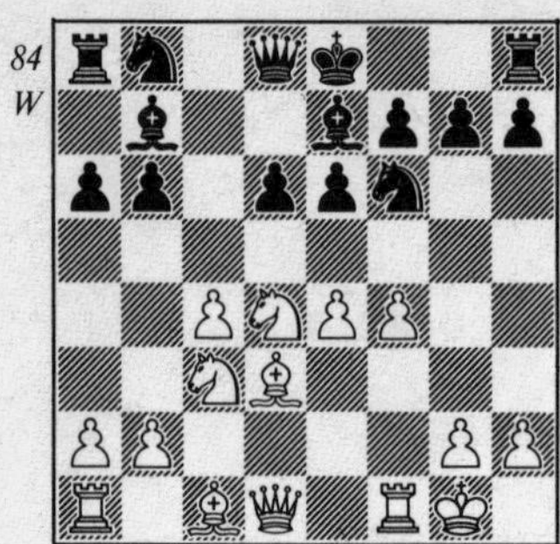

We have already hinted at how Black's scheme of development is based on the principle of flexibility, of keeping his options open and not committing himself too early; but this applies in equal measure to White. If you play through the game rapidly, it will give the illusion of being one-sided: just one more anti-Sicilian attack in which Black's K-side is laid waste. But its value lies in the fact that very accurate play was needed to make it succeed, and many things could have gone wrong. In particular White must not play e5 or f5 too early; if he does, this is an example of what may happen: 10 ♗e3 ♘c6 11 ♘×c6 ♗×c6 12 e5 d×e5 13 f×e5 ♘d7 14 ♕g4 g6 15 ♕g3 ♕c7 (Apart from the burden of protecting his weak e-pawn, White has no attack because he cannot play the natural moves to develop it, i.e. ♘e4 and/or ♗g5, without permitting too many exchanges. Nor is doubling rooks on the f-file much use). 16 ♗d4 ♘c5 17 ♗c2 ♖d8 18 ♖ad1 0–0 19 ♕e3 ♖×d4! 20 ♕×d4 ♘d7 21 ♕f4 ♘×e5 with a clear advantage (Kindermann–Gheorghiu, Zürich 1984).

The exchange sacrifice is difficult to comprehend, but its justification lies in Black's domination of the dark squares and White's difficulty in obtaining any aggressive play for his pieces. If 22 ♖de1 ♗d6 23 ♘e4 White loses his c-pawn at once by 23 . . . ♗×e4; if 22 b3 f5 (23 ♖de1 ♗f6) and the white knight has lost his only chance of activity. More generally the black minor pieces will keep the rooks out of d7, the rooks cannot use the e-file because the black knight is unshakable, and the bishop seems to be banging his head against a brick wall wherever he tries to settle; all this adds up to plenty of compensation for the material.

But we must not stray too far from the main game. The point of this interlude is to show that e5 should not be played **unless a concrete attacking continuation is available**; otherwise it creates a weak pawn, liberates the b7 bishop and obstructs its own Q-bishop. If you ask: 'Why then do we see very quick e5s and f5s in other Sicilian variations, especially Najdorfs?', the answer is that White's development advantage in the present game is nothing like as pronounced as in many of the sharper anti-Najdorf systems (6 ♗g5 and 6 ♗c4). He is playing here for a space gain and an **eventual** K-side attack, not a Blitzkrieg. The move c4 also leaves White with a potential vulnerability on the black squares: another reason to be extra careful.

10 ♔h1 . . .

This is necessary because Black may yet adopt a plan based on . . . ♘bd7. In that event White would wish to continue ♕e2 and e5, but without leaving his undefended knight at d4 open to unpleasant tactical possibilities such as the pin . . . ♗c5.

10 . . . 0–0

11 ♕e2 ♘c6

White shows every intention of aiming for e5; so the knight goes to c6. And this is a good example of the nice balance in Black's game: if White, as the player with the space advantage, avoids the exchange of knights, he cannot profit from it because Black has the manoeuvre . . . ♘d7–c5. For example: 12 ♘f3 ♘d7! 13 ♖d1 ♕c7, and White has no significant play because he cannot organise either e5 or b4: 14 ♗d2 (14 a3 ♘a5!) ♘c5 15 ♗c2 ♘b4 16 ♗b1 ♘c6 17 ♗c2 is Oltean–Gheorghiu, Romanian Championship 1983, in which Black could have continued to repeat, but chose to vary with 17 . . . ♖ad8 18 ♖ac1 ♗f6 and eventually won.

12 ♘×c6 ♗×c6

13 b3 . . .

The fianchetto gives rise to a host of attacking possibilities later on; at the same time the c-pawn receives useful support.

13 . . . ♕c7

Though his main error in the present game came with 16 . . . ♘d7, Gheorghiu was apparently not satisfied with this queen move either, and in some later games played 13 . . . ♘d7, in order to re-arrange his K-side defences one move sooner and to play . . . ♗f6 if permitted. It is not clear whether this was a good idea – certainly his plan misfired in the two instances quoted below – but it gives us a bird's eye view of the whole system by observing how White's plan has to be modified according to Black's exact moves.

We have to compare three things: (a) Vogt–Gheorghiu (East Germany–Romania match 1984); (b) Nunn–Gheorghiu No. 2 (Hamburg 1984); and (c) Nunn–Gheorghiu No. 1, the main game.

Vogt–Gheorghiu continued 13 . . . ♘d7 14 ♗b2 g6 (. . . ♗f6 is not so easy to achieve without running into other tactical problems: 14 . . . ♗f6 15 ♖ad1 ♕c7 16 ♗b1 ♖fd8 17 ♖d3 g6 18 ♖fd1 ♘c5 19 ♘d5! e×d5 20 ♗×f6 ♘×d3 21 e×d5 ♘×f4 22 ♕f3 ♘h5 23 ♗×d8 ♖×d8 24 d×c6 gives White a clear plus – Marjanović–Rajković, Yugoslavian Championship 1983; if Black tries to avoid . . . g6, ♖h3 will soon force it anyway) 15 ♖ad1 (discouraging . . . ♗f6 now; for example 15 . . . ♗f6 16 ♗b1 ♕c7 17 ♕d2, attacking d6) ♖e8 16 ♗b1; and now Black made a serious mistake and got caught up in a whirlwind: 16 . . . ♗f8? 17 e5! d×e5 18 ♗e4! ♕c7 (if 18 . . . ♗×e4 19 ♘×e4, threatening 20 ♖×d7; then 19 . . . ♗g7 20 ♗×e5 ♗×e5 21 f×e5 ♔g7 22 ♕f2 and White wins after either 22 . . . ♕e7 23 ♕f6+! ♔g8 24 ♕×e7 ♖×e7 25 ♖×d7, or 22 . . . ♖e7 23 ♘g5 ♕g8 24 ♘×f7 ♖f8 – or multiple exchanges into a hopeless rook ending – 25 ♖×d7!) 19 ♕f3 ♗×e4 (no choice now) 20 ♘×e4 f5 (loosening, but if 20 . . . ♗g7 21 f×e5 ♘×e5 22 ♘f6+ ♔h8 23 ♗×e5 wins) 21 ♖×d7 f×e4 22 ♕d1 ♕c6 23 ♗×e5 ♖ac8 24 ♕d4 ♗e7 (24 . . . ♖e7 25 ♖d6, or 24 . . . b5 25 ♕a7, or 24 . . . ♗c5 25 ♖g7+ ♔f8 26 ♗d6+) 25 f5! (the plan is 25 ♗h8 ♗f8 26 ♖g7+ ♔h8 27 ♖×g6+, but then 27 . . . e5 wrecks everything; now after 25 . . . e×f5 the line would work; if 25 . . . g×f5 26 ♗h8 ♗f8 27 ♖×f5! e×f5 28 ♖g7+ also leads to mate) ♖cd8 26 ♖×e7! e×f5 (26 . . . ♖×d4 27 ♖g7+ and mate) 27 ♖×e8+ ♕×e8 28 ♕×b6 and Black resigned.

Here e5 was justified tactically; Vogt saw that he had a real attack because he could continue generating threats after 18 ♗e4. At a guess he probably saw as far as 23 ♗×e5 in the main line (together with the supporting variations), and that after 18 . . . ♗×e4 his pressure against f6 would be crushing.

In his second game with Nunn, Gheorghiu avoided this error and played 16 . . . ♕c7. Then came the flexible move 17 ♕d3, preparing ♕d4 or ♕h3 according to circumstances, and after 17 . . . ♗f8 (17 . . . ♘c5? 18 ♕d4, threatening 19 ♘d5) 18 ♘b5! ♗×b5 (the hidden tactical point is that 18 . . . a×b5 19 ♕c3 e5 20 c×b5 ♖ac8 21 b×c6 ♕×c6 22 ♕f3, followed by f5, yields too much white-square pressure) 19 c×b5 a×b5 20 ♕×b5 White still held the advantage by virtue of his two bishops.

Comparing these two examples with the main game, we see that in Nunn–Gheorghiu No. 2 most of the action took place in the centre and on the Q-side, and that in Vogt–Gheorghiu, for all the violence of his attack, White was operating as much in the centre as on the K-side. In Nunn–Gheorghiu No. 1, by contrast, White concentrates solely on the K-side.

14	**♗b2**	**♖ad8**
15	**♖ae1**	. . .

It now becomes clear why White is thinking only in terms of the K-side. Firstly there is no point in threatening the centre by ♖ad1 because Black has securely defended d6, and secondly 15 ♖ae1 gains a tempo on account of the (strong) threat of 16 ♘d5, opening the centre to White's benefit. And, of course, there is no Q-side play this time. But he still has to take care; even now there must be no automatic e5.

15	. . .	**♗b7**
16	**♗b1**	**♘d7?** *(85)*

This is the mistake, probably a fatal one, against which Nunn had prepared his innovation. His following move 17 ♕h5 is extremely strong because the queen's threats cannot be parried unless the knight returns to f6. The queen will then withdraw to her ideal attacking square at h3 **without time loss**. And in such a sharp position the loss of two tempi is likely to be disastrous for the defender.

In the earlier games which we quoted White never had a chance to play ♕h5 because of Black's early . . . g6, and that would be his best move here. An immediate f5 would then be premature: 16 . . . g6 17 f5 e×f5 18 e×f5 ♖de8 19 f×g6 h×g6 20 ♕f2 ♕c6 and White's attack is biting on granite because he has opened the position too soon; in fact it is the black pieces which are benefiting from the open lines. That is just the kind of thing Black is hoping for in playing this system: his subtle scheme of development is reacting at once to White's mistakes. To avoid confusion, let me say that the opening of the game by vigorous pawn thrusts such as f5 is exactly the right procedure **if your opponent's development is backward or chaotic**; if, as here, it is well balanced, though seemingly restricted, you have to be much more careful.

Actually White can do better in the variation given above. The exchange at g6 is definitely wrong and he can also improve at move 18; but even then Black's position stands up well: 18 ♘d5 ♗×d5 (18 . . . ♘×d5 19 e×d5 ♖de8 20 ♖×f5! is dangerous) 19 c×d5 ♘×e4 20 ♗×e4 f×e4 21 ♕×e4 ♖de8 22 ♖c1 ♕b7 with plenty of pressure in return for a pawn, but nothing conclusive. After 16 . . . g6 17 ♕d3 is probably the most accurate, when the queen can go to h3 or the long diagonal, as appropriate.

17 ♕h5! . . .

In the earlier game Tringov had played 17 e5? here – once again premature because there is no clear attacking line to follow. Moreover, it releases one white bishop only to block the other. After 17 . . . d×e5 18 f×e5 g6 he faced the same problem as Kindermann: a weak e-pawn and lack of central control; hence no way to transfer his pieces to the K-side. If 19 ♘e4 Black could play 19 . . . ♗×e4 20 ♕×e4 ♘c5 with a very comfortable position, or he could take the pawn: 19 . . . ♘×e5 20 ♘f6+ ♗×f6 21 ♖×f6 ♘c6, followed as soon as possible by . . . ♖fe8 and . . . e5 (plus . . . ♖d7 if need be), and White really has very little compensation. So Tringov tried 19 ♕e3 ♘c5 20 ♕h6 and the sequel is an object lesson in the art of counterplay in the centre to defeat an unsound attack: 20 . . . ♕d7! (The white knight and bishops cannot help with the attack; so the only way to keep it going is ♖e3–h3, which Black will now refute by 21 . . . ♕d2. If 21 ♘d5 ♗×d5 22 c×d5 ♕×d5 and Black is still ready to play . . . ♕d2, or if 21 ♖d1 ♕c6 22 ♘d5 e×d5 23 c×d5 – 23 e6 d4! – ♖×d5 24 e6 ♖d4! 25 ♖g1 ♕×g2+!) 21 ♖e2 f5! (another fine move exploiting the back-rank weakness) 22 e×f6 ♖×f6 23 ♖g1 ♘d3 24 ♘d5 ♘×b2 25 ♘×e7+ ♕×e7 26 ♖×b2 ♕c5 27 ♖d2 ♖df8 (threatens 28 . . . ♕×g1+) 28 ♗d3 e5 29 h3 e4 30 ♗e2 ♗c6 and Black had a near-winning position.

17 . . . ♖fe8

An unpleasant move to make because the rook will be missed, should White open the f-file; but in any case Black is skating on very thin ice. 17 . . . ♘f6 18 ♕h3 leads to positions very much like the game and may actually transpose. Apart from that there are only 17 . . . g6 and 17 . . . ♗f6:

(a) 17 . . . g6 18 ♕h6, threatening 19 ♘d5; then either 18 . . . ♗f6 19 ♖e3 ♗g7 (or 19 . . . ♖fe8 20 ♖h3 ♘f8 21 ♘d5!) 20 ♕×g7+ and wins, or 18 . . . ♘f6 19 e5 d×e5 20 f×e5 ♘d7 21 ♖e3 (-h3) and wins. If here 20 . . . ♘g4 21 ♕f4 ♖d2 22 ♖e2 wins, or if Black does not exchange pawns, 19 . . . ♘g4 (19 . . . ♘d7 20 ♘d5 and 21 e×d6 wins) 20 ♕h3 h5 21 ♕g3, followed by h3, is too much of a weakness to stand.

(b) 17 . . . ♗f6 18 ♖e3 ♖fe8 19 ♖g3! (19 e5 g6 and 19 ♖h3 h6 20 ♖g3 ♔f8 are less effective, but now White really threatens 20 e5 and cuts out the defences . . . h6, . . . ♔f8 and . . . ♔h8) g6 20 ♕h6 and by now some of the tactical points are becoming familiar: 20 . . . ♗h8 (otherwise 21 ♖h3 ♘f8 22 ♘d5) 21 ♘d5! e×d5 22 ♕×h7+ and wins.

18 ♖e3 ♘f6

This is the least evil now: 18 . . . ♗f6 19 ♖g3 transposes into the previous note, 18 . . . g6 loses to 19 ♘d5! e×d5 20 ♕×h7+, and if 18 . . . ♘f8 19 ♖g3 ♘g6 (19 . . . g6 20 ♕h6 etc.) 20 f5 ♘e5 21 f×e6 f×e6 22 ♘d5! ♖f8 (22 . . . e×d5 23 ♗×e5 and 24 ♕f7+) 23 ♖e1 e×d5 24 e×d5 g6 (24 . . . h6 25 ♖×g7+ ♔×g7 26 ♕g6+ or 24 . . . ♘g6 25 ♖×g6) 25 ♗×e5 d×e5 26 ♖×g6+ wins.

19 ♕h3 . . .

Only now, with all his pieces ready, is White seriously contemplating the advance of a centre pawn, the immediate threat being 20 e5. We have emphasised that neither thrust should be made until White is certain that his opponent cannot take advantage of the weak squares which will inevitably be created, and the same principle applies to the manoeuvres ♖e3–g3 and ♕h5–h3. White is committed by these moves; he cannot toy with the idea of an attack and expect to pull his queen and the rook back if things go wrong, because the loss of time would be catastrophic. When Black hits back in the centre he would suffer the same kind of fate as Tringov did, or worse. This is especially true if g3 and h3 are occupied by pieces because White cannot eliminate the back-rank danger by making a bolt-hole for his king.

Here Nunn has decided that the adventure is justified: his opponent has wasted two tempi, his forces are all mobilised, and above all he has backed up his judgement with some concrete analysis. For example, Black must now meet the threat of 20 e5 by either 19 . . . g6 or 19 . . . h6. If 19 . . . h6 we have 20 e5 d×e5 21 f×e5 ♘d7 22 ♖g3 and White's threats are more relevant than Black's attack on the e-pawn: (a) 22 . . . ♕×e5? 23 ♘d1; (b) 22 . . . ♘×e5 23 ♕×h6 ♘g6 24 ♖×g6 f×g6 25 ♕×g6; (c) 22 . . . ♔f8 23 ♕×e6 ♘×e5 24 ♘b5; (d) 22 . . . ♗g5 23 ♖×g5 h×g5 24 ♕h7+ ♔f8 25 ♖×f7+ and mate. If Black refuses to exchange pawns, there is 20 . . . ♘d7 (or 20 . . . ♘h7) 21 ♖g3 K moves 22 ♘d5! e×d5 23 ♖×g7 etc.

19 . . . g6 is definitely a tougher defence.

19 . . . g6 *(86)*

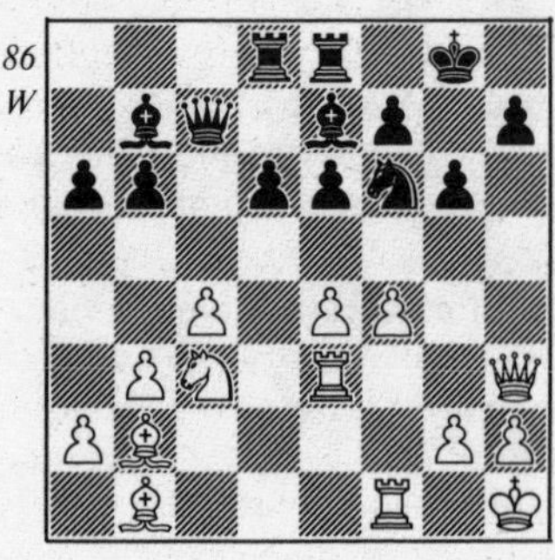
86
W

20 f5 . . .

The circumstances are now favourable for this move: e6 is under fire, the rook is missing from f8 and Black cannot occupy e5 with a piece.

20 . . . ♗c8

20 . . . e5 is a move to be avoided if at all possible, because it yields d5 without a fight, locks the centre and gives White a completely free hand on the K-side. Even so, if White adopts the wrong attacking formation it could become a useful weapon, as the note to Black's 22nd move indicates. If Black takes at f5, the square d5 is again available and White's attack is correspondingly stronger than in the game. One further point: after 20 . . . e×f5 White would recapture at once rather than be

tempted into 21 ♘d5. If (21 ♘d5) ♘×d5, then of course 22 ♕×h7+ is on again; but Black has 21 . . . ♗×d5 and the back-rank menace rears its head: 22 c×d5 f×e4!, or 22 e×d5 ♘g4 23 ♖×f5 ♗f6! (but not 23 . . . ♘×e3 24 ♕×h7+) and Black is more than holding his own.

21 ♖g3 . . .

As a general guide, the player with the initiative will prefer to keep tension in the position. In this case, for instance, 21 f×g6 f×g6 22 ♖g3 might improve Black's defensive resources by clearing the second rank and the f-file for his queen and rooks before the white rook has got into position. Therefore White moves his rook first, leaving the f7 pawn to clog up the works for at least one more move.

White is, of course, operating with direct threats whenever possible, and notice that he also knows **precisely** what he is threatening: he is not just pointing his rook at the king. That knowledge makes analysis easier because it drastically cuts down the number of defences worth considering. Here the threat is 22 e5! d×e5 23 f×g6 f×g6 24 ♗×g6, winning at once. Since 21 . . . e×f5 fails yet again to 22 ♘d5, Black has no choice.

21 . . . **♔g7**

22 ♕h4 . . .

Stepping up the pressure against f6 just when the knight cannot possibly move. The new threat is 23 f×g6 f×g6 24 ♖×f6! ♗×f6 (24 . . . ♖f8 25 ♘d5) 25 ♘d5 e×d5 26 ♕×f6+ ♔g8 27 ♕h8+ ♔f7 28 ♕g7+ ♔e6 29 c×d5 mate. If 23 . . . h×g6 here, the simplest win is 24 ♘d5 e×d5 25 ♖×f6; or White could enjoy himself with 24 ♖×f6! ♖h8 (24 . . . ♗×f6 25 ♕×f6+ ♔×f6 26 ♘d5 mate) 25 ♘d5! ♖×h4 26 ♖f×g6+ ♔h7 27 ♖g7+ etc.

22 . . . **♖f8** *(87)*

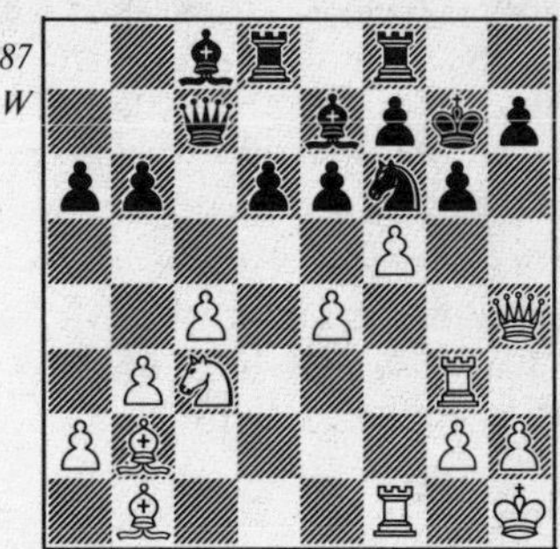

87
W

Now what? The obvious ideas are to switch to the h-file by 23 ♖h3 or to put more pressure on f6 by 23 ♖gf3. But neither of these moves will quite do because they rely on an early f×g6 to make them work, and we know that move can be too hasty. 23 ♖h3 h5! 24 f×g6 f×g6 25 ♖g3 is very tempting because of the threat of 25 e5, but Black gets in first: 25 . . . e5!, and this once undesirable move now activates his pieces! He can follow up with . . . ♘g4 and White is in trouble; the use of d5 is no consolation now. Again, 23 ♖gf3 appears to threaten the win of material, but 23 . . . e5! and if 24 f×g6 f×g6 25 ♖×f6 (hoping for an ultimate knight fork) ♗b7! refutes the combination.

So what is wrong? Simply that White is trying to win with his heavy pieces alone, when in reality the attack cannot succeed until **all** his forces have been mobilised, **including the knight and K-bishop**. Nunn's acute awareness of that fact is evident from what follows.

23 ♗c1! . . .

A real Grandmaster's move! Not only does he refuse to be tempted by 23 ♖h3, but he removes the bishop from the long diagonal just when Black has seemingly made things even worse there by playing . . . ♔g7. Nor is he interested, except as a last resort, in winning the exchange by ♗h6+. The real point of the move is that he will have to play e5 very soon in order to release his two backward pieces – that is top priority – and e5 will block the long diagonal; therefore the bishop occupies a more useful line.

23 . . . ♖de8

Another point of 23 ♗c1 is revealed. If now 23 . . . e5 24 ♗g5 (threatens a knight-fork combination again) ♗b7 (or . . . ♕b7) 25 ♖gf3 would be too much to stand. Against 23 . . . h5 White must take care for exactly the same reason as before: it is fatally easy to be lured into a premature attack. 24 f×g6? looks good, but runs into 24 . . . ♘g4! 25 ♕×h5 f×g6 (back row again) and no amount of wriggling will save him: 26 ♗h6+ ♔h7 and Black wins material. The right way is 24 e5! d×e5 25 f×g6 and the whole thing collapses on Black.

The point of the text move is to defend the bishop in case of a pin by ♗g5, and to allow further defence of f6 by . . . ♕d8.

24 e5! . . .

Winning the exchange would still leave some work to do; instead White throws every piece into the assault and brings the game to a rapid conclusion.

24 . . . d×e5

25 ♕h6+ ♔h8

25 . . . ♔g8 would lose at once to 26 f×g6 f×g6 27 ♗×g6, but with . . . ♔h8 Black is setting another horrible trap: if now 26 f×g6 f×g6 27 ♗×g6 ♖d8, he counters 28 ♗×h7? by the winning move 28 . . . ♘g4! White can play 27 ♖×g6 here, which wins two pieces for a rook after 27 . . . ♖f7 or 27 . . . ♗d8, but once again the attack is too good for that.

26 ♖h3 . . .

This is the move that carries the real punch, for if the knight cannot move Black's whole position remains constricted; meanwhile further contortions are required to deal with the threat of 27 ♗g5.

26 . . . ♖g8

27 ♗g5 ♖g7 *(88)*

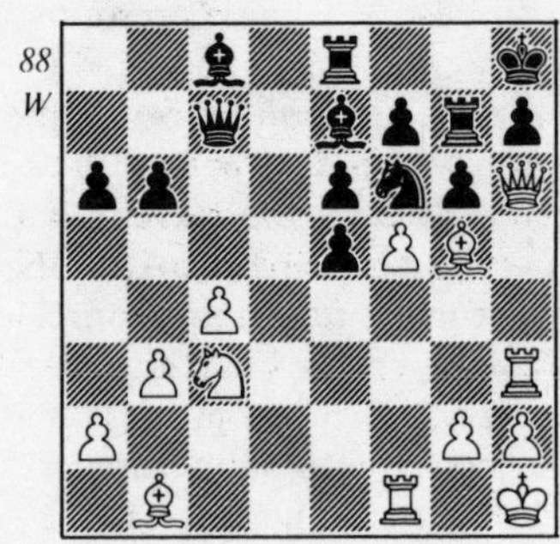

If 27 . . . ♘h5 28 f6, followed by ♕×h7+ and mate.

28 ♗×f6 . . .

There are at least two ways to win. 28 f×g6 ♕d8 29 ♗×f6 ♗×f6 30 ♕×h7+ ♖×h7 31 ♖×h7+ ♔g8 32 g×f7+ ♔f8 33 f×e8/♕+ ♔×e8 34 ♗g6+ ♔f8 35 ♖h8+ is a perfectly good alternative.

28 . . . ♗×f6

29 ♘e4 ♕d8

Even the sacrifice 29 . . . e×f5 is useless because 30 ♘×f6 would force mate at h7. White now concludes with a devastating combination.

30 f×g6 ♗e7

31 ♕×h7+! . . .

Not 31 g×f7? ♖×f7!

31 . . . ♖×h7

32 ♖×h7+ ♔g8 33 g×f7+ ♔×h7

34 f×e8/♕ 1 – 0

Game 20

King's Indian Defence
Gjøvik 1983

L. Ftačnik v. J. Nunn

1	♘f3	g6
2	d4	♗g7
3	c4	♘f6
4	♘c3	0–0
5	e4	d6
6	♗e2	♘bd7

The alternative is 6 . . . e5 7 0–0 ♘c6 8 d5 ♘e7 etc. In playing 6 . . . ♘bd7 Black exerts less pressure on d4 and does not provoke White into d5. He therefore needs to be ready to tackle either type of position – the blocked one arising if White plays d5 anyway, or the more fluid one occurring in this game.

7	0–0	e5
8	♕c2	. . .

The same rather unusual system which Korchnoi adopted in Game 12. Nunn now improves on his earlier play.

8	. . .	c6

With the rook coming to d1 Black is obviously going to need a comfortable developing square for his queen, and e7 is quite acceptable provided White cannot play ♘d5, especially in conjunction with the pin ♗g5.

9	♖d1	e×d4
10	♘×d4	♕e7
11	♗g5	♘c5
12	f3	♖e8 *(89)*

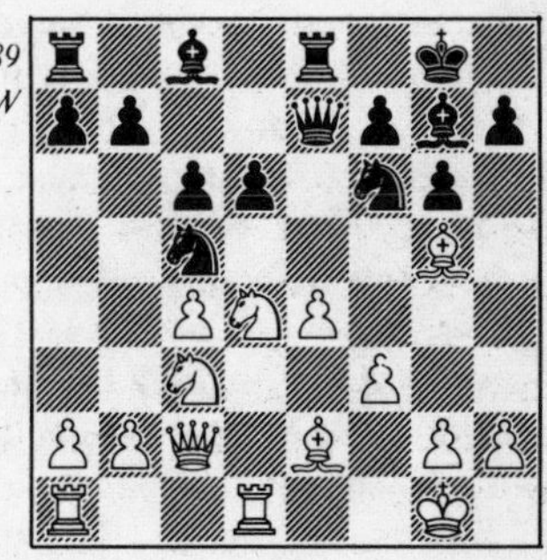

Up to here Nunn is repeating a game against F. Olafsson (England–Iceland 1982) in which the Icelander continued 13 ♕d2?, intending to attack the d-pawn and at the same time bind the K-side by preventing . . . h6. Unfortunately the move has a tactical drawback which stamps it as a blunder by Grandmaster standards. The unavoidable consequence was: 13 . . . ♘f×e4! 14 ♘×e4 (14 f×e4 ♗×d4+ is even worse) ♘×e4 15 f×e4 ♗×d4+ 16 ♔h1 (16 ♕×d4 ♕×g5 17 ♕×d6 ♕e3+) ♗f6 17 ♗×f6 ♕×f6 18 ♕×d6 ♕×d6 19 ♖×d6 ♔g7! (he would not dream of playing 19 . . . ♖×e4 20 ♖d8+ ♔g7 21 ♗f3, when White has tremendous scope) 20 ♗f3 ♗e6, with a very good ending for Black: bad white bishop, isolated e-pawn, weaknesses on the black squares, especially d4 and e5. In the event his king occupied e5, White was obliged to make a further concession by b3 and the Q-side was eventually broken up by the advance . . . a5 – a4. There is a nice blend here of complicated tactical play with a willingness to accept a simplified endgame position; a dramatic change of thinking which is typical of the strongest players.

12 . . . ♖e8 has a tactical point too, which is dealt with in a moment. One thing should be mentioned here though: in this type of position Black often secures his knight at c5 by playing . . . a5. Nunn is deliberately avoiding this, partly because he does not like the weakness at b6 which (experience has shown) White may exploit later on, and partly because he wishes to provoke b4 and use the pawn as a target for his **subsequent** . . . a5.

It turns out that Ftačnik has been in almost this position before (his previous opponent played 12 . . . ♕c7) and he now adopts the same plan.

13 b4 . . .

Before going further we need to remind ourselves that in choosing the King's Indian Black is playing with fire to some extent. It is a dangerous opening in which he accepts theoretical weaknesses (the d-pawn here) and a spatial disadvantage in the centre and relies heavily on counter-attack. Examples abound of games where the counterplay has failed and he is left with a miserable defensive position. Nunn has no intention of letting that happen; so we observe, both in the game continuation and the variations, how he insists on considering only counter-attacking moves.

For example, 13 ♔h1 would prepare the ♕d2 idea by nullifying the . . . ♘f×e4 combination. Black's intention then was: 13 . . . ♕f8 (a convenient square – it unpins the knight and supports . . . h6 and . . . f5) 14 ♕d2 ♘fd7 and now: (1) 15 b4 ♘e6 16 ♘×e6 ♖×e6 17 ♖ac1 a5, when Black gains either the a-file (after a3) or the c5 square for his knight (after b5); (2) 15 ♘c2 f5! and if 16 ♕×d6 Black equalises by 16 . . . f×e4 17 f×e4 ♘×e4 18 ♘×e4 ♖×e4 etc. (preferably leaving White to exchange at f8, when the knight will recapture). If White plays 16 e×f5 ♕×f5, the attacks on c2 and g5 will cut out his threat against d6 for a long time. Equally satisfactory for Black would be 15 ♘b3 ♘×b3 16 a×b3 ♘c5 17 ♖a3 f5.

This dynamic theme should be constantly borne in mind for the next few moves.

13 . . . ♘e6
14 ♘×e6 ♗×e6

If now 15 c5 d×c5 16 e5, Black has 16 . . . ♗f5! and it is White who loses material after 17 e×f6 ♗×c2 18 f×e7 ♗×c3. This is the tactical point referred to above which justifies 12 . . . ♖e8.

15 ♕d2 ♕c7 *(90)*

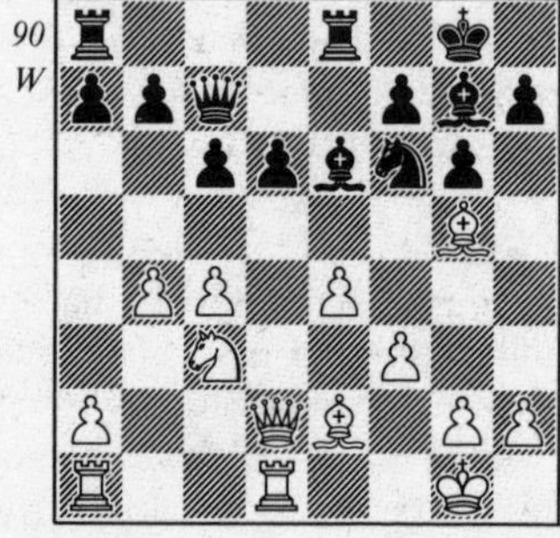

90
W

In view of a strong 16th move for White, which both players overlooked, this cannot be considered quite satisfactory. Among the alternatives, Nunn rejected 15 . . . ♖ad8 because his knight would be awkward to unpin. In fact it is not easy for White to exploit this (16 ♕f4

♘h5! for example), but all the same 16 ♕e3! makes life difficult for Black, virtually forcing a weakness in his Q-side pawn structure. With the white queen off the d-file, c5 and e5 would also become dangerous possibilities. Another idea is 15 . . . a5, but 16 b5! would be good because the b-file would open before Black's knight could get to c5: 16 . . . ♕f8 17 b×c6 b×c6 18 ♖ab1 ♘d7 19 ♘d5! c×d5 20 c×d5, for instance. Something similar happens in the game, but in circumstances much more favourable to Black; in this position White would quickly put the open file to good use. Notice too that in all these variations Black dare not touch his c-pawn. Time and again he has confidently sacrificed the d-pawn itself, but to yield White the d5 square would be an enormous concession.

The best move is probably 15 . . . ♕f8 again. Then we have: (a) 16 ♕×d6 ♕×d6 17 ♖×d6 ♘×e4 18 ♘×e4 ♗×a1 19 ♗f6 ♗×f6 20 ♘×f6+ with a draw; (b) 16 ♗f4 d5! and Black captures at e2 (or a1 first) after a mass of exchanges on d5; (c) 16 ♖ac1 ♘d7 17 ♕×d6 ♕×d6 18 ♖×d6 ♗f8 and if the rook retreats Black stands better after 19 . . . ♗×b4. White would have to try the sacrifice 19 c5 here, but he could hardly claim more than a shaky equality from it.

16 ♖ab1? . . .

Ftačnik loses this game because on three occasions (moves 16, 21 and 23) his play is not quite sharp enough. More specifically, he loses time on two of these moves, and the point is worth stressing because it highlights one of the big differences between Grandmasters and amateurs. Ftačnik's errors, of course, are subtle ones and would almost go undetected compared with the outrageous disregard for tempo which can be observed in club games. He plays 16 ♖ab1 not because he doesn't care about tempi, but because he thought (through misanalysing somehow) that he had to cover his b-pawn. But first of all we can analyse the right move: 16 ♖ac1! If 16 . . . ♕b6+ 17 ♔h1 ♕×b4? White makes use of a familiar combinative theme: 18 ♗×f6 ♗×f6 19 ♘d5! ♕b2 20 ♖c2 ♕d4 (20 . . . ♕e5 21 f4 ♕d4 is even worse, since White has the option of 22 e5, as well as 22 ♕c1) 21 ♕c1 ♕a1 22 ♕f4 and Black is obliged to surrender his queen in very unfavourable circumstances: 22 . . . c×d5 23 ♖×a1 ♗×a1 24 c×d5. If 16 . . . ♘d7 (heading for e5, his main counter-attacking motif at this point), there comes the unwelcome 17 ♘d5! and then: (a) 17 . . . c×d5 18 c×d5 ♕b6+ 19 ♗e3 ♗h6 (the only try – 19 . . . ♕d8 20 d×e6 is hopelessly inadequate) 20 ♗×b6 ♗×d2 21 ♖×d2 ♘×b6 (21 . . . ♗×d5 22 ♗f2 is also very good for White) 22 d×e6 ♖×e6 and Black faces a very unpleasant endgame; (b) 17 . . . ♕b8 18 ♘f4 and the knight stands ready to eliminate one of the black bishops. Black would then have the kind of unacceptably passive position to which I referred earlier; (c) 17 . . . ♗×d5 18 c×d5 c5 19 ♗b5! and 19 . . . b6 is forced, when the weakness at c6 is a serious matter; nor can Black conveniently unpin his knight. Finally, 16 . . . a5 17 b5 would favour White for the reasons given earlier. Nunn gives 16 . . . ♕b6+ 17 ♔h1 d5 as the best chance: it has at least the merit of muddying the water. After 18 c×d5 c×d5 19 e×d5 ♘×d5 Black survives, while 18 c×d5 c×d5 19 ♗×f6 ♗×f6 20 ♘×d5 ♗×d5 gives him prospects of a draw by reason of the opposite bishops and White's weak b-pawn.

Notice the difference as we return to the game: in a position where both sides have tactical chances **one tempo can make all the difference**. Black now seizes the initiative.

16 . . . ♘d7

Suddenly White has problems meeting the threat of 17 . . . ♘e5. Black would be quite content with 17 ♗e3 ♘e5 18 c5 d×c5 19 ♗×c5 ♖ad8, or with 17 f4 ♘b6 18 c5 d×c5 19 b×c5 ♘c4 etc.; therefore White has little choice but to play his ♘d5 trick, which is not very effective here.

17 ♘d5 c×d5

18 c×d5 ♗g4!

With his queen safe, Black, of course, does not permit the capture at e6.

19 h3 . . .

The best way to net the bishop. 19 f×g4 ♖×e4 would leave him with weak pawns at g4 and b4; what is worse, the black pieces would come surging into the game by . . . ♕b6+, . . . ♘e5 and . . . ♖ae8.

19 . . . ♗×f3

19 . . . ♗h5 would not be worth the trouble: 20 g4 and after the capture at h5 Black would have to split up his own formation or remain a pawn down.

20 g×f3 . . .

It is important to avoid the awful 'dead' position which would arise after 20 ♗×f3. The further course of the game clarifies this point because White soon gets saddled with that type of structure anyway. For the moment the pawn recapture keeps his game alive: he has long-term prospects of organising the push f4 and e5, supported by his bishops. That is why Black still has to play vigorously: he possesses only a slight plus and he must try to exploit White's temporary disorganisation and exposed king in order to break up the pawn centre.

20 . . . ♘e5 *(91)*

91
W

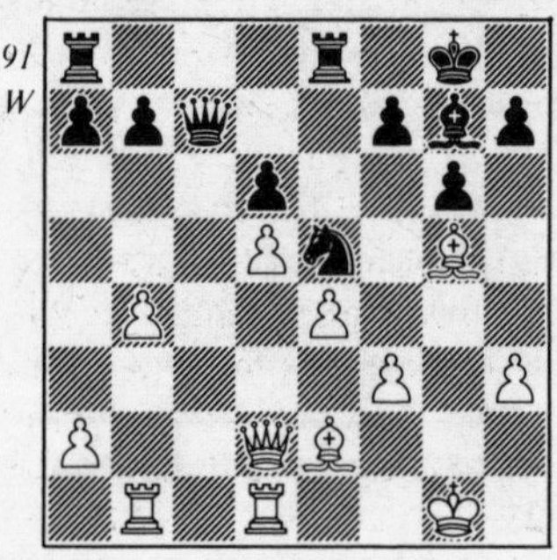

21 ♔g2(?) . . .

This is the second occasion when White's analysis fails to penetrate the position. He would like to take over the c-file with tempo gain (21 ♖bc1 and if 21 . . . ♕b6+ 22 ♗e3 ♕d8 etc.), but is afraid that Black will occupy a more desirable square (21 . . . ♕d7) and sacrifice a piece after 22 f4 by 22 . . . ♕×h3 23 f×e5 ♕g3+ and 24 . . . ♖×e5. That would indeed be a ferocious attack, but he overlooks 23 ♖c3! when Black would have insufficient compensation for the lost knight. The problem may well be psychological: the mind flinches from putting a rook opposite the black bishop, yet Black has no way of exploiting that.

21 . . . f5

Now Black can use f7 for his knight and still d7 for his queen.

22 ♖bc1 ♕d7

23 ♗e3? . . .

The third and decisive mistake,

which arose, it seems, because White already believed his position to be indefensible. But he lost heart too soon: after 23 f4 ♘f7 24 e×f5, neither 24 . . . ♕×f5 25 ♗g4 ♕e4+ 26 ♗f3 nor 24 . . . ♘×g5 25 f×g5 ♕×f5 26 ♗g4 leaves Black with more than a slight advantage because he lacks a good square (immune from attack) for his queen. A surprising feature, perhaps, on an open board, but there it is. Black may also play 24 . . . g×f5, but the splitting of his pawns would certainly not improve his chances.

More surprising is that Ftačnik's chosen move brings about the kind of dead position which a Grandmaster would normally avoid like the plague.

23	**. . .**	**f×e4**
24	**f×e4**	**. . .**

Suddenly the whole character of the game has changed and Black's advantage is permanent (backward e-pawn, command of e5, useless white K-bishop, more exposed white king). Therefore **he can take his time** and think more in general terms, using tactical control as necessary to frustrate any counterplay.

24	**. . .**	**♕e7** *(92)*

92
W

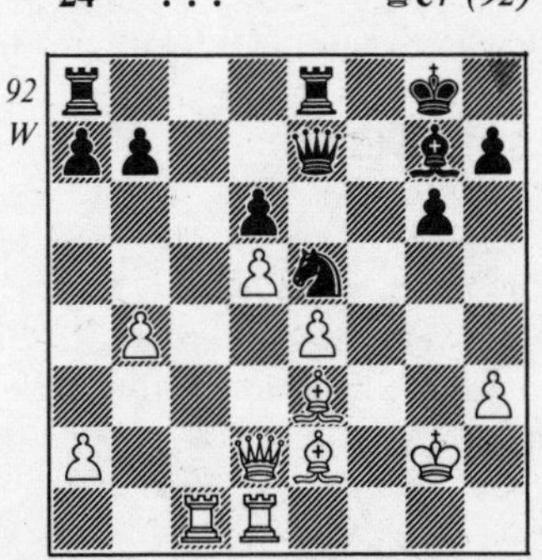

Threatens 25 . . . ♕h4, winning the e-pawn, and also prepares the exchange of dark-square bishops – standard technique for this type of position because White will remain with only his bad bishop to oppose the knight and Black's heavy pieces can overrun the undefended dark squares at their leisure.

25	**♗g5**	**♗f6**
26	**♗f4**	

Avoids the exchange, but not for long. Black has to keep his eye on the danger of ♗g4–e6+, but White never manages this: after the next move his e-pawn will require protection from the bishop.

26	**. . .**	**♘f7!**
27	**♗d3**	**♗g5**
28	**♖e1**	**♗×f4**
29	**♕×f4**	**♘e5**
30	**♗e2**	**♖ac8**

Tactically everything is well in hand: 31 ♗g4 is met by 31 . . . ♖×c1 32 ♖×c1 ♘d3 33 ♗e6+ ♕×e6; or if 32 ♕×c1 ♘×g4 33 h×g4 ♕h4 34 ♕d1 (34 g5 ♕g4+ and 35 . . . ♖e5) ♖f8 35 ♕e2 ♖f4 etc. Strategically a pure minor piece ending would be the easiest to win: the black king would occupy e5 with the knight at f6; White would defend the pawn with king and bishop and Black would then win with a passed pawn on the K-side. Any pawn ending would also be hopeless for White, of course. Black has therefore decided to exchange as much as possible in order to simplify his task.

31	**♖×c8**	**♖×c8**
32	**♖c1**	**♖×c1**
33	**♕×c1**	**♔g7** *(93)*

Black's advantage may be obvious to you, but the extent of it or the precise technique needed to force the win may be less clear. Here then are some likely variations; essentially the queen is going to walk in through the black squares, knowing that her rival dare not offer an exchange:

93
W

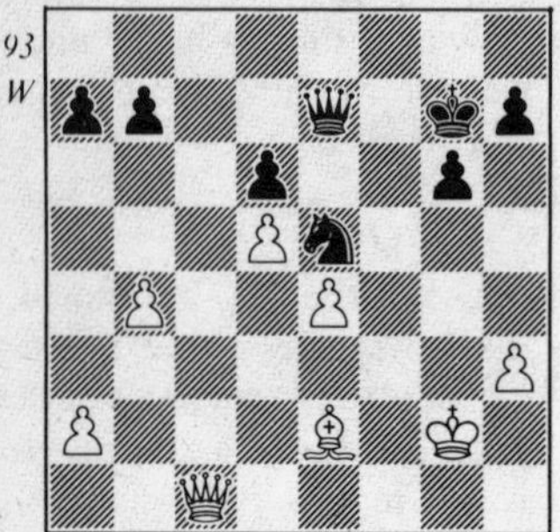

(1) 34 ♕f4 ♕f6 35 ♕g3 g5, then 36 . . . ♕f4, exchanging queens or picking up the e-pawn; (2) 34 ♕c3 ♕g5+ 35 ♔f1 (35 ♔h1 ♕f4 is worse) ♕f4+ 36 ♔e1 ♕×e4 37 ♕c7+ ♘f7 38 ♕×b7 ♕b1+39 ♔f2 ♕×a2; then the black queen recentralises, perhaps to d4 via a1, and the win is fairly straightforward because White's counterplay is at an end; (3) 34 ♕c2 ♕g5+ and then: (a) 35 ♔h1 ♕g3; (b) 35 ♔h2 ♕e3 36 ♔g2 (36 ♗d1 ♘d3 etc.) ♔h6 and the king advances to h4 or f4; (c) 35 ♔f2 ♕f4+ 36 ♔e1 ♕g3+ and 37 . . . ♕×h3, dropping back to d7 if necessary. Notice how the white queen is hamstrung in many lines by having to defend the bishop.

The importance of this tactical play, superimposed on general considerations, cannot be overstressed. It is not particularly difficult, but in each variation slightly different points have to be kept under control; and if you do not develop at least some skill in this department, no amount of theorising about bad bishops or weak squares will help you much.

Returning to the game, Ftačnik tried:

34	**♕e3**	**♕h4**
35	**a4**	**. . .**

If 35 ♕×a7 ♕×e4+ and 36 . . . ♕×b4. White can also prevent . . . ♕e1 by 35 ♗f1, but Black's invasion is irresistible: 35 . . . ♔f6 (threatening . . . ♕g5+) and if 36 ♔h1 g5 followed by . . . ♕f4, or if 36 ♕e2 ♕f4 again. Then everybody joins in – . . . h5–h4 followed by . . . g5–g4 and Black will either win by direct attack or force the queens off.

35	**. . .**	**♕e1**
36	**b5**	**♔g8!**

A ruthless move, denying White even the slightest chance. Black would like to block the Q-side by 36 . . . b6, but 37 a5 ♕×a5 (37 . . . b×a5 38 ♕×a7 is check) 38 ♕g5 leaves his queen out in the cold. After the further 38 . . . ♘f7 39 ♕e7 White is threatening to get a passed pawn by 40 e5. This may amount to nothing, but forestalling counterplay is a most important aspect of endgame technique.

37	**♔h2**	**b6!**

Now 38 a5 can be met by . . . b×a5.

38	**♔g2**	**h6**

White is paralysed; so the transfer of the knight to f4 is the simplest way to finish off.

39	**♔h2**	**g5**
40	**♔g2**	**♘g6**
41	**e5**	**♘f4+**
42	**♔f3**	**♕×e2+**

Alternatively Black can go for a mating attack by 42 . . . ♕h1+ 43 ♔f2 ♘×h3+ 44 ♔g3 ♘f4.

43	**♕×e2**	**♘×e2**
44	**e×d6**	**♘d4+**
	0 – 1	

If 45 ♔e4 ♘b3 46 ♔e5 ♔f7 etc.

Game 21

French Defence
Lloyds Bank 1983

J. Nunn v. J. Levitt

1	**e4**	**e6**
2	**d4**	**d5**
3	**♘d2**	**c5**
4	**♘gf3**	. . .

The same slightly unusual move-order as Nunn adopted against Vaganian (Game 9). We can understand the theory of this opening more easily if we begin with the commoner move 4 e×d5. In that event Black has a choice of two quite different systems: (a) 4 . . . e×d5 5 ♘gf3 ♘c6 (or 5 . . . a6, leading into Nunn–Vaganian) 6 ♗b5, the basic ideas of which are explained in Game 9. Black gets an isolated pawn, but free play for his pieces, and in practice the chances are equal. Karpov actually made seven unsuccessful attempts to win from this position in his 1974 match with Korchnoi! (b) 4 . . . ♕×d5 5 ♘gf3 (this is not a gambit; there is no way in which Black can hold the pawn for more than a couple of moves) c×d4 6 ♗c4 ♕d6 (or 6 . . . ♕d8, which is a bit passive but just about playable; for example 7 0–0 ♘c6 8 ♘b3 ♘f6 9 ♕e2 ♗e7 10 ♖d1 a6, with some advantage to White – Mestel–Petrosian, Las Palmas 1982) 7 0–0 ♘f6 8 ♘b3 ♘c6 9 ♘b×d4 ♘×d4 10 ♘×d4, with attacking chances for White based on his lead in development, but an extra central pawn for Black, which may favour him in the long run.

Now Levitt wishes to play the . . . ♕×d5 system, but is led astray by White's move-order and soon makes a serious error. He could have transposed at this point by 4 . . . c×d4 5 e×d5 ♕×d5 6 ♗c4 etc. Instead, with his following knight move, he commits himself to the pawn recapture without realising it.

4	. . .	**♘c6**
5	**e×d5**	**♕×d5?**

5 . . . e×d5 is quite satisfactory, but the text move is the mistake which we can say without exaggeration costs Black the game (incidentally, 5 . . . ♘×d4 6 ♘×d4 c×d4 7 ♗b5+ ♗d7 8 ♕e2 would also be thoroughly unpleasant). That may seem an astonishing claim to make at move five, but he is mixing his systems in a way which is bound to lead to trouble. The reasons become clear as the game progresses.

6	**♗c4**	. . .

Black's first misfortune is that he has to permit his opponent to exchange pawns at c5 instead of doing so himself at d4. And that is a burden because the recapture, whether with queen or bishop, will soon be followed by the important time-gaining move ♘e4. For example, if now 6 . . . ♕d6 there comes 7 ♘e4 ♕d8 8 d×c5 ♕×d1+ 9 ♔×d1 f5 (otherwise White keeps the pawn more comfortably – 9 . . . ♘f6 10 ♘×f6+ g×f6 11 ♗e3, for instance) 10 ♘d6+ ♗×d6 11 e×d6 ♘f6

12 ♗f4 (12 ♖e1 ♘e4 is less clear), and after that one possible continuation is 12 . . . ♘g4 13 ♖f1 ♔d7 (13 . . . e5 14 ♘xe5 ♘cxe5 15 ♗xe5 ♘xe5 16 ♖e1 is very good for White) 14 ♗b5 (better than 14 h3 e5) ♖e8 15 ♘e5+ ♘xe5 16 ♗xe5 a6 17 ♗xc6+ and the extra pawn should certainly suffice to win.

6 . . . ♕d6 looks rather obliging, but after each of the other reasonable queen moves Black runs into another very unfavourable type of position, thus: 6 . . . ♕h5 7 dxc5 ♕xc5 (7 . . . ♗xc5 8 ♘e4 is even worse – White not only threatens 9 ♘d6+, but after 8 . . . ♘ge7 has the additional option of 9 h3, preparing 10 g4 or ♘g3) 8 ♕e2, with further gain of time (♘e4) to follow; or 6 . . . ♕f5 7 dxc5 ♗xc5 8 ♗d3, with ♘e4 coming. Black's third alternative brings us back to the game.

6	**. . .**	**♕d8**
7	**dxc5**	**♗xc5**
8	**0–0**	**♘f6**
9	**♕e2** *(94)*	**. . .**

94
B

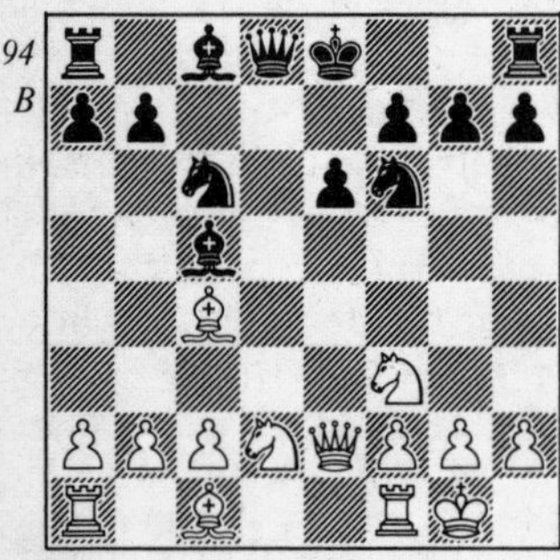

Although the black queen is not being harassed here, we have essentially the same type of position as after 6 . . . ♕h5 or . . . ♕f5. It may look tolerable for Black, but if we suppose that he now castles the difference between this game and Mestel–Petrosian becomes apparent, as follows: 9 . . . 0–0 10 ♖d1 ♕c7 11 ♘e4 ♗e7 12 ♗g5 ♘xe4 13 ♕xe4 ♗d7 14 ♗f4 ♕c8 15 ♘g5, and already White has a winning attack – 15 . . . g6 16 h4, or 15 . . . ♗xg5 16 ♗xg5, followed by ♖d3–g3 (or to h3) and ♖ad1. Black's game is desperately passive and his castled position is too exposed to survive. In this variation 13 . . . ♗xg5 14 ♘xg5 would lead to much the same thing, as would 11 . . . ♘xe4 12 ♕xe4, with 13 ♗f4 or ♘g5 to follow.

In all these lines, which spring directly from the error at move five, **the exchange of the f6 knight** is the significant point, because that piece is vital to the defence of the castled position. In Mestel–Petrosian the white knight was about to be exchanged for the c6 knight, which was much less important. Even there Black's game was passive; here the disadvantage reaches decisive proportions.

In view of this Black decides at least to delay . . . 0–0, and to keep open the option of castling Q-side. One more possibility is 9 . . . ♘d4, to exchange off an attacking piece, but then he falls badly behind in development; for example 9 . . . ♘d4 10 ♘xd4 ♗xd4 (if 10 . . . ♕xd4 11 ♘b3 ♕d6 12 ♖d1 ♕c7 13 ♘xc5 ♕xc5 14 ♗e3 etc., or alternatively 13 ♗b5+ ♗d7 14 ♗g5) 11 ♘f3 ♗b6 (or 11 . . . ♗c5, but then in many positions Black loses the chance of taking on b5 after White's bishop check and . . . ♗d7) 12 ♗b5+ ♗d7 13 ♖d1, and if 13 . . . ♕c7 14 ♖xd7 ♘xd7 15 ♘e5 ♖d8 16 ♗g5 etc.

9	**. . .**	**♕c7**
10	**♘e4**	**♗e7**

If 10 . . . ♘×e4 11 ♕×e4 and White gains more time by a subsequent ♗f4.

11 ♖e1! . . .

11 ♖d1 would be obvious, but of little value now that the queen has vacated d8, and would probably lead only to an eventual exchange. The text move, on the other hand, is a strong and subtle positional idea, the purpose of which is to gain control of e5 in conjunction with b3 and ♗b2. And why should control specifically of e5 be useful? Because Black's problem is his passive position rather than any disastrous structural weakness. Therefore White's object is to stop him completing his development comfortably. If Black manages to do that, and above all **if he can activate his Q-bishop satisfactorily**, he may ultimately equalise. Once this point is appreciated one can see that the plan of ♖e1, b3 and ♗b2 answers White's need perfectly. The bishop can only emerge after . . . e5 or by . . . ♗d7 and . . . ♗c6; and White intends to make . . . e5 unplayable and to counter . . . ♗d7 by ♘e5 as soon as the black knight moves from c6 (not necessarily intending to take the bishop, but generally to dominate the centre with his knight and to give Black another headache defending f7, if he decides to castle Q-side).

The next few moves demonstrate the power of this strategy. Whatever Black does, whichever side he castles, he cannot avoid a disadvantage of some kind. And therein lies the instructional value of this game: the way Nunn keeps control. Although it appears a very one-sided contest, Black hardly puts a foot wrong after his opening error; yet he still loses.

If we reduce all this to some concrete analysis, we can appreciate the problems Black faces: (i) 11 . . . b6 (trying to solve the problem of the Q-bishop) 12 ♗g5 ♗b7 13 ♖ad1 0–0 (13 . . . ♘×e4 14 ♕×e4 ♘a5 15 ♗b5+ ♗c6 16 ♗×e7 ♔×e7 17 ♕b4+ ♔e8 18 ♘e5 wins) 14 ♘×f6+ ♗×f6 15 ♗×f6 g×f6 16 ♕d2! (threat ♕h6) ♔g7 17 ♕d7 with a favourable ending for White; (ii) 11 . . . 0–0. Here we can follow the game continuation for another move before analysing Black's attempt to castle kingside, since the outcome is similar.

11 . . . ♗d7

12 b3 0–0–0

12 . . . 0–0 leads to 13 ♗b2 ♘×e4 14 ♕×e4, and then, for example, 14 . . . ♖ad8 15 ♕g4 e5 (or 15 . . . g6 16 ♘g5, followed by ♘e4 or ♕h4) 16 ♕h5, and White's control of e5 is paying dividends: 16 . . . g6 17 ♕h6 ♗f6, and he has the pleasant choice between 18 ♘g5 and 18 ♗a3. Without the necessary minor piece support Black cannot hope to avoid a fatal weakening of his pawn cover.

13 ♗b2 . . .

Notice how White's iron grip on the centre leaves his opponent with very few constructive moves. There is no way to improve on the following two exchanges, which damage Black's K-side pawn structure.

13 . . . ♘×e4

14 ♕×e4 ♗f6

15 ♗×f6 g×f6 *(95)*

Suddenly everything has changed. Black has gained some relief from his restricted position by exchanging, and he temporarily controls e5 himself; but far from representing an improvement in his fortunes the new situation burdens him with a whole host of fresh problems. His chief worry is that he has to defend both sides of the board - not only his battered K-side, but also his none too secure castled position, against which White is likely to advance his pawn majority. Nunn's plan, therefore, is based on the well-known theme of making threats against both flanks: first he attacks on the K-side, then, when he has tied up Black's forces, his Q-side pawns will go forward.

95
W

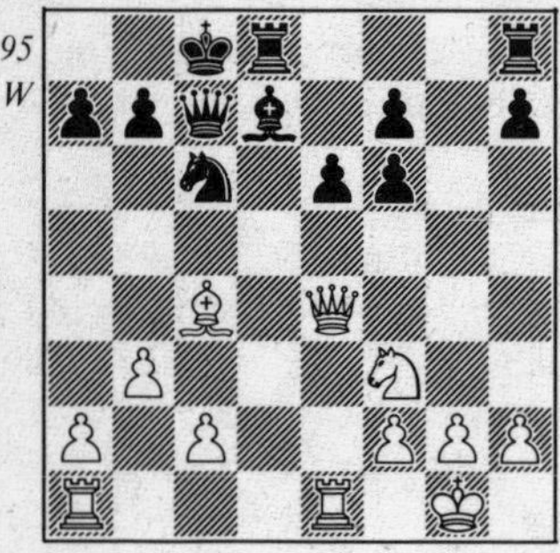

Three more general points: (1) White will avoid the exchange of queens, partly because he wishes to attack the castled position, partly because the queen's penetrating power makes her an ideal weapon for exploiting the kind of pawn weaknesses which Black possesses here (♕h4–h6). A rook might do this job (♖e4–h4), but more clumsily; (2) Black is not without chances of counterplay (by . . . ♖g8 and . . . ♗c6), and White should do all he can to hinder this; (3) White is quite happy to oppose rooks on the d-file (in fact it is an integral part of his plan); if Black permits exchanges he will lose his h-pawn, if not he will have to concede the file.

16 ♕h4 f5

Another unavoidable concession; if Black now moves his knight, to play . . . ♗c6, he will have to reckon with the reply ♘e5. In this way White attacks the pawns and simultaneously anticipates counterplay.

17 ♖ad1 ♖df8

If we analyse Black's alternatives we shall see the kind of tactical problems he is up against, and understand why he resorts to this peculiar regrouping of his forces. If he tries 17 . . . ♖hg8 White simply takes the h-pawn and escapes easily with his queen. He may even win more material; for example 18 ♕×h7 ♖h8 19 ♕×f7 ♖df8 20 ♕g7, and if 20 . . . ♖ (either) g8 21 ♕×d7+, emerging with three extra pawns. If 17 . . . ♖dg8 18 ♕f6 again makes a threat and forestalls counterplay (by . . . ♖g6 and doubling) at the same time; if then 18 . . . ♕d8 19 ♕×f7, or if 18 . . . ♗e8 White takes over the deserted d-file: 19 ♖e2 ♕e7 20 ♕c3 ♕b4 (or 20 . . . ♔b8 21 ♖ed2 f6 22 ♖d6) 21 ♕b2 ♘e7 22 ♘e5 with an extremely strong position. The passive move 18 . . . ♖f8 leads to a similar result. The only other plausible move, 17 . . . ♗e8, gives us 18 ♕f6 ♖g8 (18 . . . ♖f8 19 ♗×e6+) 19 ♕h6, picking up the h-pawn (19 . . . ♖h8 20 ♕g7), while any purely waiting move (say 17 . . . ♔b8) is met by 18 ♕f6, and Black is at least as badly off as in other variations.

The purpose of 17 . . . ♖df8 is to bring the queen to the rescue via d8 and e7, and to cover f7 in order to meet ♕f6 by . . . ♖hg8. White once again reacts by seizing the d-file.

18 ♖d2 ♕d8

18 . . . ♗e8 might have been a shade better, saving time by allowing the queen access to e7 in one move, but this is a fine point which would not have altered the essential nature

of the position. Notice how White's control of the centre, especially the black squares, now enables him to switch his pieces smoothly across to the Q-side with a speed which the defender cannot hope to match. As Black transfers his queen to e7 and commits his rooks to counterplay on the g-file, he must inevitably neglect his castled position by depriving it of piece protection. There is nothing accidental about the attack which now develops; in the nature of things Black must necessarily yield on one flank or the other.

19 ♕h6 . . .

The queen will now drop back to e3 if and when Black eventually plays . . . ♖g6.

19 . . . ♕e7
20 c3! *(96)* **. . .**

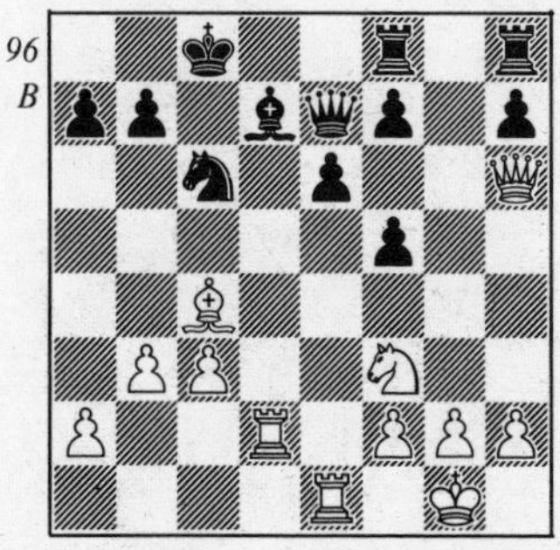

96
B

The signal for the final attack, one result of which will be to drive the black knight to a very bad square and allow its opposite number into e5; also a7 will be left undefended in the event of ♕e3. There is no decent defence against this; all Black can do is try for counterplay by 20 . . . ♖fg8 or make an attempt to exchange at least one pair of rooks on the d-file. And the second idea would fail after 20 . . . ♖d8 21 ♖ed1 ♗e8 22 ♖×d8+ ♘×d8 23 ♕g7 ♕f8 24 ♕f6 ♗c6 (24 . . . ♘c6 25 ♘e5) 25 ♘e5 ♖g8 26 g3 (threatens ♘×f7 for the second time) ♔b8 27 b4 (or 27 ♖d7), followed by b5, with an overwhelming attack.

20 . . . ♖fg8
21 ♖ed1 ♗e8
22 b4 ♖g4
23 ♗f1 . . .

Provides a solid defence for g2 and avoids the necessity of moving a K-side pawn, which might allow a little counterplay.

23 . . . f6

Black wishes to cut out ♘e5, but this allows a forced win because e6 is weakened and a white rook penetrates at once. In any event he is quite lost. The alternative is 23 . . . ♖hg8 (23 . . . a6 24 a4) 24 b5 ♘b8 25 ♘e5 ♖4g7 (25 . . . ♖e4 26 ♕×h7) 26 ♕f4, and ♕c4+ is a winning threat.

24 b5 ♘b8

24 . . . ♘a5 is at least as bad, and if 24 . . . ♘e5 25 ♘×e5 f×e5 26 ♕e3.

25 ♖d8+ ♔c7
26 ♕e3 . . .

Threatening 27 ♕×a7 and refuting 26 . . . ♕×d8 by 27 ♕c5+. Apart from 26 . . . b6, the only other conceivable defence is 26 . . . ♖a4 (26 . . . ♘d7 27 ♖1×d7+), which loses at once to 27 ♘d4 e5 28 ♘×f5 ♕×d8 29 ♕c5+ etc.

26 . . . b6
27 ♘d4! *(97)* **. . .**

This represents the main line of White's attractive combination. The rook, of course, is still invulnerable, and e6 must be defended. If 27 . . . e5, there is 28 ♘×f5 ♕×d8 29 ♖×d8 ♔×d8 30 ♕f3 ♖f4 (30 . . . ♖a4 loses to 31 ♕d1+, while 30 . . . ♖g6 31 ♕b7 and 30 . . . ♖g5 31 ♕b7 are similar to the main variation) 31 ♕b7 ♘d7 (31 . . . ♖×f5 32 ♕g7) 32 ♘e3, and the

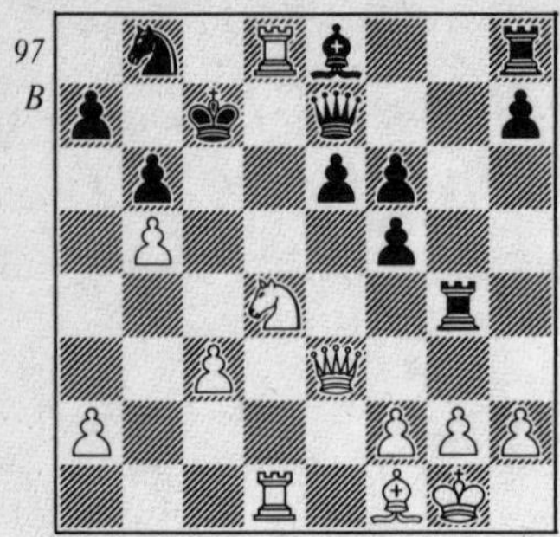

threat of ♘d5 with a mating attack cannot be averted (32 . . . ♗f7 33 ♕a8+). Which leaves only . . .

27 . . . ♖e4

28 ♕g3+ f4

Or 28 . . . e5 29 ♘×f5 ♕×d8 30 ♖×d8 ♔×d8 31 ♕d3+.

29 ♕d3 . . .

Threatening 30 ♕c4+ as well as the rook, and if 29 . . . ♕×d8 30 ♘×e6+ ♖×e6 31 ♕×d8+ ♔b7 32 ♕d5+ wins.

29 . . . f5

29 . . . ♖e5 is answered in the same way: 30 ♕c4+ and 31 ♘×e6+.

30 ♕c4+ 1 – 0

Game 22

Caro-Kann Defence
London (Phillips & Drew) 1984

J. Nunn v. Y. Seirawan

1	**e4**	**c6**
2	**d4**	**d5**
3	**e×d5**	**c×d5**
4	**c4**	**♘f6**
5	**♘c3**	**g6**

Black would like to develop his Q-bishop outside the pawn chain instead of shutting it in by . . . e6 – one of the fundamental differences between the French and Caro-Kann Defences – but the problem is that 5 . . . ♗f5 would be met by 6 ♕b3, forcing an unsound pawn sacrifice. Therefore Black must either settle for . . . e6 or make the sacrifice in a more favourable form. That is the purpose of the text move; his K-bishop develops aggressively and in the critical continuation, 6 ♕b3 ♗g7 7 c×d5, he hopes to pick up one of the weak d-pawns later. On this occasion Nunn decides to follow less familiar paths, in theory not quite so strong as 6 ♕b3, but having surprise value.

6 c×d5 ♘×d5 *(98)*

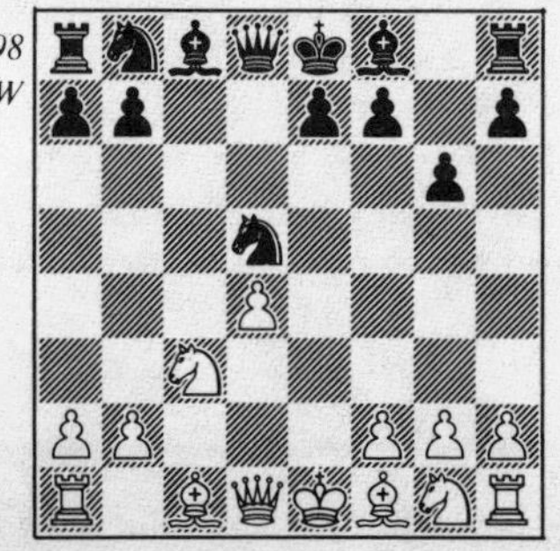
98
W

7 ♘f3 . . .

Again a relatively quiet continuation. 7 ♗b5+ ♘c6 8 ♕a4 ♘×c3 9 b×c3 gives Black another opportunity for a pawn sacrifice, quite in the spirit of this adventurous variation: 9 . . . ♗g7 10 ♗×c6+ b×c6 11 ♕×c6+ ♗d7, and his compensation lies in white-square play and generally more aggressive pieces; for example 12 ♕d5 ♖c8 13 ♘e2 0–0 14 0–0 ♗e6 15 ♕×d8 ♖f×d8 with a good position. If White declines, then 10 ♘f3 0–0 11 0–0 gives approximate equality.

Or White may play 7 ♕b3, relying on the fact that Black will certainly wish to avoid playing . . . e6 as well as . . . g6 (because of the weakness of f6 and the blocking of the bishop). And if 7 . . . ♘×c3? 8 ♗c4! forces 8 . . . e6 anyway; then, after 9 b×c3 ♘c6 10 ♘f3 ♗g7 11 ♗a3, White stands very well. So it has to be 7 . . . ♘b6, allowing 8 d5!, a point which becomes very relevant to the main game. White needs this pawn thrust to cramp his opponent and maintain some initiative; without it Black would have an easy development and would sooner or later set up a blockade on d5 (also the fianchettoed bishop would apply extra pressure against d4). But after 8 d5 the pawn is by no means easy to capture or exchange (8 . . . e6? 9 ♗b5+ ♗d7 10 d×e6, for example, would be horrendous for Black). One likely continuation might be 8 . . . ♗g7 9 ♗e3 0–0 (not 9 . . . ♗×c3+ 10 b×c3 ♘×d5? 11 ♖d1, nor here 10 . . . ♕×d5? 11 ♗×b6) 10 ♖d1 ♘a6 (10 . . . ♘bd7 11 ♘f3 ♘f6 would be a little passive, but now, if White does not take on a6, the knight obtains some play at c5; for example 11 ♗e2 ♕d6 12 ♘f3 ♘c5 13 ♕b5 – or 13 ♕c2 ♗f5 – ♘ca4!, and if 14 ♘×a4 ♗d7 – Schulz–Miles, West Germany 1983) 11 ♗×a6 b×a6 12 ♘ge2 ♗d7 13 0–0 ♖b8 14 ♗f4 ♖c8 15 ♘d4, with an edge for White (Sveshnikov–S. Garcia, Cienfuegos 1979).

7 . . . ♗g7

8 ♗c4 ♘b6

The exchange of knights at c3 is very often made in IQP positions, with the intention of transferring the weakness in White's formation from d4 to the c-file; but that is only appropriate if Black is certain that he will obtain pressure along the file. In this case the exchange would be out of place because any such pressure would not materialise for a long time; meanwhile other, more important factors are arguing against it, chiefly that Black's fianchettoed bishop would be much less effective if the d-pawn were strengthened; also White's bishop might develop aggressively at a3.

9 ♗b3 ♘c6

White's centre pawn is bound to come under such pressure in this variation that he has to think in terms of sacrificing it. That need not concern him, though; he always gets plenty of compensation, as we shall see in a moment. In passing, the idea of an early . . . ♗g4 might be worth a mention: it threatens the d-pawn and guarantees Black an exchange to relieve his restricted position. The trouble is that without the preliminary . . . ♘c6 he is likely to remain cramped. For example 9 . . . 0–0 10 0–0 ♗g4 11 d5 ♘8d7 12 h3 ♗×f3 13 ♕×f3 ♘c5 14 ♖d1 a5 (14 . . . ♘×b3 15 a×b3 would be too passive, a theme which crops up several times in what follows: unless he can win the d-pawn by this exchange, Black normally prefers to occupy c4 with his knight, then drop back to d6; that way the use of the a-file is denied White) 15 ♗c2 ♘c4 16 ♕e2 ♘d6 17 ♗e3 ♖c8 18 ♗d4, and the pawn remains a thorn in Black's side, aiding his opponent's e-file pressure (Jansa–Gaprindashvili, Vrnjačka Banja 1975). Another way is 11 . . . a5 12 a3 ♘a6 13 h3 ♗×f3 14 ♕×f3 ♖c8 15 ♖e1 ♘c5 16 ♗a2 (Nei–Belyavsky, USSR 1975) and again Black has not equalised.

For the next few moves we are concerned with the returns which White may expect if he sacrifices his d-pawn. First of all he could simply cover it by 10 ♗e3, but a continuation such as 10 . . . 0–0 11 0–0 ♘a5 12 d5 ♗g4 13 h3 ♗×f3 14 ♕×f3 ♖c8 (Keres–Tal, Tallin 1971) is unlikely to yield any advantage: White would much rather develop his bishop aggressively at g5. Secondly, the variation 10 d5 ♘a5 11 0–0 ♗×c3 12 b×c3 ♘×b3 13 a×b3 ♕×d5 is obviously inadequate since White can claim no significant lead in development. Nunn therefore sacrifices the pawn in a different way.

10 0–0 0–0

Understandably declining the offer, though it seems that the pawn could safely be taken. Only one move order is acceptable, though: 10 . . . ♗×d4?

11 ♘b5 ♗g7 (11 . . . e5 12 ♗g5 f6 13 ♘×d4 etc. is worse) 12 ♕×d8+ ♔×d8 13 ♖d1+ ♗d7 14 ♗×f7 is clearly unfavourable (14 . . . a6 15 ♗e3, followed by ♘bd4, for instance), while 10 . . . ♘×d4 11 ♘×d4 ♗×d4? 12 ♕f3 leads to either a decisive attack (12 . . . ♗f6 13 ♖d1 ♗d7 14 ♗h6 ♕c8 15 ♘e4) or the win of material by 12 . . . 0–0 13 ♖d1 ♗f5 (13 . . . ♗e6 14 ♗e3, or 13 . . . e5 14 ♗h6) 14 ♗h6 ♖e8 15 g4 ♗e6 16 ♗e3.

So it would have to be 10 . . . ♘×d4 11 ♘×d4 ♕×d4, if anything, and that gives us 12 ♕×d4 ♗×d4 13 ♘b5 ♗e5 14 ♖e1 ♗b8. All forced so far, since 14. . . f6? 15 ♖×e5 f×e5 16 ♘c7+ ♔d8 17 ♘×a8 ♘×a8 18 ♗h6 regains the pawn with a large positional advantage; but although White appears now to have a dangerous lead in development it is hard to achieve anything tangible. Best seems to be 15 ♗g5 (15 ♗h6 ♗d7 doesn't lead anywhere) e6 16 ♖ac1 (16 ♘c3–e4–f6 is ineffective without the queens, once Black has castled) 0–0 17 ♘c7 ♗×c7 18 ♖×c7 ♘d5 19 ♗×d5 e×d5, and White has only the tiniest advantage; for example 20 ♗f6 ♗e6 21 ♖×b7 ♖fb8 22 ♖×b8 ♖×b8 23 ♖c1 ♖c8. Without control of the c-file his better bishop and superior pawn structure are insignificant. Incidentally, the game position after 10 . . . 0–0 can also arise via the Grünfeld Defence and many of the quoted games started off that way.

11 d5 ♘**a5** *(99)*

The knight is quite useful here; he stands ready to occupy c4 or take the bishop, according to circumstances. On the other hand, a variation such as 11 . . . ♘e5 12 ♘×e5 ♗×e5 13 ♗h6 ♗g7 14 ♗×g7 ♔×g7 15 ♕d4+ ♔g8 16 ♖fe1 would show how easily Black can slip into a passive position if he exchanges pieces too casually. 11 . . . ♘b4 would also be unfavourable: 12 a3 ♗×c3 13 b×c3 ♘4×d5 14 ♗h6 ♖e8 (or 14 . . . ♘×c3 15 ♕c2 with advantage) 15 ♕d4 ♘f6 16 ♘e5, and then: (a) 16 . . . e6 (16 . . . ♗e6 17 ♗×e6 f×e6 18 ♕h4–g5 would be bad) 17 ♕f4 with tremendous black-square pressure; or (b) 16 . . . ♕×d4 17 ♗×f7+ ♔h8 18 c×d4 ♖d8 19 ♗b3 ♖×d4 20 ♘f7+ ♔g8 21 ♗e3 ♖h4 (forced) 22 ♖fd1 with a very dangerous initiative.

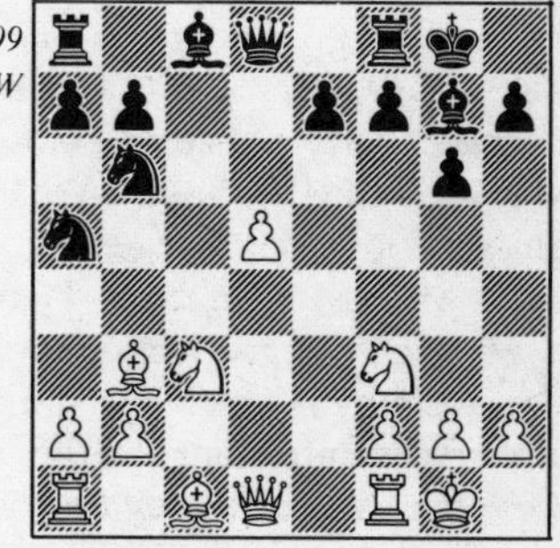

12 ♗g5 . . .

This is a difficult part of the game to comprehend, not because the following analysis is particularly complicated, but because we are having to distinguish between variations which look almost identical, but whose final positions have slight differences in the placing of the pieces.

First of all 12 ♗c2 is unplayable because 12 . . . ♗×c3 wins the d-pawn quite safely. Therefore White's choice lies between the text move and 12 ♖e1. Black for his part has to weigh up the pros and cons of capturing the bishop at b3. Sooner or later it seems he will have to do so, even if he cannot pick up the d-pawn, because he must be rid of one of his knights: to find good squares for both of them is too difficult. But after the capture White's use of the a-file and very convenient control of c4 (keeping out a black rook or the other knight) should at least compensate for the weakness of the pawns themselves; in fact, given the option, White will always take with the pawn rather than the queen.

Now we have an example of 12 ♖e1 in an earlier game (Belyavsky–Peresipkin, USSR 1976), which continued 12 . . . ♗g4 13 h3 ♗×f3 14 ♕×f3 ♕d7 15 ♗g5 ♖fe8 16 ♖ad1 ♘×b3 17 a×b3 ♘c8 18 ♖e3 ♘d6 19 g4! ♖ac8 20 ♖de1, with a slight advantage (this position closely resembles Nunn–Seirawan). What is again a more crucial question is whether Black could grab the d-pawn here. Had Peresipkin done so at move 14, he would have got a distinctly inferior ending after 14 . . . ♘×b3 15 a×b3 ♗×c3 16 b×c3 ♕×d5 17 ♕×d5 ♘×d5 18 c4 ♘f6 19 ♖×e7 etc. But what about taking at once? That would give us 12 . . . ♘×b3 13 a×b3 ♗×c3 14 b×c3 ♕×d5 (14 . . . ♘×d5 15 ♗h6 ♖e8 16 c4 is similar) 15 ♕×d5 ♘×d5 16 c4 ♘f6 17 ♖×e7 and Black has many problems, more than in the ending which we discussed in the note to his 10th move. His chief worry is that he cannot develop without losing his b-pawn; and the opposite bishops will offer no comfort while several other pieces remain on the board.

12 ♖e1 looks promising, then. Nunn's move, 12 ♗g5, is likely to lead to similar positions, but there are two reasons for giving a slight preference to the rook move. One is that after (12 ♗g5) ♘×b3 13 a×b3 ♗×c3 14 b×c3 ♕×d5 (if here 14 . . . ♘×d5 15 ♕d4 ♘f6 16 ♕e5 makes good use of the bishop and yields excellent compensation for the pawn) 15 ♕×d5 ♘×d5 16 c4 ♘f6 17 ♖fe1 the endgame is not as favourable as before because the white rook has not reached the seventh rank; and although White regains his pawn here (17 . . . ♗e6 18 ♘d4), after the best move 17 . . . h6! 18 ♗×h6 ♖e8 19 ♗g5 ♔g7 he has very little. The other reason is that Black has (12 ♗g5) h6, chasing the bishop off the e-pawn and winning a pawn in comfort after 13 ♗h4? g5 etc. And after the better move 13 ♗e3, although he still cannot grab the d-pawn safely, in view of his own loose h-pawn, he can play 13 . . . ♗g4 14 h3 ♗×f3 15 ♕×f3 ♘bc4! 16 ♗c1 ♘×b3 17 a×b3 ♘d6 18 ♖e1 ♖e8 19 ♗e3 a6 (Keres–D. Byrne, San Antonio 1972) with approximate equality. This position is again similar to Belyavsky–Peresipkin, but White has lost time moving his bishop around.

One or two points need further explanation before we leave this last variation: (1) If 15 . . . ♘×b3 16 a×b3 ♗×c3 17 b×c3, Black could safely let his h-pawn go because the queens will disappear: 17 . . . ♕×d5 (impossible before . . . ♗g4 because of simply ♗×b6) 18 ♕×d5 ♘×d5 19 ♗×h6 ♖fd8 20 c4 ♘f6 is practically equal. But White could claim a slight advantage by 17 ♗×b6 ♕×b6 18 b×c3 (Nunn–Miles, London 1977) in view of the weakness in Black's K-side formation. (2) If White plays 13 ♗f4, trying to avoid the time loss when the knight comes to c4, he no longer has the option of taking on b6 and Black again has 13 . . . ♗g4 14 h3 ♗×f3 15 ♕×f3 ♘×b3 etc., with equality.

12 . . . ♗g4

13 h3 ♗×f3

14 ♕×f3 ♘×b3(?)

Black's timing is out here. He correctly plans . . . ♕d7, followed by . . . ♘c8–d6, but the capture on b3 should be delayed until White has played ♖ad1; the Black will not lose a tempo (or weaken b6) by being obliged to play . . . a6 before using his Q-rook.

15 a×b3 ♕d7

This time Black cannot quite equalise by taking the d-pawn. If 15 . . . ♗×c3 16 b×c3 ♕×d5 17 ♕×d5 ♘×d5 18 c4; then 18 . . . ♘f6 19 ♖fe1 ♖fe8 20 ♗×f6 e×f6 21 ♖×e8+ ♖×e8 22 ♖×a7 gives White a favourable ending, while 18 . . . ♘c7 or . . . ♘b6 19 ♗×e7 is different from a previous position (note 1 at the end of the note to White's 12th) in that the bishop is much better placed than at h6 and the knight is worse. If Black tries 19 . . . h6 here (in the first line, after 19 ♖fe1), there is 20 ♗×f6 e×f6 21 ♖e7 with advantage (21 . . . ♖fb8 22 ♖d1 etc.), or if 15 . . . h6 16 ♗e3 ♗×c3, then 17 ♗×b6, as in Nunn–Miles.

16 ♖fd1! *(100)* **. . .**

100
B

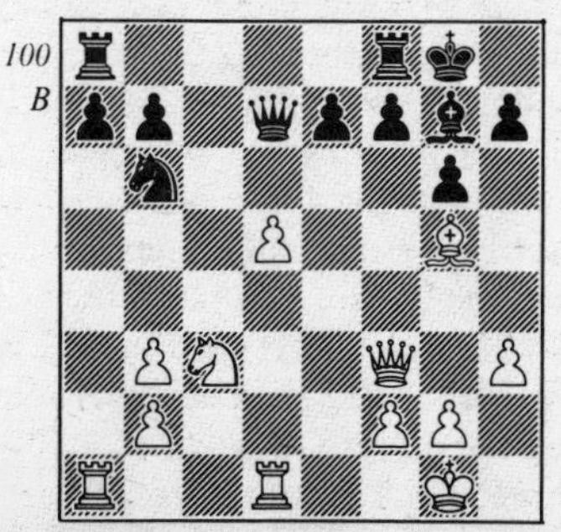

With this move a new phase of the game opens. Black no longer has the option of taking the d-pawn, and the position must be assessed according to the long-term strength or weakness of that pawn. (We are not talking about a typical IQP position here, as it is normally understood, because the pawn is on the fifth rank; but still some of the same rules apply.) Obviously it restricts Black, but equally it would be a weakness in a simplified position. Therefore White's guiding principle will be to avoid premature exchanges. The same applies to the b-pawns: they keep the black pieces out of c3 and c4, but in a rook ending they would be catastrophic liabilities; meanwhile their doubling provides White with the use of the a-file. In short, White has all the dynamic advantages, while Black hopes that he will survive the intervening phase and emerge with a superior endgame. And that is quite fitting because Seirawan is a player who tends to think in terms of static values, while Nunn's style is altogether more energetic. That kind of comparison needs to be kept in perspective, though; style among Grandmasters is a subtle business because they are by definition balanced and complete players. We are only referring to slight preferences for one type of position or another – nothing more.

In this case it is interesting to note that during the game both players thought that they stood better at this point! Natural optimism to some extent, no doubt, but it shows how difficult the positional play has become. The further course of events indicates that with correct play the game is still about equal.

Now Nunn's last move is very logical and instructive. 16 ♖fe1 would be routine, but the pressure against e7 would not bother Black much and could not be effectively augmented with White worrying about his own d-pawn. By securing the d-pawn he releases the knight for other duties; meanwhile the other rook stays at a1, forcing . . . a6 before long, and when the black knight moves to d6 (as it must) the white knight will go to a4 and make use of the new weakness at b6. If you say: 'Why waste a rook in order to activate a knight?', the answer is that the rook is doing an important job guarding the unpleasant d-pawn; it is at e1 that it would be wasted.

16 . . . ♘c8

17 ♕e3! . . .

White has no immediate attacking prospects; so for the moment he is making the transfer of the knight to d6 as tedious as possible. More positive action will depend on Black's response. Later he may wish to exchange Black's aggressive bishop, but not yet: his own bishop is too useful depriving the black queen of squares (after the next move, that is).

17 . . . ♖e8

18 ♗f4 a6

If 18 . . . e5 19 d×e6 ♕×e6 20 ♕×e6 f×e6 21 ♖d7 and Black loses at least a pawn: 21 . . . b6 (or 21 . . . ♖e7 22 ♖d8+ ♔f7 23 ♗d6) 22 ♘b5 ♖f8 23 ♘c7 and wins.

19 ♘a4 *(101)* **♕f5?**

A miscalculation which has terrible consequences. The queen should occupy b5, leaving f5 for the knight; Black's regrouping will not work the other way round because the white knight seizes b6. After 19 . . . ♕b5

101
B

20 ♖ac1 ♘d6 is quite safe because 21 ♖c5 ♕b4 does not trap the queen; and if 21 ♘b6 ♘f5 22 ♕c5 ♕×c5 23 ♖×c5 ♗d4! is fine. Therefore White's only attempt at gaining advantage would be 20 ♗c7! If then 20 . . . ♘d6? 21 ♘b6 and 21 . . . ♘f5 is now countered by 22 ♕d3 ♕×d3 23 ♖×d3 ♖a7 24 ♖e1 ♔f8 (nothing else will do; 25 d6 is threatened anyway) 25 d6 and wins: 25 . . . ♘×d6 26 ♖×d6, or 25 . . . e×d6 26 ♖×e8+ ♔×e8 27 ♗b8. If Black plays here 21 . . . ♖a7, then 22 g4! suddenly and surprisingly paralyses him; one possible finish might be 22 . . . ♗×b2 23 ♖a2 ♗f6 24 ♖e1 (threatens ♗×d6) ♔f8 (or 24 . . . ♖f8 25 ♗×d6 e×d6 26 ♘d7, or 24 . . . ♕b4 25 ♖a4) 25 ♖a5! ♕b4 26 ♘d7+ ♔g7 27 ♗×d6 ♕×a5 28 ♘×f6 and wins.

So at first glance 20 ♗c7 looks promising, but the snag is that Black can simply withdraw his queen: 20 . . . ♕d7. And there, unfortunately, the game might well have ended in something of an anti-climax, for it seems that White dare not avoid the repetition by 21 ♗f4 ♕b5 etc. If 21 ♕c5 or ♖ac1, 21 . . . b5 is good, while if 21 ♗e5 ♗×e5 22 ♕×e5 ♕b5, followed quickly by . . . ♘d6 and . . . ♖ac8, he can scarcely claim sufficient attacking chances to offset his weak pawns. He might try something based on h4–h5, but it would be risky.

After 19 . . . ♕f5, on the other hand, Black's game collapses with astonishing speed.

20 ♖ac1 . . .

Now 20 . . . ♘d6 is met by 21 ♘b6 ♖ad8 22 ♖d2 and again Black is desperately short of moves. For example: (a) 22 . . . ♕e4 23 ♕×e4 ♘×e4 24 ♖e2 ♘d6 25 ♖c7 with heavy pressure; (b) 22 . . . ♘b5 23 ♗c7 ♘×c7 24 ♖×c7 with a similar effect; (c) 22 . . . ♘c8 23 g4 ♕f6 24 ♖×c8 ♖×c8 25 ♘d7 ♕h4 26 ♗g5 and wins; (d) 22 . . . e5 23 d×e6 ♖×e6 24 ♖×d6! ♖e×d6 (or 24 . . . ♖d×d6 25 ♖c8+ ♗f8 26 ♗h6) 25 ♗×d6 ♖×d6 26 ♘c8 and wins. Seirawan must have appreciated all or most of that when he played 19 . . . ♕f5, and with his next move no doubt planned to drive the knight back and follow up with . . . ♘d6. Probably it was White's 21st which he overlooked; at the same time he is creating a serious weakness at c6.

20 . . . b5

21 g4! . . .

The knight not only refuses to retreat, but hangs on grimly at a4 for another seven moves!

21 . . . ♕f6

The other way is 21 . . . ♕d7. Then 22 ♖c7 ♕d8 23 ♘c5 etc. is obviously good, but more instructive is Nunn's intended continuation: 22 ♘c5 ♕a7 (forced; if 22 . . . ♕d8 23 ♘e6! f×e6 24 ♕×e6+ ♔h8 25 ♗c7), and now a change of theme, a lightning switch to the K-side because the black queen has been driven to a7 and **because White is thinking in terms of the whole board**, not just the c-file which has recently been the centre of attention: 23 ♗e5 ♘d6 24 ♗×g7 ♔×g7 25 h4!, with a very dangerous attack based on h5–h6. Black dare not touch his K-side pawns, nor can he bring his reserves across to defend the threatened sector: the knight at c5 and the d-pawn effectively cut his position in half.

22 ♖c6 e6?

The second mistake allows the d-pawn to run through and White wins by force. The only hope, though a faint one, is 22 . . . ♘d6, after which Nunn's intention was to paralyse him, as before, with 23 ♘b6 ♖ad8 24 ♖d2. He then threatens ♖c7, followed by ♘d7 or ♖a7, and Black has no decent moves at all. Not even 24 . . . e5 is possible now (25 ♗g5). Black could free himself a little by throwing away a pawn: 24 . . . h6 25 ♗×h6 ♗×h6 26 ♕×h6 ♕f3; but 27 ♕e3 ♕×e3 28 f×e3 should be quite sufficient to win. White would probably begin with ♔f2–f3 and e4, then release his knight by ♖c7 and ♘d7.

23 d6! . . .

Now 23 . . . b×a4 24 d7, followed by ♗g5, loses at least the exchange; 23 . . . ♘a7 24 ♖×a6 b×a4 25 d7 ♖f8 26 ♖×a7 is equally hopeless; and 23 . . . ♘×d6 24 ♘b6 ♘b7 25 ♘×a8 ♖×a8 26 ♖c7 ♘a5 27 ♖dd7 ♖f8 28 ♗d6 also wins easily for White; if here 24 . . . e5, there is 25 ♖d×d6 e×f4 26 ♕×e8+ etc.

Black tries instead to neutralise the pawn by luring it to e7, but White can liquidate into a won ending.

23 . . . ♘e7

24 ♗g5 ♘d5

If 24 . . . ♕e5 25 ♗×e7 b×a4 26 d7 and wins.

25 ♖×d5 e×d5

26 ♗×f6 ♖×e3

27 **f×e3** **♗×f6**
28 **d7** **♖d8**
29 **♘c5** *(102)* . . .

102
B

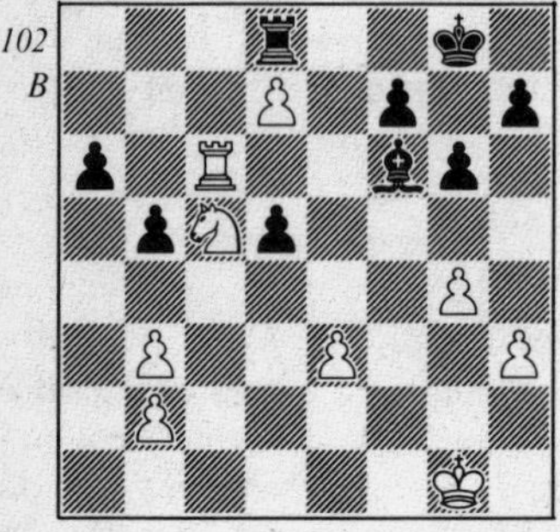

The stronger side can usually expect to win a piece or the exchange from this kind of position, provided the defending king cannot approach quickly, and in making all the exchanges beginning with 24 ♗g5 Nunn has satisfied himself that he can in fact win the bishop. He would not have wished to simplify as he did, if the best he could now do were to swap his d-pawn for, say, the black a- and b-pawns.

However Black now rescues his bishop, 30 ♖c8 will win: 29 . . . ♔g7 30 ♖c8 any 31 ♖×d8 ♗×d8 32 ♘b7, or 29 . . . ♗e7 30 ♖c8 ♔f8 31 ♘b7.

29 . . . **♗×b2**
30 **♖c8** **♗f6**
31 **♘b7!** . . .

There is still something to learn from the final few moves, especially for inexperienced players. White's 31st and 32nd are the kind of finesses which always seem to give a Grandmaster that extra bit of power and make the task of winning so much easier. How many people would have grabbed the piece at once here? 31 ♖×d8+ ♗×d8 32 ♘b7 would no doubt win the game, but after 32 . . . ♗c7 33 d8/♕+ ♗×d8 32 ♘×d8 a5 Black has counterplay; and using a knight against widely separated passed pawns is always awkward. At the very least the game would drag on in a depressing sort of way. But by the simple process of looking at all his possible moves Nunn makes life more comfortable for himself. 31 ♘b7 is better because it drives the black rook to a useless square where it blocks its own king.

31 . . . **♖f8**
32 **b4!** . . .

And the second finesse cripples Black's pawn majority and ends his resistance. There is no hurry to win the bishop; even after the desperate 32 . . . a5 33 ♘×a5 it cannot be saved.

32 . . . **♔g7**
33 **♔f2** **♗e7**
34 **♖e8** **♗h4+**
35 **♔f3** **h6**
36 **♖×f8** **♔×f8**
37 **d8/♕+** **♗×d8**
38 **♘×d8** **♔e7**
39 **♘b7** **1 – 0**

Game 23

Sicilian Defence
Salonika Olympiad 1984

J. Nunn v. U. Andersson

1	e4	c5
2	♘f3	e6
3	d4	c×d4
4	♘×d4	♘c6
5	♘c3	a6
6	f4 *(103)*	. . .

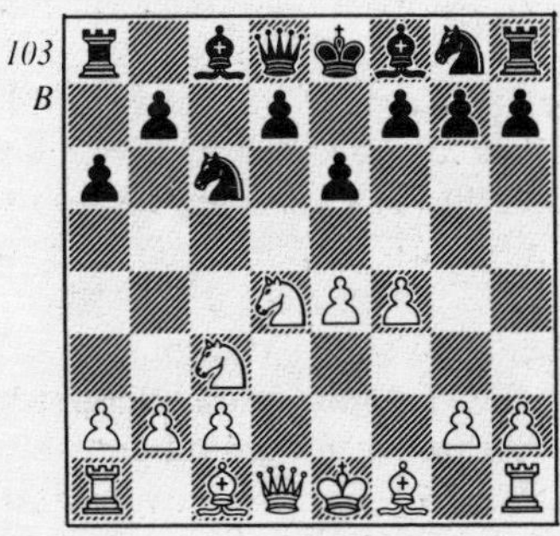

This unusual move took Andersson by surprise and caused him to spend twenty minutes on his reply. If that seems excessive, remember that there is such an abundance of Sicilian theory nowadays that even an expert may take quite a long time to sort out all the possible transpositions and decide which order of moves would suit him best.

Here Andersson has started off with a Paulsen system, while retaining the option of a transposition into the Scheveningen by . . . d6 (compare the remarks on Game 13). But one of the ideas behind 6 f4 is that such a transposition (6 . . . d6 or 6 . . . ♕c7 and 7 . . . d6) would give rise to a variation in which it is considered best for Black to avoid . . . a6 and concentrate on slightly faster piece development. A second point is that against . . . d6 White could advantageously try a plan based on ♗e3, ♕d2 and 0–0–0, instead of the quieter 0–0 lines. Against such sharp play Black normally likes to hit back by means of . . . e5, but here the loss of tempo involved in . . . a6 will cause trouble if he opens the centre.

These considerations represent the favourable aspects of 6 f4. Its dark side is that White is committing himself very early and could end up with an unpleasantly rigid pawn formation (pawns at e5 and f4); in that event a further advance would be difficult and he might not be able to find a suitable plan.

Andersson finally decides to stick to normal lines with 6 . . . ♕c7, instead of trying to refute White's move. We could briefly sum up his alternatives as follows:

(1) 6 . . . ♘ge7, and then either 7 ♗e2 ♘×d4 8 ♕×d4 ♘c6, which would be a regular line of Taimanov's system, or, more originally, 7 ♘f3 (avoiding the exchange and thus obliging the K-bishop to occupy g6) b5 8 ♗d3 ♘g6 9 ♗e3 ♗b7 10 0–0, followed by ♕e1-g3, and White may get attacking chances based on f5.

(2) 6 . . . ♗c5 (trying to take

advantage of another possible drawback to f4, the weakening of some black squares, but the attack rebounds) 7 ♗e3 ♕b6 8 ♘a4 ♕a5+ 9 c3 ♗×d4 (9 . . . ♕c7 10 ♘×e6) 10 ♗×d4 ♘×d4 11 ♕×d4, and Black suffers from the weakness of b6 and his dark squares generally, a frequent problem in the Taimanov.

(3) 6 . . . d5 (The most natural and probably the best move. After 7 e×d5 e×d5 the isolated d-pawn would not matter much; more significant would be White's weakness at e4 and the useless placing of his f-pawn, doing nothing and blocking the Q-bishop) 7 ♗e3 ♗b4 8 e5 ♘ge7 9 a3 ♗a5 10 ♗d3 ♘×d4 11 ♗×d4 (Nunn–Timman, London 1984) ♗b6 12 ♘e2 ♗×d4 13 ♘×d4 ♕b6 with equality.

Some of the finer points of this last variation require further explanation: (a) White avoids 7 e5 because 7 . . . ♘ge7 (-f5), together with . . . g6 and possibly . . . h5, would saddle him with that rigid pawn structure, and finding a good plan would be difficult. (b) If Black plays 7 . . . ♘f6, then 8 e5 ♘d7 9 ♕g4 would be a different matter, partly because of the time gain and partly because the black knight could not reach f5. White has attacking chances here too: if 9 . . . ♘e7 10 0–0–0 g6, for example, there is the sacrifice 11 ♘×e6. (c) It follows that Black's choice lies between 7 . . . ♗b4 and 7 . . . ♘ge7, both of which are satisfactory. 7 . . . ♘ge7 could lead to 8 ♘f3 d×e4 9 ♕×d8+ ♘×d8 10 ♘×e4 ♘d5 11 ♗d2 ♘c6, which is about equal, while 7 . . . ♗b4, though it forces White's e5, commits Black's better bishop to an early exchange (otherwise it is useless at a5) which could be dangerous in this type of pawn formation. To exchange it at c3 would leave a serious dark-square weakness, hence the main line. In the final position Black seems to be in trouble with his bad bishop, but 13 . . . ♕b6 guarantees him reasonable play; for instance 14 b4 ♘c6 and White cannot do better than 15 c3 because he must watch his own weakness at e3 (or if 15 ♘×c6 b×c6, with . . . c5 and/or . . . a5 coming). Therefore 15 c3 ♘×d4 16 c×d4 ♗d7 17 ♗e2 ♗b5 etc., and Black has no worries. A similar thing would happen after 14 ♖b1.

6 . . . ♕c7

7 ♗e2 ♘×d4

After 7 . . . d6 White has ♗e3, ♕d2, 0–0–0 etc., or he could try the even sharper line 8 f5 ♘f6 9 f×e6 ♗×e6 10 ♘×e6 f×e6 11 0–0 ♗e7 12 ♗g4, then ♗h3 with pressure against e6. Black, of course, would be unwilling to play . . . e5 here because of the fresh weaknesses which would appear at f5 and d5.

Apart from that Black has several options: (a) 7 . . . ♗c5 8 ♗e3 d6 9 ♕d3 ♘ge7 10 0–0–0 0–0 11 ♘×c6 ♗×e3+ 12 ♕×e3 b×c6 (otherwise the d-pawn is weak) 13 g4!, and White is well on the way to developing a dangerous attack because the natural counterplay in the centre (13 . . . d5) once again falls into the trap of creating black-square weaknesses (14 ♖hf1 followed by ♕c5). (b) 7 . . . ♗b4 (preparing . . . ♘f6, but White can take immediate advantage) 8 ♘×c6 b×c6 9 ♕d4 ♗f8 10 e5 d5 (otherwise ♘e4) 11 e×d6 ♕×d6 12 ♕×d6 ♗×d6 13 ♗f3 ♗b7 14 ♘e4 ♗e7 15 ♗e3 (-c5) with a clearly better ending. (c) 7 . . . b5 (Typical Taimanov play, concentrating on his

Q-side counter-attack at the expense of conventional development. White exchanges knights at this point because any delay will permit Black to recapture with the bishop after 8 . . . ♗b7 and then play . . . ♕b7; or if he does not exchange knights at all, Black will happily continue with his counterplay by . . . ♗b7, . . . ♘a5 and . . . ♘c4. In short, he does best to disrupt Black's plans without further ado) 8 ♘×c6 ♕×c6 (8 . . . d×c6 9 0–0 ♗b7 10 ♗e3 ♘f6 11 e5 ♘d5 12 ♘×d5 c×d5 would turn into a French Defence type of position, not unlike the earlier reference Nunn–Timman, but favourable to White this time because of the lack of counterplay) 9 ♗f3 ♗b7 10 e5 ♕c7 11 ♘e4 ♖d8 12 ♕e2 (or possibly 12 ♕d4 ♕×c2 13 ♗e3, which is a bit speculative) d5 13 e×d6 (not 13 ♘g3 g6, Parma–Soos, Titovo–Uzice 1966, when White's f4 is showing up in a most unfavourable light) ♗×d6 14 ♘×d6+ ♖×d6 15 0–0, with an edge for White.

With the text move Black avoids the capture at c6 and plans to drive the white queen back later. At the same time he experiences certain problems in completing his development.

8 ♕×d4 b5

The other obvious continuation is 8 . . . ♘e7, against which White has quite an elegant manoeuvre to seize control of the black squares: 9 ♕f2! ♘c6 10 ♗e3 b5 11 0–0 ♗e7 12 e5, followed by ♘e4 and ♗c5. Notice that 11 . . . d6 (to prevent e5) would be too dangerous on account of 12 f5.

9 ♗e3 . . .

Sometimes an early . . . b5 can be exploited by a4, but not here: 9 a4 b4 10 ♘a2 ♕×c2 11 ♘×b4 ♕c5! is fine for Black; or if 11 ♗e3 ♕×a4 and White does not have the development to justify a two-pawn sacrifice.

9 . . . ♗b7

9 . . . b4 10 ♘a4 ♕×c2 is bad because of 11 ♘b6 ♖b8 12 ♖c1, trapping the queen, while 9 . . . b4 without the capture at c2 merely exposes b6, this being one occasion when a4 happens to be a good square for a knight. The only other move which suggests itself is 9 . . . ♘e7. That enables Black to complete his development more conveniently, but it depends on a tactical factor: 9 . . . ♘e7 10 ♗×b5 a×b5 11 ♘×b5 is unplayable because of 11 . . . ♕a5+, but if White has castled the variation wins for him; therefore Black must play the knight move immediately or not at all. After 9 . . . ♘e7 one possible variation would be 10 0–0 ♘c6 11 ♕d2 ♗b7 12 ♖ad1 ♗e7 13 a4 b4 14 ♘d5! e×d5 15 e×d5 ♕d6 16 d×c6 ♕×d2 17 ♖×d2 ♗×c6 18 ♗f3 with a small advantage to White.

10 0–0 . . .

Not 10 0–0–0 because after 10 . . . ♖c8 the threat of 11 . . . b4 is very hard to meet.

10 . . . ♖c8

Again 10 . . . b4 11 ♘a4 ♕×c2 is far too dangerous: 12 ♘b6 ♖d8 13 ♗d3 ♕c7 14 ♖ac1 ♕b8 15 f5, threatening ♗f4, and White has a huge attack.

On the subject of modern Sicilians generally and Taimanov's variation in particular, Black seems to be breaking the rules on every side. How can he justify his apparent neglect not only of development, but of the centre as well? In fact experience has shown that his tough pawn structure d7, e6 and f7 can withstand quick attacks quite capably, provided he does not loosen it by a transposition into the Scheveningen (. . . d6) at an unfortunate moment. If White plays an early f5, the e-pawn has plenty of defence in reserve; if he plays e5, Black may occupy the holes left behind at f5 and d5. In other words, White's control of the centre is by no means as overwhelming as it may appear. Black's influence there is subtler, and any crude attacks by his opponent or any attempts to seize too much advantage are liable to rebound. That is why Black is able in some degree to delay his conventional development and catch up later. Of course, he is walking a tightrope and the slightest error is likely to have grave consequences. Here, for instance, it is important to play 10 . . . ♖c8 before developing the knight, in order to have the simplifying move . . . ♗c5 available when required. If 10 . . . ♘f6 11 ♗f3 threatens 12 e5 and Black has problems. Another point arises in this connection at move 12.

11 ♖ad1 . . .

Better than the slow move 11 a3, since . . . b4 is no threat. As an example of that slower treatment, here is Ghizdavu–Matera (USA 1976) in which Black obtained the typical Sicilian endgame advantage, one of the basic themes of the whole defence: 11 a3 ♘f6 12 ♗f3 ♗e7 13 ♖ad1 (or 13 e5 ♗×f3, as in the main line) 0–0 14 e5 (if 14 ♖f2, to cover the c-pawn, 14 . . . ♗×a3 15 ♘×b5 ♗×b2! is good for Black) ♗×f3 15 g×f3 (because 15 ♖×f3 ♘g4 16 ♔h1 ♘×e3 17 ♕×e3 d6 would be worse; White would miss his dark-square bishop) ♘h5 16 ♕×d7 (othrwise Black gets a positional plus by . . . g6 and . . . ♘g7) ♗c5! 17 ♖fe1 ♘×f4 18 ♕×c7 ♖×c7 19 ♗×c5 ♖×c5, and White has several pawn weaknesses which eventually cost him the game.

11 . . . ♘f6

There is a possible exchange sacrifice here which may have tempted Andersson, but in the end he rightly rejected it. After a flurry of tactics White's superior development not surprisingly carries the day. It begins with 11 . . . ♗c5 12 ♕×g7 ♗×e3+ 13 ♔h1, and now Black can try one of three things: (a) 13 . . . ♗×f4 14 ♗h5! (puts more pressure on and captures the rook with check) ♘h6 (nothing else) 15 ♕×h8+ ♔e7 16 ♕×h7, threatening 17 ♘e2 and leaving Black with no compensation for the material; (b) 13 . . . ♔e7, which looks promising because 14 ♕×h8 ♘f6 15 ♕g7 ♗×f4 leads to trouble, as shown in the next variation, but which is actually answered by the devastating move 14 f5!; (c) 13 . . . b4 14 f5! (again it is far stronger to keep the attack going; 14 ♕×h8 is countered by 14 . . . ♔e7 15 f5 – or 15 ♕g7 b×c3 – ♘f6 16 ♕g7 ♖g8, trapping the queen, and 14 ♗h5 ♘h6! is unclear) b×c3 15 f×e6 d×e6 16 ♗h5 ♘h6 17 ♕×h8+ ♔e7 18 ♕g7 (threatening ♖×f7+) ♖f8 (if 18 . . . ♗d2 19 ♕×h6!, or if 18 . . . ♔e8 19 ♗×f7+ ♘×f7 20 ♕g8+) 19 ♕f6+ ♔e8 20 ♖d3 (but not 20 ♕×e6+ ♕e7) and Black loses his bishop or his knight (20 . . . ♗d2 21 b×c3).

Now after 11 . . . ♘f6 White has little alternative but to simplify. 12 ♗f3 is tempting, since 12 . . . ♗c5 13 ♕×c5 ♕×c5 14 ♗×c5 ♖×c5 15 e5 ♗×f3 16 ♖×f3 is definitely favourable, but with his development now more advanced and tactically with his rook at c8 Black can at last safely take the c-pawn: 12 . . . b4 13 ♘a4 ♕×c2, and if 14 ♘b6 ♗c5!

12	**e5**	**♘d5**
13	**♘×d5**	**♗×d5**
14	**♗f3**	**♗×f3**
15	**♖×f3** *(104)*	. . .

104
B

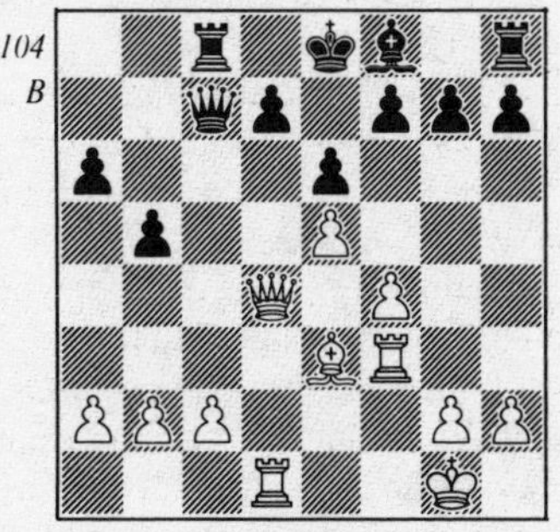

Here Black faces a tough decision: 15 . . . ♗e7 or 15 . . . ♗c5? Or does it matter? In fact . . . ♗c5 is right; the other move, as played, is unsatisfactory. But in making his choice he has to see that after 15 . . . ♗c5 16 ♕×c5 ♕×c5 17 ♗×c5 ♖×c5 18 c3 (18 ♖fd3 ♖×c2 19 ♖×d7 0–0 is all right) ♔e7 19 ♖fd3 ♖c7 20 ♖d6 ♖a8 his temporarily passive position can soon be put right by the undermining move . . . f6 (before White gets a real grip on things). Incidentally, 19 . . . ♖d8 20 ♖d6 ♖c6 would not be a good way to defend because White has 21 ♔f2 and 22 ♔e3, threatening to liquidate all four rooks and march to c5. Nor would one exchange help Black: 21 ♔f2 ♖×d6 22 ♖×d6 ♖a8 23 ♔e3 ♔d8 24 ♔d4, reaching c5 again.

After 20 . . . ♖a8 the position looks like one of the typically favourable endings which you find in all the books. But it is deceptive, partly because . . . f6 is available and partly because d7 is not a serious weakness with the king handy to defend it. If anything a6 is a weaker point, but Black can cope with that if he defends himself vigorously. For example: (a) 21 ♖a1 f6 22 a4 f×e5 23 f×e5 ♖c5 with equality; (b) 21 a4 b×a4! 22 ♖a1 ♖b8 with equality; (c) 21 ♖b6 f6 22 e×f6+ g×f6 23 ♖dd6 a5 24 ♖a6 ♖×a6 25 ♖×a6 b4!, again equalising; (d) 21 ♔f2 f6 22 e×f6+ (leaving Black to swap and follow with . . . ♖c5 always seems worse) g×f6 23 ♔e3 a5, with . . . b4 to follow, or if here 23 ♖b6 ♖c6 24 ♖b7 ♖d6 etc. Against a good defence White can achieve absolutely nothing.

16 ♕d2 0–0 17 c3 seems to offer White rather more chances; for example 17 . . . ♖fd8 (17 . . . f6 allows 18 ♕×d7 and the e-pawn is *en prise* with check) 18 ♗×c5 ♕×c5+ 19 ♔h1, followed by ♖d3, and . . . d5 is prevented.

15	. . .	**♗e7?**
16	**c3**	**0–0**
17	**♕b6!**	. . .

It is unlikely that Andersson was deceived into thinking that the four-rook ending would be bad for him. Rather he thought that 15 . . . ♗e7 was at least as good because he underestimated this harmless-looking move. Of course, White cannot take the d-pawn (17 ♕×d7? ♖fd8), but what is more interesting is that without 17 ♕b6 he has no hope of gaining the upper hand. His control of the centre seems impressive, but there is actually no other way in which he can increase his pressure on the d-pawn before Black eliminates it by . . . ♖fd8 and . . . d6. Nor can he seriously contemplate an attack on the castled position since (a) Black has no weakness there; (b) he has a minor piece handy to defend the king; and (c) White himself lacks the necessary minor pieces to build up anything convincing. Against ♕e4 and ♖h3 Black simply plays . . . g6 and White is wasting his time.

But 17 ♕b6! really hits the nail on the head. If Black exchanges queens he loses the d-pawn: 17 . . . ♕×b6 18 ♗×b6 ♗d8 (or 18 . . . ♖c6 19 ♖×d7) 19 ♗f2 ♖c7 20 ♖fd3; if not he must cover the a-pawn, since a line such as 17 . . . f6 18 e×f6 ♗×f6 19 ♕×a6 merely complicates matters without offering him any real play. Unfortunately the only available defence, 17 . . . ♕c6, permits 18 ♕×c6 d×c6 19 ♖d7 ♖fe8 (19 . . . ♗d8 20 ♖a7) 20 ♖f1 ♖cd8 21 ♖fd1 ♔f8 22 ♔f2 and Black is in a kind of Zugzwang. If he exchanges rooks he cannot prevent ♖a7 or ♖c7, or if 22 . . . ♖c8 23 ♖a7 ♖a8 24 ♖dd7 and he is paralysed.

Andersson takes his only other chance; he sacrifices the d-pawn, opens the c-file for himself and tries to hold a rook ending.

17	**. . .**	**b4**
18	**c×b4**	**♕×b6**
19	**♗×b6**	**♗×b4**
20	**♖×d7**	**♖c1+**
21	**♖f1**	**♗c5+**

Black is obliged to exchange his awkward bishop. 21 . . . ♖c2 22 a3 ♗d2 23 b4 would be unpleasant because the bishop would be very short of good squares, while White's could settle happily on c5.

22	**♗×c5**	**♖×c5**
23	**♖fd1**	**h6!** *(105)*

Andersson is a great endgame player, and until his slight error at move 42 he puts up the maximum resistance in these trying circumstances.

Here he is preparing to attack the one weakness in White's game, the pawn chain f4–e5. The reason why this is a weakness is that after . . . g5 White will either have to accept an isolated e-pawn or defend by g3. And after g3 and an exchange at f4 the king will have a harder job defending his f- and h-pawns than if the formation were at, say, f3 and e4 because there are more open spaces and hence more opportunities for the black rooks to cause trouble. Of course . . . h6 and . . . g5 also weakens Black, but he has to risk that. His task is to stir things up, create as many loose pawns as possible and try to reduce the overall number of pawns to a minimum.

105
W

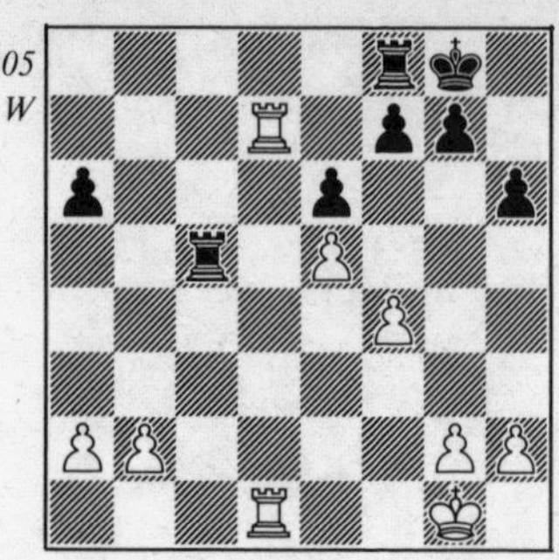

24	**g3**	**g5**
25	**♔f2**	**. . .**

Developing the king and generally consolidating his position. Now 25 . . . f6 is an interesting alternative to Black's next move; quite a few pawns are likely to disappear and White has to find the most accurate response. On the other hand, Black is putting his own king in jeopardy and the chances are that he would lose more rapidly. The analysis would be: 25 . . . f6 26 e×f6 and then (a) 26 . . . ♖×f6 27 ♖b7! (covering the b-pawn so that he will not be left only with rook-pawns in any subsequent pawn massacre, and also preparing mate threats or a double seventh) ♖c2+ (or 27 . . . g×f4 28 ♖d8+, leading to a similar ending to the game, but with Black's king confined to the back rank) 28 ♔f3 ♖×h2 29 ♖d8+ ♖f8 30 ♖dd7 ♖f6 31 ♖g7+ (standard double-seventh play; White achieves his object, in this case the transfer of the rooks to a7 and b7, with tempo gains) ♔f8 32 ♖h7 ♔g8 33 ♖bg7+ ♔f8 34 ♖a7 ♔g8 35 ♖hg7+ ♔f8 36 ♖gb7 ♔g8 37 ♖×a6, and wins with two united passed pawns and the black king still in a bad position; (b) 26 . . . g×f4 27 ♖g7+! (gaining a tempo shortly by the back-rank mate threat) ♔h8 28 g×f4 ♖c2+ (28 . . . ♖×f6 29 ♖a7 ♖×f4+ 30 ♔e3 ♖f8 31 ♖dd7, threatening mate and the a-pawn, and obtaining two united passed pawns, as before) 29 ♔e3 ♖×b2 30 ♖dg1!, with a decisive attack, i.e. 30 . . . ♖×a2 or . . . ♖×h2 31 f7 and wins, or 30 . . . ♖bb8 31 f7, followed by ♔e4–e5–f6, ♖1g6 and ♖×h6 mate!

25	**. . .**	**♔g7**
26	**♔e3**	**♔g6**
27	**♖d8**	**♖×d8**
28	**♖×d8**	**♖c2**

Against the direct attack 28 . . . g×f4+ 29 g×f4 ♔f5 White has prepared 30 ♖d7, and if 30 . . . f6 31 ♖f7; if here 29 . . . ♖c1, there is 30 ♖g8+ ♔f5 31 ♖g7.

29	**♖d2**	**♖c1**

Or 29 . . . g×f4+ 30 g×f4 ♖c1 31 ♖g2+ ♔f5 32 ♖g7 ♖e1+ 33 ♔d2, as before. So far so good; White has consolidated. But to make progress he must use his king aggressively. And that means the f-pawn must be liquidated; otherwise, after 30 ♔d4 g×f4 31 g×f4 ♔f5, it would be too much of a liability.

30	**f×g5!**	**h×g5**

Or 30 . . . ♔×g5 31 ♖f2; either way White can now use the backwardness of the f-pawn to cancel out his own weakness at e5.

31	**♔d4** *(106)*	**. . .**

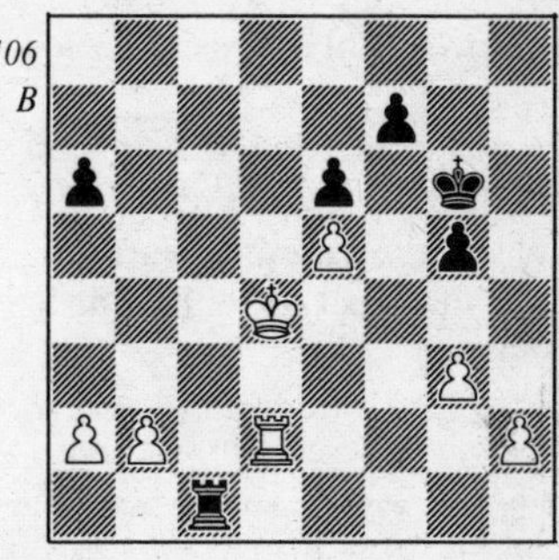

Black has no compensation for his lost pawn here; if anything White's centralised king gives him what positional advantage there is. But for all that the winning process is far from easy. There are two reasons: one is that the black rook is quite active and progress will be difficult until it has been driven into a defensive position. It is impossible to overstate this point. At present the rook is capable of harassing any of the opposing pawns, and if White rushes things one possible outcome is a premature pawn massacre with the game being reduced to two pawns vs. one, or even one vs. none, the result of which may well be uncertain. The second difficult aspect is also a peculiarity of rook endings. White cannot simply make a passed pawn without due preparation; the circumstances (i.e. the placing of the pieces) must first be made as favourable as possible. If, for instance, Black can place his rook behind a newly created passed pawn, or blockade it with his king, it may well become a liability in need of protection from its rook. But if White can support it with his king **in the absence of the defending king**, he is well on the way to winning. Better still would be a passed pawn with its own rook behind it, forcing the other rook into a terribly passive position in front of the pawn.

Since White can make a passed pawn on either side of the board here, the black king should centralise in readiness to blockade either the h- or the b-pawn, according to White's choice. And that is just what Andersson does; he follows with two very good moves which make the winning task as difficult as possible.

31 . . . a5!

Against passive play White can make a passed b-pawn at once, because his king is on hand and its rival is far away. The process would be: 31 . . . ♔g7 32 b4 ♔g6 33 ♖b2 ♔f5 (or 33 . . . ♖d1+ 34 ♔c5 ♖e1 35 ♔b6 and the connected pawns will decide – or most likely the b-pawn alone here; Black would need a strong, advanced passed pawn of his own even to consider seriously such a possibility) 34 ♖f2+ ♔g6 35 ♖f6+ ♔g7 36 ♖f3! (taking advantage of the fact that a3 is vacant to drive the black rook into a passive position) ♖c2 37 ♖a3 ♖c6 (again 37 . . . ♖×h2 38 ♖×a6 would be hopeless) 38 ♖c3 ♖b6 39 ♔c4 ♖b5 (or 39 . . . ♖c6+ 40 ♔b3) 40 ♖e3 ♔g6 41 a4 ♖d5 42 b5 and wins.

After 31 . . . a5 the creation of a passed pawn is not so easy; White has to inch forward by b3, ♖b2, a3 and b4 (not a3 at once on account of . . . a4!), and consequently cannot use a3 for his rook.

32 b3 f6!

Again the best chance, bringing his king nearer to the b-pawn and making a passed pawn of his own. The passive defence line would now run as follows: 32 . . . ♔g7 (32 . . . ♔f5 33 ♖f2+ is no improvement) 33 a3 (White has to sacrifice a pawn; if 33 ♖b2 ♖d1+ 34 ♔c4 ♖e1) and then (a) 33 . . . ♖b1 34 ♔c4 ♖e1 35 b4 a×b4 36 a×b4 ♖×e5 37 b5 ♖e1 38 ♖b2 ♖c1+ 39 ♔d4 ♖c8 40 b6 ♖b8 41 b7 ♔f6 42 ♔c5 ♔f5 43 ♔c6 e5 44 ♔c7 ♖×b7+ 45 ♔×b7 ♔g4 46 ♔c6 e4 47 ♔d5 and wins; or (b) 33 . . . ♖a1 34 b4 ♖×a3 35 b5 ♖b3 36 ♔c5 and wins, if necessary by hiding his king from checks on the a-file (36 . . . ♖c3+ 37 ♔b6); otherwise, for example, 36 . . . ♔f8 37 b6 ♔e7 38 ♔c6 a4 39 b7 a3 40 ♖a2 g4 (or 40 . . . ♔d8 41 ♖×a3) 41 ♔c7 and wins (but not this time 41 ♖×a3? ♖×a3 42 b8/♕ ♖c3+).

33 e×f6 ♔×f6 *(107)*

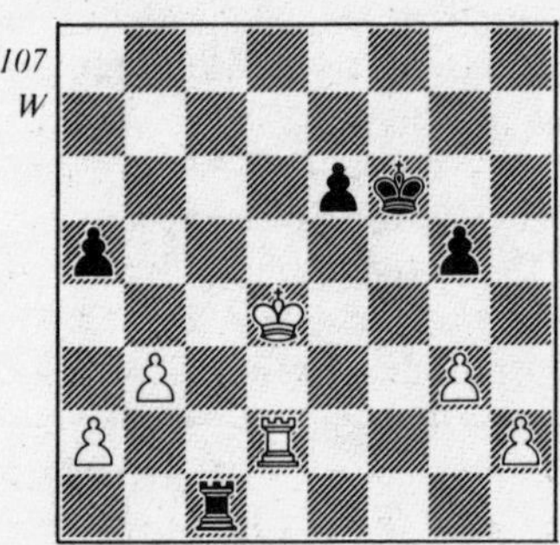
107
W

34 ♖f2+ . . .

Strictly speaking, this is not the best move because White can force a win by the immediate 34 a3. But in practice it was certainly the wisest course to adopt. The point is that the variations arising from 34 a3 are now much more critical since Black has his own passed pawn. The analysis would be as follows: 34 a3 ♖a1 (34

. . . e5+ 35 ♔d5 ♖c3 36 ♖f2+ ♔e7 37 ♖b2 ♖e3 38 b4 is far worse) 35 b4 ♖×a3 36 b5 ♖b3 (this time 36 . . . e5+ 37 ♔d5 ♖b3 38 ♖f2+ ♔g6 39 ♔c6 e4 would simply transpose into the main line) 37 ♖f2+! (this check is no optional extra – the king must be driven back; if 37 ♔c5? e5 38 b6 e4 39 ♔c6 e3, followed by . . . ♔e5 and Black's pawn is as good as White's), and then (a) 37 . . . ♔e7 38 ♔c5 ♖c3+ (or 38 . . . ♔d7 39 ♖a2, or 38 . . . a4 39 ♖a2 a3 40 ♔c4 ♖f3 41 ♔b4) 39 ♔b6 a4 40 ♔a7 and wins; or (b) 37 . . . ♔g6 (to support the e-pawn better) 38 ♔c5 e5 39 b6 e4 40 ♔c6 e3 41 ♖f1! (41 ♖e2 ♔f5) a4 (41 . . . e2 42 ♖e1 ♖b2 43 b7 a4 44 ♖×e2) 42 b7 a3 43 ♔c7 e2 44 ♖e1 a2 45 b8/♕ ♖×b8 46 ♔×b8 ♔f5 47 h3 (forcing Black to sacrifice) a1/♕ 48 ♖×a1 ♔e4 49 h4 and wins.

You will appreciate that the slightest miscalculation in all this could easily have thrown away the win, and in fact Nunn did not even bother to look at the line during the game. Apart from any other considerations he is now only six moves from the time-control and preferred to adjourn in order to analyse more thoroughly. But in any case Grandmasters do not play endings in such a reckless way if they can possibly avoid it, especially if they feel the game should be won anyway by quieter methods. So from now until move 40 White is content to improve the position of his pieces, at the same time setting a few traps.

34 . . . ♔e7
35 ♔e4 . . .

Threatening ♔f3–g4.

35 . . . ♖c3
36 ♖b2 ♔d6
37 ♔d4 . . .

Not 37 a3 because the black king is close enough to blockade the passed pawn which would arise after b4, . . . ♖×a3 and b5. White is thinking more in terms of driving the rook off the third rank and generally making it passive.

37 . . . ♖f3
38 ♔e4 . . .

38 ♖d2 is tempting, but after 38 . . . ♖f1 39 ♔c4+ ♔c6 40 ♖e2 Black has 40 . . . ♖c1+ before . . . ♔d6, thus keeping the king out of both b5 and e5.

38 . . . ♖c3
39 ♖d2+ ♔e7
40 ♖d4! . . .

Here is the great lesson of this endgame: pieces before pawns! Remember the remarks we made in connection with White's 31st move and notice above all what emphasis Nunn lays on the correct placing of his king and rook. At this stage he is far more concerned with attacking the enemy pawn weaknesses and tying up Black's pieces than with making a passed pawn. This principle will stand out most clearly when we come to the note to White's 42nd move. Meanwhile, the point of 40 ♖d4 is to chase the black rook off its ideal position on the third rank; while it remains there the very important winning idea of ♔f3–g4 is thwarted. The threat is 41 ♖c4, and since Black cannot permit two united passed pawns to appear (by 41 . . . ♖c2 42 ♖a4 ♖×h2 43 ♖×a5) he must occupy c5, either now or on the next move.

40 . . . ♖c5
41 ♖c4 ♖f5
42 ♖c2 *(108)* **. . .**

Covering f2. Now Black is eager to

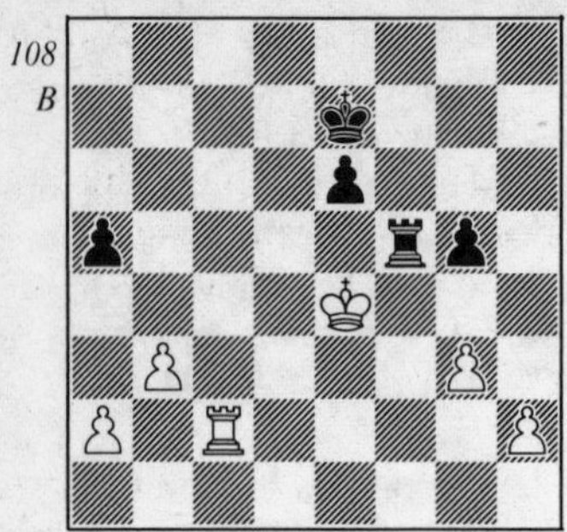
108
B

regain his aggressive position by . . . ♖f1, hence the following move (if 42 . . . ♖f1? 43 ♖c5); but in deserting the Q-side he permits White to win fairly quickly. The strongest defence is 42 . . . ♔d6!, which also prepares . . . ♖f1, but keeps the king's position flexible. After that there is a wide choice of plans, but Nunn's preference is to keep improving the placing of his pieces by the subtle move 43 ♔e3! And that is very interesting because, apart from its more positive aspects of controlling f2 and opening the fourth rank for the rook (. . . g4 ♖c4, for instance), it puts Black practically in Zugzwang. Here are the variations, quite easy to understand if you bear in mind the principle of pieces before pawns and the typical endgame theme of attacking on one side or the other, according to the black king's movements:

(1) 43 . . . ♖e5+ 44 ♔f3 ♔e7 (otherwise White has ♔g4, ♖f2, **cutting off the king**, and **only then h4**) 45 ♔g4 ♔f6 46 ♔h5!, and Black is tied up because he dare not abandon his g-pawn and allow White two connected. White, of course, will now exploit his Q-side majority, for example 46 . . . ♖f5 47 ♖c3 (a little more convenient than 47 a3 ♖f3 48 ♖b2; White can take his time) ♖f2 48 h3 ♖f5 (48 . . . ♖h2 49 ♖f3+ and 50 g4) 49 a3 ♖b5 (or 49 . . . ♖f1 50 b4, always relying on the fact that the black rook cannot leave his g-pawn) 50 ♖f3+ ♔g7 51 b4 a×b4 52 a×b4 ♖d5 53 ♖c3 ♔f6 54 ♖c5 ♖d4 55 b5 and wins.

(2) 43 . . . ♖b5 (43 . . . ♖d5? 44 ♖d2) 44 ♔f3 ♖b4 45 ♖c4, followed by ♔g4.

(3) 43 . . . ♖f1 44 ♖f2 and since 44 . . . ♖d1 (heading for d4) is unplayable Black again cannot prevent ♔f3–g4.

(4) 43 . . . ♖f8 44 h4! (now quite appropriate because the black rook will have to go in front of the h-pawn, taking two moves to reach h5, and because 44 . . . g4, looking for counterplay by . . . ♖f3+, is met by ♖f2, then ♖f4) g×h4 45 g×h4 ♖h8 46 ♖h2 ♖h5 (or 46 . . . ♔e5 47 h5 ♔f5 48 a3 etc.) 47 ♔f4, then ♔g4 and the pawn advances.

(5) 43 . . . g4 (43 . . . e5? 44 ♖f2) 44 ♖c4 ♖h5 45 ♖a4 and wins by ♔f4.

(6) 43 . . . ♔d5 44 ♖f2 ♖e5+ 45 ♔f3 ♖f5+ 46 ♔g2 ♖e5 47 ♖d2+ ♔c5 48 ♔f3, then ♔g4 and h4, with the black king now stranded on the c-file.

(7) 43 . . . ♔d7 44 ♖f2 ♖e5+ 45 ♔f3 ♖f5+ 46 ♔g2 ♖d5 (or 46 . . . ♖e5 47 ♖d2+ and ♔f3) 47 ♔h3 ♖d4 48 ♖f7+ ♔d6 49 ♖g7 ♖d2 50 a4 ♖d5 51 ♔g4 and wins.

(8) 43 . . . ♔e7 (the most resilient defence) 44 ♖c7+ and then: (a) 44 . . . ♔d6 45 ♖g7 (tying up the rook completely because he must stop ♔f3; therefore Black can only move around with his king; if 45 . . . e5? 46 g4) ♔c6 46 h3 ♔c5 47 ♔e4 ♔c6, and now White needs just a little more pressure somewhere to decide the game: 48 a4! and Black must allow

♖b7–b5 because 48 . . . ♔b6 is answered by 49 ♖e7. Therefore 48 . . . ♔c5 49 ♖b7 ♔c6 50 ♖b5 ♖×b5 51 a×b5+ ♔×b5 52 h4 and wins. If here 48 . . . ♖c5, then 49 ♖e7 (easier than 49 ♔f3 etc.) amounts to the same thing. (b) 44 . . . ♔f6 45 a4! (Once again the seizure of b5, augmenting the power of the rook is stronger than creating an immediate passed pawn. Notice one difference: when the black king goes to f6, as in the game, and the white rook is still at c2, then a3 and b4 is the simplest way because the rook can go behind his passed pawn) g4 (or 45 . . . ♖e5+ 46 ♔d3 ♖d5+ 47 ♔c4 ♖d2 48 ♔b5 ♖×h2 49 ♔×a5, then ♖c3, to cover the g-pawn, and White wins) 46 ♖b7 ♖f3+ 47 ♔e4 ♖f2 48 ♖b5 ♖f3 (48 . . . ♖b2 49 ♔f4) 49 ♔d4! (not 49 ♖×a5 ♖×b3; White wants nothing less than two united passed pawns) ♖f2 50 ♖×a5 ♖×h2 51 ♔e4! (better than 51 ♖b5 ♖g2; by this finesse White gets one square nearer the g-pawn at the end, yet without tempo loss) ♖f2 52 ♖b5 ♖f3 53 a5 ♖×g3 54 a6 ♖g1 55 b4 and wins.

42 . . . ♔f6(?)
43 a3 g4

If Black tries to correct his error by 43 . . . ♔e7, White continues 44 b4 a×b4 45 a×b4 ♔d6 46 ♔d4! threatening to support the b-pawn with his king. After 46 . . . ♖d5+ (46 . . . ♖f1 47 ♖b2 ♔c6 48 b5+ ♔b6 49 ♔e5 ♖e1+ 50 ♔f6) 47 ♔c4 ♖e5 48 ♔b3 and 49 ♔a4 Black's king is cut off and the b-pawn can advance. Another defensive plan is to activate Black's e-pawn, but White answers 43 . . . ♖f1 by 44 ♖b2 ♖e1+ (or 44 . . . ♖a1 45 b4, as in the game) 45 ♔d4 e5+ 46 ♔c4 e4 47 ♔b5 e3 (47 . . . ♖a1 48 a4) 48 ♔×a5 ♔e5 49 b4 ♔e4 50 b5 ♖d1 51 b6 ♖d2 52 ♖b8, winning easily.

44 b4 ♖f3

Hoping for 45 b×a5? ♖×a3, with his rook behind the passed pawn.

45 ♖b2 ♖×a3
46 b5 ♖c3
47 b6 ♖c8
48 ♔d4 1 – 0

Black's king and pawns are too backward to stand a chance. The variations are:

(a) 48 . . . a4 49 b7 ♖b8 50 ♔c5 a3 51 ♖f2+ ♔e5 52 ♖e2+ ♔f5 53 ♔c6, or here 50 . . . e5 51 ♔c6 e4 52 ♔c7 ♖×b7+ 53 ♔×b7 ♔e5 54 ♔c6 e3 (54 . . . ♔d4 55 ♖a2) 55 ♖a2 etc. (b) 48 . . . e5+ 49 ♔d5 ♖d8+ 50 ♔c6 e4 51 b7 e3 52 b8/♕ ♖×b8 53 ♖×b8 ♔e5 54 ♖b5+, and White will always win with his last pawns after sacrificing his rook at e1.

Incidentally, Rook vs. One or Two Pawns (whether the rook has any of his own pawns left or not) crops up time and again as the final stage of these endings, and is undoubtedly one of the most useful aspects of endgame theory with which to familiarise yourself. On a more general matter, bear in mind the importance of learning to analyse in the endgame, something which many people neglect. Although White's piece manoeuvres here were intended to make the win as certain and as easy as possible, there is a limit to what you can do in that respect. In the end there is no guarantee that you will not have to work out some critical variations, and you will get nowhere if you rely solely on positional play. For instance, Nunn avoided 34 a3 because he judged it both reckless and unnecessary in the circumstances; but he might have had to return to that, had there been no better line. As it turned out, he needed only to calculate the relatively straightforward 43 a3 etc., but even that, I imagine, would have been beyond many players.

Game 24

King's Indian Defence
Wijk aan Zee 1985
A. Belyavsky v. J. Nunn

1	**d4**	**♘f6**
2	**c4**	**g6**
3	**♘c3**	**♗g7**
4	**e4**	**d6**
5	**f3**	**0–0**
6	**♗e3**	**♘bd7**

Around this time Nunn was dissatisfied with his results against the Sämisch variation, using the commoner systems of 6 . . .e5 and 6 . . . ♘c6; so he decided to look for improvements in some lesser known line. There is plenty of theory on 6 . . . ♘bd7, but is is not generally regarded as very promising. However, a week spent reassessing the material given in the theoretical books produced a number of new ideas for Black.

Now after 7 ♕d2 c5 White has a choice of two systems: he can block the centre by 8 d5, as in the main game, or he can play a half-open position, leaving Black to exchange on d4. The second plan is of some interest because it shows how the evaluation of an opening can alter over the years. For example, Perkins–Nunn (GLC Weekend Open, 1984) continued 8 ♘ge2 a6 9 ♘c1 c×d4 10 ♗×d4, reaching a position which the books regarded as at least slightly favourable for White. This judgement was based on an old game (Ivkov–Bukić, Yugoslavia 1962), which proceeded 10 . . . ♘c5 11 ♗e2 ♘e6 12 ♗e3 ♗d7 13 0–0 ♖b8 14 ♘d3 b5 15 c×b5 a×b5 16 ♘b4 ♕a5 17 a3, and White does indeed have rather the better of it here.

But Nunn gives the whole thing a new twist with 10 . . . b6!, intending to set up a 'hedgehog' position. The hedgehog is a modern idea, a type of structure rather than the name of an opening or a variation, though it does tend to arise frequently out of Sicilians, and Maroczy Binds in particular. If you consult the opening notes to Game 19 (Nunn–Gheorghiu) you will find more information on it. Broadly speaking, Black is restricted, though not uncomfortably so, and to judge the correct time and place to launch an attack can be extremely difficult for White; he can easily overdo it. Moreover, Black's piece distribution in a hedgehog is subtle and flexible, ready to react at a moment's notice to any mistake on White's part, or to any disharmony in his position. And in the variation we are discussing the placing of the knight at c1 (and to some extent the bishop at d4) is awkward and therefore potentially dangerous. Here are the remaining moves of Perkins–Nunn, with few further comments except to point out the difference between Black's play in this game and the relatively crude moves of Ivkov–Bukić: 11 ♗e2 e6 12

0–0 ♕c7 13 ♖d1 ♘e5 14 ♘b3 ♗b7 15 ♖ac1 ♖ad8 (using this rook because he anticipates a later attack by . . . f5) 16 ♘a4 ♘fd7 17 ♕e3 ♘c5 18 ♘c3 (18 ♘a×c5 d×c5 changes the pawn structure in Black's favour, on account of the hole at d4) f6 (intending . . . ♘c6) 19 ♕f2 f5! 20 e×f5 ♖×f5 21 ♕e3 ♖df8 22 ♘d2 ♖f4 23 ♗×c5 d×c5 24 g3 ♖4f7 25 ♘ce4 ♘g4 26 ♕b3 ♗d4+ 27 ♔h1 ♕e5 28 ♕×b6 ♘f2+ 29 ♘×f2 ♕×e2 30 ♘fe4 ♗×e4 0–1 (if 31 f×e4 ♗e3 wins).

7 ♕d2 . . .

In another recent game (Salonika Olympiad 1984) Gheorghiu played 7 ♘h3, upon which Nunn reverted to an . . . e5 system, and that game continued 7 . . . e5 8 d5 ♘h5 9 ♕c2 (if 9 g4 Black would sacrifice a pawn by 9 . . . ♘f4 10 ♘×f4 e×f4 11 ♗×f4 ♘e5, with . . . f5 to follow) ♘c5 10 ♘f2 a5 11 0–0–0 f5 ♘d3 b6 with equality. The difference is apparent at move eight of the main game. If 7 ♘h3 c5 8 d5 ♘e5, the development of White's K-side would not be hampered as it is in Belyavsky–Nunn; his knight would already be out and he could continue 9 ♘f2. In that event Black's strategy would be pointless and he would not have another good plan available at move 8 (being unable to play . . . e6). Against 7 ♕d2, on the other hand, 7 . . . e5 would lead back into a critical line of one of the older systems which Nunn is trying to avoid. Moreover, White would retain the option of playing his knight to e2 for a recapture on d4 (retaking with the bishop is more awkward) and would not be obliged to commit himself at once to a blocked position by d5.

7 . . . c5
8 d5 . . .

Black's problem now is that he cannot chip away at White's centre by an immediate . . . e6. Prior to this game, therefore, the *Encyclopedia of Chess Openings* suggested either Q-side action by . . . a6 or preparation of . . . e6 by 8 . . . ♖e8, neither of which is very attractive. An alternative idea is to look for some way of activating the knights, and that is the basis of Nunn's explorations: he has tried to discover a way to make 8 . . . ♘e5 work without having the knight driven back at once.

8 . . . ♘e5 *(109)*

109
W

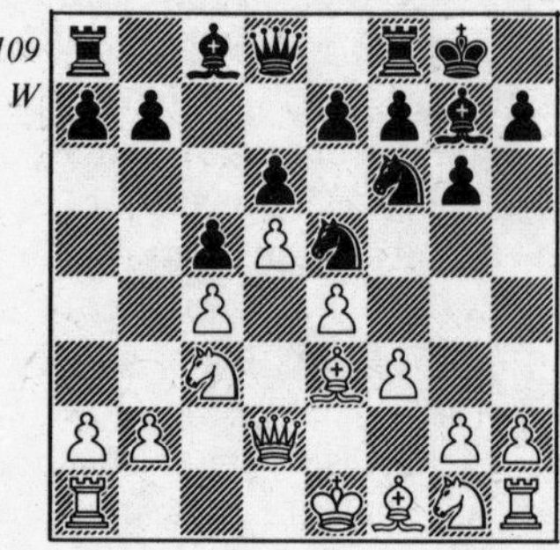

The first justification for this is that 9 f4 is met by 9 . . . ♘eg4, exchanging the important bishop, and the second is that the developing moves 9 ♘ge2 and 9 ♘h3 are both ruled out. Furthermore, castling Q-side, which is a necessary part of White's plan in many Sämisch lines, would be extremely dangerous here because the long diagonal is open: . . . c5 instead of . . . e5 makes all the difference in this respect. After 9 0–0–0 Black would immediately begin an assault by . . . a6 and . . . b5, probably sacrificing a pawn as in the Benkö Gambit.

That makes 9 h3, preparing f4, the most obvious attempt at a refutation, and most of Black's home analysis has been aimed at ensuring that he can keep the initiative thereafter, even if he has to sacrifice something. It might be added that the Sämisch variation, strong and dangerous though it is, is peculiarly vulnerable to such lightning attacks by Black, partly because White's piece development is a little slow, partly because a slight weakness is apparent on the dark squares.

9 h3 is Belyavsky's choice, then. But it seems not to be the strongest. In a later round at Wijk aan Zee Timman played 9 ♗g5! against Nunn, avoiding the knight's attack at g4, and got a good position by 9 . . . a6 10 f4 ♘ed7 11 ♘f3 b5 12 c×b5 a×b5 13 ♗×b5 ♕a5 14 0–0 ♘×e4 15 ♘×e4 ♕×b5 16 ♗×e7 ♕×b2 17 ♕×b2 ♗×b2 18 ♖ae1 ♗a6 19 ♖f2 ♖fe8 20 ♘×d6 ♖eb8 21 ♘e4 ♗c4 22 ♗d6 ♖b7. Here Timman should have played 23 ♗e5! (23 . . . ♘×e5 24 f×e5, or 23 . . . ♗×e5 24 ♘×e5), when Black would have been in big trouble; instead he played 23 ♘e5 and only drew after 23 . . . ♗×e5 24 f×e5 ♗×d5 25 ♘×c5. At present that is just about the last word on the variation; unless Black's play here can be improved, 8 . . . ♘e5 appears to be not quite satisfactory.

9	**h3**	**♘h5**
10	**♗f2**	. . .

Probably best. The knight cannot be allowed into g3 (10 f4 ♘g3 11 f×e5 ♘×h1 12 e×d6 e×d6 is not justified, nor here 12 ♗f4 d×e5 13 ♗h2 f5; or if 11 ♖h2 ♘×f1 12 ♔×f1 ♘×c4); so White's choice lies among 10 ♗f2, 10 ♕f2 and 10 ♔f2. Of these three, 10 ♔f2 is unwise because of 10 . . . e6, when . . . ♕h4+ is hard to stop: 11 g3 f5 etc., or 11 ♗g5 ♗f6 and he faces the same problem – 12 h4 h6. Therefore we need only pay attention here to 10 ♕f2, which produces the following analysis:

(a) 10 . . . f5 (premature) 11 e×f5 (White must never allow a bind by . . . f4) ♗×f5 (if 11 . . . ♖×f5 12 g4 ♘f4 13 ♕d2!, winning material for insufficient returns, or if 11 . . . g×f5 12 f4 ♘g6 13 ♘ge2 – Black must avoid such a passive position, come what may) 12 g4 ♗×g4 13 h×g4 ♘×g4 14 ♕d2, and Black's compensation for the piece is inadequate, whether he exchanges at e3 or tries 14 . . . ♘g3 15 ♖h3 ♘×f1 16 ♔×f1.

(b) 10 . . . ♕a5 (an interesting switch to the Q-side, threatening . . . ♘×c4, but still not quite good enough), and now: (i) 11 g4 ♘×f3+ (not 11 . . . ♘×c4 12 ♗×c4 ♗×c3+ 13 ♔d1!) 12 ♘×f3 (12 ♕×f3 ♗×c3+ and . . . ♗×b2) ♗×c3+ 13 ♔d1 (or 13 b×c3 ♕×c3+ 14 ♔e2 ♕×c4+ 15 ♔d1 ♕a4+, which would most likely end in perpetual check because interposing the white queen would permit a final . . . ♘g3, picking up a fourth pawn) ♘g3! (Black keeps his bishop in preference to the knight, at the same time deflecting the queen from b2) 14 ♕×g3 ♗×b2 15 ♖b1 (or possibly an exchange sacrifice by 15 ♖c1, which Black would be well-advised to leave alone) ♕a4+ 16 ♔e1 (not to the second rank because of . . . ♕×a2) ♕c2 17 ♖d1 (17 ♘d2? ♗c3) ♗c3+, followed by . . . ♕×e4, with a very obscure position; chances for both sides is about all you can say; (ii) 11 ♗d2 ♕b4! 12 ♘d1 (12 b3 ♘d3+, or 12 g4 ♕×b2 13 ♖b1 ♕c2 14 g×h5 ♘×c4 15 ♗×c4 ♗×c3, or here 15 ♖c1 ♕×d2+ 16 ♕×d2 ♘×d2 17 ♔×d2 ♗h6+, regaining the material, or 15

♖b3 ♘b2 16 ♗e2 c4 17 ♖a3 b5, and Black stands well every time) ♘f4! 13 ♕e3 (or 13 ♕g3 ♘ed3+, winning the c-pawn safely, or 13 ♗×b4 ♘ed3+ and Black gets a good ending) ♘ed3+ 14 ♗×d3 ♘×g2+ 15 ♔e2 ♘×e3 16 ♗×b4 ♘×d1, and Black is doing very well; (iii) 11 ♖c1! (the best reply to 10 . . . ♕a5, bolstering up c3 and meeting 11 . . . ♕b4 by 12 g4 etc.; so Black switches to the K-side) f5 12 e×f5 ♗×f5 13 g4 ♗e4 (another point of . . . ♕a5, but still not good enough to equalise) 14 g×h5 ♘×f3+ 15 ♘×f3 ♖×f3 (15 . . . ♗×f3 16 ♖h2 ♗×h5 17 ♕d2 is inadequate) 16 ♕d2, and Black cannot do better than regain his piece by 16 . . . ♖×e3+ 17 ♕×e3 ♗×h1. The trouble then is 18 h×g6, when he dare not recapture (18 . . . h×g6 19 ♕e6+ and 20 ♗d3, and White for once takes over the attack decisively). His bishop must therefore remain out of place at h1, and he does not even hold a slight material advantage as compensation.

(c) 10 . . . e6! Definitely the best reply to 10 ♕f2. Black is using every available tactical resource to keep his knights in position. 11 f4 can now be parried by 11 . . . ♗f6!, when White curiously does not have a convenient move – 12 g3 ♘×g3, or 12 h4 ♘g4, or 12 ♘f3 ♘×f3+ and 13 . . . ♗h4+. The other dangerous thrust 11 g4 is dealt with by 11 . . . e×d5 12 c×d5 (12 g×h5 d4 and 12 ♘×d5 ♘f6 are both good for Black) ♗f6 13 h4 ♗×g4 14 f×g4 ♘×g4, and this time he is quite favourably placed, with three extra pawns and domination of the black squares in return for his piece. f4 and g4 are the only two moves with which he need concern himself at this stage; as long as White refuses to drive the knights back he will find it impossible to develop naturally.

10 . . . f5

11 e×f5 . . .

Against 11 f4 Black keeps his pieces working to good effect by 11 . . . ♗h6 12 g3 f×e4 13 ♘×e4 ♗f5; or he could try the typical pawn sacrifice 13 . . . b5 14 c×b5 c4.

11 . . . ♖×f5

One of the main ideas behind 8 . . . ♘e5 is about to be revealed. 11 . . . ♗×f5? 12 g4 simply loses a piece for nothing, while 11 . . . g×f5 12 f4 ♗h6 13 g3 does not provide the necessary activity, as it did above: here the c8 bishop is shut in, and the threat of ♕e2 forces an immediate knight retreat. But with 11 . . . ♖×f5 he is offering a piece merely to keep the initiative; specifically his intention is to maintain the knight at e5.

12 g4 . . .

If the offer is declined, . . . ♘f4 and . . . ♗h6 can follow and Black gets an aggressive position all the same.

12 . . . ♖×f3

13 g×h5 . . .

Again White cannot do better. If 13 0–0–0 ♖f7! 14 g×h5 ♕f8, and Black always regains his piece favourably; for example 15 ♘e4 ♗h6 16 ♗e3 ♗×e3 17 ♕×e3 ♖×f1. If 13 ♗e2 ♖×f2 14 ♔×f2 ♕f8+, followed by . . . ♘f4 and perhaps . . . ♗h6, with a pawn and a tremendous black-square grip in return for the exchange.

13 . . . ♕f8 *(110)*

It is not always easy to state the exact point at which home analysis ends, especially if the position becomes as much a matter of judgement as further calculation; but in the main Nunn had ended his investigations here. He examined briefly several of

White's most natural 14th moves, none of which is quite satisfactory, and beyond that judged (correctly) that his powerful initiative and the poor position of White's king should offset the material disadvantage.

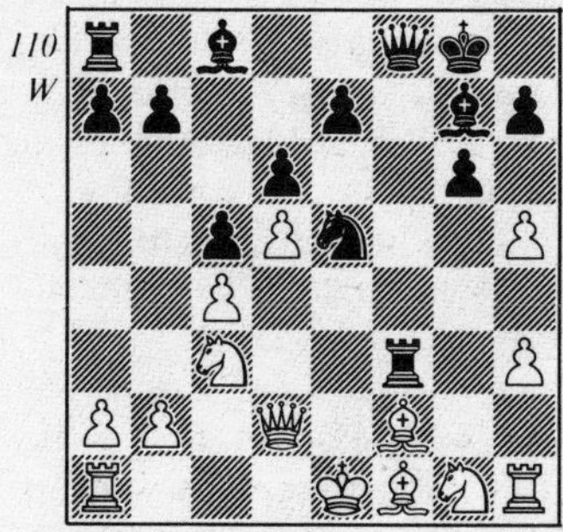

110
W

First of all, White obviously cannot move his g1 knight or either bishop; so what is left? Here are a few possible defences:

(a) 14 ♖d1 ♗f5, and the threat of . . . ♗h6 puts the queen in a tight spot (15 ♕e2 ♗d3, or 15 b3 ♘d3+). In fact White does not have a decent move here.

(b) 14 h×g6 ♗f5 (14 . . . h×g6 is less good because a little later the queen comes to bear on g6 – see the note to Black's 18th move) 15 g×h7+ ♔h8, and again White is grievously short of moves – 16 ♗e2 ♖×f2 17 ♔×f2 ♗e4+, for instance, or 16 ♗e3 ♖×f1+ 17 ♔×f1 ♗e4+, when Black regains his material and the dominant knight gives him a much superior position.

On the whole, White's best hope is to surrender his queen and play an endgame with unbalanced material (typically queen + 2 or 3 pawns against a rook and two minor pieces); but he has to contrive this in exactly the right way because his position is bound to be exposed. For example, 14 ♖h2 ♗h6 15 ♕e2 might be tried, but then comes 15 . . . ♕f4 16 ♖g2 ♘d3+ 17 ♕×d3 ♖×d3 18 ♗×d3 ♕d2+, and the idea fails disastrously. If here 15 ♕d1 ♕f4 16 ♖g2 ♗f5, and Black gets a strong attack every time: 17 ♘ge2 ♖e3! 18 ♗×e3 ♕×e3; or 17 ♗e2 ♖×f2 18 ♖×f2 ♕g3 19 ♔f1 (19 ♘f3 ♗e3) ♗e3 20 ♖g2 ♗×h3 21 ♘×h3 ♖f8+; or 17 ♘×f3 ♘×f3+ 18 ♔e2 ♘d4+ 19 ♗×d4 c×d4, or here 19 ♔e1 ♘c2+ 20 ♔e2 ♘×a1 21 ♕×a1 ♕d2+ 22 ♔f3 ♖f8 etc.

A better attempt is 14 ♕e2 ♘d3+ 15 ♕×d3 ♖×d3 16 ♗×d3 ♗f5 17 ♖d1 (or 17 ♗e2? ♗×c3+ 18 b×c3 ♗e4 19 ♖h2 ♕f4, trapping the rook; or 17 ♗×f5 ♗×c3+ 18 b×c3 ♕×f5 19 ♘e2 ♖f8 20 ♗g3 ♕e4, with a very favourable position, as in the main line; or 17 ♘e4 ♗×b2 18 ♖d1 ♗×e4 19 ♗×e4 ♕f4 20 ♗d3 ♗c3+ 21 ♔e2 ♖f8, again with very good winning chances), but even so Black gets excellent winning prospects by 17 . . . ♗×d3 18 ♖×d3 ♕f5 19 ♖f3 (must somehow prevent . . . ♗×c3+ and . . . ♕e4+) ♗×c3+ 20 b×c3 ♕b1+ 21 ♔e2 ♕×a2+ 22 ♔d3 (must protect the c- and d-pawns) ♕b1+ 23 ♔e2 a5.

We begin to appreciate the problems facing White, which can be summed up as follows: (1) He cannot develop properly because Black's pieces are interfering vigorously with the process; (2) He can never organise Q-side castling because of . . . ♗h6 and because of the pressure down the f-file; (3) The very heart of his position has been laid bare to Black's threats in a most unusual way: white squares, black squares, everything is wide open, and he is in continual danger of losing material back; (4) In many variations even the exchange of queens leaves Black on top, because his bishops are so powerful in the endgame.

After considerable thought Belyavsky comes up with the best defence, an idea which Nunn had overlooked.

14 ♘e4! . . .

This excellent move should have enabled him to equalise, because 14 . . . ♗f5 can now be met by 15 ♘g5 ♗h6 16 h4, taming one of the black bishops. Or if 14 . . . ♖f4 15 ♕e2! (not 15 ♘g5 h6 16 ♘e6 ♗×e6 17 d×e6 ♕f5 18 ♖h2 ♖f8, which once again yields Black tremendous pressure) ♗f5 16 ♗g2, and with the knight established at e4 he can halt the flood of black pieces through the centre.

14 . . . ♗h6

15 ♕c2? . . .

But this leads to trouble. In playing 14 ♘e4 White had to appreciate that now was the time to surrender his queen, thus: 15 ♕e2! (15 ♕d1? ♕f4) ♘d3+ (no choice because his rook is now genuinely under attack; if 15 . . . ♕f4? 16 ♘×f3 ♘×f3+ 17 ♔d1 ♗f5 18 ♗g3) 16 ♕×d3 ♖×d3 17 ♗×d3 ♕f4 (threatening . . . ♗f5 and meeting 18 ♘e2 by 18 . . . ♕f3, or a knight move by . . . ♕d2+; but compared with the earlier variation – 14 ♕e2 – White's b-pawn is not now under fire and this time his position just holds) 18 ♖d1 (forced) ♗f5 19 ♘e2 ♕f3 20 ♘2g3 ♗e3! (very dangerous for White; if he takes there is the neat variation 21 ♗×e3? ♕×e3+ 22 ♔f1 ♗×e4 23 ♘×e4 ♕f3+ 24 ♘f2 ♖f8 and wins; if 21 ♘×f5 g×f5 22 ♖g1+ ♔h8 obviously loses material, or if 21 ♖h2 – 21 0–0 ♗×h3 – ♗×e4 22 ♘×e4 ♗f4! and wins) 21 ♖f1! (21 ♖g1 is also all right) ♗×e4 (about the best Black can do; if 21 . . . ♗×h3 22 ♗e2 drives him back) 22 ♘×e4 ♗×f2+ 23 ♖×f2 ♕×h5, and the game is roughly level because White's pawn position is not crumbling at the edges, as it has been in other similar variations.

All this is a great deal to see over the board, of course, apart from the need to anticipate Black's following move. 15 ♕c2 is inferior because . . . ♗f5 will now be a pin; therefore Black can leave his rook *en prise* for one more move.

15 . . . ♕f4!

Sacrificing another exchange. The remainder of the game is pure tactics and in a sense self-explanatory, but a few general hints may be useful. Black keeps the game under control by observing three principles (subconciously in the case of a Grandmaster): (1) He avoids time loss and operates with threats where possible; (2) He takes every reasonable white reply into account at each move (in other words he analyses thoroughly without dropping his guard for a moment), and pays particular attention to the queen's activities (see especially move 20); (3) He is prepared to reduce the game to a favourable ending if necessary (i.e. he avoids being greedy).

If White now takes the rook, he gets a typically inferior endgame: 16 ♘×f3 ♘×f3+ 17 ♔d1 (17 ♔e2 ♗f5 18 ♗g3 ♕e3+ is worse) ♗f5 18 ♗g3 (there is no alternative; if he counter-sacrifices by 18 ♗d3 ♘d4! 19 ♗×d4 ♕f3+ 20 ♕e2 ♕×h1+ 21 ♔e2 ♕×a1, he has nothing) ♕e3 (because White's next move is forced, and in the endgame the bishop will be slightly worse at f2 than at g3) 19 ♗f2

♕×e4 20 ♕×e4 ♗×e4 21 ♗g2 ♖f8. Here Black already has one pawn for the exchange and the clumsy white rooks will be no match for his energetic bishops. Against a passive move he may continue with . . . ♗d3, shutting in the king completely (22 . . . ♗d3 23 ♗f1? ♗×f1 24 ♖×f1 ♘d2). The c-pawn is also in trouble, and 22 b3 is defeated by 22 . . . ♗g7 23 ♖c1 ♗b2. There are hidden dangers everywhere in this line – 22 ♔e2 ♘d4+ 23 ♔f1 (23 ♗×d4 ♗×g2 24 ♖hg1 ♗f3+) ♗d3+ 24 ♔g1 ♘e2+ 25 ♔h2 ♗f4+, for instance; or if on the previous move 21 ♗e2 ♘d4 22 ♖f1 (22 ♖g1 ♘c2 23 ♖b1 ♘e3+ is worse) ♘c2 23 ♖b1 ♘e3+ 24 ♗×e3 ♗×e3 25 ♖a1 ♗g2 and the rook is trapped – 26 ♖e1 ♗f2. If 21 h×g6 Black would simply recapture 21 . . . h×g6.

Apart from 16 ♘×f3, and faced with the threat of . . . ♗f5, the text move 16 ♘e2 is the only thing White can seriously consider. 16 ♗e2 is easily refuted by 16 . . . ♗f5 17 ♗×f3 (17 ♘×f3 ♗×e4) ♘×f3+ 18 ♘×f3 ♗×e4 etc., while any variation such as 16 ♘g3 ♖×g3 17 ♗×g3 ♕×g3+ 18 ♕f2 ♕g5 is almost an automatic win for Black: he follows up with . . . ♗d7 and . . . ♖f8 and White is hopelessly exposed. The material difference is quite irrelevant here.

16 ♘e2 ♖×f2
17 ♘×f2 ♘f3+

Bear in mind that in choosing 15 . . . ♕f4 Nunn has had to see that 17 . . . ♕h4? 18 ♕e4 and 17 . . . ♕e3? 18 ♗g2 ♗f5 19 ♕c1 are both bad, and that after the correct continuation (as played) White has no satisfactory defence to the threat of 19 . . . ♕×f2.

18 ♔d1 ♕h4! *(111)*

Again not 18 . . . ♕e3? 19 ♘g4. And compare note (b) to Black's 13th move: had 14 h×g6 h×g6 been interposed before ♘e4, the black g-pawn would now be *en prise* with check!

111
W

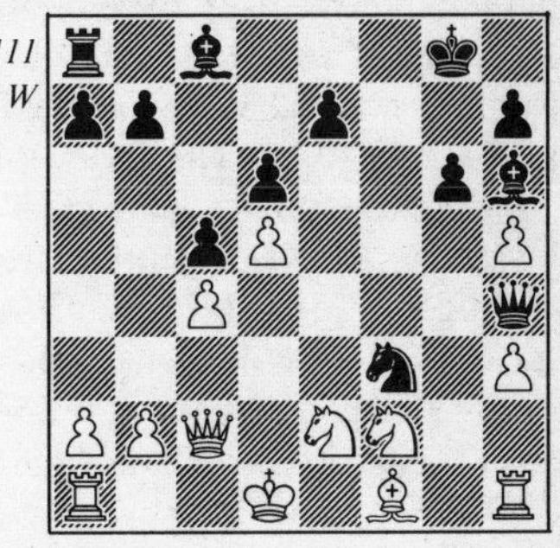

19 ♘d3 . . .

The only way to save the knight without allowing mate at e1. If the e2 knight moves 19 . . . ♘d4 wins a piece, or if 19 h×g6 (the only possible counter-attack), there is 19 . . . ♕×f2 20 g×h7+ ♔h8 21 ♕g6 ♕e1+ 22 ♔c2 ♕d2+ 23 ♔b3 ♕e3+ 24 ♔c2 (24 ♔a4 ♗d7+ 25 ♔a5 ♕d2+ 26 ♘c3 ♕×b2 and wins, or 24 ♘c3 ♗f5, and the queen has to retreat, leaving Black with a crushing attack) ♗d7! (threatening chiefly 25 . . . ♕d2+ 26 ♔b3 ♗a4+), and if 25 ♕d3 (or 25 ♖d1 ♖f8 26 ♘g3 ♘e5 27 ♕h5 ♗f4, when the knight cannot move because of . . . ♕e4+), either 25 . . . ♕f2, threatening 26 . . . ♗f5, or 25 . . . ♕×d3+ 26 ♔×d3 ♗f5+ 27 ♔c3 ♗g7+ 28 ♔b3 ♘d2+ 29 ♔a3 (29 ♔a4 ♗c2+ is no better) ♘×c4+ 30 ♔b3 ♘d2+ 31 ♔a3 b5, with an overwhelming position.

19 . . . ♗f5

This time the threat is 20 . . . ♘e1, and if 21 ♘×e1 ♗×c2+ 22 ♘×c2 ♕g5 and wins. In a way this variation sums up the peculiar flavour of the whole game: for the square d2 to be undefendable at move 22 is amazing! Since 20 ♗g2 ♘e5 costs a piece, White's choice is once more severely restricted. In playing 20 ♘ec1 he strengthens the knight at d3, but leaves himself open to another danger because the black queen is allowed access to e4. The following note makes this point clear; meanwhile we can analyse his other two possibilities, 20 ♕c3 and 20 ♘c3.

The first can be dealt with in a rather long but forced variation, as follows: 20 ♕c3 ♗g7 21 ♕b3 ♗×d3 22 ♕×d3 ♕e1+ 23 ♔c2 ♕×a1 24 ♕×f3 ♕×b2+ 25 ♔d1 ♕a1+ 26 ♘c1 (if the king moves, two more pawns go, leaving Black with four against a knight) ♗h6 27 ♕a3 ♖f8 (threatens . . . ♖f3) 28 ♗e2 ♖f2 29 ♖e1 ♖h2 (threatens . . . ♖×h3) 30 ♔c2 ♗×c1 31 ♕×c1 ♕×a2+ 32 ♔d1 (32 ♕b2 ♕×c4+) ♖×h3, and Black has four pawns for the bishop, a continuing attack and an immediate threat of 33 . . . ♖b3.

20 ♘c3 is met by 20 . . . ♘d2! (The same theme as in the game; with this unusual idea the white queen is shut out from the K-side. Notice that other moves would be inferior: 20 . . . ♘e1? 21 ♕f2, or 20 . . . ♘d4 21 ♕f2 ♕×f2 22 ♘×f2 ♗c2+ 23 ♔e1 ♘f3+ and Black has only a draw), and now Black's theme is either . . . ♘×f1 or . . . ♘×c4, according to which defence is adopted: (a) 21 ♗e2 ♘×c4 22 ♕b1 ♘e3+ and 23 . . . c4, or if 22 ♕b3 ♘e3+ 23 ♔c1 (or d2) c4 24 ♕×b7 ♖f8 and wins; (b) 21 b3 ♘×f1 22 ♖×f1 ♕×h5+ 23 ♕e2 (or 23 ♔e1 ♕×h3, when 24 ♖d1 can be met by 24 . . . ♕g3+ 25 ♖f2 ♗e3; White would therefore have to sacrifice by 24 ♖×f5 ♕×f5, but Black still gets three good pawns and a dangerous attack for his piece; if 23 ♘e2 ♕×h3 is similar) ♗×d3 24 ♕×h5 g×h5, and it is interesting to observe just how good this endgame is for Black. 25 ♖f3 is answered by 25 . . . ♖f8! 26 ♖×f8+ (or 26 ♖g3+ ♔h8 27 ♖g1 ♖f2 and White is hopelessly passive) ♔×f8 27 ♔e1 (27 ♘e2 ♗g7 28 ♖c1 ♗b2) ♗e3! 28 ♘e2 (28 ♖d1 ♗c2) h4 29 ♔f1 ♔f7, and the king's advance is decisive. On the first move 25 ♖g1+ ♔h8 leaves White no better off – 26 ♔e1 ♖f8 etc.; (c) 21 ♕×d2 ♗×d2 22 ♔×d2 ♕×c4, and White's position is ragged and exposed, unlike the compact one he had in the note to his 15th move. Here . . . ♕d4 followed by . . . c4 is a very dangerous threat, and Black's initiative should at least win him the d-pawn, with every chance of victory.

Against 20 ♘c3, then, Black would still have a fight on his hands; after the following move his task is easier.

20 ♘ec1(?) ♘d2!

Again this strangely powerful move, threatening above all 21 . . . ♕e4 22 ♖g1 ♕e3, and if 23 ♖h1 ♕f3+.

21 h×g6 h×g6

Not 21 . . . ♕e4 without recapturing at g6 because White gets counterplay: 22 g×h7+ ♔h8 (or 22 . . . ♗×h7 23 ♖g1+, or 22 . . . ♔×h7 23 ♘e1!, which shows how alert Black has to be) 23 ♖g1 ♕e3 24 ♕c3+ ♔×h7 25 ♖g7+ ♗×g7 26 ♕×d2 etc. Now, however, he must pay attention to the threat. Belyavsky struggled to find a defence until he had only a few minutes left to reach move 40, but all in vain despite his extra rook. If he takes the knight his chances are even more meagre than before: 22 ♕×d2 ♗×d2 23 ♔×d2 ♕×c4, and with no knight at c3 the d-pawn disappears at once – 24 ♗g2 ♕d4 25 ♔e2 c4, and . . . ♕×b2+ if the knight moves. 22 ♖g1 is refuted by 22 . . . ♕d4 23 ♖h1 ♕e4 etc., and 22 ♘e2, 22 ♗e2 and 22 ♘b3 are all decisively met by 22 . . . ♘×c4 (–e3+), as given earlier.

22	**♗g2**	**♘×c4**
23	**♕f2** *(112)*	**. . .**

112
B

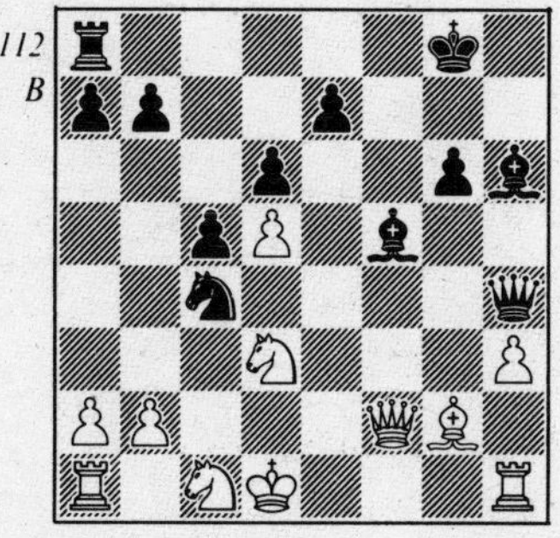

The only other possible attempt, 23 ♖e1, is defeated at once by 23 . . . ♕h5+ and 24 . . . ♘e3+.

23	**. . .**	**♘e3+**

Black is justified in playing for more than just a favourable endgame by 23 . . . ♕×f2 24 ♘×f2 ♘e3+.

24	**♔e2**	**♕c4!**

There seems to be something slightly comical about this switch to the Q-side, just when the white queen has managed to crawl painfully across to f2! The chief threat is 25 . . . ♗×d3+ 26 ♘×d3 ♕c2+ 27 ♔e1 ♕×d3 etc., 25 ♕×e3 being met by 25 . . . ♕c2+

25	**♗f3**	**♖f8**

Black has plenty of time to strengthen his position before taking at d3. If 25 . . . ♗×d3+ 26 ♘×d3 ♕c2+ 27 ♔e1 ♕×d3, White hangs on by 28 ♗d1.

26	**♖g1**	**♘c2**

Even stronger than 26 . . . ♗×d3+, because . . . ♘d4+ will win two pieces.

27	**♔d1**	**♗×d3**
	0 – 1	

Index of Openings

King-side

Queen-side